STUDIES OF THE AMERICAS

edited by
James Dunkerley
Institute for the Study of the Americas
University of London
School of Advanced Study

Titles in this series are multi-disciplinary studies of aspects of the societies of the hemisphere, particularly in the areas of politics, economics, history, anthropology, sociology, and the environment. The series covers a comparative perspective across the Americas, including Canada and the Caribbean as well as the USA and Latin America.

Titles in this series published by Palgrave Macmillan:

Cuba's Military 1990-2005: Revolutionary Soldiers during Counter-Revolutionary Times
By Hal Klepak

The Judicialization of Politics in Latin America
Edited by Rachel Sieder, Line Schjolden, and Alan Angell

Latin America: A New Interpretation
By Laurence Whitehead

Appropriation as Practice: Art and Identity in Argentina
By Arnd Schneider

America and Enlightenment Constitutionalism
Edited by Gary L. McDowell and Johnathan O'Neill

Vargas and Brazil: New Perspectives
Edited by Jens R. Hentschke

When Was Latin America Modern?
Edited by Nicola Miller and Stephen Hart

Debating Cuban Exceptionalism
Edited by Bert Hoffmann and Laurence Whitehead

Caribbean Land and Development Revisited
Edited by Jean Besson and Janet Momsen

Cultures of the Lusophone Black Atlantic
Edited by Nancy Priscilla Naro, Roger Sansi-Roca, and David H. Treece

Democratization, Development, and Legality: Chile, 1831-1973
By Julio Faundez

The Hispanic World and American Intellectual Life, 1820-1880
By Iván Jaksić

The Role of Mexico's Plural *in Latin American Literary and Political Culture*
By John King

Faith and Impiety in Revolutionary Mexico: God's Revolution?
By Matthew Butler

Cultures of the Lusophone Black Atlantic

Edited by

Nancy Priscilla Naro,
Roger Sansi-Roca, and
David H. Treece

CULTURES OF THE LUSOPHONE BLACK ATLANTIC
Copyright © Nancy Priscilla Naro, Roger Sansi-Roca, and
David H. Treece, 2007.

First published in 2007 by
PALGRAVE MACMILLAN™
175 Fifth Avenue, New York, N.Y. 10010 and
Houndmills, Basingstoke, Hampshire, England RG21 6XS
Companies and representatives throughout the world.

PALGRAVE MACMILLAN is the global academic imprint of the Palgrave Macmillan
division of St. Martin's Press, LLC and of Palgrave Macmillan Ltd.
Macmillan® is a registered trademark in the United States, United Kingdom
and other countries. Palgrave is a registered trademark in the European
Union and other countries.

ISBN-13: 978–0–230–60047–8
ISBN-10: 0–230–60047–6

Library of Congress Cataloging-in-Publication Data

Cultures of the lusophone Black Atlantic / edited by Nancy Priscilla Naro,
Roger Sansi-Roca and David H. Treece.
p. cm.
Includes bibliographical references and index.
ISBN 0–230–60047–6 (alk. paper)
1. Portuguese-speaking countries—Civilization—African influences.
2. Blacks—Portuguese-speaking countries—History. 3. Hybridity (Social
sciences) I. Naro, Nancy Priscilla. II. Sansi-Roca, Roger. III. Treece, Dave.

DT594.C85 2007
305.896′017569—dc22   2007006826

A catalogue record for this book is available from the British Library.

Design by Newgen Imaging Systems (P) Ltd., Chennai, India.

First edition: October 2007

10 9 8 7 6 5 4 3 2 1

Printed in the United States of America.

Contents

Part III   Hybridity, Multiculturalism, and Racial Politics

Contributors

Matthias Röhrig Assunção (MA Paris 1979, PhD Freie Universität Berlin, 1990), Senior Lecturer in the Department of History, University of Essex. His research deals with plantation society, slave and peasant revolts, and popular culture in Maranhão, northern Brazil, as well as martial arts in the Black Atlantic. His most recent book is *Capoeira. The History of an Afro-Brazilian Martial Art* (Routledge 2005).

Stefania Capone (MA Anthropology UFRJ-Brazil and PhD University of Paris X-Nanterre), Senior Researcher of the CNRS and has taught at the University of Paris X-Nanterre since 1997. She is the author of many works on candomblé, santería in United States and the transnationalisation of Afro-American religions, including *La quête de l'Afrique dans le candomblé. Pouvoir et tradition au Brésil* (Paris: Karthala, 1999) and *Les Yoruba du Nouveau Monde. Religion, ethnicité et nationalisme noir aux Etats-Unis* (2005).

Roquinaldo Ferreira (PhD UCLA, 2003), Assistant Professor, Department of History, University of Virginia. He has been a fellow at the W.E.B. Du Bois Institute for African and African American Research (Harvard University); the David Rockefeller Center for Latin American Studies (Harvard University); and the Gilder Lehrman Center for the Study of Slavery, Resistance, and Abolition (Yale University). His research focuses on Central Africa (Angola and Kongo) and the African Diaspora to Brazil. His forthcoming book is provisionally entitled *Angola and Brazil in the Atlantic World : Trade and the Social and Cultural Landscapes of Slaving (ca.1680–1830)* and will be published by Cambridge University Press.

Kesha D. Fikes (PhD UCLA, 2000), Assistant Professor, Department of Anthropology, University of Chicago. She has worked in Lusophone Africa and Portugal on race and the bureaucracies of spatial mobility, the relationship between colonial migrant labor projects and postcolonial/postindependence migrant labor phenomena.

Peter Fry (PhD University of London, 1969), Professor of Anthropology, Federal University of Rio de Janeiro. He has recently published *A persistência da raça: ensaios antropológicas sobre o Brasil e a África austral* (Rio de

Janeiro: Civilização Brasileira, 2005), "Cultures of Difference: The Aftermath of Portuguese and British Colonial Policies in Southern Africa" (*Social Anthropology*) and "O significado da anemia falciforme no contexto da 'política racial' do governo brasileiro 1995–2004" (*História, Ciências, Saúde – Manguinhos*).

Milton Guran (PhD UNICAMP, 1986), Photographer and anthropologist, academic coordinator for the undergraduate course in Social Sciences and the postgraduate course *Photography as a Research Tool in the Social Sciences* in the Institute for the Humanities, Instituto de Humanidades da Universidade Candido Mendes. He is the author of *Agudás – os brasileiros do Benim* (Ed. Nova Fronteira / Ed. Gama Filho, 2000) and *Linguagem fotográfica e informação* (Ed. Gama Filho, 2002, 3rd ed). He won the VITAE Prize (1990), the X Marc Ferrez FUNARTE Prize (1998), and the Pierre Verger Prize of the Associação Brasileira de Antropologia (2002). Coordinator of *FotoRio – Encontro Internacional de Fotografia do Rio de Janeiro*.

Philip J. Havik (PhD Leiden University, The Netherlands, 2004), Researcher at the Centre for African and Asiatic Studies of the Instituto de Investigação Científica Tropical (IICT) in Lisbon, Portugal, and visiting professor at the Department of History, Federal University of Brasilia, Brazil. Recent publications include "Silences and Soundbytes: The Gendered Dynamics of Trade and Brokerage in the Pre-colonial Guinea Bissau region" (Muenster 2004), "Les Noirs et les 'Blancs' de l'Ethnographie Coloniale: discours sur le genre en Guinée Portugaise (1915–1935)" (2005), and *Creole Societies in the Portuguese Colonial Empire* (coedited with. Malyn Newitt, forthcoming).

Luiz Mott (PhD Unicamp, Brazil), Professor of Anthropology at the University of Bahia and a political activist. He has worked extensively on popular religion and the Inquisition in Brazil. His publications include *Rosa Egipcíaca: Uma Santa Africana no Brasil Colonial.* (Editora Bertrand 1993) and *Escravidão, Homossexualidade e Demonologia.* (Editora Icone 1988). He founded the Grupo Gay da Bahia and has worked on Gay rights and AIDS prevention.

Nancy Priscilla Naro (PhD University of Chicago, 1981), Lecturer at the Pontifícia Universidade Católica do Rio de Janeiro (1976–1983), and the Universidade Federal Fluminense Rio de Janeiro (1983–1995); currently Reader in Brazilian History at King's College, London and Co-Director of the project "Cultures of the Lusophone Black Atlantic" at the Centre for the Study of Brazilian Culture and Society, King's College London. She has worked extensively on the transition from slave to free labor. She is the author of *A Slave's Place, a Master's World. Fashioning Dependence in Rural* Brazil (Continuum 2000); editor and contributor *Blacks, Coloureds and national identity in nineteenth-century Latin America* (ILAS 2003).

Roger Sansi-Roca (PhD University of Chicago, 2003), Lecturer, Department of Anthropology, Goldsmith's College, and Co-Director of the project "Cultures of the Lusophone Black Atlantic" at the Centre for the Study of Brazilian Culture and Society, King's College London. His publications include "Catholic Saints, African Gods, Black Masks and White Heads: Tracing the History of Some Religious Festivals in Bahia." (*Portuguese Studies*) and *Fetishes and Monuments: Afro-Brazilian Art and Culture in Bahia* (forthcoming).

Clara Saraiva, Senior Researcher at the Lisbon Institute for Tropical Scientific research (IICT) and Professor, Department of Anthropology, Universidade Nova de Lisboa. She has carried out fieldwork in Guinea-Bissau on funerary rituals and religion among the Pepel, and on issues of transnational religion among migrants in Lisbon.

David H. Treece (PhD University of Liverpool, 1987), Camoens Professor, Department of Portuguese and Brazilian Studies and Director of the Centre for the Study of Brazilian Culture and Society, King's College London. His publications include *Exiles, Allies, Rebels: Brazil's Indianist Movement, Indigenist Politics, and the Imperial Nation-State* (Greenwood Press 2000) and "Rhythm And Poetry: Politics, Aesthetics and Popular Music in Brazil since 1960," in Anny Brooksbank Jones and Ronaldo Munck (eds.), *Cultural Politics in Latin America* (Macmillan 2000) He has done research on literary Indianism and indigenous politics, Brazilian Cultural History; twentieth-century Brazilian poetry and popular music; contemporary Brazilian fiction and its translation. He is currently finalizing a manuscript on black music in Brazil.

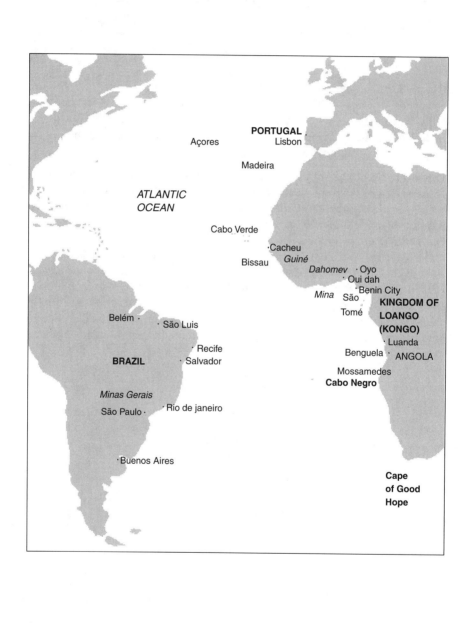

Introduction

The Atlantic, between Scylla and Charybdis

Nancy Priscilla Naro, Roger Sansi-Roca, and David H. Treece

"*It is not a matter of sailing between lands, since their situation would be unknown and their existence only a hypothesis. The reversal that is being proposed is quite more radical: only the travel is real, not the land, and the routes are replaced by the rules of navigation.*"[1]

"Routes, routes, routes, routes, routes, routes, routes"[2]

After decades of obsession with "difference," historians, anthropologists, and other students of culture are directing their gaze to the seas and oceans as historical spaces of cultural production. Hidden dangers abound because, as historical and cultural spaces, the seas possess no visible boundaries, no inscribed landmarks, and no entitled owners; such dangers can and do, however, afford new opportunities. The seas loom up as seamless wholes that can absorb and reflect human history with the same plasticity with which they absorb and reflect the rays of the sun. They allow us to suspend for a moment our rigid and dogmatic dichotomies between nations, civilizations, Us and Them, Europe and Africa, the West and the Rest.

These dichotomies have historically been constructed by a denial of the oceanic space as a space of culture, by its transformation into a kind of abstract passage, "the middle-passage." Retrospectively, the oceans have been seen as passages through which one agent—the imperial agent, the West—exported and imposed itself throughout the world, to the Rest. Or alternatively, as a passage through which resistant identities of the Rest of the world have confronted the West. But in fact, both the West and the Rest are a result of this passage: it is not only a means to their own reproduction, it is their foundation.

From the 1960s and 1970s, dependency and world-systems theories (Braudel 1975; Gunder Frank 1978; Rodney 1972; Wallerstein 1976; Wolf 1982) argued that history and the social sciences should take as their primary subject of analysis not only individual nations, but the world-systems into which they were integrated. As far as the formation of the West was concerned, this meant the capitalist world-economy (Wallerstein 1976). The expansion of capitalism and industrialization in Europe was understood to be directly related to the colonial exploitation of the slave trade in Africa and raw materials such as sugar, cotton, and coffee in the Americas and Asia. In the last twenty years, the attention of anthropologists and historians has shifted from the economic means of production of these world-systems to the cultural and ideological foundations that sustained them. A pioneering work in this direction was Mintz and Price's *The Birth of African-American Culture*, where they described colonial slave societies in the Americas not simply as an encounter between two "bodies" of belief and value, Africa and Europe: rather slaves in the Americas began to share a culture precisely by creating it in the New World, in the colonial context (Mintz and Prize 1992 [1976]: 14).

It must be pointed out that the scope of Mintz and Price's work was limited to "African-American" cultures described as a sort of unintended consequence of the economic world system that created colonialism and slavery. Europe, Africa, and the Americas were still implicitly described as different players in this system, with different positions in the African-American equation: Africa provided the labor force and its culture; this culture was radically transformed, not to say destroyed, by the capitalist world economy, controlled by Europe; and the consequence was and is an African-American "Creole"[3] culture that redefines aspects of the African past in the new framework of the world economy. In this narrative, Europe was the main agent, Africa a passive victim, and the New World the space of transformation.

The arguments of Mintz and Price generated a violent reaction since its publication, and they still do today. One of the main criticisms to their "creolization" model is that it denies the agency of Africans or the influence of African cultures in the Americas. In contraposition to this creolization model, a school of historians of Africa and the slave trade has taken an "Afrocentric" position (Lovejoy 1997, Thornton 1992, Heywood 2001) that claims to reassess the influence of Africa in the formation of the Americas. In *Africa and Africans in the Making of the Atlantic World* (1992), John Thornton clearly states that the history of Africa as a diverse continent in a deep transformation was central to the formation of Atlantic trade and American societies. But still, the dynamism with which the historical transformations of Africa are described by Thornton is a bit lost on the second half of the book, *Africans in the New World*, which is basically concerned with the cultural continuities between Africa and the Americas. Thus Africans are shown taking change in their own hands, while African Americans are preserving the past.

Thornton's fascinating previous work on Kongo had shown how many of the cultural transformations that were supposed to have taken place in the Americas in fact had an African origin: the case of the Christianization of Kongo (Thornton 1984, 1988) and its influence on popular religion in the Americas is extremely important in this sense. In many ways, his work did bring back the issue of creolization to Africa, and not just to the Americas, even if he did not directly follow the model of Mintz and Price. In fact, as Price says (2003), when getting down to the particular historical facts, the contraposition of the creolization and the Afrocentric schools seems a bit overdrawn by the latter, perhaps for political reasons.

The differences are bigger, however, when we get to the level of the more general formulations. The problem with an Afrocentric model is its paradoxical closeness to the "Eurocentric" model that world-systems theory was trying to overcome. In the same vein that Eurocentric models of history describe a historical geography in which Europe imposes its civilization on the Americas, the Afrocentric model can easily fall in the same trap praising Africa as a sort of "matrix" civilization (*matriz civilizadora*, as often referred to by intellectuals and the media in Brazil) that gave birth to African-American cultures. In fact, both perspectives are not contradictory, but complementary: both Africa and Europe are reified as coherent totalities defined in a past (the Old World) of which the Americas are the present (the New World). What was revolutionary about the creolization model was that it did break up the genetic geography that posited the Old World as the origin of the New World. The creolization model proposed that American cultures were fully historical cultures: they were not just the result of transposition from here to there; this was not only a new land, but a new situation that generated *unprecedented* exchanges and transformations. The "creole" is not just the hybrid, half-blood offspring of black and white, but something entirely and historically new and different from its predecessors. This is not just a question of genetics but of historicity. The historicity of the creolization of slaves in North America is brilliantly described for example in the works of Ira Berlin (1998), who has shown the gargantuan complexity of these processes in which early "creolized" regions were re-Africanized by new populations, who then became creolized or quite simply American, if in different terms.

Despite their apparent confrontation with the creolization model, the best work of the Afrocentric literature seems to bring into the picture the clear perception that not only was the New World changing constantly, not only were the Americas the place of creolization or historical change, but also Africa was a place where the Atlantic trade had produced deep historical transformations that were not just the result of European imposition, but of the internal dynamics of African societies. In the end, Europe also, by the same token, was not only an agent of transformation, but also a result of it: Europe was also changed by the new Atlantic World. Europe and Africa have always been as creole as the Americas, in spite of the laborious task of historical erasure taken by nationalist narratives for centuries.

All these issues seem evident, but it is necessary to state them clearly to understand why it is important to shift our gaze toward the Atlantic. We have to look at the Atlantic not just as a passage, a separation, between Old and New, agents and patients of History, but as a dynamic space that puts in circulation all the actors involved both as agents and patients of the history that is being produced and reproduced *by* and not only *through* the seas. Shifting our attention from the continents to the Atlantic, we have gained different perspectives. The long process of colonialism formed and transformed not only the cultures of the New World, but also the Old World; and we should understand these transformations simultaneously, as mutually constitutive.

The notion of an Atlantic World has been around for many decades, but traditionally the emphasis has been on Euro-American civilization.[4] Alternatively, the Afrocentric school has emphasized the African input in this Atlantic World (Lovejoy and Rogers 1994; Sollow 1993; Thornton 1992; Heywood 2001), but rarely questioning the historical geography of this Atlantic World as constituted by an "Old" and a "New" world that were related as cause and consequence by the seas.

It was Paul Gilroy, in his seminal work *The Black Atlantic* (1993), who more powerfully argued for the oceans as a space, and not just a passage of culture. He proposed that "cultural historians could take the Atlantic as one single, complex unit of analysis in their discussions of the modern world and use it to produce an explicitly transnational and intercultural perspective" (1993: 15). His objective was to shift the focus of Black studies from African-American cultures to broader dimensions in which Great Britain would also play a formative part in the dialogue of the Black Atlantic identity. For Gilroy, the Black Atlantic can be seen as a "counter-culture of modernity" a living, utopian critique of the contradictions and injustices of capitalist modernity (1993: 38).

The Atlantic metaphor is powerful because it liberates us from the pigeon-holes of the past: we do not just have to "rethink" (Mann and Bay 2001), but we can finally overcome notions of African-American cultures or the African Diaspora that contained the intervention of Africa, Africans, and descendants in the modern world in a secure, protected box, leaving the grand narrative of history to Europe. Did anybody write about the European Diaspora or about Euro-American cultures in the same terms that these post-Africas have been so clearly delineated by scholars? Not that we know of; probably because the history of the European Diaspora is just the grand narrative of modernity. The hyphenated histories and the diasporas always come as second characters to this narrative. They remain as "others" to the big story. Talking about the Black Atlantic as part of modern history, Gilroy tried to open the box and let the sea flows take the lead.

Gilroy's work was actually inspired by Peter Linebaugh and Marcus Rediker's *Many-Headed Hydra* (1990, 2001), a work that addressed the Atlantic space more in terms of class than race. Describing the formation of an international proletariat of sailors, slaves, prostitutes, pirates, and renegades throughout the history of western Atlantic colonialism, these authors claim that from the very outset of the capitalist colonial project, the egalitarian revolutionary ideals of this Atlantic working class constituted a counterforce.

Linebaugh and Rediker's argument encompasses Gilroy's subsuming the Black counterculture into a more general idea of a mongrel Atlantic proletariat, a "Red" Atlantic (Armitage 2001). However, in their attempt to define class or race as a coherent and continuous presence, both *The Multi-Headed Hydra* and *The Black Atlantic* may lead to a similar problem. Both seem to be looking for long and transnational processes of identity formation built in opposition to another Atlantic, the "Capitalist" or "White" Atlantic. Although both argue for the transformative potential of these "countercultures of modernity," it is often unclear if these countercultures are in fact transforming the imperial model they are built against, or if they are only resisting from its periphery. Struggling to define long-lasting, transatlantic countercultures, they may at some points fall into the trap of identity and "difference," which in many ways limits the productive potential of the seas as a master trope. Their treatment of the way in which these identities "resist" the dominant powers still carries a notion of radical and irredeemable difference between One and the Other. The White and the Black Atlantic, the Capitalist and the Proletarian Atlantic, Hercules and the Hydra are in confrontation, but they remain separate like Scylla and Charybdis. This difference implies a hierarchy: the White and the Capitalist always make the first move imposing their will, their "manifest destiny"; while the Black and the Proletarian always resist, sometimes heroically, but never really take the lead. Like Africa and the Other, in these narratives the "alternative" Atlantics are ultimately condemned to be overcome by the force of the West. Defining specific identities as constructed "against," in resistance to modernity or capitalism, these authors spend more time trying to define what constitutes these countercultures, rather than explaining how these identities may in fact be central to what they call modernity; how the Black Atlantic or the Proletarian Atlantic may not be just a reaction to, but constitute an integral part of the modern world.

Maybe we should talk, in more general terms, of an Atlantic modernity. In *Wizards and Scientists* (2002), Stephan Palmié identifies Western Modernity and Afro-American tradition in Cuba as "perspectival refractions of a single encompassing historical formation" (Palmie 2002: 15). For Palmié, there is little reason not to view them as constitutive of each other on an even more viscerally "embedded" level of description" (2002: 61).

These perspectival refractions of the Atlantic ultimately call into question the coherence, the unity, and the lasting success of the project of modernity. They show that the history of colonization has never been a single narrative, the narrative of the imposition of the West over the Rest. Historical anthropologists like Ann Stoler and Nicholas Thomas have argued that we cannot see colonialism simply as the imposition of predetermined political agendas over the colonized. For Thomas, a close examination of colonial situations shows that

> Colonialism cannot be understood if it is assumed that some unitary representation is extended from the metropolis and cast across passive spaces, unmediated by perceptions or encounters, Colonial projects are construed, misconstrued, adapted and enacted by actors whose subjectivities are fractured- half

here, half there, sometimes disloyal, sometimes almost 'on the side' of the people they patronize and dominate, and against the interest of some metropolitan office (Thomas 1994: 60).

The West, like the Rest, is not a coherent, integrated, unchanging structure. It is constituted by a myriad of interests, subjects, discourses, voices that are not necessarily coherent or stable, but historically contingent. In other terms, colonialism is a cultural, historical process. Ultimately, colonialism created its own forms of culture, not reducible to its constitutive elements, neither West nor Rest. And this colonial culture is not just present in the Americas, but has affected the whole of the Atlantic World, and the colonial world in general, including the metropolis. In and through the process of colonial expansion, the West was also transformed. The colonial cultures are not just countercultures or cultures of resistance: they not only resisted the West, but transformed, expanded, and enriched it. Perhaps they should rather be seen—or heard—as *counterpoints*,[5] to invoke a musical analogy, as distinct yet simultaneously resonating voices weaving a polyphonic texture. There is no better example of the contrapuntal movement of Atlantic history than the fate of black music-making whose conceptions of time, space, and motion have so profoundly reshaped those of Western, or even global musical culture. Indeed, it may be that the most fertile resource of conceptual language for theorizing the Atlantic is the field of musical practice. Musical experience—itself a central thread of Atlantic cultural history—is in many ways akin to the fluid, temporally dynamic, multidimensional fabric of oceanic space. In both, a formless reservoir of possibilities, the energetic potential of waves, pulses and currents is harnessed by human initiative so as to set in motion complex patterns of continuity and change, networks of resonance and dissonance, dramas of conflict, dialogue, and transformation. This "ocean of sound" is a virtual, contingent space, structured and made meaningful only insofar as it is "performed" in real time, in the historical present, by those voices, bodies, vessels, and instruments that vibrate and move across it. Music can therefore encourage us to think of the colonial experience with a simultaneous attention to its historical and geographical dimensions, as a temporal and spatial process, a dynamic field of resonances, rather than as a static entity, a unitary map of frontiers and pathways.

Looking at these particular colonial histories, we can offer new perspectives on how these grand narratives were constituted as polyphonies. This does not mean that we have to surrender to a radical historical particularism. One can argue that the West and Rest are not transhistorical entities, but this does not mean that we cannot talk about them. We can, however, only talk about them in relation to each other: there would be no concept of the West if this had not been built in opposition to something else; and both emerge in relation to each other through this relationship. We are observing *the relation* that constructs these oppositions and identities, a relation that is constitutive of the related elements. As Lévi-Strauss said in more poetic terms, "what is real is the voyage, not the land." It is the passage, or even better, the multiple passages, the seas that constituted the land; these multiple passages of the Atlantic built Europe, Africa, and the Americas into what they are at present.

Colonial Cultures and the Portuguese Empire

Charles Boxer (1991) stated that the Portuguese were the first to form a colonial empire in the Atlantic, and the last to surrender it. From the first Portuguese discoveries to the end of the Portuguese Empire in Africa, the Portuguese colonial experience lasted almost six centuries. However, the Portuguese relationship with the Atlantic, of long-standing interest to scholars of the transatlantic slave trade, remains largely ignored or overlooked in many English-language publications on the Atlantic World,[6] reproducing its status as a "marginal" player in the European colonial system (Miller 1993). On the other hand, Lusophone cultural history has traditionally been centered on imperial expansion (e.g., Boxer 1991; Russell-Wood 1992), or has been limited to national boundaries (Russell-Wood 1982), or to the early colonial period (Russell 1995). From our point of view, it has been a mistake to look for a coherent, enduring narrative of the Portuguese Empire, as was proposed in the last century by Gilberto Freyre's "Lusotropicalism" (Freyre 1956, 1962, 1971), and enthusiastically adopted as state ideology in Brazil and in Portugal. Lusotropicalism extolled the peculiarities of Portuguese colonialism. The Lusophone Empire was supposedly more humane and convivial than other European imperial projects. The Portuguese, as opposed to the English or the Dutch, were not racist, it was argued, but generously embraced miscegenation as a form of incorporating colonial peoples into the Portuguese nation.

The fallacies of this approach have been widely and roundly critiqued since the wars of independence and the April 1974 Revolution and it is not our intention to rehearse these arguments again here.[7] In any case, the works in this volume demonstrate how untenable the idea of an all-encompassing, culturally specific and transhistorical Portuguese colonial project is. The diversity of the forms of exchange and cultural production in the different periods, and spaces of the Portuguese colonial world is not reducible to the general model of a "lusotropical" culture. Quite the opposite, the long history of colonial contact in the Lusophone world produced a myriad of colonial cultures.

Historians and anthropologists working in Portuguese-speaking Africa and Brazil are bringing together intellectual history, former national histories, and local histories of colonial cultures, finding complex networks of peoples, religions, and culture in circulation. These new approaches are addressing not only the disjunction within and beyond the empire, but also the unexpected connections and reshufflings that emerged from its margins. The ships did not always sail in the same directions: and like the ships, people, words, and values circulated in the most unexpected ways: Africans from the Americas and the Atlantic islands returned to Africa, and Portuguese, Brazilians, and Africans traveled to and from Brazil, the Atlantic islands, and Portugal during and after the Portuguese Empire (Verger 1968; Carneiro da Cunha 1985; Guran 2000; Mann and Bay 2001).

Local societies and their unexpected world connections are also coming under renewed scrutiny in the conjuncture of the Black Atlantic. For Luiz Felipe de Alencastro (2000, 2004), the dynamics of local societies influence the impact they make on the unity of the Portuguese colonial empire. Alencastro has explored the local agendas at play as the British government increased its pressure on Portugal to suspend the transatlantic slave trade agreed in 1831 with Brazil, but only implemented nearly two decades later at mid-century. For Alencastro, it is imperative to include Mozambique among the local or microagendas in the South Atlantic because of the ongoing British penetration into the area that resulted in major changes in Portuguese colonial aspirations and trade relationships there and beyond. Likewise, by considering the multiple actors and their agendas in the broad South Atlantic conjuncture, Alencastro also reconfigured the chronological dimensions of Brazil's independence, extending the 1808–1822 watershed to mid-century (Alencastro 2004).

The notion of the Black Atlantic is also making its way into the anthropological literature on Afro-Brazilian culture and racial relations. And yet, these studies remain essentially concerned with the present national context (Sansone 2003), or with general narratives of the Black Atlantic formation of Afro-Brazilian religions (Matory 2005). But the larger historical context of the Lusophone Black Atlantic has not been directly addressed up to now. In general terms, historical research and anthropology have largely followed independent trajectories. One of the main objectives of this volume is to finally bring them back together.

The Lusophone Black Atlantic

The purpose of this book is to discuss the advantages, possibilities, and even the limitations of proposing the Lusophone Black Atlantic as a space of historical and cultural production. We are not claiming to unveil a grand narrative of the Portuguese colonial empire or a counternarrative of Black resistance to this empire in Africa and the Americas. Our objective is to demonstrate how the historical continuities throughout this historical space are in fact composed of a myriad of local and specific discontinuities, local cultures, "perspectival refractions" that extend their influence well beyond the Lusophone context, and can be useful in projecting a different perspective on the history of the Atlantic. We understand the history of the Atlantic to be a process of construction of colonial cultures, as cultures of relation, sometimes through identity, sometimes through confrontation. These relations took different forms, from relations between different religions to relations between economies, politics, and races. The Lusophone and the

Black elements in this historical space are not stable identities, but are counterpoints that link these local colonial cultures to the grand narratives of empire. In this sense, this volume addresses the formation of local histories in the context of colonialism, like the Kristons of Guinea (Havik), or the *agudás* of Benin (Guran); but it also looks at how these colonial cultures, from the periphery, were central to the formation of modern notions of labor (Fikes), or of the value of objects through the idea of the *fetish* (Sansi-Roca).

Earlier versions of the contributions to this volume were presented and discussed at two conferences held in 2005: "The Lusophone Black Atlantic in a Comparative Perspective" and "The Portuguese Atlantic: Africa, Brazil and Cape Verde." They present a variety of perspectives and locations bringing together current research in history, anthropology, and cultural studies in different countries including the United States, the United Kingdom, France, Brazil, Portugal, and Lusophone Africa. The book is divided into three parts that range from studies of early colonial encounters to contemporary racial politics.

The chapters in Part I, *Colonial Formations*, address the construction of colonial cultures in the early period of the Portuguese expansion and the enduring influence that some aspects of these cultures were to have in the formation of the Atlantic World as a whole. Religion and sorcery are a recurrent issue in these chapters. Religion was, for the first centuries of Atlantic colonialism, the language through which identity and alterity were objectified more significantly. Religious conflicts and the persecution of sorcery provided a narrative for much broader political, economic, and cultural conflicts that shaped the modern states of Europe during their colonial expansion. The confrontations between Christians and Muslims and the persecution of the Jews lay at its very origins; the opposition between Christians and Pagans emerged, as unknown lands were encountered; but it was especially the conflict between Catholics and Protestants that infused the historical space of the Atlantic with radical divisions. In this section, religious identities are as paramount to the discussions of the early cultural formations of Afro-Atlantic societies as are the ways in which the Portuguese and Spanish empire attempted to control these cultural formations through religious institutions like the Inquisition and accusations of heresy and sorcery. In "Kriol without Creoles: Rethinking Guinea's Afro-Atlantic Connections (Sixteenth to Twentieth Centuries)," Philip Havik describes how the Kriston communities in Guinea became mediators between the Catholic Atlantic and the societies of inland Africa through their command of the religions and languages of both worlds. In more general terms, in "The Fetish in the Lusophone Black Atlantic," Roger Sansi-Roca describes the long and convoluted history of the term fetish. From the Portuguese *feitiço* (magical spell) it arrived on the coasts of West Africa in the context of formation of an Atlantic cultural complex of sorcery (*feitiçaria*) that involved both Europeans and Africans. But by the eighteenth century, the Portuguese origin of the term had been almost forgotten, and Protestant north European travelers identified the *fetish* and *fetishism* as the religion of the Africans, misrecognizing its creole, transcultural origin. In the following centuries, paradoxically, these concepts would be used to demonstrate the backwardness and inferiority of "fetishist" Africans in relation to Europeans. Another aspect of the Atlantic discourse on sorcery is presented in Luiz Mott's chapter "Historical Roots of Homosexuality in the Lusophone Atlantic," where he discusses the persecution of sodomy and its association with sorcery in the Inquisition trials.

The contributors to Part II of the book, *Migrations and Colonial Cultures*, bring to the discussion different populations at the margins of the Lusophone world. The ambiguity of the relationship of these peoples with the core of the Portuguese Empire requires a more nuanced and critical vision of the Lusophone Atlantic and its colonial cultures than the traditional narratives of empire. In "Atlantic Microhistories: Mobility, Personal Ties, and Slaving in the Black Atlantic World (Angola and Brazil)," Roquinaldo Ferreira looks at the life histories of Brazilian slave traders in Angola, and how the links with the two sides of the South Atlantic can be described almost independently of its imperial center in the North Atlantic.

A common issue in this set of chapters is migration and cultural relocation. In "Colonial Aspirations: Connecting Three Points of the Portuguese Black Atlantic," Nancy Naro describes the reconfiguration of the Portuguese Empire after the independence of Brazil from the perspective of Portuguese exiles from independent Brazil resettling in Angola so as to reinvent the colony. In "Agudás from Benin: 'Brazilian' Identity as a Bridge to Citizenship," Milton Guran presents the case of the Agudás, ex-slaves who returned to Africa and reconfigured their identity there as Brazilians—cultural mediators between Europeans and Africans. Finally, in "Emigration and the Spatial Production of Difference from Cape Verde," Kesha Fikes presents the formation of the Cape Verdian "difference," its "racial ambivalence," from the perspective of Cape Verdians in the islands and the diaspora. Instead of defining Cape Verde as a space *in between*, Fikes describes it as a space *from*, a space of origin, not just of encounter and mixture.

Finally, Clara Saraiva in "African and Brazilian Altars in Lisbon" shows how African and Brazilian immigrants reinvent their religious traditions in the motherland, Portugal. On the other hand, Portuguese reappropriate the religious practices of Afro-Brazilian Umbanda. In both cases, elements of the culture and the traditions and elements of the local culture of the metropolis are reconfigured in particular ways, creating new, unprecedented synthesis.

Beyond general ideas about identity and its politics, the invention of tradition, and "imagined communities," two common and concrete issues—work and the family—emerged as key to an understanding of the continuities and discontinuities in these colonial cultures. Work, and its opposite, "vagrancy" (*vadiagem*) often appear in relation to each other: the migrants are often accused of being vagrants by local elites, when in fact they are precisely the contrary—they are former slaves. On the other hand, these migrant communities often only have one clear source of identity and solidarity—their extended families. More than in alliance or opposition to the state, the nation, or the ethnic group, these migrant communities in unstable spaces build their life histories and their cultures around these more grounded institutions.

Black Lusophone cultural formations have often been invoked as exemplary cases of hybridity, miscegenation, and syncretism. And yet, in recent years, political and cultural movements have laid claim to a more nationalist and essentialist notion of "Africanity" and cultural purity. These transformations are also related to changes in cultural policy and the influence of transnational discourses on race and ethnicity. The chapters in Part III *Hybridity, Multiculturalism, and Racial Politics,* address these current transformations. In "History and Memory in *Capoeira* Lyrics," Matthias Assunção describes how the history of *capoeira* and the history of Brazil are reflected in the lyrics of *capoeira* songs. Particularly interesting is his observation of the shift toward more explicitly political lyrics than those related to African roots and slave resistance. In "The *"Orisha* Religion" between Syncretism and Re-Africanization," Stefania Capone describes the process of re-Africanization of Candomblé in Brazil, and how the creation of international networks between different African-American religions is resulting in a further reinscription and reinvention of its practices and values.

Transnational political models of multiculturalism, based on ideals of cultural (and racial) "purity" and "authenticity" are also redefining previous models of the miscegenated nation. In the final chapter of this volume, "Undoing Brazil: Hybridity versus Multiculturalism," Peter Fry reflects on the unpredictable consequences of this process in Brazilian cultural politics.

A final consideration about this volume concerns the biographical and intellectual trajectories of its contributors, which in many ways resemble the processes of "perspectival refraction" or the cultural counterpoint that the chapters collectively address. There is a certain irony in that, just as the Anglophone academic world was won over by a postcolonial theory critical of ethnocentrism, much of the academic production of this postcolonial turn adopted an Anglophone perspective. The "Anglocentric" hegemony of intellectual production became consolidated in recent decades even when it was led by "subaltern" studies.[8]

The Black Atlantic has not been an exception to this rule. A counterpoint has evolved in the Lusophone world (particularly in Brazil) where intellectuals are *au fait* with the intellectual production of their Anglophone counterparts. Their research reflects the earnestness and vigor of an intellectual tradition that questioned the now fashionable terms "hybridity" and "syncretism" well before they were rediscovered by their Anglophone counterparts. Many of the contributors to this volume are Lusophone scholars who had academic training in European and American universities; the rest are European and North American scholars who not only carried out research in the Lusophone world, but continue to work in Lusophone countries and, in some cases, have become naturalized Brazilians or Portuguese. But despite that, often they are not considered "cosmopolitan" scholars, because their publications in foreign languages have been relatively unknown or neglected in the English-speaking centers of cosmopolitan academic production. They have become "local" or provincial scholars of "exotic" cultures whose research, as cutting-edge as it is, is largely acknowledged only by a small body of specialists in their particular area.

In this respect, it would be unfair not to recognize that although many of the authors of this volume have lived and done research in that continent, none of them is from Lusophone Africa. This is at least in part a reflection of the fact that academic production in Angola, Mozambique, Cape Verde, and São Tomé has still not achieved the level of recognition enjoyed by Brazilian and Portuguese history and anthropology. But this is just a partial excuse. Following volumes should make an effort to represent more fully the intellectual, as well as thematic scope of the Atlantic space.

Finally, we wish to emphasize that this is not a collection that transposes the latest theories of Anglophone cultural and postcolonial studies to a "forgotten" part of the world. It is not just an invitation to extend the scholarly gaze of the cosmopolitan to the Lusophone Black Atlantic. In fact, we would hope that it would be the other way around: that Anglophone scholars working on the Atlantic might take on board questions and interpretations that derive *from* other perspectives and gain unanticipated insights into their own fields of interest.

However, this does not mean that the different contributors to this volume share the same perspective on the Lusophone Black Atlantic; that is almost inevitable in a volume with such a wide range of topics, disciplines, and scholarly traditions. In the same terms that we do not defend the unity of an imperial Lusotropical culture but the plurality of colonial cultures in the Lusophone space, we also want to acknowledge the diversity of voices and "scholarly cultures." Our first objective was to offer an overarching view of the field, to open this space, and propose some questions and ideas to discuss in wider arenas, not just within Atlantic studies, but through the Atlantic, into the interrelated fields of History, Anthropology, and Cultural Studies in general. If we achieve this objective, we will be more than satisfied.

Notes

1. Il ne s'agit pas de voguer vers d'autres terres, leur situation fût-elle inconnue et leur existence hypothétique. Le renversement qu'on propose est beaucoup plus radical : seul le voyage est réel, non la terre, et les routes sont remplacées par les règles de navigation (Claude Lévi-Strauss, *Mythologiques, le Cru et le Cuit* [Paris: Plon, 1964], 33).

2. "Roteiros. Roteiros. Roteiros. Roteiros. Roteiros. Roteiros. Roteiros" (Oswald de Andrade, "Manifesto Antropofágico," *Revista de Antropofagia* 1(1) 1928: 2).

3. The term Creole, *crioulo* in Portuguese, means both a descendant of Europeans born in the New World (as in Spanish) or a descendant of Africans born in the New World, However, the second meaning is dominant in Brazil.

4. For a historiography of the use of these terms, see Gabaccia 2004.

5. Counterpoint is understood here not only as a feature of post-medieval European art music, but also of jazz and other African-American musical forms.

6. In the journal *Atlantic Studies*, launched in 2004, for example, despite one contributor's claim to deal with the state-of-the-art of past and current research on the Atlantic, the Portuguese contribution to the Black Atlantic is largely unaddressed. The article draws on the issues of division and unity of national identities on either side of the Atlantic prioritizing the North Atlantic and, specifically, studies concerning the United States (Gabaccia 2004).

7. For postcolonial criticisms of the Lusotropicalist ideology see Amilcar Cabral (1978), Mário Pinto de Andrade (1975), Margarido (1975). More recent assessments of Lusotropicalism can be found in Chabal (2000), Thomaz (2002), and Vale de Almeida (2005).

8. Bourdieu and Wacquant's explicit argument about these questions in "On the Cunning of Imperialist Reason" (1999) generated an interesting reaction including Fry (2000) and others in *Theory, Culture & Society* 17(1): 2000.

Bibliography

Alencastro, Luiz Felipe de. 2000. *O Trato dos Viventes: Formação do Brasil no Atlântico Sul Séculos XVI e XVII* São Paulo: Companhia das Letras.

————. 2004. "Continental Drift: The Independence of Brazil (1822), Portugal and Africa," in Olivier Pétré-Grenouilleau, ed. *From Slave Trade to Empire. Europe and the Colonisation of Black Africa 1780s–1880s*. London: Routledge, pp.98–109.

Almeida, Miguel Vale de. 2004. *An Earth-Coloured Sea*. Oxford: Berghahn books.

Andrade, Mário Pinto de. 1975. *Antologia temática da poesia africana*. Lisbon: Sá da Costa.

Armitage, D. 2001. "The Red Atlantic." *Reviews in American History* 29(2001): 479–586.

Berlin, Ira. 1998. *Many Thousands Gone: The First Two Centuries of Slavery in North America*. Cambridge, Mass.: The Belknap Press/Harvard University Press.

Bourdieu, P. and L. Wacquant. 1999. "On the Cunning of Imperialist Reason." *Theory, Culture, Society* 16(1): 41–58. Trans. D.M. Robbins and L.Wacquant.

Boxer, C.R. 1991. *The Portuguese Seaborne Empire, 1415–1825*. Manchester: Carcanet.

Braudel, Fernand. 1975. *The Mediterranian and the Mediterranian World in the Age of Phillip the II*. London: Collins.

Cabral, Amilcar. 1978. *Obras Escolhidas*. Porto: Seara Nova.

Carneiro da Cunha, Manuela. 1985. *Negros Estrangeiros. Os escravos libertos e sua volta à Africa*. São Paulo: Brasiliense.

Chabal, Patrick, with David Birmingham, Joshua Forrest, Malyn Newitt, Gerhard Seibert, and Elisa Silvia Andrade. 2000. *A History of Postcolonial Lusophone Africa*. London: Hurst and Company.

Freyre, Gilberto. 1956. *The Masters and the Slaves (Casa-Grande & Senzala): A Study in the development of Brazilian Civilization*. London: Weidenfeld and Nicolson.

————. 1962. *O Brasil em face das Áfricas negras e mestiças*. Rio de Janeiro: Federação das Associações Portuguesas.

Freyre, Gilberto. 1971. *Novo mundo nos trópicos*. São Paulo: Companhia Editora Nacional.

Fry, Peter. 2000. "Politics, Nationality, and the Meanings of "Race" in Brazil." *Daedalus* 129(2): 83–118.

Gabaccia, Donna. 2004. "A Long Atlantic in a Wider World." *Atlantic Studies* 1(1): 1–27.

Gilroy, Paul. 1992. *The Black Atlantic: Modernity and Double-Consciousness.* Cambridge, Mass.: Harvard University Press.

Grenouilleau, Olivier Pétré, ed. 2004. *From Slave Trade to Empire.* London: Routledge.

Gunder Frank, André. 1978. *Dependent Accumulation and Underdevelopment.* London: Macmillan.

Guran, Milton. 2000. *Os Agudás. Os "brasileiros" do Benim.* Rio de Janeiro: Nova Fronteira/Universidade de Gama Filho.

Heywood, Linda, ed. 2001. *Central Africans and Cultural Transformations in the American Diaspora.* Cambridge: Cambridge University Press.

Linebaugh, Peter and Marcus Radiker. 1990. "The Many-Headed Hydra: Sailors, Slaves, and the Atlantic Working Class in the Eighteenth Century." *Journal of Historical Sociology* 3(3): 225–253.

———. 2002. *The Many-headed Hydra: Sailors, Slaves, Commoners, and the Hidden History of the Revolutionary Atlantic.* London: Verso.

Lovejoy, Paul E. 1997. "Identifying Enslaved Africans: Methodological and Conceptual Considerations in Studying the African Diaspora." UNESCO. SSHRCC Summer Institute, York University.

Lovejoy, Paul and Nicholas Rogers, eds. 1994. *Unfree Labour in the Development of the Atlantic World.* London: Frank Cass.

Mann, Kirstin and Edna G. Bay, eds. 2001. *Rethinking the African Diaspora. The Making of a Black Atlantic World in the Bight of Benin and Brazil.* London: Frank Cass.

Margarido, Alfredo. 1975. "Le colonialisme portugais et l' anthropologie," in Copans, Jean, ed. *Anthropologie et Impérialisme.* Paris: Maspero, pp.134–155.

Matory, Lorand J. 2005. *Black Atlantic Religion: Tradition, Transnationalism, and Matriarchy in the Afro-Brazilian Candomblé.* Princeton: Princeton University Press.

Miller, Joseph. 1993. "A Marginal Institution on the Margin of the Atlantic System: The Portuguese Southern Atlantic Slave Trade in the Eighteenth Century," in Barbara Sollow, ed. *Slavery and the Rise of the Atlantic System.* Cambridge: Cambridge University Press, pp.120–150.

Mintz, Sidney W. and Richard Price. 1991 (1972). *The Birth of African-American Culture.* Boston: Beacon Press.

Palmié, Stephan. 2002. *Wizards and Scientists : Explorations in Afro-Cuban Modernity and Tradition.* Durham, NC: Duke University Press.

Price, Richard. 2003. "O milagre da Creolização: Retrospetiva." *Estudos Afro-Asiáticos* 25(3): 383–419.

Rodney, Walter. 1972. *How Europe Underdeveloped Africa.* London: Bogle-L'Overture.

Russell, P.E. 1995. *Portugal, Spain, and the African Atlantic, 1343–1490.* Variorum: Aldershot.

Russell-Wood, A.J.R. 1982. *The Black Man in Slavery and Freedom in Colonial Brazil.* London: Macmillan.

———. 1992. *A World on the Move: The Portuguese in Africa, Asia and America, 1415–1808.* Manchester: Carcanet.

Sansone, Livio. 2003. *Blackness without Ethnicity: Constructing Race in Brazil.* New York: Palgrave MacMillan.

Sollow, Barbara, ed. 1993. *Slavery and the Rise of the Atlantic System*. Cambridge: Cambridge University Press.

Stoler, Ann Laura. 1995. *Race and the Education of Desire: Foucault's History of Sexuality and the Colonial Order of Things*. Durhan, NC: Duke University Press.

Thomas, Nicholas. 1994. *Colonialism's Culture: Anthropology, Travel and Government*. Cambridge: Polity Press.

Thomaz, Omar Ribeiro. 2002. *Ecos do Atlântico Sul*. Rio de Janeiro: Ed. UFRJ-Fapesp.

Thornton, John. 1984. "The Development of an African Church in the Kingdom of Kongo 1491–1750." *The Journal of African History* 25(2): 147–167.

———. 1988. "On the Trail to Voodoo: African Christianity in Africa and the Americas." *The Americas* 44(1988): 261–278.

———. 1992. *Africa and Africans in the Making of the Atlantic World*. Cambridge: Cambridge Universiy Press.

Verger, Pierre. 1968. *Flux et reflux de la traite de nègres entre le Golfe du Bénin et Bahia de Todos os Santos du XVIIème au XIXème siècles*. Paris/Le Haye: Mouton & Co.

Wallerstein, Immanuel. 1976. "A World-System Perspective in the Social Sciences." *The British Journal of Sociology* 27 (September 1976): 343–352.

Wolf, Eric Robert. 1982. *Europe and the People without History*. Berkeley, CA: University of California Press.

Part I

Colonial Formations

Chapter 1

The Fetish in the Lusophone Atlantic

Roger Sansi-Roca

The term "fetish" has a long and complex story bound to the history of the Atlantic. It originates from the Portuguese term *feitiço*, magic charm, and *feitiçaria* (sorcery). The Portuguese recognized many of the ritual practices they encountered in Africa as forms of sorcery. References to the fetish date from the seventeenth century, in Dutch and English travel accounts of the West Coast of Africa. Travelers often misrecognized the Portuguese origin of the term, and defined the fetish as a specifically African religion. For these Protestant travelers, this African religion was particularly deviant: it seemed to be based on self-interest, chance, and the worship of material things. From the eighteenth century on, theories of "fetishism" became central to Western discourses on Africa. For enlightened philosophers, African fetishists would be unable to distinguish objects from subjects, religion from economy, and good from evil. Fetishism sent Africans far back in history to the dark origins of humanity at an impossible distance from enlightened Europe.

Since the late nineteenth century, anthropologists have rejected the terms fetish and fetishism as false concepts that projected a perverse and disrespectful image of African religions. For Mauss, the theory of fetishism is an *immense malentendu*, an "enormous misunderstanding" (Iacono 1992). A misunderstanding that, in fact, may reveal more about the ideologies of the Westerners who invented it, than about the African religions it was supposed to describe. Marx and Freud were well aware of that fact when they described the implicit fetishism of Western bourgeois society, from commodities to sexuality.

William Pietz explained this story in "The Problem of the Fetish" (Pietz 1985, 1987, 1988). His central thesis is that "the fetish, as an idea and a problem, and as a novel object not proper to any prior discrete society, originated in the cross-cultural spaces of the coast of West-Africa during the sixteenth and seventeenth centuries" (Pietz 1985: 5). For Pietz, "The fetish, then, not only originated from, but remains specific to, the problematic of the social value of material objects as revealed in situations formed by the encounter of radically heterogeneous social systems."

Pietz's writings on the fetish and fetishism have had a seminal influence in the last twenty years (Apter and Pietz 1993; Spyer 1998; Latour 1996; Graeber 2005). However, most of Pietz's followers have been more interested in the final part of his account: how the African fetish became the European discourse on fetishism. But how did the Portuguese *feitiço* become the African fetish in the first place?

The Portuguese disappear from most travel narratives at a very early stage. They are presented exclusively as the picturesque southern European people from whom the word was borrowed. But the presence of the Portuguese in Africa was not limited to the spread of some unusual words. European travelers were not encountering only African societies, but Creole societies that were both African and European in many ways. The Portuguese and other Europeans had been trading and mixing with Africans for almost two centuries by the time these travelers started discussing the fetish. However, the silence of Protestant travelers in reference to the Portuguese is quite clearly an intentional misrecognition that resulted from a long war in which the Dutch, the English, and the Danes replaced the Portuguese predominance on the coast. Eliminating the Portuguese and the Creoles from the travel accounts was nothing but a consequence of their defeat.

The relevance of the Portuguese and the Creoles is greater than has been acknowledged by Pietz and his readers, who readily reduced this story to a dualist confrontation between Westerners and Africans when, in reality, the characters in this story were "in between." North European travelers appeared to be profoundly disturbed about the creolization of societies on the African coast, and did not quite know how to address it. Although creolization had involved Europeans of all nations and creeds since the first contacts with Africa, the enemies of the Portuguese specifically identified it with the latter. They were seen to be the archetypes of a former kind of colonialism that was too improvised and precarious, and that had to be obliterated and replaced by more effective strategies of trade, settlement, and appropriation. Moreover their religion, Catholicism, was described as being very similar to Fetishism, the religion of the Africans.

The criticism of fetishism then was not only addressed to Africa in itself, but more widely to the Afro-European Atlantic societies of the coast that presented a more definite threat to the European travelers due to their proximity to them. In addition to building a discourse on the irredeemable difference between Africa and Europe, it was also vital to deny the possibility of any intermediate space, a space that could be European and African at the same time.

If the discourse of fetishism denied the possibility of an intermediary space, what happened to all the Creole societies that had emerged at the rims of the Atlantic? They would be refused their place in history even more emphatically than Africa. Africa, at least, was in the primitive past. But where would be Cape Verde or Brazil, outposts of a decadent empire? What would be their place in history? In the following centuries, intellectuals from the Lusophone world attempted to adapt the philosophies of the Western Enlightenment to their own reality. In the late nineteenth century, Brazilian social scientists like Raymundo Nina Rodrigues struggled to divide their society into its European and African components. Replacing the *feitiço*, the Creole, miscegenated discourse on sorcery, with the scientific discourse on fetishism was central to this endeavor. In spite of the absolute rejection today of the scientific racism of these authors, it is possible to trace their influence on the countless scholars who continue to search for an authentic Afro-Brazilian culture.

In the following pages I plan to unravel the traces of the history of the fetish in the Atlantic from a Lusophone perspective. I will initially interrogate how Portuguese discourse and practices of sorcery, the *feitiço* and *feitiçaria,* spread throughout West Africa along with creolization. Secondly I will look at how the Portuguese *feitiço* and *feitiçaria* became "the fetish" and "fetishism." I will show how throughout the eighteenth century, the creolized, Afro-Portuguese discourse on sorcery was reinterpreted by Protestant traders as a specifically African discourse on religion, fetishism, the religion of the fetish. And finally, I will return to the Lusophone world to show how notions of the fetish and fetishism were appropriated in late nineteenth century Brazil. Here, some social thinkers proposed to redefine practices of *feitiçaria* as fetishism. In other words, they classified local forms of sorcery as a foreign, primitive, and essentially *different* African fetishist cult. In so doing, they were proposing to build an intellectual separation in Brazilian society between a European and an African Brazil. A separation that, I will argue, did not really exist at that time nor does it exist today.

Sorcery in the Lusophone Atlantic

Portuguese accounts of the discoveries in West Africa are not very prolix in describing the everyday life of the Africans they encountered. Occasionally one finds the discoverers asking the native kings to give up their idolatries and sorceries (*idolatrias* e *feitiçarias*) and convert to Christianity.[1] *Idolatria* and *feitiçaria* appear together but they are not the same thing. Idolatry is an erudite term of the medieval church that makes reference to the organized cult of idols, or false gods, essentially in the form of images and sculptures of human resemblance. It was assumed that pagan peoples were idolaters, and that idolatry was inspired by the Devil and by their ignorance of the Word of God. (Bernand and Gruzinski 1988). *Feitiçaria*, sorcery, was linked to idolatry, but they were not the same. Idolatry is a religious cult, with priests and acts of religion toward gods, even if these are false gods or idols. *Feitiçaria* or sorcery is not religion; it is magic—the techniques of enchantment. *Feiticeiros* are not priests, but private practitioners of the arts of magic—people who make spells and charms of love, wealth, and death. The objective of *feitiçaria* is not worship but the solution of practical problems of life.

The persecution of the practices of sorcery in modern Portugal and Spain by the Inquisition came quite late, and was secondary to its main objective: the persecution of other religions—heresy. Sorcery was not heresy or the practice of another creed, but a singular contract with the Devil. In most cases, the pact with the Devil could not be proved and the accused were declared innocent (maybe after years of preemptive imprisonment and torture) (Bethencourt 1994).

This was not a persecution of other religions, but of personal contracts with the Devil. As such, sorcery was a universal phenomenon, not culturally specific, and it was also a personal crime committed by single individuals.[2]

The Inquisition records reveal that in Portugal, magical rituals had a great plasticity and easily adjusted to the needs and aspirations of people from different social origins (Bethencourt 1987). From the rural midwife who gave abortive plants to a pregnant girl to the cosmopolitan alchemist, there were a wide range of people, practices, and techniques that may have had nothing in common except for the fact that they were suspected at one point or another of deceit and dishonesty if they failed or of having a contract with the Devil if they succeeded.

The practices and objects described by the Inquisition records had two main aims: to protect against unfortunate events and to propitiate fortunate events. On the one hand, the body is seen as a place of potential danger where devils and beasts can enter (Bethencourt 1987: 57), and therefore it is necessary to protect it—"sealing the body" (*fechar o corpo*) as it is still said nowadays. On the other hand, amulets were also supposed to influence people, or to use the correct term, achieve "grace" ("Alcançar graça com quem quisesse" [Bethencourt 1987: 68]) particularly in love or social affairs.

The elements that went into the making of amulets were also in some ways exceptional: the rope of a hanged man; a broken mirror (Bethencourt 1987: 52), parts of bodies of beasts (Bethencourt 1986: 53), bones of dead people, or the saliva of somebody dying ("a baba de uma pessoa que estivesse à hora da morte" [Bethencourt 1987: 85]).

The actual origin and forms of collecting these things is perhaps more important to understand their value than what they represent: more significant than the symbolism of the rope and the saliva, whatever that may be, is the collection of these items from the most exceptional events, such as the transition from life and death, and that makes them the indexes of the event. The collection of any saliva or rope would not do since these have power, they are *feitiços*. Their power is more a result of this indexicality, this causal relationship with the supernatural event, than what they represent, their symbolism.[3]

To achieve grace, the *pedra d' ara* (altar stone) is one of the more frequently used amulets. The altar stone was a "portable altar," a "piece of marble with an opening where relics of holy martyrs were placed and over which priests consecrated the communion host and wine" (Souza 1986: 132). Consecrated holy hosts were also commonly used. However, the value of the *pedras d' ara* and the holy hosts should not be taken exclusively in symbolic terms. They are valuable because they have been through the Eucharist, the most miraculous of events, and they are indexes of the power of the Christ. It is interesting to note that the first Mass had to wait for the arrival of the *pedras d' ara*, altar stones from Portugal—as if only these could take the place of the local idols (Brasio 1952: 66). In fact, at the end of the nineteenth century, the place where the first mass with the *pedras d' ara* took place had become a rain charm, a fetish called Sa Manuela, after Manuel, the first convert, formerly the Mani Soyo, uncle of the King (MacGaffey 1988: 207).

The plasticity of magical practices is a consequence of the unpredictability of the relationship between humans and beings from the other world. Since Evans-Pritchard (1937), it is known that sorcery, or magic in its positive incarnation, is not ignorant of the laws of nature. On the contrary, it is very much grounded in them. However, when an event cannot be explained in relation to these laws, when something extraordinary happens, one should look for an effective cause behind these laws in some personal agencies—gods, spirits, or sorcerers. The power of the *feitiço* is intimately related to this extraordinary event.

This point could be better understood by reading Bluteau's definitions of *feitiçaria* and *feitiço* in the first Portuguese dictionary, *Vocabulario Portuguez e Latino* of 1713. He gives two possible definitions of *feitiço*. For one, he says, a *feitiço* is an event that in itself would not have any consequences, if it was not caused by the Devil.[4] For example, in reference to a salamander that is scrambling up the front door of a house, he argues that it could be just that, a salamander; but it could also be a sign of the Devil. A *feitiço* is an *event* that cannot be reduced to its natural causes. The second definition of *feitiço* is an artifice,[5] some thing invented to seduce and enchant people. *Feitiço*, in this second sense acquires a more material presence than in the first sense, where it is more an event than a thing. But obviously both questions are connected: a *feitiço* is an event that becomes objectified in a thing—it contains the consequences of this action, indexing it.

What is socially described as *feitiçaria* is therefore more a loose body of beliefs and practices related with fear and desire, the unexpected, the marvelous, and fate, than a positive and systematized body of knowledge. The loose complex of *feitiçaria* seems to be inevitably relevant for the seafarers who crossed the oceans where they would have to face the more randomly dangerous events and adventures. These seamen wore amulets and recognized *feitiços* in the extraordinary things and people they found on their way—for example, in Africa.

On the West Coast of Africa, the conversion of the idolaters was not a priority of Portuguese tradesmen who did not actively promote Christianity since they had no intention of occupying the African hinterland. However, on the coast of Guinea, "freelance" *tangomãos* and *lançados* brought elements of Christianity and European culture (Brooks 2003). Many were former sailors, *degredados* (outcasts), Jews, or mixed-race Portuguese who knew the land and spoke the local languages. In connection with trade, communities of Christianized African traders, the Kriston, emerged throughout the coast (Havik, this volume). Europeans who questioned the Portuguese ancestry and Christianity of these *tangomãos* and Kriston often disdainfully observed that their knowledge of Christianity was reduced to wearing large crucifixes and rosaries.[6] The European distrust and rejection of the Kriston Creole communities occurred because they were articulate both in African and European ways that gave them a commercial advantage.

Cultural contact often brought together different cultures, religions, and bodily adornments in strange ways. Christians wore huge rosaries and crosses around their necks, Muslims wore their amulets and *gri-gris*; and sometimes, both: Gaspar Vaz, a Mandingo Muslim who had been a slave in Cabo Verde, showed European travelers how he still wore a Catholic rosary under his Muslim clothes and amulets, as a symbol of trust and recognition (Brooks 2003: 62).

Africans were not the only ones who wore Catholic rosaries under their amulets; Europeans also wore Muslim amulets under their rosaries. Such usage did not necessarily imply conversion to Islam: the amulets were worn for protection from sorcery, or so it was said. In Guinea, the Portuguese encountered Mandingo Muslim marabous who practiced as oracles and made amulets with fragments of the Coran.[7] By the mid-seventeenth century, Mandingo magic was clearly in use by the Portuguese. In 1656, in Chaceu, Ambrósio Gomes, "a white man," tied some magical strings he got from the Mandingos around the arm of Crispina Peres, a mulatto woman who was giving birth, to protect her. (Sweet 2003: 182) By the beginning of the eighteenth century, the fame of "Mandingo bags" had spread throughout the empire, making *feitiçaria* and *mandinga* almost synonymous terms in the Portuguese world. In 1700, a Capeverdean slave, Francisco, was selling a variety of *bolsas* (pouches) in Lisbon that protected its owners from fights, helped to win games and to seduce. In 1729, Luis de Lima, a native of Ouidah, confessed to the Inquisition that he had used *mandinga*s in Porto and Pernambuco, Brazil. He also named twenty-six other slaves from the Mina coast who used *mandinga*s. Most of them had spent time in Brazil before coming to Portugal. One of them, a Bahian-born slave, Manuel da Piedade, sold ingredients for *bolsas de Mandinga*. Other Africans from Ouidah were later accused of manufacturing *mandinga*s. It is interesting to note that none of the people I mentioned were actually Mandingo or even from Guinea. Their clients were both slaves and masters, black and white, African and Portuguese (Sweet 2003: 183, see also Calainho 2004: 53).

What did the Inquisition judges find in these *bolsas de Mandinga*? Altar stones, pieces of paper with Christian orations, rocks, sticks, roots, bones, hair, animal skins, feathers, powders, and consecrated particles. The usual stuff of *feitiçaria*: random objects collected in the more extraordinary situations.

These pouches were also used at the remote extremes of the colonial world. By the beginning of the eighteenth century, Vicente de Morais, a freed man and soldier in the backlands of Angola, was accused by the

Inquisition of being a *mandingueiro*, that is, making *mandinga* pouches. It is interesting to note that in this case, the name for the pouches is not always *mandinga*: sometimes they are called, Sallamanca, Cabo Verde, São Paulo. Vicente confessed that he had a pouch to protect him in combat. In it the judges found a pebble of an altar stone, and a Catholic prayer. Vicente also confessed that a white friend had given him a pouch, but he could not "test it," because he had given it to somebody else (Pantoja 2004: 129–130).

Recently, Sweet (2003) and Harding (2000) described the Mandinga pouches as objects of African resistance against the Portuguese Empire and slavery. Harding sees the *bolsa de Mandinga* "as part of the continuing effort to re-order a world fractured by slavery . . . they were also an effort in the direction of adjusting the balance of power, of moderating the caprice of the dominant order. The *bolsas* and other *feitiços* represented a counterforce" (Harding 2000: 31–32).

Since Bastide (1978), it is commonly held that *feitiçaria* was used by slaves in the Portuguese colonial world as a tool for survival. It is less clear why it is necessary to reduce *feitiçaria* to a cure of the psychological trauma of slavery, a tool of slave resistance against their masters, or even of cultural resistance in general. First, this argument does not explain why the actual material components of these pouches and the spells and rituals prayed upon it were not necessarily African. On the contrary, they were mostly Catholic. Second, the argument of slave resistance ignores the discourses of the practitioners of *feitiçaria* as they are recorded: the objective of the *bolsas de mandinga* was to seal the body, *fechar o corpo*, against the influence of spirits (Souza 1986: 132). These spirits of the dead and the Devil were real social agents for the people who used the *bolsas*, as real as slaves and masters. Third, it does not account for the fact that the *bolsas* were used by people of all social origins and social classes, slaves and free, blacks and whites. *Feitiçaria* was a part of everyone's everyday life (Souza 1986: 133).

Mandinga pouches blended European, African, and maybe even indigenous practices (Souza 1986: 131). The truth contained in these bags was common to all the peoples traveling through the colonial world: the fragility of the body, the foolishness of desire, the burden of social hierarchies, and the constant presence of death. In the Portuguese colonial world, these facts transcended differences of race, origin, and even of religion to create a new kind of object that we could call Atlantic: the Mandinga pouch.

This does not mean that it is necessary to downplay the conflicts and violence generated by slavery. On the contrary, the Portuguese colonial society was an extremely violent and unfair social system. But this violence was not reducible to a slave/master, black/white contradiction, it took many other forms: from religious persecution against Jews and Muslims, to class conflict between noblemen and the populace, metropolitans and colonials, men and women, even conflicts between slaves of different origins, slaves and free men, and so on. The discourse of the Mandinga pouch and of *feitiçaria* in general, is in many ways a discourse about everyday power and the violence of all against everything that preceded and succeeded the Atlantic slave trade.

This is clearly shown in the numbers of the Inquisition trials. The Inquisition cannot easily be reduced to an institution that repressed slaves and their African culture. Only 62 of the 652 cases of *feitiçaria* denounced to the Portuguese Inquisition between the seventeenth and the eighteenth centuries were blacks and mulattos, that is less than 10 percent. Of these, almost 49 percent were free and 18 percent were *forros* (freed): only a third were slaves (Calainho 2004: 62–63). The Inquisition was not persecuting slaves and Africans per se: it was persecuting the Devil. It is however true that more and more Africans were accused of sorcery as colonization and slavery increased in the eighteenth century.[8] Why were Africans progressively identified with *feitiçaria*? Maybe for the popular imagination, the Devil often took the face of the stranger within. Bethencourt (1986) discusses cases in seventeenth century Portugal in which many of the *feitiçeiras* are Muslim and Jewish converts, *moriscas* and *cristãs novas*. By the late eighteenth century, Jews and Muslims had clearly been replaced by Africans. But their clients were the same: poor and rich, black and white, Portuguese and African.

The paradox of sorcery seems to be that the apparently powerless foreigner, the outsider, the unknown, is the most powerful sorcerer. It is interesting to note the variations on the origin of the pouch from the case of an Angolan soldier: In Angola, the pouch may not be just Mandinga, but Cabo Verde, São Paulo, Sallamanca: the four corners of the Atlantic. The important thing, more than the origin itself, is that it is not from *here*, but from somewhere else, from some strange and exceptional place that, like the contents of the bag, is exceptional. What is objectified in the pouches is not an African origin: the pouch contains the relics and traces of exceptional events in which the world of the living and the dead meet. Indexing these events, they help people to confront the unexpected in their lives. The symbolism of the objects is not as important as the fact that it "works," that it makes miracles. In the case of the Angolan soldier, he clearly stated that he did not know it was magical until it "worked." The miraculous event is necessary, and the pouch is an index of this miracle.

This is an important point. Pouches needed to be tested: they had to work in crucial situations so that people could recognize their power. Only then did they become their *bolsa*, their personal index, their fetish: in an event that defines one's life in relation to this object. For Pietz, this is one of the central questions of the problem of the fetish, what he calls "personalization." Finding a fetish is an event that cannot be predicted. It is a single happening in which people find something unforeseen that they recognize as a part of themselves, something that becomes personified. Pietz explains this point wonderfully, making reference to Leiris and the surrealist notion of the *objet trouvé*, "these crisis moments of singular encounter and indefinable transaction between the life of the self and that of the world become fixed, in both places and things, as personal memories that retain a peculiar power to move one profoundly" (Pietz 1985: 12).

The *bolsas de Mandinga* are the objectifications of these events, of these personal histories. They are not just symbols of tokens of one or another religion, one or another culture, one or another race or continent, but indexes of the personal lives of people in the Lusophone world, a life marked by trade, transience, and uncertainty.

From *Feitiços* to Fetishes—and Fetishism

In the Portuguese colonial world, sorcery was a system of exchange of objects, practices, and beliefs that circulated throughout the seas and was personalized and reappropriated in countless ways. In this context, the term *feitiço* and the practices associated with the *feitiço* may have expanded throughout the coasts of Africa well beyond Portuguese influence.

Since 1500, the Portuguese had built forts and traded gold and slaves in the ports of the Gulf of Guiné in places like São Jorge da Mina and Ouidah, but in the words of one of their later captains, never a human soul was converted.[9] On the other hand, the area was of great interest to the rivals of Portugal. From relatively early in the sixteenth century, we have accounts from Dutch, English, Danish, and French travelers who were competing for a trading space on the coast with the Portuguese and finally overcame them by the mid-seventeenth century. The travelers were the most critical of the population of half-castes, the "mulattos," who were deceitful and nasty, both with Africans and Europeans (Bosman 1705). The travelers were equally surprised and annoyed at the *fetissos*. These travelers said that the Africans used the word *fetisso*: we do not know to what extent this had become a Creole word (a word that Africans used when talking to each other) or it was used by Africans just as a pidgin, to answer the questions of the Europeans, assuming that they understood the term. Probably the exchange between Europeans and Africas was often mediated by Portuguese speakers, maybe these mulattos that Bosman mentions. The paradoxical result was that for the Europeans, the *fetissos* became an African thing.

But for Protestants like De Marees and Bosman, the *fetissos* were not just magic charms; they were the gods of the Africans and their priests were the *fetisseros*.[10] The Portuguese distinction between sorcery and idolatry was superfluous: magic and religion was the same thing. The religion of the Africans was the *fetisso*, and this placed them at an irredeemable distance from Protestant Europeans. In this way, similar to the way in which *mandinga* became synonymous with sorcery in the Portuguese colonial world because it was foreign and strange, the Portuguese *feitiço* became synonymous with African religion in the trading ports of West Africa.

The *fetisso, fetish, fetiche* started then to be associated directly with Africa, regardless of the Portuguese, who, as mentioned earlier, disappeared from the accounts. The new Protestant travelers refused to recognize the agency of the Devil or the spirits of the dead behind the cult of fetishes. The fetishes were held to be artifices made by humans in their stupidity and greed, God being a remote creator in a disenchanted world. The story and the enchantment of the fetish would then become purely a work of deception of a false priest who was nothing else but a charlatan.

Willem Bosman's account of fetish worship in Guinea is illustrative. He makes no mention of the Devil as the cause of the fetish: it is only the stupidity and greed of Africans.[11] He explains that when he asked an African how many gods they had, the African answered laughing that they had as many as they wished. They just made one when they needed one! They knew that they made artificial gods, and yet they worshiped them! For Bosman, this was clear proof that their religion was only guided by interest (Bosman 1705: 367). In one of his cases, Bosman refers to the snake cult in Ouidah. He tells of a snake that abandoned his worshipers and went speedily to the town of their enemies, "at which they were overjoyed" (Bosman 1705: 367). The former enemies became the new worshipers of the runaway snake.

For Bosman "How their Gods are represented to them, or what Idea they form of them, I never yet could learn, because indeed they do not know themselves" (Bosman 1705: 155).What troubles Bosman is the difficulty he has to explain the fetish in terms of representation—and indeed it cannot be understood as a representation, or a symbol or something else. It is clear that they do not represent anything: they are the object of cult themselves. The snake of Ouidah was not the symbol of anything but the object of the cult itself.[12]

I have pointed out that the *feitiço* is essentially an index—a sign that does not stand for an object through a mental representation, but which is the consequence of an act; an index of an exceptional event that becomes an entirely new being, with its living breath. Maybe this, for a man of the Enlightenment like Bosman, was impossible to accept, since the modern theory of agency of the Enlightenment is anthropocentric—only humans have agency: their action is guided by intentions, or better still by their will, while other events are natural and nature is guided by laws, not intentions. Therefore, for a modern thinker, a sacred snake speeding to the enemies would not necessarily imply that it wanted to be worshiped by them, because a snake is a stupid animal that follows the laws of nature and has no will—only humans do. In the traveler's accounts it is commonly stated that Africans worship the first thing they find on their way, the first thing they fancy, they recognize as their fetish. This was seen by European thinkers as a demonstration of their ignorance, their lack of understanding that beings in the world do not have a will, but are ruled by natural laws. For Hegel, this would place Africans outside of history since their relation to the world was not mediated by understanding but by pure fancy. One might return to Evans-Pritchard (and maybe even invoking Wittgenstein) and claim that Hegel was wrong: magic is not ignorant of the laws of nature; it only looks for human meaning behind events when these events are uncannily exceptional. It is not any snake that becomes a god but if that sacred snake crosses fields in the middle of a battle, it is difficult not to believe that this has a meaning—that there is a will behind it.

But is this magical thinking so far removed from the cosmology of the Enlightenment? I do not think so. Bosman compares fetish worship to Catholicism: "If it was possible to convert the Negroes to the Christian Religion, the Roman-Catholics would succeed better than we should, because they agree on several particulars, especially on their ridiculous Ceremonies" (Bosman 1705: 154 quoted in Pietz 1985: 39). Other Protestant traders agreed. For the Huguenot Barbot, "these people have fetishes...just like Roman Catholics have their saints" (Barbot 1992: 578). It should be no wonder that in the early eighteenth century after long and bloody wars of religion and commercial wars throughout the world, Protestant and free-thinking traders would despise and reject anything that suggested Papism. What they found in common between these religions was their "external-ism," the relevance they gave to rituals, displays of objects, the hierarchical power of religious congregations, and in particular their transactional character—that they were based on exchanges with the divine through made-up mediators like fetishes, spirits, saints, and priests. They made and sold the divine. In contrast, the Protestants understood their own puritan practice as a private relationship between individuals and God, through their thought and faith, not through made-up objects or rituals, or performances, in a relationship that was not based in transactions, exchanges, and making deals. On the contrary, production and exchange belonged to the economy, as Marx explained very well; in fact the economy *can* be understood in terms of fetishism: it is a human institution, an artifact that has acquired its own agency, the "hidden hand" independent from the will of humans, acquiring quasi-natural status—but not quite. But of course, Bosman and those like him would never recognize that—it would be like recognizing the hybrid nature of modernity.

In these terms, I would not be so sure that the likes of Bosman would not really understand the fetish: in fact they organized their economy around it. It was religion, more than the fetish that troubled them. In *Du Culte des Dieux Fétiches*, Charles De Brosses finally developed a full-fledged theory of the fetish, and invented the term fetishism. Arguing that fetishism, or the cult of things, is the origin of all religion, De Brosses organized the most powerful argument against religion that was ever made in a century of skepticism. By identifying the worship of objects as a first step in a process leading to more spiritual forms of religion, it was finally possible to integrate the criticism of religion to a general theory of progress that would see the Enlightenment as the last, logical end of human achievement: in modern Europe, men had finally managed to relate to objects just in the terms of their true value as commodities sepa-rating their religious beliefs from material things altogether. Or at least that is what they thought, until Marx demonstrated that the way they worshipped commodities was also fetishism. But that is another story that has been robustly addressed by many others.[13] I would like to empha-size, however, that from then on Africa was not only distant from Europe in space, but also in time. In fact for Hegel, Africa was outside of history altogether. What happened then to all the colonies in the world that were ruled by neither enlightened Europe nor Africa, but by backward and decadent empires, like Portugal? Were they outside of history too?

Feitiçaria and Fetishism in Brazil

We find the first traces of the progressive distance between the Portuguese and the African *Fetiche* even in Bluteau's definition of *feitiço*. He says that one possible origin of the word, is the African term *fetiche*, "name that the peoples of Guinea give to the idols they worship" ("nome que os povos de Guinè, na Africa dão a os idolos que eles adorão" Bluteau 1713: 66). He probably refers to Dapper, a Dutch geographer who had been translated into French.[14] Curiously enough, Bluteau has inverted the facts; he does not recognize that *fetiche* comes from *feitiço*, but he thinks that it is the other way around! It is, however, important to note that the term *fetiche* is not used in Brazil as a synonym of *mandinga*. European travelers did sometimes use the term *fetish* in reference to things they saw in Brazil, and that looked "Africanesque."[15] On the other hand, Lusophone intellectuals, at least since Bluteau, knew the term, but *fetiche* and its derivative *fetichismo* were certainly not popular terms from African or indigenous languages (like *mandinga*), but erudite terms coming from French. Their usage was not common prior to the mid-nineteenth century, when the visibility that they started to enjoy was probably due to the influence of Positivism (Corrêa 1998) The term *fetichismo* starts to appear in Bahian newspapers around the 1860s in cases of police persecution[16] but is much more infrequent than the traditional terms, *feitiço* and *feitiçaria* that had always been systematically used in these cases. At this point, it is important to make clear that when the authorities were persecuting *feitiçaria*, they were not going after another culture, but were against practices of magic and spiritism that they perceived as criminal. As Maggie has explained in *Medo do Feitiço* (1992), policemen and judges in the late nineteenth century did not persecute *all* magical and spiritist practices as such, but their use for *evil* purposes and fraud. Analyzing court cases of the early Republican period, Maggie concludes that all the discussion is built around a common belief: the existence of spirits that can be incorporated and the possibility that some of these spirits produce evil charms, *feitiços*. The persecution of these activities, as was true in colonial times, was never systematic; it depended more on public opinion, scandal, and the personal interest of the law enforcement agents in some cases (see Lühning 1996).

Yet, the uses of the term *fetishism* in newspapers also imply a moral and a cultural argument about the evils that were inherent to Brazilian culture, as a backward, decadent culture that mixed inferior civilizations—essentially African cultures—with the culture of an inferior, second-rate colonial power, Portugal, whose customs and religion where in fact not so far from this fetishism. In fact, the Catholic religion, more than any other institution, was seen as being mainly responsible for the backwardness of Brazil amongst many of the new "positivist" intellectuals. For example, Tobias Barreto in "Moisés e Laplace," an article of 1870, discusses the fetishist cult at the origins of humanity, but he thinks that fetishism is at "a grande distância de nós," far away in time. He does not seem to contemplate the possibility of living with actual fetishists in his own time. On the other hand, he also says that :"Entretanto, aquele mísero culto fetíchico, tão grosseiro e tão ridículo, é credor de maior soma de bens reais de que certo monoteísmo barbaro que ajeza a humanidade, sob a vigilância do látego divino e tem as mãos cruentas de sufocar auroras e garrotear idéias" (Barreto 30: 1990). In this text, he uses the classical argument of fetishism as causally linked to contemporary religions—like the monotheistic Catholic religion. And he uses this argument to criticize Catholicism as a modern fetishism that enslaves the ignorant masses. This is an important point I think, to understand the uses of the term fetishism in Brazil. Contained in any theory in fetishism is an implicit criticism of religion as a social institution—essentially of Catholicism. This is particularly important in Brazil at the end of the Empire and Abolition when the Church was going through a certain identity crisis. The Brazilian church is seen by liberal intellectuals like Barreto as an archaic, medieval, obscurantist institution. Popular, traditional Catholic practices are positively despised when not feared by the new elites of educated intellectuals who aspire to live in a modern European society, and view religion as a factor of "backwardness." Even the hierarchies of the Church urge a renovation, initiating a process of "Romanization" as they attempt to eradicate magical practices and impose the authority of priests. This context of religious reform will also affect the way in which Candomblé and other similar forms of ritual practices are seen in Brazilian society. Forms of popular religious expression that were traditionally framed as Catholic—like the "lavagens," were now seen as "Candomblés a céu aberto" (open air Candomblés), and persecuted both by the police and the Church (Sansi 2005).

In this context of intense national crisis Raymundo Nina Rodrigues wrote his classical book, *L' animisme fétichiste des nègres de Bahia*, in which he planned to study the persistence of African fetishism in Brazil.[17] For Nina Rodrigues, Candomblé was not *feitiçaria*, or sorcery, but a fetishist cult, a religion. A primitive religion, but still a religion, and it had to be observed and researched as a resistant African culture. Looking for the "pure" African tradition, the researcher had to leave aside everything that had the mark of mixture, racial, cultural, or religious. He proposed a number of prophylactic measures in an environment that he otherwise saw as completely contaminated. First, it was necessary to separate, at least conceptually, what was African from what was European. And a good starting point was to look at something that for Nina was purely African: Candomblé cults.

Being a form of *feitiçaria*, or sorcery, Candomblé was seen by most Bahians as a magical practice commonly used regardless of class or skin color. But Rodrigues saw Candomblé as fetishism and wanted to cast it as something essentially *different* and *strange*, an African, non-Brazilian primitive religion. The genial paradox of Nina Rodrigues is that, despite the general

criticism that his racist approach received afterward, he became the founder
of a school of research that defended the African cultural autonomy of
Candomblé, as a *different* African culture that was incrusted in Brazilian
society. This assumption is still common amongst many contemporary
researchers. The paradox of Nina Rodrigues is the paradox of generations of
intellectuals from outside the "core" of Western civilization, who have faithfully followed European theories that radically separated the world into
two—the West and the Rest, when they lived in situations in which they
were both, and maybe something else.

Conclusion

In general terms, the paradox of the story of the fetish is that it is both about
appropriation and exchange, and misrecognition and disavowal. It is also
both about the formation of a colonial culture and its repression and oblit-
eration. The first part is the story of the colonial formation of an Atlantic
complex of sorcery, from *feitiço* to fetish; the other side, the story of the
Western discourse on value, from fetish to fetishism. Most scholars have up
to now been more interested in this second part of the story of fetishism, a
story of reification, disavowal, and irredeemable difference. But the first part
of this story, the story of the fetish, is more about historicity, appropriation,
and the formation of colonial cultures. The objects, personas, and practices
of sorcery that circulated through the Atlantic relied on a kind of common
language built on the value given to extraordinary events, miracles, and revelations, and their enduring power through objects that indexed them. The
central point that this raises, I think, is the *historicity* of the fetish. Pietz
notes that "the fetish is always a meaningful fixation of a singular event; it is
above all an 'historical' object, the enduring material form and force of an
unrepeatable event" (Pietz 1985: 12). This is what was interpreted as
"caprice" or "arbitrary" choice by European travelers; but is in fact the recognition of the singular values generated by events that cannot be explained
by the elements that become a part of the situation before it happens (Latour
2001: 131).

   This historicity founded in events is radically different from Hegelian history, as teleology. But this is the notion of historicity that we find at the roots
of anthropology, the historical particularism of Boas, when he insisted that
like causes did not produce like effects; and the new historical anthropology
that emerges from the work of Marshall Sahlins (1981) is centered on the
relevance of the event in the "structure of the conjuncture," to explain processes of cultural change and exchange. An important point in Sahlins' for-
mulation of the structure of the conjuncture is that social actors perceive the
conjuncture as repeating traditional structures, when in fact, by repeating
these structures, they change. This is precisely the point I want to underscore: the event in which the fetish is "found" is not perceived by the person
as arbitrary, but necessary. The value found in the object is not randomly
attributed by the person, but it is seen as an immanent value of the object,

something inchoate that was always there waiting for this particular person, something that he/she recognizes. It is as if the thing was offering itself to the person: as if they always belonged together. In this sense, this is a process of mediated exchange,[18] between the person and a hidden value that is giving itself to the person. Thus, contextual values and historical changes are perceived as immanent values and mediated exchanges. In the case of the fetish, for example, it is precisely this historicity that turns it into an object of "intercultural mediation" that literally incorporates Christian, African, and Muslim elements in one bag recognizing in these elements a potential value that could be encompassed by the fetish.

Beyond that, this is the story of a terrible misunderstanding that began in the seventeenth century, when Protestant travelers like Bosman explained that they could not understand what fetishes represented. As I argued, it is possible to see this statement as one of the first steps toward a particular way of addressing the relation of things and humans, and economy and religion as two separate spheres of value. Bosman is one more in a lineage of thinkers who decided that the world was divided in two: either you are with us, Enlightened Europe, Civilization, and Commerce, or you are against us, with Fetishist Africa, Barbarism, and Religion. Either you understand the real value of things, or you just reify your irrational beliefs in objects to obtain power over others. This practice of reification, for Bosman or Barbot, was not exclusive to Africans: African fetishism was, in fact, uncannily similar to Papism. But then the accusation would turn against the accuser, when Marx showed that, in fact, Western capitalism too, was reifying the value of objects to enslave people.

But again, that story has been told countless times. Beyond the consequences of fetishism, we have been looking here at its causes. In this chapter, I have proposed to decenter the story of the fetish from the West versus Africa divide. Introducing the "Lusophone" particle in the Atlantic, we introduce a third factor—a world that has never been fully recognized as the one or the other, West or Rest, but that has been present in the European colonial adventure from its very beginning to its very end. This space may help us to think of the relation of the West and Africa not in terms of radical alterity but of mutual constitution. It was through Lusophone categories that northern Europeans understood Africa: and it was in fact as an extension to the cultural war against Catholicism that the radical criticism of the fetish was developed. As we all know, northern Europeans won this cultural war, and intellectuals of the Lusophone world in the following centuries, like Nina Rodrigues, tried to adapt its rigid dualisms to a social reality that contradicted them entirely. The paradox of Nina Rodrigues is the paradox of generations of intellectuals from the periphery of Western civilization, who have faithfully followed European theories that radically separated the world into two—Us and the Rest, when they lived in situations in which they were both, and maybe something else.

Notes

I want to thank many friends who have helped me write this paper, but in particular Luís Nicolau of the Universidade Federal da Bahia whose encouragement and knowledge have been fundamental to my research in Bahia.

1. For example, when Diego Cão arrived in the Congo, according to Rui de Pina, he talked to the king, "encomendandolhe que arrengasse os Idollos e feitiçarias . . ." (Rui de Pina, chap. LVII, in Brasio 1952: 35) and on the discovery of the kingdom of Benin, in 1486, the Portuguese gave the king "santos e muy católicos conselhos, com louvadas amonestações pera a Fé, reepreendendo muito, as heresias, e grandes ydolatrias e feitiçarias de que naquella terra os negros muito usam" (Rui de Pina, chap. XXIV, in Brasio 1952: 52). The king of Benin in the early sixteenth century asked for missionaries, but then lost interest, made them prisoners, and almost starved them to death. According to João de Barros (*Decadas,* I, chap III), he was only interested in the missionaries in order to become powerful amongst his neighbors. In one case though, as it is well known, Christianity became the religion of the state: in Congo, the king and his son converted to Christianity, and ordered the burning of the idols, according to the chroniclers. In any case, the first Christian king of Congo, João also had a moment of weakness in his old age. The chronicler João de Barros explains how the priests requested him to renounce his large harem and keep only one wife, as a Christian. But the king was not ready to accept it, and this provoked a conflict with his son Alfonso, who was a devout Christian. According to Barros, some people in the king's court, inspired by the Devil, conspired against Alfonso and told the king that he had become a powerful sorcerer, thanks to the Christian priests, and that he flew at night from the distant city where he lived to his father's harem, to have sex with his wives. To test if this was true, the king played a trick: he sent a *feitiço,* a charm, wrapped in a cloth to one of his wives, whom he suspected. The messenger who brought the *feitiço* told her that it was from her lover, the prince, and that he sent it to protect her from the king—since he was intending to kill all his wives. The wife, shocked by this story, ran to tell her husband the king about it. This was enough proof for the king that he was ill advised, and that his son was loyal. This is the first and more specific reference to a *feitiço* in Barros' *Asia* ("Por se mais certificar da verdade á cerca do filho, ordenou El Rey hum feitiço que se usava entre elles" (Barros *Asia, Decadas* I chap. X).

2. Originally, *Feitiçaria* was more an object of Christian law than of Christian theology (Pietz 1987: 31) In 1385 and 1403, King João I of Portugal made laws against it, in which he forbids his subjects to use or effect charms (*obra de feitiços*), or bonds (*ligamentos*), or summoning up of devils (*chamar os diabos*), since *Feitiçaria*, like Idolatry, is inspired by the Devil. *Feitiçaria* is always an accusation; no one would admit to being a *feiticeiro*. But this official discourse on sorcery could be bypassed by the practitioner of magic affirming the contrary, that one was practicing magic against the Devil, not for it, and against the evil spirits that haunted living people. They could do this since it was not their techniques and instruments that constituted the *feitiçaria* but the inspiration from the Devil. This introduced a considerable ambiguity in its persecution.

3. Here I am using Peirce's distinction between index and symbol, where the first would be a sign that is causally linked to its object, while the second is only an abstract representation of the object that has to be decoded (Peirce 1955). As such, anybody can recognize an index if they see its object, but only people who are competent in the code of the symbol language, for example, can understand the connection between object and sign. The classical peircean example is fire and smoke: smoke is an index of fire. But the word "fire" in English is a symbol of fire.

4. "He huma cousa, que em si naturalmente não tem o effeyto, que obvio, causando-o só o Demonio, com aquillo, que por permissão Divina le ajunta, para que possa obrar." (Bluteau 1713: 66).

5. "Cousa não natural, feita por arte" (Bluteau 1713: 66).

6. La Courbe, a French traveler, talks about these tangomaos, saying that "They always wear a large Crucifix around their neck and call themselves by a saint's name, although for the most part they are neither baptized, nor show any evidence of Christian religion" (quoted in Brooks 2003: 153). Another traveler, Olivier, talks about a certain Dom Joan of Rufisque, who had "several wives . . . He prayed two Missionaries . . . to baptize his children . . . I was astonished to see that this man was very devout, having always a large Rosary in his hands, & several images of Our Saviour, of the Virgin, & of the Saints around his bed / The same with his wives or concubines, who carry'd also large Rosaries around their necks (Olivier, quoted in Brooks 2003: 153).

7. Lemos, a traveler, talks about the "dexerims," "Letrados da Ley . . . e escrevem em lingua Arabica . . . prezao-se de grandes adevinhadores, e feitiçeiros" (Lemos 1953: 25). The Jesuit Father Balthazar Barreira, in Guiné in the early sevententh century, made comments about the bags that Muslim priests make for "tricking people"(Sweet 2003: 181).

8. Particularly in Brazil, in eighteenth-century Minas Gerais, 71.8 percent of the accused were black (Nogueira 2004: 7).

9. In the foundation of the Castle of São Jorge del Mina, in 1482, the Portuguese thank God "for allowing them to praise and glorify Him in the midst of idolaters" (from the *Asia* of João de Barros, quoted in G.R. Crone 1937). In fact they had provoked the locals to take up arms when, in order to build the Castle and Chapel, they had taken stones from their "saint hill" ("seus sanctos penedos" [Barros, chapter III, in Brasio 1952: 20]). This was a bad beginning for the cause of Christianity in the Gold Coast, without any doubt, and the chronicles from Elmina confirm that it never got much better: "A Mina há noventa annos que hé descoberta. Nunca em todo este tempo se coverteo huma alma, nem se tratou disso . . . (Brasio 1953: 97).

10. De Marees: "They weare strange wreathes, which they call Fetissos (which name they derive from their Idolatry) for when they eate and drinke, then they power meat and drinke upon them: and first gave them to eate and drinke" (Purchas 1605: 267). He also says that "They have also a Priest, who in their speech they call a *Fetissero*, hee upon their Sabbath day sits upon a stole" (Purchas 1605: 290).

11. He explains that Africans say that when God created the world he made men white and black. He gave to the black man the option to choose first between two gifts: gold or "the knowledge of the arts of reading and writing" (Bosman 1705: 146). He chose gold. Therefore, with time he became the slave of the white man, who with his arts took the black man's gold and his own body.

Here we have the proof that dependency theory was born in Africa. But Bosman interpreted the story in other terms, as a corroboration of his idea that Africans were ignorant people led simply by greed and interest, and that their fetish priests misled them to worship their fetishes, making them think.

12. Albert de Surgy, working amongst the Ewe-speaking peoples of the coast of Togo and Benin, discusses the uses of the fetishes in this area. He explains that the term is applied to two kinds of things: the *bo* and the *vudu*. Among the Akan, we have the similar ideas of *suman* and *abossom*. The *vodu* are spirits fixed in altars, and they require worship, while the *bo*, are only activated objects (amulets) that protect people and influence others. They accumulate many hidden things, from plants, to human and animal remains, stones, pieces of machinery, and even mementos of particular events, like train tickets. In both cases, their power, according to De Surgy, is not reducible to what they represent or to the natural properties of its elements, but stems from the breath of life (*gbogbo*, or *Afoxé* in Yoruba) that founded it (Le fétiche doit sa puissance (*nyuse*) non pas a des propriétés physicochimiques, et non pas à des formes représentatives ou dénotatives d'autre chose, mais au "soufflé" (*gbogbo*) des ingrédients dont il se compose [Surgy, 1994: 56]). That is to say, the "breath" instaurates the fetish as a unique object that is the result of a unique event, not reducible to its components. Among the Yoruba, we find the same notion of *Axe* or *Afoxé* as the breath of life infused on altars, also conceived as living entities: a unique event that has resulted in a unique object. Like the Portuguese *feitiço*, or the *minkissi*, or Angola, the *bo* and *vodu* are living objectifications of exceptional events.

13. See, for example, Graeber 2005.

14. The same definition is given by the *Encyclopédie Française* of Diderot and D'Alembert some fifty years latter (I quote the first edition, p.598: "Fétiche, f, F. (Hist.mod) Nom que les peuples de Guinée en Afrique donnent à leurs divinités. Ils on une fétiche pour toute une province, & des fétiches particuliers pour chaque famille. Cette ici o est un arbre, une tête de singe, un oiseau, une quelque chose de semblable, suivant leur fantaisie" (Dapper 1686, *Description de l'Afrique*, Amsterdam: Boom and Somerer). Their reference is the XVII century Dutch geographer Dapper, who was translated to French and probably read in that language by Bluteau.

15. For example, Kidder and Fletcher, English travelers in Bahia in 1839 say, "You can scarcely look into a basket in which the *quitandeiras* (the women that sell food in the street) carry fruit without seeing a 'fetisch.' The most common is a piece of charcoal, with which, the abasted darkey will inform you, the 'evil eye' is driven away" (Kidder and Fletcher 1857: 137–138).

16. "O fetichista Grato, africano que foi preso pela polícia em uma casa do Conceição do Boqueirão, no meio do seu laboratório para prever a sorte, e que era pai de terreiro de seu candomblé foi deportado pela polícia para a costa da África, na barca portuguesa D. Francisca" (*Jornal da Bahia*, July 17, 1859).

"Chico Papae, gran-sacerdote do fetichismo, fallecido ha mais de 5 annos, na rua da Poeira" (*O Alabama*, June 23, 1870).

Noticia sobre o caso do feiticeiro Juca Rosa (José Sebastião Rosa) no Rio: "encontrou-se um templo horrivel levantado a um monstruoso fetiche, no qual celebrava-se uma especie de lithurgia tao extraordinaria e tao abominavel que o incenso era queimado dentro de craneos humanos, de mistura com gottas de sangue de gallo preto ou cinzento...o idolo a quem eram tributadas essas sacrilegas oblações era appellidado Manipanco" [February 25, 1871, p.2].

"A sacerdotisa do fetichismo enche a casa de mulheres de toda laia e de rapazes de vida solta, os quaes são attraidos por ali, mais por causa de umas creoulinhas, escravas sem subordinação da mesma, do que pelos seus embustes." [March 11, 1871, p.3].

17. "A persistencia do fetichismo africano como expressão do sentimento religioso dos negros bahianos e seus mestiços, é facto que as exterioridades do culto catholico apparentemente adoptado por elles, não conseguiram disfarçar nem nas associações hybridas que com esse culto largamente estableceu o fetichismo" (Nina Rodrigues 1906).

18. Marilyn Strathern, in *The Gender of the Gift* (1988), introduces the notion of the "partible person" in Melanesia—what Gell calls the "distributed" person (1998). For Strathern, in Melanesia "Objects are created not in contradistinction to persons but out of persons" (Strathern 1988: 172). Through gifts, people give a part of themselves. They are not something that *stands* for them, a symbol, but they are "extracted from one and absorbed by another" (Strathern 1988: 178). This continuity between people and things is what Strathern calls a "mediated exchange," as opposed to the unmediated exchange of commodities that is based in a fundamental discontinuity between people and things (Strathern 1988: 192).

Bibliography

Apter, Emily and William Pietz, eds. 1993. *Fetishism as Cultural Discourse*. Ithaca, New York: Cornell University Press.

Atkins, John. 1735. *A Voyage to Guinea, Brazil and the West Indies*. London: C. Ward and R. Chandler.

Barbot, Georges. 1992. *On Guinea*. London: Hakluyt Society.

Barreto, Thobias. 1990. *Crítica da Religião*. Rio de Janeiro: Editora Record.

Barros, João de. 1553. *Ásia, Décadas*. Lisbon

Bastide, Roger. 1978 (1960). *The African Religions of Brazil*. Baltimore: Johns Hopkins University Press.

Bernand, Carmen and Serge Gruzinski. 1988. *De l'idôlatrie: une archéologie des sciences religieuses*. Paris: Seuil.

Bethencourt, Francisco. 1987. *O Imaginário da Magia: feiticeiros, saludadores e nigromantes no século XVI*. Lisbon: Projeto Universidade Aberta.

———. 1994. *História das Inquisições: Portugal, Espanha e Itália*. Lisbon: Projeto Universidade Aberta Círculo de Leitores.

Bluteau, Raphael. 1713. Vocabulário Portuguez e Latino. Coimbra.

Bosman, Willem. 1705. *A New and Accurate Description of the Coast of Guine*. London: James Knapton.

Brasio, Antonio. 1952. *Monumenta Missionaria Africana-Africa Occidental (1471–1482)*. Lisbon: Agencia Geral do Ultramar.

Brooks, George E. 2003. *Eurafricans in West Africa*. Cleveland: Ohio University Press.

Brosses, Charles de. 1988 (1760). *Du Culte des Dieux Fétiches ou Parallèle de l'ancienne Religion de l'Egypte avec la Religion actuelle de Nigritie*. Paris: Fayard.

Calainho, Daniela. 2004. "Africanos penitenciados pela inquisição portuguesa." *Revista Lusófona de Ciência das Religiões* 3(5): 47–63.

Corrêa, Mariza. 1998. As *Ilusões da Liberdade. A Escola Nina Rodrigues e a Antropologia no Brasil.* Bragança Paulista: Estudos CPAPH.

Crone, G.R. 1937. *The Voyages of Cadamosto,* London: Hakluyt Society.

De Surgy, Albert. 1994. *Nature et fonction des fétiches en Afrique Noire, le cas de Sud Togo.* Paris: L'Harmattan.

Evans-Pritchard, E.E. 1937. *Witchcraft, Oracles and Magic among the Zande.* Oxford: Oxford University Press.

Graeber, David. 2005. "Fetishism as Social Creativity: or, Fetishes are Gods in the Process of Construction." *Anthropological Theory* 5: 407–438.

Harding, Rachel. 2000. *A Refuge in Thunder. Candomblé and Alternative Spaces of Blackness.* Bloomington: Indiana University Press.

Hegel, Friederich. 1956. *The Philosophy of History.* New York: Dover.

Iacono, Alfonso M. 1992. *Le fétichisme. Histoire d'un concept.* Paris: P.U.F.

Kidder, Daniel P. and Fletcher, James C. 1857. *Brazil & the Brazilians.* London: Childs & Peterson, pp.137–138.

Latour, Bruno. 1996. *Petite réflexion sur le culte moderne des dieux faitiches.* Paris: Synthélabo.

———. 2001. *L'Espoir de Pandore.* Paris: Éditions de La Découverte.

Lemos Coelho, Francisco de. 1953. *Duas Descrições seiscentistas da Guiné.* Academia Portuguesa de História.

Lühning, Angela. 1996. "Acabe com este Santo, que Pedrito vem aí...." *Revista da USP* 28: 194–220.

MacGaffey, Wyatt. 1988. "Complexity Astonishment and Power: The Visual Vocabulary of Kongo Minkisi." *Journal of Southern African Studies* 14(2): 188–203.

Maggie, Yvonne. 1992. *Medo do Feitiço: Relações entre Magia e Poder no Brasil.* Rio de Janeiro: Arquivo Nacional.

Nogueira, André. 2004. "Da trama: práticas mágicas/feitiçaria como espelho das relações sociais—Minas Gerais, século XVIII." *Mneme, Revista Virtual de Humanidades* 5(11) July–September 2004: 1–17.

Pantoja, Selma. 2004. "Inquisição, Degredo e Mestiçagem em Angola no século XVIII." *Revista Lusófona de Ciência das Religiões* 3(5/6): 117–136.

Peirce C.S. 1955. *Philosophical Writings.* New York: Dover.

Pietz, Willam. 1985. "The Problem of the Fetish, I." *Res, Anthropology and Esthetics* 9 (Spring): 5–17.

———. 1987. "The Problem of the Fetish, II: the Origin of the Fetish." *Res, Anthropology and Esthetics* 13 (Spring): 23–45.

———. 1988. "The Problem of the Fetish, IIIa: Bosman's Guinaea and the Enlightenment Theory of Fetichism." *Res, Anthropology and Esthetics* 16 (Fall): 106–123.

Preston Blier, Suzanne. 1995. *African Vodun.* Chicago: University of Chicago Press.

Purchas, Samuel. 1605. *Hakluytus Posthumus or Purchas: His Pilgrimages In Twenty Volumes. Volume VI* Glasgow: James MacLehose and Sons.

Reis, João José. 2001. "Candomblé in Nineteenth-century Bahia: Priests, Followers, Clients," in Kristin Mann and Edna Bay (eds.) *Rethinking the African Diaspora.* London: Frank Cass, pp.91–115.

Rio, João do. 1951. *As Religiões no Rio.* Rio de Janeiro: Organização Simões.

Rodrigues, Raimundo Nina. 1906. *O Animismo Fetichista dos Negros Bahianos.* Rio de Janeiro: Civilização Brasileira.

Romero, Silvio. 1888. *Historia da literatura Brasileira.* Rio de Janeiro: Garnier.

Sahlins, Marshall. 1981. *Historical Metaphors and Mythical Realities*. Ann Arbor: The University of Michigan Press.

Sansi, Roger. 2005. "Catholic Saints, African Gods, Black Masks and White Heads: Tracing the History of Some Religious Festivals in Bahia." *Portuguese Studies* 21(1): 182–200.

Souza, Laura de Mello e. 1986. *O Diabo e a Terra de Santa Cruz*. São Paulo: Companhia das Letras.

Spyer, Patricia, ed. 1998. *Border Fetishisms*. London: Routledge.

Strathern, Marilyn. 1986. *The Gender of the Gift*. Cambridge: Cambridge University Press.

Sweet, James H. 2003. *Recreating Africa. Culture, Kinship, and Religion in the African-Portuguese World, 1441–1770*. Chapel Hill: University of North Carolina Press.

Verger, Pierre. 1968. *Flux et Reflux de la traite des Esclaves entre le Golfe de Bénin et Bahia*. Paris: Mouton.

Chapter 2

Kriol without Creoles: Rethinking Guinea's Afro-Atlantic Connections (Sixteenth to Twentieth Centuries)

Philip J. Havik

Introduction

Since the mid-1990s the idea of a "Black Atlantic," as proposed by Gilroy (1993), has opened a whole new perspective upon the cultural aspects of transatlantic interactions. The various populations that make up this dynamic, interactive space began to "get" a joint history, characterized by composite practices and identities in a constantly changing world as people on the move linked and recreated continents and islands. Far from dissipating, this breath of fresh air in the social sciences has since provoked a multidisciplinary debate, obliging its respective disciplines to reposition themselves within this new universe. However, its principal proponents have essentially focused on the northern Atlantic and on its Anglophone aspects, thereby largely neglecting the southern hemisphere (Coates 2005). While some scholars have reminded their readers of the latter's importance with regard to the all-pervading transatlantic slave trade, their writings have not, so far, been identified as exponents of this new current of thought.

In the 1930s, Africanists and Americanists alike began to reconstruct parts of the Atlantic puzzle by focusing on certain groups and phenomena that bridged the divide (Freyre 1933; Herskovits 1938). In the 1950s and 1960s, a series of studies saw the light of day that traced the growth of Europe's maritime empires with a strong emphasis on the slave trade (De Armas 1956; Chaunu 1957; Boxer 1957, 1969; Mauro 1960). Studies on the transatlantic slave trade proliferated from the 1970s, and have since become a major area of study (Miers and Kopytoff 1977; Daget 1988; Solow 1993, Klein 1999). At the same time, the imperial thread that continued was paralleled by works that took a closer look at the impact Atlantic exchanges had upon coastal African societies (Birmingham 1966; Ryder 1969; Rodney

1970; Hopkins 1973; Curtin 1975; Northrup 1978; Lovejoy 1983; Miller 1988; Law 1991; Inikori and Engerman 1992; Thornton 1992; Klein 1999). Last but not least, the African roots of communities in the New World have also been subject to a reappraisal (Hall 1992; Eltis 2000; Bond 2005; Gruzinsky 1999; De Alencastro 2000). The contributions of these and other scholars opened up an Atlantic perspective that gradually shifted from a one way, economicist and historicist approach to an interactive Afro-American-Atlantic paradigm that laid the foundations of a heterocultural formation, now commonly known as the Black Atlantic.[1]

However, relatively little has been written about the cultural history of this fascinating Afro-Atlantic mosaic and of the Creole vernaculars that characterize it. Although the importance of the cultural nexus that bridges the Atlantic has indeed been studied for some time by linguists, and above all by creolists, their incursions have essentially been limited to idiomatic and syntactical issues. The emergence of Creole languages has been studied on either side of the Atlantic, that is, in the Caribbean and the neighboring Latin-American littoral, as well as on Atlantic islands such as Cape Verde and São Tomé and Príncipe, and some parts of the West African coast. The trans-atlantic slave trade has been identified as the main vehicle of diffusion lead-ing to the formation of a series of Creole languages with French, English, Spanish, and Portuguese roots on the one hand, and African origins on the other (Hall, 1966; Valdman, 1977; Bickerton, 1981; Holm, 1988; McWhorther, 1999; Huber & Parkvall, 1999; Gilbert, 2002). Their emer-gence as contact languages has been and is still the subject of intensive debate. Despite a number of historical studies covering segments of the period examined here that focus on the formation of "Luso-African" communities (Da Mota 1951, 1954; Carreira 1983; Boulègue 1989; Brooks 1993, 2003, Mark 2002; Horta 2000), a social history of their vernaculars has still to be written. In the case of the Portuguese-based or Lusolexed Creoles in Cape Verde, and in the Casamance and Guinea Bissau regions, the first contribu-tions date back to the late nineteenth century (Barros 1885; Vasconcelos 1899). The first grammar and dictionary of Guinean Creole or Kriol was produced by a Guinean born Franciscan priest and appeared in a Portuguese review around the turn of the nineteenth century.[2] He was also the first to publish an overview of Kriol stories and songs. During the *Estado Novo* or New State period in Portugal (1926–1974), little was produced on Guinea's lingua franca, whereas Cape Verdean Creole benefited from a cultural revival from the 1940s that resulted in the first serious attempts to codify its vocab-ulary and grammar in the 1950s and 1960s. From the 1980s, several dic-tionaries have been published of either Creole, mostly in conjunction with a linguistic analysis, and in the case of Kriol including stories and proverbs (Scantamburlo 1981, 1999; Biasutti 1987; Rougé 1988; Pinto Bull 1989; Massa 1996). At the same time, the first publication on the origins and expansion of Kriolu—and to a lesser extent Kriol—appeared that gave a sociohistorical perspective on these processes (Carreira 1982). More recently, scholars have taken a closer look at the transatlantic context of Creole languages, including those with a lusophone lexical base, testing various hypotheses on their formation and evolution (Martinus 1996).

One may conclude therefore that the above mentioned ideas about a "black" Atlantic space as a medium for social and cultural (ex)change are in urgent need of an interdisciplinary approach. However, the notion of a mediated, Atlantic space that produced novel sociocultural and linguistic phenomena in the case of the region is not entirely new. Receding a few decades, the work of the Cape Verdean anthropologist, Luis Romano, reveals a notable awareness of such a universe and its implications when discussing the islands' Creole society in a broad, Atlantic perspective (Romano 1970). Amounting to a critique on the neglect of Afro-Atlantic relations in contemporary literature, the author stated that the archipelago was—at the time of writing—"a land awaiting researchers, almost untouched, full of important treasures regarding its origins and the ethnic complexity of its inhabitants, both in time and in space" (Romano 1970: 8). Viewing the islands as an "anthropological link between the African coast and Brazil," he proposed studying its inhabitants as a heterogeneous "Atlantic population" (Ibid.: 14). In opting for a South-South, rather than a North-South approach, he praised the knowledge of "black women-cooks" and "female healers" who constituted "authentic archives" that were replete with revelations of "other times" (Ibid.: 8–9). Romano also observed the extent to which the speech of islanders denoted a "double consciousness" when alternately expressing themselves in Portuguese and Kriolu, depending on the situation and the recipient.

More recently, creolists such as Manuel Veiga, basing himself on Paul Teyssier, proposed the idea of Portuguese language and culture as an "open space" and Kriolu as an "identitary space" (Veiga 1998). Whereas the former was a means for establishing "fertile conviviality," the latter was a space that "translated, signified and symbolized" (Ibid.). Besides the Luso-African Creoles that emerged in an insular context such as Cape Verde and São Tomé and Príncipe, another Lusolexed variant, Kriol, became an important *lingua franca* in the Guinea Bissau and neighbouring Casamance region on the West African coast. The latter has a composite lexical base, including Portuguese and African languages, such as Mandé and Temne, is one of the few examples of a continental West African Creole together with *Krio* spoken in Sierra Leone and *Aku* in the Gambia. What essentially distinguishes Kriol from its neighboring Creoles is the simultaneous interaction between trading communities on the coast with the African interior on the one hand and with the Cape Verde Islands on the other that shaped the language and its different regional dialects into what it is today, that is, a vibrant regional *lingua franca*. However, rather than European languages functioning as the Atlantic transmission belt for interaction, a creolized pidgin emerging on the Cape Verde islands such as Santiago and Fogo acted as a means of establishing contact in the Guinea Bissau region in conjunction with African languages such as Mandé—and further South also Temne.

As a result, rather than centering upon the axis of Portuguese and Creole languages, in the case of the Guinea Bissau region, including the Casamance,

Creole and "ethnic" African languages acted both as an "open" and an "identitary" space in an Afro-Atlantic context. The growth of communities of Christianized Africans, the so-called Kriston, inhabiting coastal and riverine trading towns such as Geba, Cacheu, Farim, Ziguinchor, and Bissau, is paradigmatic for this duality. Their multiethnic origins and intrinsic spatial and social mobility commuting between these locations and the interior, as well as between the coast and the Cape Verde islands allowed them develop and diversify a coastal pidgin into fully fledged Creole dialects by the seventeenth century. Whilst the relay trade provided them with an extensive regional network of clients, the practice of wardship strengthened their relations with African societies in the interior. The latter custom worked both ways: whereas the Kriston in coastal trade settlements placed their siblings with their relatives in the interior, the latter also left their descendants with their relatives in the towns. This process, called *kriason* in Kriol, bolstered the interactive status of Creole languages and their adaptability across geographical and cultural frontiers. It also enabled its speakers, who in the case of the Kriston born and raised in trade settlements usually learned Kriol as a first language—while their relatives in the interior acquired it as a second or third language—to assume various identities in accordance with requirements of the context of encounters. Thus, Kriol functioned as a window to the Atlantic, whereas native languages such as Mandé provided access to the interior. At the same time, the use of these languages associated its speakers with clearly defined but different cultural spaces thus attributing parallel identities to them.

The emergence of these Creole languages form part of a broader dynamic that anthropologists have termed "transculturation," whereby imported practices, objects, and ideas are appropriated and transformed by populations that recreate and reinvent them in(to) their own cultural environment.[3] This ongoing (re)negotiation of practices and identities as a result of cultural encounters contributed to the formation of communities that developed novel means of communication molded on their multicultural social base and novel patterns of mobility. Whereas Kriolu and its Windward and Leeward variants, and Kriol with its urban variants in Ziguinchor, Cacheu, Bissau, and Bolama constitute a linguistic expression of a cross-cultural Afro-Atlantic nexus, they also interacted with each other over a period of centuries.[4] Far from wishing to theorize about the actual formation and development of these languages and dialects, the present chapter intends to provide a historical perspective upon the way these vernaculars were represented in written—and mostly locally produced—sources from the sixteenth to the twentieth centuries.

Guinea's Afro-Atlantic Connections

One of the most characteristic Afro-Atlantic features of coastal societies in West Africa are the Creole languages spoken in the Gambia, Sierra Leone, the Cape Verde islands and the Guinea-Bissau region. In the 1970s, scholars assumed that the "Portuguese pidgin that was one of the results of the Portuguese commercial expansion in the fifteenth and sixteenth centuries" was of "central importance to the whole debate because it was the first to develop in the general European expansion which left similar contact systems...spread out over Africa, Asia and America" (Naro, 1978: 314). Much of the discussion on pidgins focused on the reasons for them taking root in one particular area, that is, West Africa, and on the impact of Portuguese on their formation and development. Giving rise to various theories,[5] the existence of Portuguese Creole languages on the (Upper) Guinea coast has been, alternately or in conjunction, associated with a metropolitan, a Cape Verdean and a Guinean connection.

In the first case, it is identified with the *fala da Guiné* (the chatter of Guinea) or *fala dos negros* (the chatter of the negroes) mentioned in early modern Portuguese sources. Written references were invariably accompanied by depreciatory remarks on its allegedly "bastardized" or "miscellaneous" character, while also being the object of ridicule.[6] The spread of these new dialects is recorded from the mid-1400 onward, that is, soon after the arrival of the first slaves from West Africa in the 1440s (Saunders 1994: 137; Tinhorão 1997: 212–225). The distinction made in Portuguese sources between the *negros boçais* and their more educated *ladino* counterparts was not only based on appearance and vocational training, but also on the ability to speak Creole or Portuguese. The presence of large communities of Africans working as slaves and freepersons in households, towns, and farms had allowed them to develop their own distinctive cultures in a European environment (Ibid.: 97–120). With time the Portuguese spoken by Africans gave rise to the publication of pamphlets forming part of the popular *literatura de cordel* that was distributed among a broad section of the literate population in urban areas. The great earthquake that shook Portugal in 1755 provided an opportunity for diviners and astrologers to capture a growing market for their almanacs versed in the satirical *lingua de preto* (the language of the blacks).[7]

Secondly, the colonization of the Cape Verde islands was another source of Portuguese Creole dialects spoken in the region. From 1460s, communities of European—mainly Portuguese—settlers on the islands of Santiago and Fogo were soon joined by an increasing number of Africans shipped in from the Guinean coast as slaves, many of whom were reexported to Portugal, Spain, and the Americas. The role of these islands as locations for Afro-Atlantic entrepôts and the site for (a highly unstable) extensive plantation agriculture and cattle rearing turned it into an important source of cross-cultural interaction. By the late 1500s, besides a small minority of whites, mulattos, and free blacks, the population of the two islands consisted of 13,000 Africans of which 11,000 had been baptized or attended confession and 2,700 were catechized.[8]

Among them, one also found free Christianized Africans, who traded and commuted between the coast and the archipelago.[9] The different Creole dialects that formed in these insular locations were each influenced by the varying composition of the immigrant population. While missionaries from Europe mostly spoke Latin, locally recruited Roman Catholic lay priests were also instrumental in the diffusion of Creoles as *linguas francas*. The obligation imposed upon slave owners to have their slaves baptized within a period of six months after acquisition also contributed to this process.[10] The twin processes of Christianization and *ladinization* laid the foundations for a Creole culture on the islands that fanned out to the coast via Afro-Atlantic interaction and trade networks (Carreira 1982; Martinus 1996: 123–130).

Thirdly, the Kriol dialects spoken in the Guinea-Bissau region as well as those spoken in the Gambia and Sierra Leone have generally been associated with the presence of private trader-settlers and their descendants. In the former case, the *lançados* and *tangomãos* have been identified as the progenitors of a Creole pidgin (Da Mota 1951: 10; Naro, 1978: 341; Carreira 1982: 33, 1983: 120). But the *grumetes* who acted as pilots, rowers, sailors, and interpreters and formed part of Kriston communities were also described as agents of diffusion (Carreira 1982: 27, 31; Pinto Bull 1989: 78; De Couto 1994: 32).[11] Rather than being a "plantation Creole" such as that which developed in an insular, colonized context, for example, in the Caribbean, Cape Verde or São Tome and Príncipe, Kriol emerged in and around riverine trade settlements on the continent. Much emphasis has been placed on the economic impact of the aforementioned trader-settlers, some from Europe and others from the Cape Verde islands upon coastal regions, and also on their contribution to the formation of a Luso-African Diaspora.[12] But in demographic terms their number was very small, living in highly dispersed locations along hundreds of miles of coastline and riverbanks. Indeed, far from the creolophone base being circumscribed to a few incoming traders and adventurers some of whom went native and were absorbed into the African population, its continuum and expansion was guaranteed by Christianized Africans living in trade settlements. Constantly commuting between entrepôts, the African interior, and the Cape Verde islands, they developed institutions and traditions of their own that survived centuries of change and interaction (Havik 2004: 129–145). Still labeled as the *língua* (or rather *fala-*) Kriston in the Casamance, the linguistic roots of Kriol denote the influence of Bañun in trade settlements such as Ziguinchor, Mandé in Geba and Farim, Pepel in Cacheu and Bissau and Manjaku and Mankañe in Bolama (Rougé 1988: 11).[13] Notably, Mandé as well as Temne idiom comprise 60 percent of African idiom in important sixteenth and seventeenth century travel accounts (Rougé 1995: 94).[14]

The role of African languages in the formation of Kriol dialects has long been underestimated, that is, until the 1970s. Mandé was the African language with the greatest diffusion in the West African region from first contact until the mid-nineteenth century. It was used by the itinerant *djila* trader and the Islamized *muru* preachers who traveled far beyond Kaabu's borders into the Guinean littoral. But it was also spread by multilingual Christianized Africans who despite their residence in Afro-Atlantic trade settlements remained in contact with their cultural base and heritage. Given the great importance of the Geba settlement that would for centuries harbor the largest Kriston community in the region, it is no coincidence therefore that Guinean Kriol, as well as Cape Verdean Kriolu, contain many Mandé loanwords. In seventeenth century Gambia, two *linguas francas* dominated, that is, Mandingo and Creole, the *Portingall tongue* (Jobson 1968: 30).[15] In the Cape Verdean archipelago Creole, the influence of Mandinga was (still) very noticeable in the early eighteenth century, besides including "a corrupt Portuguese and other words."[16] The influence of the Kaabú confederation that dominated exchanges in the interior between the sixteenth and nineteenth centuries was fundamental in this respect: "Kabou is inhabited by a mixture of several nations; the Mandingos are the most numerous and their language the only one in use."[17] But the strong influence of Bañun and Pepel on Kriol dialects of Ziguinchor and Cacheu and the Pepel and Biafada on Bissau also illustrate regional diversities and their long-standing roots, thus testifying to the key role of Kriston as cultural go-betweens. In addition, this process is further enhanced by influence of Temne idiom into certain Kriol and Kriolu key-words (*tabanka, irán, polón,* and *funku*; see below) on account of the coastal kola trade. The employment of such keywords that are still in use indicates the strong influence of Temne in the early phase of Luso-African interaction, above all in the fifteenth and sixteenth centuries.

Thus, patterns of commercial and cultural interaction in the region produced a composite, vibrant Afro-Atlantic dynamic that hinged upon these three connections in combinations that varied over time. In the following pages the case of Kriol will be looked at in some detail by taking into account these linkages and their impact upon its evolution and the way it was depicted in written sources from the sixteenth century.

Agents of Diffusion: The Kriston

One of the earliest sources on the West African coast dating back to 1456 provides elucidative observations on the way in which the first contacts were established between traveling traders and Africans.

> We discussed sending one of our turgimãos (i.e. interpreters), because all our ships had black turgimãos brought along from Portugal, these turgimãos are black slaves sold by that king of Senegal to the first Portuguese Christians who came to discover the land of the Negroes; those slaves were converted into Christians in Portugal and learnt the Hispanic language well; we obtained them from their masters with the reciprocation and payment that we would give them a slave in return for each (slave bought). To be chosen from our mount for their work of turgimania [the act of translating]: and when each of these turgimãos gave their master four slaves, they would set them free. Thus, many slaves were manumitted, by means of this turgimania. (Peres, 1988: 149)

This excerpt demonstrates the direct correlation between mercantile strategies and linguistic change with regard to the Guinea coast that led to the formation of contingents of converted interpreters, or *xalona* (also *chalona*) as they were called along the Upper Guinea coast. It also informs strategies that promoted the manumission of converted Africans on account of their *ladino* status and contributed to the early formation of Christianized groups. The method in question was repeated with other (male) individuals, often captured, from coastal communities whose languages were as yet unknown, in order to obtain information on their societies after a "crash course" in Portuguese (Peres, 1988: 178). The fact that a female slave kept in Lisbon at the time managed to converse with her captured countryman in a common language (Ibid.), indicated that in those early days the Afro-Atlantic connection was already operative via Portugal. The said "language policy"[18] was applied from the 1430s as the caravels moved southward along the West African coast, but soon shifted toward one that employed the said *turgimãos* as agents in the slave trade itself.

> These turgimãos that speak Portuguese, some of them are captives, others are free, and besides their wages they have the advantage of negotiating a male or female slave and bring them back to the ship.[19]

From the sixteenth century onward, references are made to the existence of "Portuguese," in all likelihood a Portuguese pidgin or proto-Creole in the initial phase of Afro-Atlantic contact (Rougé 1995: 91, 92).[20] The fact that it was termed "Portuguese" is in itself a sign that in this early phase of contact it was not regarded as the chatter of the negroes but rather as a local variant of Portuguese. Various authors mention the widespread use of "Portuguese," for example spoken by a Pepel "king of Cacheu,"[21] by Bañun and Biafada *gurumetes* and *tungumás* (Almada 1964: 76 and 97–98); by the *Portingall* on the Gambia River (Jobson 1968: 30); by a Biafada *djagra* with a Kriston curriculum.[22] Until the eighteenth century, the term "Portuguese" is used as a synonym for Creole dialects spoken along the coast. The apparent ease with which inhabitants of coastal settlements master "Portuguese" and the self-evidence with which the fact was presented, show that Creole dialects were regarded as forming an integral part of Afro-Atlantic networks. For example, among the Bañun in the Buguendo area on the Cacheu river many

> Negroes, both men and women, make themselves well understood [speak Kriol] and serve our traders, and accompany them to other rivers as gorumetes, gaining wages as if they were brought up amongst us, in security. (Almada 1594/1964: 84)

Then and now, the capacity to speak the local trading idiom such as Mandé or Kriol produced significant differences in receptivity of and access to an African clientele to outsiders. The use of interpreters was not only common but constituted a sine qua non for guaranteeing favorable conditions for bargaining and hospitality for strangers who wished to trade with or convert local inhabitants. In addition, the services of interpreters would allow Atlantic traders to obtain bargains, getting commodities "on the cheap" (Donelha 1977: 148).

Notably, the shift of the centre of the regional slave trade from Cape Verde to the coast in the seventeenth century gave a strong impulse to the consolidation of Creole dialects in Afro-Atlantic trade settlements such as Geba, Ziguinchor, Cacheu, and Bissau. It no coincidence that the Kriston communities in these locations gain greater visibility at the time, for example with respect to their control over relay networks with the interior. At this stage Christianized women living in trade settlements, that is, the *tungumás*, also gain notoriety as traders and mediators in their own right in Afro-Atlantic networks, and are recognized as authoritative local actors in coastal trade settlements (Havik 2004: 148–199). *Tungumás* and *gurmetes*, who formed the core of the Kriston communities in coastal and riverine towns, epitomized the universe of bilingual or multilingual Creole speakers. During the first two centuries of Afro-Atlantic interaction, *gurmetes* of Bañun and Biafada origin, among whom most interpreters and pilots were recruited, were singled out for their great knowledge of languages (Almada 1594/1964: 84, 97, 98; Sandoval 1625: 47; Vitoriano Portuense 1694, in: Da Mota 1974: 70; Labat 1728: 243; Araújo 1753, in Peres 1952: 8).The presence of *chalonas* or interpreters was recorded at almost all transactions and palavers with Africans from the sixteenth century. Officials, traders, and missionaries relied heavily on their services.

> The (cabo) Barnabé Lopes, who being of heathen stock, was baptized many years ago and converted his mother and his relatives, whilst serving as interpreter (Vitoriano Portuense 1696, in Da Mota 1974: 99).[23]

The existence of Kriston communities all along the West African coast and rivers from Senegal to Sierra Leone testified to its widespread diffusion.

> Many Christians inhabit the Sierra Leone, Nunez and Pongo rivers, and all speak Portuguese owing to the contacts and blood ties they have. Every year a priest serving the residents of Bissau goes there to preach, confess, baptize and marry them.... (Francisco da Guarda 1694, in Da Mota 1974: 146)

Indeed, in the late eighteenth century, the term *gremeta* is still in use on the Sierra Leone coast among Kriston communities who still call themselves Portuguese.[24] Generally, some confusion remains on the question of "which" Creole they spoke, given that different Creoles also emerged on the windward and leeward Cape Verde islands. The fact that many Christianized inhabitants of the region spoke Creole *línguas francas*, did not necessarily mean that they all spoke the same dialect. A somewhat confusing terminology was commonly applied to vernaculars with Lusophone roots used in commercial exchange on the African coast. An English source from the mid-sixteenth century (approximately 1564), describes the *Portingalls* as the guides in their *almadias* or *canoas* employed by traders on the coast: clearly they were

Africans rather than Europeans.[25] The usage of terms like "Portuguese," *the Portingall tongue* (Jobson, 1968: 30), "Christians...who speak some Portuguese with which they make themselves understood as well as possible" (Anguiano 1957: 268), "Latin Creole" (Cultru 1913: 230),[26] or "Creole Portuguese" (Moore 1738: 39) all indicate the existence of Creole *línguas francas* spoken on the 'Rivers of Guinea of Cape Verde' as they were called in the early days of Afro-Atlantic exchange. It should be noted however that such designations were invariably employed by strangers, that is, non-native speakers. In the case of Crispina Peres, a *tungumá* from Cacheu, without naming it as Creole, it is clear that Portuguese inquisitors could not understand her "Portuguese" so that they were obliged to employ an interpreter (Havik 2004: 158).

Early references to Kriol terminology can be found in travel accounts, official reports, and missionary correspondence. The first direct reference to idiom identified with a specific Kriol dialect pertains to the term *rónias* (worship of shrines) commonly used in Cacheu that forms part of *the Crioulo of Cacheu* (Coelho 1990: 153). By the late seventeenth century, the term *Crioulo* is used clearly distinguishing the language from Portuguese and indigenous African languages.[27] The fact that despite their ability to speak Creole, Pepel *régulos* insist on employing a Kriston *chalona* or interpreter indicated that it was a second language for many African dignitaries, typically used as a commercial vernacular. The use of Kriol therefore clearly bore social implications, associated with the status of the speaker, the person being addressed and the context in which it was spoken. The customs that defined these spatial and social distinctions appear to indicate a hierarchy of linguistic practice in the region, alternating between African, Creole, and European languages.

Evidence has been found in archival deposits for the existence of creolized versions of Portuguese in written form dating back to the last quarter of the eighteenth century, which suggest that Kriol speakers took recourse to a written Portuguese when addressing officials. Significantly, despite the fact that the original is quite readable and understandable, Portuguese officials regarded spelling and idiom as "too close for comfort" to Kriol for the authorities in Cape Verde and Lisbon (Arquivo Histórico Ultramarino-AHU, Conselho Ultramarino, Guiné, Cx. 10, 8-8-1775). It amounted to a passionate plea directed to the commander of the Bissau garrison written by *gurmetes*, who after having attacked an English vessel on the orders of the Bissau governor were "put in irons" by the former. It is one of the few surviving documents written by Kriston themselves and illustrates their use of what could be qualified as a "creolized Portuguese" in order to address the governor of Bissau. Note the religious tone adopted in the text typically associated with Kriol denoting many similarities with that commonly employed by Roman Catholic missionaries at the time. The Kriston petitioners presented themselves here as *gurmetes* in conformity with Creole pronunciation that is translated by *gorometes* in the Portuguese transcription.

Snr. governador desta praza de saon joze de Bisaõ que digo ar d(eo)s guarde por nos amparo

Dinacio Jose de Voao (Port: Ignácio José de Bayão).

Meu snr. A todos nosso dezeireoros voza senhoria logra saude egoal os nossos dezech(?) para empregar em zervis de D(eo)s nos senhor Anos aqui estamos pasando com for me avontade de Deos

Savera V.Sa. que Aqui estamos perzo por bem as nozas corsoes nos dis sia e nos naõ queriamos vir A sera lioa este ano por que vem zaviamos o que estamos Aesprementar aqui estamos pagando o que naõ comemoz nem os nos parentes e nosso viemos na ovidienza de V.Sa. agora aqui estamos as espera da ordem de V Sa. Amais de Snres da Copa. Os ingles naõ quer rem senaõ a sua zente e seu dro. E a emBarcacaõ e nos naõ terem remedo senaõ termos paçenza com os feros, ate vir Aordem de V.Sa. pois, aqui estamos carregados de ferros por toda forma nos peis na maõ anote corente no pescos e naõ emfado mais a Vsa. Que Deos que Depor Ills ? ann de Vosa Senhor Atodos os Gurmetes desta povoação.[28]

Note that the original is full of spelling mistakes, which reflect the phonetic transcription of Creole speech altering prefixes by adding consonants before vowels (*Dinacio/Ignacio*); substituting V's for B's (*Voao/Bayão*) and z's for g's (*zente/gente*), omitting open and plural suffixes (*pescos/pescoços*), and deleting double consonants (fero/ferro). In addition, the syntactical order is often inverted (*por bem as nozas corsoes nos dis sia/bem nos dizião as nossas corações*) as in Kriol. The text demonstrates that the Kriston were not simply Creole speakers but that—at least some among them—were also literate Lusophones, able to speak and write Portuguese.[29] In addition, it also shows that they were versatile linguists who could switch from Creole to Portuguese—and of course back to African languages—whenever the situation required. This provided them with an unusual measure of social mobility, quite in keeping with their role as commercial and political intermediaries in the region.

In fact, by the eighteenth century, Kriston communities in trade settlements such as Bissau had consolidated their institutions among which the *juiz do povo* (the judge of the people), chosen among Kriston elders and brotherhoods wielded considerable power and authority. They levied taxes and tolls, fixed prices, charged for their services, while their courts exercised jurisdiction over transactions; they owned their own riverine vessels and canoes, and businesses, while also being armed, which gave them a considerable leverage over both African and Portuguese authorities. They controlled the riverine relay trade in slaves, gold, ivory, hides, and beeswax between coastal trade settlements such as Ziguinchor, Cacheu, and Bissau on the one hand, and the ports of Kolda, Farim, and Geba hundreds of miles upstream in the interior. By the last quarter of the eighteenth century, their number had grown to about five thousand in these towns, while totaling about fifteen thousand by the turn of the nineteenth century (Havik 2004: tables 1 and 3). Their number would increase throughout the nineteenth century as the latent tensions between African dignitaries, Kriston elders, and Cape Verdean and Portuguese officials erupted into open, armed conflict. In this highly explosive atmosphere that was largely induced by the quest for land on the part of European powers, above all Portugal and France, the tropes regarding Creole languages shifted to sheer ignorance or a dismissive attitude toward "Africanized" Kriol, while showing tolerance or openly favoring "Europeanized" Kriolu.

Stratifying Creole

The use of the term Creole to designate individuals or groups in the Guinea-Bissau region is recorded in various sources from the early seventeenth century. However, the term *Creoulo* or '*Criolo* was only reserved for those originating from the Cape Verde islands.[30] For example, "a Creole Negro who travelled with me from the Cape Verde islands" (AHU, Conselho Ultramarino, Guiné, Cx. 4, 23-4-1699). They were looked upon distrustfully by missionaries who complained about the "the creoles born of Negroes and Negresses that live on the plantations, and who give us a lot of trouble with confessions" (Barreira 17-7-1611, in Brásio, IV 1968: 464) The presence of an increasing number of Spanish speakers, traders, as well as Roman Catholic priests during the period of Spanish rule over the Peninsula (1580–1640) was probably associated with the wider diffusion of the term. Whereas the latter used the term *criollos da terra* (in Cacheu) to describe the offspring of Afro-Atlantic cohabitation, Portuguese speakers would use the expression *filhos da terra* (children of the land; Anguiano 1957: 154).[31] The term *pardo*, that is, brown, is used for those born as a result of concubinage or mixed marriages between Cape Verdean settlers and African women in trade settlements. Lists of residents inhabiting settlements distinguished between *preto* (P: black), *pardo* (P: brown), and *branco* (P: white) (AHU, Guiné, 31-3-1733).

The denunciation by a Cacheu governor of a local conspiracy against "whites and creoles" implied that they were regarded as outsiders (AHU, Guiné, 14-8-1736), as did references to *crioulos das ilhas de Cabo Verde* (creoles from Cape Verde; AHU, Guiné, 30-11-1752, 2-12-1755, 19-7-1755). The term mulatto was rarely employed (AHU, Conselho Ultramarino, Guiné, Cx. 10, 20-5-1773); much more common for Guinean born individuals from mixed marriages was the term *pardo* (Kr: *pardu*), that is, brown. Few cases are recorded of the simultaneous coinage of the terms *pardo* and *mulato* (AHU, Guiné, 1815, doc: 54); in others different interpretations of the term mulatto circulate with regard to the same population:

> The rest of the population [of Geba, apart from three Europeans] which amounts to seven hundred and fifty individuals is composed of blacks or mulattos who are nevertheless called whites because all who are free claim that distinction. (Mollien 1820: 323)

Twenty years later, a Portuguese official observed that

> The garrison town of Geba [is] a Portuguese village of black Christians, a few mulattoes and five or six whites. (Lima, 1844: 108)

Another term *mestiço* is also rarely used, but again typically in relation to Cape Verde: see for example *mistiços de Cabo Verde* (AHU, Conselho Ultramarino, Guiné, Cx. 22, 22-9-1817). One of the very few references to the term Creole used by Guinean born individuals to designate themselves was employed by *Criolas naturais de Cacheu*, that is, Creoles born in Cacheu (AHU, Conselho Ultramarino, Guiné, Cx. 22, 21-2-1818). Judging by the fact that these women were employed in the household of a Cape Verdean trader-official, such terminology was in all likelihood circumscribed to those circles. Another rare reference is coined by a Cape Verdean official who in the 1830s refers to "the free residents and creoles of Bissau" (AHU, Conselho Ultramarino, Guiné, Cx. 25, Manuel António Martins approx. 1830-5). Another contemporary source also includes them in the stratum of "creole individuals of the settlement" (AHU, Cape Verde, Pasta 9, 15-10-1844). In the 1850s, a high- ranking Cape Verdean official, himself a Creole speaker, stated that "the greater part of the gurmetes of Bissau seemed to me to be 'mestiços'" (i.e., mulattoes; Monteiro 1853: 231). Thus, sources indicate a gradual shift, already noticeable in Portuguese written sources from the eighteenth century, in which the two meanings became, at least temporarily, intertwined.

In the meantime, an increasing variety of Kriol idiom had surfaced in written sources from the seventeenth century, above all those transcribed by missionaries. The use of Kriol vernacular was common among outsiders such as traders, officials, priests, and ship captains; see for example the case of food-related keywords as *chabéu* (Kr: palm oil; Álvares 1616, 1990: 38); *mankara* (Ibid.: 8); *fundé* (Kr: finger millet), *kakri* (Kr: small crab), and *mafé* (Kr: sauce served with fish and rice; Anguiano 1957: 269). In addition, terms such as *tongomá* (Spanish Capuchins, in Da Mota 1974: 124, 127), *kuñadadiu*, *baloba* (Kr: ancestral shrine), *chúr* (Kr: funeral), *chai* (Kr: adultery trial), *dono di furto* (Kr: criminal judge), *rónia* (Kr: ancestor worship), *laba kabesa* (Kr: baptism) were also common knowledge in the seventeenth century. Terms such as *tabanka* (Kr: fence, village), *funku* (Kr: hut, slave quarters),[32] and *bolaña* (Kr: paddy rice field) also regularly appear in texts. Even short Kriol sentences were reproduced such as *candelaria amitabai* (Kr: *Candelaria, ami ta bai*; Candelaria, I am leaving; Dias 1945).[33] References to Kriston interpreters or *chalonas* hired to mediate contacts between incoming traders and local dignitaries were increasingly common in reports, illustrating how important Kriol vernacular was for Afro-Atlantic relations. Contrasting with the matter of fact nature of these observations, occasionally Creole as in the case of *caixeiros* or sales clerks, were officially reprimanded for speaking in a "scandalous tongue" (AHU, Conselho Ultramarino, Guiné, Cx. 11, 1776). But respect for the authority of African dignitaries and elders by the Kriston inhabitants of Geba is also recorded with the Kriol term *grandesa* (AHU, Conselho Ultramarino,Guiné, Cx. 12, 5-8-1780). *Baraka* (P.: *barraca*, hut or trading post; see *barracoon*) which first appeared in the eighteenth century (AHU, Conselho Ultramarino, Guiné, Cx. 9, 24-6-1765), came to be used with increasing frequency in the nineteenth century at the outset of the groundnut boom, when settlers negotiated usufruct rights to land with ruling African lineages (AHU, Conselho Ultramarino, Guiné, Cx. 23, 28-7-1828). The Kriol term *kamarada* became a common designation in the 1800s for the local intermediary in villages who dealt with strangers.[34] Terms such as *palabra* (Kr: palaver) and *daxa* (Kr: tribute) were commonly used from the seventeenth century onward as a result of ongoing bargaining between African dignitaries and trader-officials from coastal towns.

When the first attempts at colonization and cultivation are made in the late eighteenth century, settler-traders, who were obliged to master at least its most common idiom and phrases, recognized the widespread usage of Portuguese words in the West African region.

> Many Portuguese words are incorporated into all the African coast languages; indeed a kind of Portuguese patois, which may be called the commercial language of the sea coast, current with them all (i.e. grumetes). (Beaver 1805: 320)

Among the military ranks, only a few high-ranking officials were fluent in Portuguese, while most of the garrisons spoke Cape Verdean or Guinean Creole and an African language. Reports illustrate the association made between skin color and Creole speakers.

> In the Bissau garrison there are only six officials and two soldiers are white; all the others are Black soldiers of inferior rank who do not generally speak Portuguese and many do not even understand it; all speak Creole and Pepel. (AHU, CV, Pasta 3, 13-5-1837)

The incredulity expressed by Portuguese officials at the fact that the *lingua franca* spoken by Cape Verdeans showed little resemblance to Portuguese, provided some insight into contemporary views on its usage:

> For some inexplicable reason, the Portuguese language has fallen into disuse for daily intercourse in the towns and in the countryside; in its place a mestizo mishmash of African terms and Old Portuguese . . . is pronounced rapidly with guttural endings, which they call the Creole language, without any grammar or definite rules, that varies between the islands. (Lopes de Lima 1844: 109)

Travelers remarked upon the fact that "the Creole of the island of Santiago [which historically had the longest and most intensive contact with the continent] is closest to the Guinean version" (Chelmicki and Varnhagen, vol. 2, 1841: 328). This observation is interesting coming as it did from a non-Portuguese official, that is, of Polish origin, who clearly distinguished insular and continental Creoles while also recognizing the similarities and differences between the two. Other sources stated that the Creole of Guinea was "similar to that of the Cape Verde Islands," but that in the case of the latter the change from the "Kriolu badiu" of the interior of the island of Santiago to that of the capital Praia implied a "progressive resemblance to Portuguese" (Ibid: 76). On the continent it is "impossible for a Portuguese who settles there not to speak Creole: . . . words, expressions and creole phrases are found in his conversation and writing . . . and he often ends up by speaking a language which is neither Creole nor Portuguese . . ." (Ibid.: 77). Describing a process that shows some similarities with trade settlements in the Guinea Bissau region, the writer, a Portuguese official, went on to say that

> The whites promote its use, learning Creole as soon as they arrive from Europe, and using it in a domestic context and in the education of their children, to the exclusion of "Português limpo" or pure Portuguese. During meetings between people of certain rank Portuguese is still spoken in towns; but the Nhánhas [free women; from P: *senhora*, or lady] always speak in Creole. (Lima, 1844:109)

Indeed, other sources confirm that "the Portuguese who reside in the Cape Verde islands and in Guinea speak Creole as a common, daily language" (Chelmicki and Varnhagen 1841: 196). Some however assume the existence of a hierarchy of dialects within Creole, depending on the social status of those who spoke them. The belittling of *Kriston ladinu* discourse which is deemed imperceptible by Portuguese officials who demand its translation during palavers is reinforced by considerations which appear to favor certain intermediaries whose command of African languages and African ways is deemed useful, thus enabling them to bypass Kriol (AHU, Fundo do Governo da Guiné, Livro 34, 7-12-1844). The first tentative approach to Kriol was produced by a French trader and naturalist who maintained that besides noting similarities between Cape Verdean and Guinean Creoles, it was the differences that counted. The author noted that the diversity of African idiom was reflected in the variety of Kriol dialects spoken in the region. "In every place, idiom and even grammar are different in accordance with the dominant [African] language which then modifies the Portuguese language and which is everywhere [contributes to] the foundation of Creole."

> Kriol varies from place to place. That of Bissau is mixed with Pepel, that of Ziguinchor with Felupe and Banhun, that of Farim with Mandinga. The way Kriol is spoken defines the social rank of the speaker.[35]

Even though he admitted that "there exists something called the Creole Portuguese language," he refused to go beyond the statement that "Creole Portuguese is no more than an alteration of the Portuguese language." An interesting remark from a European who had married an African woman of Kriston origin, that is, a Kriol speaker. His opinions are shared for example by native Creole speakers of Cape Verdean origin.

> It is composed of many words of that language, some of which are still in use today, of Spanish words, and others are loanwords from peoples which live in the vicinity of factories. (Ibid.: 76)[36]

He provides the example of "a *Pepel-Manjaku" gurmete* who was designated as "Portuguese," having become a sergeant in the French garrison of Sedhiou upstream on the Casamance River from Ziguinchor. This officer had "been unable to learn French, but had adapted our language by the mechanism of the Creole Portuguese language . . . his superiors had great difficulty in understanding him" (Ibid.: 75). The inhabitants of the town of Ziguinchor who all spoke Portuguese [i.e., Kriol] were said to be very similar in terms of education to the 'gourmets' [or *laptots*] and 'maîtres langues' of St- Louis" (Simon, 1859: 127).

The evocation by a high ranking Portuguese official of a night spent in a Bissau ward most frequented by "*gurmetes* . . . these badly domesticated people" gives some idea of local Kriston culture and the less than favorable opinion certain performances aroused among outsiders.

> all night they went to and fro in the streets shouting at the top of their voices or having returned to houses in the vicinity . . . chanting ladainhas in between bursts of strident laughter and furious yells, or mornas, batuques and other dances which are capable of scaring off the coarsest of Europeans. (Almeida, 1859: 50)

The traditional *ladainhas* or laments which had their origin in Roman-Catholic liturgy were sung at religious ceremonies and official occasions, such as All Souls or *Dia dos Finados* (Brooks, 1984) by the "people of the lower classes" (AHU, FGG, Livro 72, 1-11-1864). On the other hand, the more irreverent Cape Verdean music and dance, that is, the said slow and sad *mornas* from the islands and the stirring-up tempo *batuques* with their continental roots were also performed by the Kriston in the settlement. Apart from language, names, dress, and residence also indicated differential social status. For instance, according to a Cape Verdean official, *grumetes*, or the "Christians" sported Portuguese names (but Kriol *nomi di kasa* or nicknames associated with one's lineage) and professed Portuguese appurtenance.

> The grumetes also call themselves Portuguese, because they speak the Creole of Cape Verde with some variations and because their dress resembles more that of the Europeans than of the Pepel. (Monteiro, 1853: 231; Barros, 1885–1886: 152–55)

They wore Afro-Atlantic dress (women wore long white cotton dress and headdress (scarf) or turban and men wore half-length, striped cotton trousers, the so called *chacoal*, with long white shirt, and straw hat) which distinguished them from their relatives who traditionally wore hides.[37]

> Almost all [grumetes] wore cotton trousers, course or striped, a shirt of blue "zuarte" worn over them, and tapered around the waist by a "banda" of Geba, and on her heads they wore a straw hat. (Ibid.)

Various examples from archival sources demonstrate the association made between dress and certain social strata. When a Capuchin abbot of the Bissau hospice was accused of slave trafficking, running a brothel on the premises, and of having a daughter with his mistress, shocked witnesses declared that they had seen him "walking around drunk and dressed in sailors trousers" (AHU, Guiné, Cx. 14, 13-3-1795). Another case that caused a "great stir" was that of a European official who, having deserted his post in Bissau, was caught scaling the *tabanka* or town fence "disguised as a grumete and having painted his face and arms black" (AHU, Cabo Verde, Pasta 36, 13-7-1863).

During the nineteenth century, the increasing social mobility and cultural diversity of the Kriston stratum became more apparent: "the Kasanga, Pepel, Balanta, Biafada and Bijagó who currently compose the Christian Negro population in Portuguese Guinea, and are known by the name of grumetes" (Valdez 1864: 324). Naturally, these changes had an impact on the Afro-Atlantic linguistic spectrum resulting in inflexions of local African languages in Kriol. The establishment of rudimentary health services in Guinea's coastal towns such as Bissau in the 1840s, also produced a number of Kriol terms for illnesses (Kr: *númú*, from Mandé; sleeping sickness; Kr. *barrê pé*, cholera morbus) recorded by Cape Verdean doctors stationed there (AHU, CV, Cx. 132, January 1872). Travelers held that these lexical and phonetic variations were limited to the "Christians" of Bissau, Cacheu, Geba, and Bolama (Doelter 1884: 191), the same towns that symbolized metropolitan authorities' colonial ambitions. The growing contrasts between these groups emerge from local sources that underscored the humble origins of many Africans who migrated to these towns in search of commercial opportunities:

> The Creole of these people [grumetes] who form the popular mass of Guinea, by being less pure and correct, is called the Creole of the "descidos", those who came from the high grounds in the interior to the Portuguese establishments at sea level. (M.M. de Barros 1897–1899: 297)

The same author, himself Guinean born and a native Creole speaker, was the first to assemble a Kriol or "Guineense" dictionary, and called the Creole spoken by the Kriston "the low Creole spoken by the people called *grumetes*" (M.M. de Barros 1906: 307).[38] He associated the "better spoken" Creole with towns such as Bissau and Cacheu that were or had been the residence of government. On the other hand, he singled out Kriston women—now also called *grumetas*—for their poetical and musical vein whose verse is contained in what amounts to the first publication of songs, stories, and parables in Kriol (Barros, 1900). The songs composed and sung by the *kantadêras* who often competed for the favors of their public produced "an unending source of beautiful images and comparisons" (Ibid.: 57). Often remaining anonymous, they were baptized slaves but also free women, who roamed garrison town markets and streets as *bidêras* or market traders (Ibid.: 59, 74).

Apart from having some knowledge of Portuguese, French, or English, *gurmetes* also spoke their own native African tongue. It was transmitted from generation to generation by means of an apprenticeship system that included their relatives in villages in the interior. In Ziguinchor in the Casamance region for example

> It is certain that all of them [grumetes], without exception speak Banhun and Felupe dialects, with the same perfection as Creole. It is unusual for a father not to send his children [sons] to spend some time in Banhun and Felupe territory, thus creating an intimacy with these people from an early age onwards which they acquire later on due to the commercial transactions they effectuate there. (Geraldes, 1887: 503)

This reciprocal interaction enabled the Kriston to act as exchange agents and maintain their bilingual traditions. By the late nineteenth century

> . . . from the mouth of the Casamance river to Sedhiou [a French entrepôt upstream from Ziguinchor] it is the Creole dialect that one hears, both from the Banhun, the Felupe and the Balanta. (Geraldes 1887: 506)

The Creole dialects of Bissau, Cacheu, Geba, and Bolama were "only spoken by the Christians in those settlements" (Doelter 1884: 191). The whites in Guinea not only spoke Creole when talking to the locals, but also among themselves, even employing it in correspondence (Ibid.: 192).

> Portuguese [i.e. Creole] is spoken from Sierra Leone to Gorée; it is the language of [commercial] relations. (Galibert 1889/1890: 276)

Members of Kriston communities also played a key role as go-betweens at the highest level, that is, as interpreters or *xalonas*, between authorities and outside residents on the one hand, and African dignitaries on the other. Overhearing one of these conversations, a Cape Verdean official concluded that Pepel lineage chiefs or *djagras* on the island of Bissau spoke "Creole very badly," suggesting difficulties on the part of native Cape Verdean Creole speakers to understand local Kriol dialects (Monteiro 1853: 421). Palavers were usually conducted in Kriol, such as in the case of the friendship treaty agreed upon by the Manjaku ruler of the Ilhetas (Jeta and Pecixe) and the colonial authorities. Having captured a number of *gurmetes*, the former held the latter as collateral in order to wrest the assurance of free passage and trade for all their canoes in all ports of the region from the administration (Boletim Oficial da Guiné Portuguesa, 22 and 23, 1883). Thirty years before the military occupation of the territory, the ceremony including the recitation of the minutes of the treaty of "subservience and loyalty" signed by the same "king" onboard a Portuguese schooner, reflected the contemporary political context that had changed little despite the colonial staging

> Everything has been well explained and translated to the *régulo* [chief] by his own son and grandchildren who are well versed in Creole, the dialect in which the representatives of the government made their exposition. (AHU, Fundo Viegas, 16-4-1885)

Suppressing Creole Languages

Although they were regarded as indispensable, the role of interpreters was the subject of increasing concern on the part of authorities; some commented that they

> are the worst element that exists here . . . and are people who have great influence in the eyes of the Blacks who speak to the government through them . . .; generally, the interpreters talk in accordance with their interests, i.e. in favour of those from whom they receive more heads of cattle . . . They are the reason why the government does not properly answer the questions raised by the chiefs and the people. (AHU, Guiné Portuguesa, Pasta 418, 8-1-1904)

At the turn of the nineteenth century, references to religious ceremonies spoken in Kriol caused visitors to comment that "it was somewhat more difficult than the Creole of Cape Verde but even so I could perfectly understand it."[39] Soon Kriol would spread further into the interior given the presence of mulattos of Cape Verdean extraction who propagated Creole dialects throughout the colony:

> There is no indigenous village where one does not find Blacks who in increasing numbers understand or can make themselves understood in Creole.[40]

However, the military occupation in 1915 of the continental part of the territory allotted to Portugal at the Berlin Conference (1885) and by the Franco-Portuguese frontier treaty (1886), had a profound impact upon colonial tropes. These changes in the political configuration in the territory would soon lead the recently established administration to outlaw the use of Creole from public services (1917), a measure that followed the introduction of laws that divided the inhabitants of "Portuguese" Guinea into "civilized" and "indigenous" individuals. The author of this measure proclaimed that it was unacceptable that Creole rather Portuguese was the "national language" spoken in Guinea's administration, mainly by Cape Verdeans but also by Kriston officials. Despite such measures, the language question would continue to concern Portuguese officials who remained a small minority in the administration in comparison to Cape Verdeans throughout the colonial period (1915–1974). The latter occupied about half to two thirds of all posts from the 1920s until the end of colonial rule in 1974, a fact that caused resentment amongst (some of) their Portuguese counterparts.[41] The Cape Verdean contingent rarely expressed itself in Portuguese which was only spoken by a few Portuguese civil servants and traders (Caroço 1923).[42]

> It is really depressing for us Portuguese who for centuries have covered Guinea with our blood, that arriving here we have the impression that we find ourselves in a foreign territory. . . . The foreigners, who are forced to learn the language of the colony as a result of their commercial activities, learn Creole, thinking it is Portuguese. (Ibid.)

The situation on the ground was reflected in the problems that primary teachers faced when having to continually correct the errors made by Kriol speakers in Portuguese.[43] Little changed during the colonial period despite educational reforms in the 1930s and the establishment of missionary schools following the concordat with the Vatican in 1940. In the 1930s official reports by Guinea-based Portuguese officials regularly complained about the fact that lower ranking officials, who were often of Guinean origin, rendered dispatches illegible. The declared aim of promoting the spread of Portuguese throughout the colony was not only thwarted by the notorious lack of investment in education, but also by

> various people and of [higher] social status who like to and boast speaking Creole . . . In stead of colonising it seems that these people have come to be colonised by the natives . . . It cannot be the case that civil servants speak creole, including their families. This is as unacceptable as it is humiliating.[44]

On his visits to the interior, the then governor found that the children of European or assimilated Africans working as civil servants and traders by interacting with black servants were assimilating Creole speech and African habits for not having a school in their vicinity to attend.[45] Travelers, such as an English journalist visiting Guinea in the mid-thirties remarked upon the "dominating position of Creole as the lingua franca of the colony (Lyall, 1938: 244). Concluding that "the lingua franca of Guinea and the Casamance is still Capverdian Creole," he observed that "although since it is spoken by natives and Europeans as well as by Capeverdians it has become slightly modified," on account of the influence of "African languages and Europeanised pronunciation" (Ibid.: 178). He thus saw it as an "interesting example of cross-fertilization" between Guinea and Cape Verde. A Portuguese anthropologist was of a similar opinion that the local dialect spoken by *grumetes*, mulattoes, as well as by the Pepel and Manjaco was essentially an adaptation of Cape Verdean Creole.[46] Although he underlined its "poor nature," he praised the way Cape Verdeans "elegantly" expressed themselves in Creole, whilst acknowledging that some even produced prose and poetry worth mentioning (Ibid.: 31).[47] Indeed, colonial reference works on literature from the Portuguese colonies that first begun to appear in the mid-twenties, now included a few samples from Cape Verde as well as from Guinea.[48] While reiterating the idea that the Creole spoken in Guinea was a dialect based upon Kriolu, according to the author, the only Creoles who lived in Guinea were Cape Verdeans (Oliveira 1944: 214).

The first inspection of civil services in the wake of the reforms introduced in the early thirties, reveal that Creole is in fact the regional *lingua franca* and used in commercial transactions. It stated clearly that any trader had to learn Creole—without specifying which variety, which would have undoubtedly been Kriol. The examples given put the onus on the Syrian/Lebanese trading diaspora in the interior which apparently mastered Kriol quickly. Their trade houses and shops which had spread throughout the interior from

1910 onwards were seen as "schools for Creole" which provoked "denation-alisation in a colony which has been Portuguese for a number of centuries, and where Portuguese is hardly spoken by the natives" (Salvação Barreto, 18-3-1938; AHU, Inspecção Superior Administrativa Ultramarina, 1665).[49] In addition, the report also squarely laid the blame on the shoulders of the large numbers of Cape Verdeans "who do not speak Portuguese (and boast not speaking it)." It was about time, the inspector stated, that "Portuguese is spoken in our colonies and that we should end the denationalising impact of Creole" (Ibid.). A few years on, another report directly correlated the sup-pression of Kriol with Christian proselitism by stating that: "It is obvious that in Guinea combating the use of Creole and spreading the Christian faith is a necessity. The use of Creole is a result of the infiltration of the Capeverdean (tongue) and has to be countered."[50] Evidently, expatriate groups such as Lebanese traders and Cape Verdean officials are identified here as the culprits and not, by implication, the Guinean population at large. The population census of 1950 actually confirmed this situation: of the more than eight thousand *civilizados* registered in the colony, only 641 (i.e., 7.7 percent) were able to read and write Portuguese, despite it being a precondi-tion for acquiring the status of *civilizado* (Mendy, 1994: 307).

However, in the 1940s, tell-tale signs of a debate within governmental circles begin to appear. Some official reports then began to distinguish between the different Creole tongues with a view to defending the use of Cape Verdean Creole as an "intermediate language" that would, it was argued, facilitate the teaching of Portuguese (Jones da Silveira, 20-5-1941, AHU, ISAU, 1669).[51] While Kriol was generally ignored, such proposals favoring Kriolu appear to signify the gradual acceptance of its status quo in some metropolitan quarters, thus denoting a marked shift from the hard line taken twenty-five years earlier. But then again, some official reports also underlined existing concerns with "the terrible obstacle" that Creole repre-sented for the diffusion of the Portuguese language.[52] The colonization of Guinea by Cape Verdeans was seen here as the main reason for this "lamen-table" situation, whilst the use of "indigenous dialects" by the Catholic missions had also contributed to their importance (Ibid.). On the other hand, some administrators, notably of Cape Verdean extraction, doubted the feasibility of suppressing Creole given that it was the only and most effective—means of communication in the interior (Conferência dos Administradores de 1941, 1942: 357). Similar opinions were held by admin-istrators, who distinguished the two Creoles and saw Kriol as a kind of Esperanto the suppression of which would lead the indigenous population to distance itself from the authorities (Ibid.: 124). Others, taking a firm stance, defended the suppression of the use of Creole dialects, including the expul-sion of civil servants from the colony whilst appointed native chiefs who did not command Portuguese should be excluded from office (Ibid: 179, 384). In sum, opinions among civil servants differed, while there appeared to be no clearly defined language policy in the colony where Kriolu was the main language spoken among the many civil servants of Cape Verdean extraction.

However, district administrators' reports underlined that despite the official ban on its use of 1917 that was reinforced in 1943, Kriol was actually the *lingua franca* in urban and rural areas for commercial transactions.

Only with the publication of the monumental study on Guinea by the historian Teixeira da Mota, working closely with the then governor, Sarmento Rodrigues, who later became minister of colonies (*Ultramar*), the legitimacy of Creole languages and the crucial importance of Kriol were recognized (Mota 1954, I: 227–233). Based on extensive archival and field-work, this naval historian saw the Kriston of the *praças* or towns as the historical demographic nucleus of trade settlements and as the principal movers behind the diffusion of Kriol in the region. Rather than accepting the hypothesis that Guinean Creole was a mere derivation of Cape Verdean Kriolu, or simply ignoring it,[53] he held that the two creoles evolved simul-taneously (Da Mota 1954, I: 232), what has become known as the ambigen-esis theory. And instead of viewing Kriol as a threat to Portuguese, the author saw it as a regional evolution of his native language, resulting from the "interaction between races, cultures and idioms."[54] In addition, he argued that Guinea's recent colonization had increased the influence of Portuguese upon Creole, whilst at the same time intensifying the cultural exchange between the latter and native languages as "ethnic" frontiers were broken down. In sum, Kriol was now depicted as a fascinating cultural mosaic, rapidly expanding on account of cross-cultural interaction in a ter-ritory where twenty languages were spoken, that demanded understanding rather than suppression. The few fellow countrymen who did concur recog-nized the need for the further diffusion of Kriol as a language by means of which Guineans could communicate amongst each other and with "civi-lized" persons. The local press also began to pay attention to the issue of Creole, illustrating that there was a lively, ongoing debate on the character-istics of Creole languages in Guinea and Cape Verde (*O Bolamense*, May, 1958; March, May, 1961). Nevertheless, influential, high ranking metro-politan officials blamed the diffusion of Creole on the dominance of Capeverdeans in Guinea which resulted in the—intolerable—insignificance of Portuguese culture (Silva Cunha, 1959: 62). Whereas Cape Verdean Creole began to be studied in earnest by Kriolu speakers in the 1950s, lin-guistic research into Kriol remained the province of "foreigners."[55] When nationalist movements emerged as the internal opposition to the colonial regime in Guinea during the 1950s under the leadership of Creolophones, Kriol was immediately employed as a fundamental tool of mobilization, so that it rapidly spread throughout the interior. But that is another story which falls beyond the scope of this chapter.

Conclusions

Distinct patterns emerge from the data presented above that demonstrate marked shifts in the way in which Creole languages in West Africa with a Luso-African lexical base were depicted over more than four centuries in a variety of written sources. Creole dialects rapidly developed in Afro-Atlantic trade settlements on the continent from the sixteenth century, and were used as a *lingua franca* in regional trade networks. Whilst the coastal slave and goods trade expanded, the growing Kriston communities in these locations consolidated their near monopoly over riverine transactions with peoples in the interior from the seventeenth century. Having created their own autonomous institutions, these communities disseminated Kriol through trade networks and social mechanisms such as intermarriage and, above all, the custom of wardship or *kriason*, thereby maintaining a regular cultural interaction with neighboring groups. In the Cape Verdean archipelago, Creole dialects also developed since contact in a society founded upon slave labor imported from the Guinea coast. The isles' decline as a slave entrepôt from the middle of the seventeenth century accelerated existing divergences between the Creoles spoken in the two regions.

Owing to the barter trade and the droughts that periodically hit the islands, there was a constant flux of people and commodities between the coast and the archipelago. Therefore, both Kriol and Kriolu were spoken in the fortified towns on the Guinea coast and rivers, albeit that the latter's native speakers formed a tiny minority. Initially, precolonial sources acknowledge the emergence of local Creole dialects in these locations and quote related idioms as well as identifying the Kriston as their speakers. However, from the late eighteenth and early nineteenth century, Portuguese sources denote a change in attitude toward these communities and their language. Whereas Cape Verdeans had for centuries been banned into exile in Guinea in order to serve as soldiers, they were now increasingly seen as potential settlers and colonizers of a future "Portuguese" Guinea. As the cultivation of export crops such as groundnuts spread throughout West Africa from the 1820s and 1830s, the Portuguese administration saw Cape Verdeans as the vanguard of new settlements that would regenerate the Guinean economy almost exclusively based upon slave exports. The serious famines that hit the Cape Verdean archipelago during the nineteenth century provoked an exodus toward the western Atlantic and to the Guinea coast, causing considerable numbers of impoverished islanders to rebuild their lives on the continent. Meanwhile, the Christianized Africans who monopolized transactions with the coastal towns' hinterland, were increasingly seen as unreliable on account of their privileged relations with African societies and as a threat to Portuguese expansion in the region.[56]

As a result, written sources attributed an increasingly negative status to the Kriston whilst the Cape Verdean Creoles were progressively seen as "suitable" actors for mediating Portuguese intervention in the region. Concomitantly, as indigenous Creole vernacular on the coast took on a pejorative connotation or was simply ignored, Cape Verdean Kriolu gained a certain measure of acceptance, also on account of its greater lexical and grammatical proximity to Portuguese. In addition, the complex processes of transculturation that laid the foundations for the emergence of these languages of mediation were also accompanied by nationalist and racialist tropes that drew comparisons between the two spaces and their purported levels of civilization. As coastal towns were converted into the administrative centers of an embryonic Portuguese colony with clearly defined political frontiers, the Kriston were no longer treated as legitimate go-betweens but rather depicted as Africanized actors who stood in the way of colonial modernization. Cape Verdean Creoles however, used their 'civilized' status to their advantage in order to integrate themselves into the expanding colonial administration.

Relations between Kriol and Kriolu speakers thus came to be imbued with strongly hierarchical elements, thus reinforcing latent tensions between the different groups and spaces. Racial preconceptions which emerged in the mid nineteenth century and were progressively codified into law with the imposition of the "indigenato" or native regime from the early 1900s, further accentuated this distinction, amplifying and deepening it. As a result, the two Creoles whose diffusion was a direct but unintended "side-effect" of Portugal's occupation and colonization of the territory were associated with distinct social strata and cultural contexts. These paradigm shifts strongly affected colonial tropes that hinged upon sociocultural differentiation: whereas ambivalent identities of Cape Verdeans implied the alternation between insular dialects and Portuguese, continental Kriol speakers shifted between Guinean Creole and African languages. By excluding Portuguese, this continental duality was considered, at least until the 1950s, as a negation of centuries of imperial presence in the region. However, it was precisely this twilight zone that gave rise to a debate on the origins and utility of these languages in a colonial perspective. On the one hand, both languages were considered to be threats to the diffusion of Portuguese culture and of the Portuguese language, which were a condition sine qua non for progress and civilization. On the other, Kriol and African languages were depicted as "closed," inward looking and Africanized, while Cape Verdean Kriolu was seen as "open" showing a measure of permeability to Lusophone influences. These currents of thought surfaced in a debate that began in earnest in the early 1950s, centering above all on the issues of race and nation that came to dominate the contested political arena as African colonies gained independence. It was by no means coincidental that the positive assessment of Guinean Creole was directly correlated with the rejection of racialist precepts and of corporatist metropolitan nationalism associated with the *Estado Novo*. The fact that Kriol became a vehicle of dissent and mobilization in "Portuguese" Guinea against the colonial regime during the anti-colonial war (1963–1974), showed that it had lost none of its dynamics as a regional *lingua franca*. Building upon its secular role as a language of Afro-Atlantic and intra-African contact and mediation, Kriol in fact reinforced its presence in the interior during the colonial period and its aftermath to such an extent that it is now the de facto national language of independent Guinea Bissau.

Notes

Modified version of the paper presented at the conference "The Portuguese Atlantic: Africa, Brazil and Cape Verde," July 2005, Mindelo, Cape Verde.

1. See special issue of *Itinerário* (1999, 2) on Atlantic History. As well as other recent works such as Armitage and Braddick 2002; Egerton et al. (2007).
2. See Barros (1897–1906). The term Kriol is henceforth used in text for Guinean Creole, and Kriolu for Cape Verdean Creole.
3. The concept of transculturation was popularized by Fernando Ortiz, the author of a number of studies on Afro-Cuban culture; see by this author, *Cuban Counterpoint: tobacco and sugar*, Durham (NC), Duke University Press, 1995.
4. Maria Dulce de Oliveira Almada, *Cabo Verde: contribuição para o Estudo do Dialecto Falado no seu Arquipélago* (Lisboa: JIU, 1961); Marlyse Baptista *The Syntax of Cape Verdean Creole: The Sotavento Varieties* (Amsterdam/Philadelphia: John Benjamins, 2002); Manuel Veiga *La Creole du Cap Vert* (Paris: Karthala, 2000); Mafalda Mendes, Nicholas Quint, Fatima Ragageles, and Aires Semedo, *Dicionário Prático Português-Caboverdiano (varianti di Santiagu)/Disionari Purtues-Berdianu, Kiriolu di Santiagu* (Lisbon: Priberam, 2002) (see also online version: www.priberam.com); Juergen Lang (ed.) *Dicionário do Crioulo da Ilha de Cabo Verde (Santiago)* (Tubingen: Guenther Narr Verlag, 2002); Francoise and Jean Michel Massa, *Dictionnaire Encyclopedique et Bilingue Cabo Verde/Cap Vert* (Rennes: EDPAL, 2001).
5. For an overview of Creole's Atlantic background, see Martinus, *The Kiss of a Slave*, 118–191.
6. For an analysis of the emergence of creolized African speech in Portugal, see Paul Teyssier *La Langue de Gil Vicente* (Paris, Librairie C. Klincksieck, 1959).
7. These were alternatively known as *folhinhas, prognósticos, lunários*, and *sarrabais* (Ibid., 226).
8. Francisco de Andrade "Relação de Francisco de Andrade sobre as Ilhas de Cabo Verde, 1582," in Antonio Brásio, *Monumenta Missionária Africana*, vol. 3, Lisbon, AGU/Academia Portuguesa de História, 1964: 99–102.
9. Francesco Carletti, *Reis om de Wereld (1594–1606)* (The Hague: Kruseman's Uitgeversmaatschappij, 1967).
10. Baptismo dos Escravos da Guiné, 24-3-1514, in António Brásio *Monumenta Missionária Africana*, II, 1963: 69–70.
11. For the Cape Verdean hypothesis, see, Baltasar Lopes da Silva, *O Dialecto Crioulo de Cabo Verde* (Lisbon: Imprensa Nacional/Casa da Moeda, 1984), 31 and Cabral (1984): 79.
12. See Da Mota (1951), Brooks (2003), Mark (2002). Also, Maria da Graça Nolasco da Silva, "Subsídios para o Estudo dos Lançados na Guiné," in Boletim Cultural da Guiné Portuguesa, Bissau, XXV, 1970: 25–40, 217–232, 396–420, 513–560. Rodney (1970): 71–94; and Carlos Alberto Zerón, "Pombeiros e Tangomãos: intermediários de escravos em África," in Rui Manuel Loureiro and Serge Gruzinsky, eds. *Passar as Fronteiras* (Lagos: Centro de Estudos Gil Eanes, 1999), 15–38.

13. The strong influence of Mandé on both Guinean and Cape Verdean (Santiago island) creole languages has been sustained by several authors, including Baltasar Lopes da Silva in A. Lessa and J. Ruffié, eds. *Mesa Redonda sobre o Homem Cabo Verdiano* (Lisbon: Junta de Investigações do Ultramar, 1957), 138. See also Rougé (1995).

14. The association with Temne derived from the *kola* and salt trade carried on by *tangomãos* and *grumetes* between Sierra Leone and the Guinea-Bissau region (Ibid), and areas controlled by the Soninké/Mandinga such as Geba and Farim, and Kantor on the Gambia River; see Thuray (1979), who provides examples of an early "pidgin Temne-Portuguese" vocabulary based on loanwords and tonal assimilations, while retracing semantic changes.

15. The purest (and oldest) form of Kriol, or *Kriol fundu* is supposed to be that of Geba.

16. George Roberts, 1725, in Bonnafoux, Desiré *As Ilhas de Cabo Verde nos anos 1720: quatro anos de viagens do capitão George Roberts*, Sarcelles, 1980: 38–39.

17. G. Mollien, *Travels in the Interior of Africa*, T.E. Bowdich, ed. (London: Colburn, 1820), 321.

18. See Jeanne Hein, "Early Portuguese Efforts to Communicate while Opening the Sea Route to India," unpublished conference paper, 1987.

19. Valentim Fernandes, "Descripção da Costa de África de Senegal ao Cabo do Monte" (1506), in Antonio Brásio, *Monumenta Missionária Africana*, I, 1958: 694.

20. Rougé deduces the existence of such a "pidgin" idiom in the earliest European travel literature, such as Fernandes (1506), in Brásio, I, 1958: 672–739. Generally, compilers' principal sources were private traders operating in the region who were familiar with the local trading vernacular.

21. Avelino Teixeira da Mota, "Primeira Visita de um Governador das Ilhas de Cabo Verde a Guiné," in *Ultramar*, VIII, 32, 4, 1968: 57–69; op. cit. 65.

22. Relação de Frei André de Faro sobre as Missões da Guiné, 1663–1664, in António Brásio *Monumenta Missionaria Africana*, IV, 1968: 249.

23. His intervention in the baptism of a Pepel *djagra* was amply praised, even "against the will of many" (Ibid.: 105).

24. See John Matthews, *A Voyage to the River Sierra Leone on the Coast of Africa* (London: White & Son, 1788), 13, 78.

25. Richard Hakluyt, "The Hawkins Voyages," in *The Principal Navigations; Voyages, Traffiques and Discoveries of the English nation*, 12 vols. (Glasgow: James MacLehose & Sons, 1904), vol 7, 21.

26. Cultru (1913): 230. When the French traveler, La Courbe, visited Cacheu in 1686 and attempted to converse in Latin in seventeenth-century Guinea, he was told that instead of speaking "Portuguese Latin" he would have to make himself understood in "Creole Latin" (Ibid.).

27. Avelino Teixeira da Mota, *As Viagens do Bispo D. Frei Vitoriano Portuense a Guiné e a Cristianização dos Reis de Bissau* (1694–1696) (Lisbon: CECA/ JICU, 1974), 69–70.

28. Copy of the enclosed letter which was written by the Gorumetes who went in the schooner Our Lady of the Rosary who insulted and raided the English on their way to Sierra Leone, upon leaving this port, the content of which is the following:

> Sir, the Governor of this praça of São José of Bissau, Ignácio José de Bayão, God be with him for our protection

Dear Sir, all of us wish you are in the best of health equal to our wishes to act in the service of God, our Lord; we are currently here in accordance with God's will.

You know Sir that we have been incarcerated, our hearts had indeed warned us, as we did not want to go to Sierra Leone this year because we know (now) what we are going through, we are paying here for what we do not eat, not even our relatives, and we send (this letter) in obedience to you Sir; now we are awaiting an order from You Sir and from the other gentlemen of the Company (Grão Pará e Maranhão); the English only want their people and their money, and the ship, and we have no alternative but to be patient with the fetters, until your order comes in, Sir; here we are burdened by irons, around are feet, our hands and during the night a chain round our necks, we will not bore you any further, sir, God be with You Sir for many years to come. To all the gurmetes of this settlement. (AHU, 8-8-1775)

29. On the question of the relation between orality and writing with regard to Kriol, see Wilson Trajano Filho, "A Tensão entre a Escrita e a Oralidade," *Soronda*, Revista de Estudos Guineenses, July 16, 1993: 73–102.

30. Baltasar Barreira, 17-7-1611; in Brásio, IV, 1968: 464; Sebastião Gomes, 27-5-1617, in Brásio, IV, 1968: 613; AHU, Guiné, 23-4-1699; AHU, Guiné, 2-6-1752.

31. The same seventeenth-century source stated that Roman Catholic missionaries were already transcribing African languages. Whether that included Creole dialects is not clear from the text (Ibid: 182). The term *fidjus di tchon* derived from the Portuguese (*filhos da terra*, children of the soil) did survive in Kriol; however creole as a designation for people was not used in Kriol, given that local idiom such as *djagasidu* (derived from Bañun, i.e., mixed) already existed.

32. The term *funku* in the sense of slave house still appeared in nineteenth century sources (AHU, Guiné, 3-4-1810; Lopes de Lima 1844: 94). *Funku*, derived from the Temne *an-funk* or covered gallery, is also used for traditional hut on Santiago Island in Cape Verde; see Mendes et al. *Dicionário Prático Português-Caboverdiano*, 2002, op.cit.

33. This expression refers to the patron saint of Bissau, *Nossa Senhora da Candelaria*, and was commonly used as a farewell when leaving on a trade- or war-mission, or in the case of fleeing from an imminent threat.

34. J.J. Lopes de Lima, "Felupe: gentios da Guiné Portuguesa," *Archivo Popular* Lisbon, 3 (40) 1839: 317–318; 3 (41) 1839: 322–324.

35. See Bocandé (1849), T. 12: 76.

36. He is the first to point out that the gender of words is determined by adding adjectives on to the noun, that is, *femea* (female) and *machu* (male) and the simplification of the conjugation of verbs by adding adverbs and altering the pronouns.

37. This dress was clearly identified with *Kriston* culture. When a Roman Catholic priest was accused of keeping female concubines in his house, one of the testimonies at the trial indignantly stated that he had been "seen several times wearing sailors' trousers and getting drunk," clearly underlining the pejorative meaning associated with *gurmete* attire (AHU, Guiné, Cx. 14, 13-3-1793).

38. Other Portuguese authors also started to pay attention to "Portuguese Creole" at the time, but mainly to Cape Verdean dialects; see Leite de Vasconcelos (1897–1899).

39. Ferreira F. Da Silva and Na Guiné, *Apontamentos para a História da Diocese e da Organisação do Seminário Lyceu* (Lisbon: Minerva Central, 1899), 84.

40. Pereira (1914): 30. Like many if his contemporaries, this Portuguese governor regarded the "Creoulo" of the Cape Verde islands as a degenerated form of his own native tongue.

41. An English traveler visiting Guinea in the 1930s confirms the enmity between the said governor and Cape Verdean residents reproducing hearsay on a rumor "that a blacklist circulated of all the whites whom the Cape Verdeans were going to massacre on a given day . . . it is significant that it was taken dead seriously at the time"; from Lyall (1938): 179.

42. Caroço (1923): 25. The said governor's report contains diatribes against Cape Verdeans, mainly working as civil servants or traders at the time, whom he saw as the main obstacles to the colony's development. Such attacks also appeared in the local press; for example, see Voz da Guiné, no. 5, 1-6-1922.

43. Anuário da Guiné, 1925; Bolama, Imprensa Nacional, 1925: 161. At the time there were only five or six primary schools in the whole of Guinea.

44. Ricardo Vaz Monteiro, in Conferência dos Administradores de 1943 (1944): 50.

45. Luiz António de Carvalho Viegas, Bolama, 3-7-1935 to Minister of Colonies, Lisbon; AHU, DGENS, 2344.

46. António de Almeida "Prefácio," in Monografia Catálogo da Exposição da Colónia da Guiné, Sociedade de Geografia de Lisboa, Lisbon, 1939.

47. Another equally well-known Portuguese anthropologist, conspicuously ignored Kriol in his account of a scientific mission to Guinea in the 1940s, although admitting that "as we didn't even command creole, we had take recourse to interpreters in order make ourselves understood to natives who do not speak Portuguese or did not understand it"; António Mendes Correia, *Uma Jornada Científica na Guiné Portuguesa* (Lisbon: Agência Geral das Colónias, 1947), 61.

48. Oliveira (1944): 21–66. The stories included from Guinea had already been published by Marques de Barros in his *Litteratura dos Negros* (1900). The first novels about Guinea appeared in the 1930s, written by a Cape Verdean official based there, one of them winning a colonial literary prize; see Fausto Duarte *Auá, Novela Negra,* Lisbon, Livraria Clássica Editora 1934, containing a number of Kriol words and expressions. About the author, see Benjamin Pinto Bull *Fausto Duarte: a la recherché de l'identité Guineenne?* (Paris: Fondation Calouste Gulbenkian, 1985).

49. Salvação Barreto, 18-3-1938; AHU, Inspecção Superior Administrativa Ultramarina, 1665. This situation was confirmed by officials who stated that "commercial establishments contribute most to the spread of Kriol"; Fernando Rogado Quintino, "Conferência dos Administradores de 1941," Bolama, 1942: 357.

50. Nunes de Oliveira, 27-11-1943; AHU, ISAU, 1697.

51. Interestingly, at the same time Portuguese publications show a rapprochement toward Creole culture in the case of Cape Verde, where the *Claridade* literary movement had emerged in the 1930s . Extensively quoting Kriolu idiom some saw the culture of the isles as "the symbiosis of souls joining Africa and Portugal in a new social type, a civilization that has a character of its own and honours us." in Augusto Casimiro, *Portugal Crioulo* (Lisbon: Edições Cosmos, 1940), 17.

52. Nunes de Oliveira, 1-8-1942; AHU, ISAU, Mç. 1664.
53. In the account of his travels in Cape Verde and Guinea the Brazilian sociologist, Gilberto Freyre (1953), voiced his aversion to "the capeverdean dialect" (p.248), without however mentioning Kriol at all.
54. Notably, the same author also challenged "racialists," that is, those who applied racialist theory to the study of African populations, which he maintained, could by no stretch of imagination be regarded as "pure" as a result of centuries of interaction and intermarriage.
55. See Wilson (1959: 569–601) and (1962). Following Da Mota's line of thought, this author considered that Kriol, being essential for Guinea's social cohesion, should be taught at schools; these ideas were picked up by Amilcar Cabral in the 1960s and Paulo Freire in the 1970s and more recently by Hildo Honório do Couto arguing it being instrumental to learning Portuguese; see do Couto, "Kriol as a Bridge to Portuguese in Guinea Bissau," in Fodor, István, Hagège, Claude (eds.). 1999. *Language Reform: History and Future*, Vol. 5 (Hamburg: Helmut Buske Verlag), 203–216.
56. See for an account of these shifts, Havik (2004): 129–147 and René Pélissier, *Naissance de la Guiné: Portugais et Africains en Sénegambie (1841–1936)* (Orgéval: Éditions Pélissier, 1989).

Bibliography

Alencastro, Luis Felipe de. 2000. *O Trato dos Viventes: a formação do Brasil no Atlântico Sul, Sécs. XVI-XVIII*. São Paulo: Companhia das Letras.

Almada, André Alvares de. 1964. *Tratado Breve dos Rios de Guiné de Cabo Verde*, (1594), Lisbon: LIAM.

Almeida, J.C. de. 1859. *Um Mez na Guiné*, Lisbon: Typographia Universal.

Anguiano, Mateo de. 1957. *Missiones Capuchinas en Africa, II: Missiones al Reino de la Zinga, Benim, Abda, Guinea e Sierra Leona*. Madrid: CSIC, Instituto Santo Toribio de Morgovejo.

Armas, Antonio Rumeu de. 1956. *España en el Africa Atlântica*. 2 vols. Madrid: CSIC, Instituto de Estudios Africanos.

Armitage, David and Michael J. Braddick, eds. 2002. *The British Atlantic World, 1500–1800*. London: Palgrave.

Barros, Frederico de. 1885–1886. "Lingua Creola da Guiné Portugueza do Archipelago de Cabo Verde." *Revista de Estudos Livres* 3–4: 152–155.

Barros, Marcelino Marques de. 1897–1899. "O Guineeense." *Revista Lusitana* V–VI: 74–317; VII, 1902: 82–96, 166–188, 268–282; IX, 1906: 306–311.

———. 1900. *Litteratura dos Negros: contos, cantigas e parabolas.* Lisbon: Typographia do Commercio.

Biasutti, Pe. P.A. 1987. *Vokabulari Kriol-Portugís*. Bubaque: Missão Católica.

Bickerton, Derek 1981. *Roots of Language*, Ann Arbor, Karoma.

Birmingham, David. 1966. *Trade and Conflict in Angola*. Oxford: Oxford University Press.

Bertrand Bocandé, Bertrand. 1849. "Sur la Guinée Portugaise ou Sénégambie Méridionale." *Bulletin de la Societé de Géographie de Paris* 3 e Série, Tomo 1: 265–350; T. 12, 57–93.

Bond, Bradley, ed. 2005. *French Colonial Louisiana and the Atlantic World*. Baton Rouge: Louisiana State University Press.

Boulègue, Jean. 1989. *Les Luso-Africains de Sénégambie*. Lisboa: Instituto de Investigação Científica e Tecnologica.

Boxer, Charles. 1957. *Dutch in Brazil 1624–1654*. Oxford: The Clarendon Press.

———. 1969. *The Portuguese Seaborne Empire (1415–1825)*. London: Hutchinson.

Brooks, George E. 1984. "The Observance of All Souls Day in the Guinea Bissau Region." *History in Africa* 13: 1–34.

———. 1993. *Landlords and Strangers: Ecology, Society and Trade in Western Africa, 1000–1630*. Boulder: Westview Press.

———. 2003. *Eurafricans in Western Africa: Commerce, Social Status, Gender and Religious Observance from the Sixteenth to the Eighteenth Century*. Athens: Ohio University Press, Oxford: James Currey.

Cabral, Nelson Eurico. 1984. "Les Créoles Portugais en Afrique de l'Ouest." *Revue Internationale des Sciences Sociales* 36 (1): 77–85.

Caroço, Jorge Vellez. 1923. *Relatório do Governador da Guiné de 1922*. Coimbra: Imprensa da Universidade.

Carreira, António. 1982. *O Crioulo de Cabo Verde: surto e expansão*. Lisbon: Author's edition.

———. 1983. *Os Portugueses nos Rios de Guiné (1500–1900)*. Lisbon: Author's edition.

Chaunu, Pierre and Huguette. 1957. *Séville et l'Atlantique (1504–1650)*. 12 vols. Paris: Armand Collin.

Chelmicki, J.C.C de, and Varnhagen, F.A. de. 1841. *Corografia Cabo Verdiana*. 2 vols. Lisbon: Typographia C.C. da Cunha.

Coates, Timothy. 2005. Review of Bernard Bailyn, *Atlantic History: Concepts and Contours*. Cambridge: Harvard University Press, in: e–journal of Portuguese History, 3(1), Summer 2005 (www.brown.edu/Departments/Portuguese_Brazilian_Studies/ejph).

Coelho, Francisco de Lemos. 1990. *Duas Descrições Seiscentistas da Guiné (1669/1684)*. Damião Peres (ed.) Lisbon: Academia Portuguesa de História.

Conferência dos Administradores de 1941, 1942, Bolama, Imprensa Nacional.

Conferência dos Administradores de 1943, 1944. Bolama, Imprensa Nacional.

Conferência de Administradores de 1944, 1945. Bolama, Imprensa Nacional.

Couto, Hildo Honório do. 1994. *O Crioulo Português da Guiné Bissau*. Hamburg: Helmut Buske Verlag.

Cultru, Pierre. 1913. *Premier Voyage du Sieur de la Courbe faite a la Coste d'Afrique* (1686), Paris: Eduard Champion & Emile Larose.

Curtin, Philip D. 1975. *Economic Change in Pre-colonial Africa: Senegambia in the Era of the Slave Trade*. Madison: University of Wisconsin Press.

Daaku, Kwame. 1970. *Trade and Politics on the Gold Coast, 1600–1720*. Oxford: Oxford University Press.

Daget, Serge, ed. 1988. *De la Traite á Esclavage*. 2 vols. Nantes/Paris: CRHMA/SFHOM.

Dias, António J. 1945. "Crenças e Costumes dos Indígenas da Ilha de Bissau no Século XVIII." *Portugal em África* 2: 159–165 and 223–229.

Doelter, C. 1884. *Ueber die Capverden nach dem Rio Grande und Futa Djallon*. Leipzig: Paul Trohberg Verlag.

Donelha, André. 1977. *Descrição da Serra Leoa e dos rios de Guiné e do Cabo Verde* (1625). Lisbon: Junta de Investigação Científica do Ultramar.

Egerton, Douglas R., Alison Games, Jane G. Landers, Kris Lane, and Donald R. Wright. 2007. *The Atlantic World: A History, 1400–1888*. Wheeling, IL: Harlan Davidson.

Eltis, David. 2000. *The Rise of African Slavery in the Americas*. Cambridge: Cambridge University Press.

Fernandes, Valentim. 1958. "Descripção da Costa de África de Senegal ao Cabo do Monte," (1506), in Antonio Brásio, *Monumenta Missionária Africana* I, 1958: 672–739.

Freyre, Gilberto. [1933] (1963). *Casa Grande e Senzala*. Brasilia: Universidade de Brasilia.

———. 1953. *Aventura e Rotina*. Lisbon: Livros do Brasil.

Geraldes, F.A. Marques. 1887. "Guiné Portugueza." *Boletim da Sociedade de Geografia de Lisboa* 7a Série, 8: 503.

Gilbert, Glenn G. 2002. *Pidgins and Creole Languages in the Twenty First Century*. New York, Peter Lang.

Gilroy, Paul. 1993. *The Black Atlantic: Modernity and Double Consciousness*. Cambridge, Mass.: Harvard University Press.

Gruzinsky, Serge. 1999. *La Pensée Metisse*. Paris : Librairie Arthème Fayard.

Hall, Gwendolyn Midlo. 1992. *Africans in Colonial Louisiana*. Baton Rouge, Louisiana State University Press.

Hall, Robert A. 1966. *Pidgin and Creole Languages*. Ithaca, Cornell University Press.

Hansen, Thorkild. 2006. *Coast of Slaves*. East Lansing: Michigan State University Press.

Herskovits, Melville J. 1937. *Dahomey: An Ancient African Kingdom*. 2 vols. New York: J.J. Augustin.

Havik, Philip J. 2004. *Silences and Soundbytes: the Gendered Dynamics of Trade and Brokerage in the Pre-colonial Guinea Bissau Region*. Meunster/New Brunswick: LIT/Transaction Publishers.

Holm, John. 1988. *Pidgins and Creoles: theory and structure*. 2 vols. Cambridge, Cambridge University Press.

Hopkins, A.J. 1973. *An Economic History of West Africa*. Cambridge: Cambridge University Press.

Horta, José da Silva. 2000. "Evidence for a Luso-African Identity in Portuguese Accounts on Guinea of Cape Verde." *History in Africa* 27: 99–130.

Huber, Magnus and Parkvall, Mikael, eds. 1999. *Spreading the Word: the Issue of Diffusion among the Atlantic Creoles*. London: Battlebridge Publications, Westminster Creolistic Series.

Inikori, Joseph and Stanley L. Engerman, eds. 1992. *The Atlantic Slave Trade: Effects on Economies, Societies and Peoples in Africa, the Americas and Europe*. Durham, NC: Duke University Press.

Jobson, Richard. 1968. *The Golden Trade*. Amsterdam/New York: Da Capo Press/ Theatrum Orbis Terrarum.

Klein, Herbert. 1999. *The Atlantic Slave Trade*. Cambridge: Cambridge University Press.

Law, Robin. 1991. *The Slave Coast of West Africa, 1550–1750: the Impact of the Atlantic Slave Trade on an African society*. Oxford: Oxford University Press.

Lima, J.J. Lopes de. 1844. *Ensaio sobre a Estatística das Ilhas de Cabo Verde no Mar Atlântico e suas Dependências na Guiné Portuguesa ao Norte do Equador*. Lisbon: Imprensa Nacional.

Lovejoy, Paul. 1983. *Transformations in Slavery: A History of Slavery in Africa*. Cambridge: Cambridge University Press.

Lyall, Archibald. 1938. *Black and White makes Brown: A Journey to the Cape Verde Islands*. London, Heinemann.

Mark, Peter. 2002. *Portuguese Style and Luso-African Identity: Precolonial Senegambia, Sixteenth to Nineteenth Centuries.* Bloomington: University of Indiana Press.

Martinus, Frank. 1996. *The Kiss of the Slave: Papiamentu's West-African's Connections.* Amsterdam: Universiteit van Amsterdam.

Massa, Françoise and Jean, Michel. 1996. *Dictionnaire encyclopedique et Bilingue: Guinée Bissau.* Rennes: EDPAL.

Mendy, Pater Karibe. 1994. *Colonialismo Português em África: a tradição da resistência na Guiné Bissau (1879–1959).* Bissau: INEP.

Miers, Suzanne and Igor Kopytoff. 1977. *Slavery in Africa: Historical and Anthropological Perspectives.* Madison: University of Wisconsin.

Mauro, Fréderic. 1960. *Le Portugal et l'Atlantique qu XVIIe siècle (1570–1670). Étude Economique.* Paris: S.E.V.P.E.N.

McWhorther, John, ed. 1999. *Language Change and Language Contact in Pidgins and Creoles.* Amsterdam: John Benjamins.

Miller, Joseph. 1988. *Way of Death: Merchant Capitalism and the Angolan Slave Trade, 1730–1830.* Madison: University of Wisconsin Press.

J.M. de Souza and J.M de Souza. 1853. "Estudos sobre a Guiné de Cabo Verde.: *O Panorama* 10.

Moore, Francis. 1838. *Travels into the Inland Parts of Africa.* London: Edward Cave.

Mota, Avelino Teixeira da. 1951. *Contactos Culturais Luso-Africanos na Guiné de Cabo Verde.* Lisbon: Sociedade de Geografia de Lisboa.

———. 1954. *Guiné Portuguesa.* 2 vols. Lisbon: Agência Geral de Ultramar.

Mota, Avelino Teixeira da. 1974. *As Viagens do Bispo D. Frei Vitoriano Portuense a Guiné e a Cristianização dos Reis de Bissau* (1694–1696). Lisbon: CECA/ JICU).

Naro, Anthony. 1978. "A Study of the Origins of Pidgin." *Language* 54(2): 314–346.

Northrup, David. 1978. *Trade without Rulers: Pre-colonial Economic Development in South-Eastern Nigeria.* Oxford: The Clarendon Press.

Oliveira, José Osório de. 1944. *Literatura Africana.* Lisbon: Agência Geral das Colónias.

Pereira, Carlos. 1914. *La Guinée Portugaise,* Lisbon, A Editora Lda.

Peres, Damião, (ed.) 1952. *Relação da Viagem da Fragata Nossa Senhora da Estrela a Bissau em 1753.* Lisbon: Academia Portuguesa de História.

Peres, Damião, ed. 1988. *Viagens de Luis de Cadamosto e Pedro de Sintra.* Lisbon: Academia Portuguesa da História.

Pinto Bull, Benjamin. 1989. *O Crioulo da Guiné Bissau: filosofia e sabedoria.* Lisbon/ Bissau: ICALP/INEP.

Pratt, Mary Louise. 2001. *Imperial Eyes: Travel Writing and Transculturation.* London/New York: Routledge.

Rodney, Walter. 1970. *A History of the Upper Guinea Coast.* Oxford: The Clarendon Press.

Romano, Luis. 1970. *Cabo Verde: renascence de uma civilização no Atlântico médio.* Lisbon: Editora Revista Ocidente.

Rougé, Jean Luis. 1988. *Petit Dictionnaire Etymologique du Kriol de Guinee Bissau e Casamance.* Bissau: INEP.

———. 1995. "A Propósito da Formaçaõ dos Crioulos de Cabo Verde e Guiné." *Soronda, Revista de Estudos Guineenses* 20: 81–97.

Ryder, A.F.C. 1970. *Benin and the Europeans.* New York: Humanities Press.

Saunders, A.C. de C.M. 1994. *História Social dos Escravos e Libertos Negros em Portugal.* Lisbon: Casa da Moeda.

Scantamburlo, Pe. Luigi. 1981. *Gramática da Lingua Criol da Guine Bissau.* Bologna: Coop Servizio Missionario.

———. 1999. *Diccionario do Guineense.* vol. 1. Lisbon: Edições Colibri.

Silva Cunha, J.M. 1959. da Relatório da Campanha de 1958 (Guiné), Lisbon, Missão de Estudo dos Movimentos Associativos em África, Centro de Estudos Politicos e Sociais, Junta de Investigações do Ultramar.

Simon, Eugène. 1857. "La Casamance et les Peuplades qui en habitent les Bords." Paris: Bulletin de la Societé de Geographie de Paris, 4e Série, T. 13, 115–142.

Solow, Barbara. 1993. *Slavery and the Rise of the Atlantic System.* Cambridge: Cambridge University Press.

Thornton, John. 1992. *Africa and the Africans in the Making of the Atlantic World, 1400-1680.* Cambridge: Cambridge University Press.

Tinhorão, J. Ramos. 1997. *Os Negros em Portugal, uma presença silenciosa.* Lisbon: Editorial Caminho.

Trajano Filho, Wilson. 1998. "Polymorphic Creoledom: the 'Creole' society of Guinea Bissau." Unpublished PhD thesis, Philadelphia: University of Pennsylvania.

Turay, A.K. 1979. "The Portuguese in Temneland: an Ethnolinguistic Perspective." *The Journal of the Historical Society of Sierra Leone* 3 (1–2), December: 27–35.

Vasconcelos, J. Leite de. 1879–1899. "Dialectos Crioulos Portugueses de Africa." *Revista Lusitana* 5: 241–261.

Valdman, Albert, ed. 1977. *Pidgins and Creole Linguistics.* Bloomington: Indiana University Press.

Veiga, Manuel. 1998. "O Português: espaço aberto; o Crioulo: espaço identitário." *Novas Literaturas Africanas de Lingua Portuguesa.* Lisbon: Ministério da Educação, pp.31–40.

———. 1995. *O Crioulo de Cabo Verde: introdução à gramática.* Santiago: Instituto Caboverdiano do Livro (ICL).

Wilson, A.A. 1959. "Uma volta linguística na Guiné." *Boletim Cultural da Guiné Portuguesa* 14 (56): 569–601.

———. 1962. *The Crioulo of Guiné.* Johannesburg: Witwatersrand University Press.

Chapter 3

Historical Roots of Homosexuality in the Lusophone Atlantic

Luiz Mott

The Myth of the Nonexistence of Homosexuality in Africa and the Introduction of this "Vice" by White Colonizers

Officially, the first claim about the nonexistence of homosexuality in the African continent is found in 1871 in the British historian Edward Gibbon's book *The History of the Decline and Fall of the Roman Empire*: "I believe, and hope, that the negroes, in their own country, were exempt from this moral pestilence."[1] Unedited manuscripts of the Portuguese Inquisition preserved at the *Torre do Tombo* in Lisbon suggest that we should go at least as far back as the seventeenth century to find the genesis of this myth. In 1630, Cristovão Cabral, the new governor of the Island of Cape Verde, was denounced to the Holy Office for being a self-professed perpetrator of numerous acts of sodomy. In their report the Inquisitors reaffirmed the myth:

> It would indeed be against the service of God and of His Majesty to have in Cape Verde a Governor so immersed in this nefarious/execrable sin and so long disgraced, to [go to] this land where he will sin without hesitation or limit, *and where he will introduce this abominable transgression....* As to his mistakes, it is prudent to prevent [them] from the outset and not to allow Cape Verde to become a Sodom...*for with his objectionable habits* [he could] *contaminate the people of that land*[2] [author's emphasis].

Two decades later a twenty-eight-year old native of Cape Verde, canon Gabriel Dias Ferreira, was arrested and accused of committing sodomy with eighty-two mostly black youths. Referring to this case, the Inquisitor Pedro Castilho commented: "this immoral criminal is harmful for having committed the sin of sodomy with many boçais black boys, *and* [for] *being one of the first* [to be] *denounced in that territory, where it seems there was no notice of such a crime before...*"[3] [author's emphasis]. In 1905, the clergyman,

Henrique A. Junod from the Swiss mission in South Africa, made the same assumption for the region of Maputo:

> Greek paganism knew of this immorality [pederasty], and practiced it; but Bantu paganism, at least in our tribe, despite its corruption, was not aware of it. And even today, although it is believed that this type of vice has infiltrated certain parts of [Tonga] tribal territory, such as Maputo, the native population has a true horror of it.[4]

Another version of this myth recognizes the presence of homoeroticism among African peoples since at least the mid-nineteenth century. However, it attributes the dissemination of such practices in the African continent to the Arab slave traders, Turks, or converted Muslim Africans. The Sudanese claimed Turkish pirates were responsible for the spread of the "vice" (1848), whilst the eastern Bantu groups blamed the Nubians for the same evil (1885).[5]

The supposed "exceptionality of Africa" regarding homoerotic practices was reinforced by several anthropologists whose views were obscured by a Victorian homophobia. Evans-Pritchard, Alan Merriam, Melville Herskovits, and Geoffrey Gorer were amongst those scholars who denied, hid, or underplayed the presence of such practices amongst the Zande, Bala, Dahomeans, and Shona.[6]

Behind the myth of the nonexistence of homoeroticism in precolonial Africa dwell other myths that draw on no less prejudiced ideas. Firstly, black people's sexuality is seen as something instinctive. Driven by animal instincts Africans would be ignorant of the unnatural vices practiced by white people. Secondly, their supposed physical superiority is contrasted with the peculiarly effeminate way of the civilized world.

The Presence of Homosexuality in Precolonial Africa

African Homosexuality is neither random nor accidental – it is a consistent and logical feature of African societies and belief systems.

Murray, E. 1998: XV[7]

Leaving aside the rock paintings of the caves of San attributed to the Bushmen of Southern Africa and dated as being fifteen thousand years old, where "egregious sexual practices such as group anal or inter-crural sex" are evident, the first documented case of an African who practiced "the love that dares not speak its name" is that of a transvestite prostitute arrested by the Portuguese Inquisition in Lisbon in 1556.[8] Antonio was a black slave and a native of the Kingdom of Benin. He is described in the following terms; "when one calls him a man, he is not pleased. Generally, he is called Vitória and only wants to be called Vitória, and he would run after and throw stones at whoever called him Negro." He was an imposing figure: "large, haunted, beardless, and very black."[9] Outraged by the unfair competition that Antonio represented, the prostitutes who worked around the riverbank in Lisbon denounced this "black person, dressed and adorned like a black woman, who seduced the boys, young men and *ratinhos*,[10] passing workers, and he would take them to a secret place behind some of the razed houses. He [Antonio] would beckon to them with waves and gestures, like a woman enticing them to sin. And [one] saw seven or eight men enter together while the others looked on and laughed outside."[11]

During the day Antonio dressed in some ambiguous and bizarre costumes: "He had a very white cloth over his head, with a hat over this and a wicker basket over the hat, a white doublet laced at the front, and an overall open at the front." When asked in the street; "Why do you call out to men if you are a Negro man? He answered: "I am a black woman and not a man! And showed his breasts..."[12] Before moving to Lisbon, the transvestite Vitória lived in Ponta Delgada on the island of São Miguel in the Azores. There he wore a red jacket, breeches, and a hairnet and at night, he went out dressed as a woman. It is reported that when he was captured as a slave, "he pretended to be a negro woman and for this they put him with the black women and only afterwards, when they saw the documents, was the mistake noticed..."[13] Audaciously, Vitória did not hide her homoerotic preferences. She once said to a person who saw her with a bowl of honey and some bread: "look, my husband gives me this; and he [the witness] asked who is your husband and the Negro answered: white man, and asked; do you want me to be your husband? And the Negro responded: you do not have, show me, show me now, demanding that he show his nature, and added: if you are my husband, I will soon give you many things..."[14]

Arrested in Ribeira, Antonio was taken to the prisons of the Holy Office. Due to his insufficient Portuguese an African interpreter was called in order that he could be understood by the Reverend Inquisitors. He said that he "was a woman and had a hole in the island." Intrigued, the priests of the Holy Office asked if "the hole that he has was made by him or [if] somebody else made it because of some inferiority, or if he was born with it? He said that he was born with the said holes and that there were many people in his land who had the same holes and were born with them...."[15] The inquisitors did not accept this claim and ordered the prison officers to inspect Antonio in order "to see if he was a man, a woman or hermaphrodite."[16] In order to be better examined he was then tied to a ladder with his hands behind his back and his legs open. The officers concluded their technical report with the following words: "We swear that the said Antonio has the nature of a man, without having any holes or anything else of a woman's nature."[17] He was condemned to permanent exile in the galleys of the king where he served as a rower in the Algarve.[18]

Still in the sixteenth century, the manuscripts of the Portuguese Inquisition provide us with another example of an African accused of homoerotic practices. In 1591, during the first Visitation of the Holy Office to Bahia, an old Christian from Lisbon named Matias Moreira made an accusation against

Francisco Manicongo, a shoemaker and slave belonging to Antonio Pires living on the Ladeira da Misericórdia, a street in Salvador. Moreira claimed that Manicongo,

> is infamous amongst the negroes of this city for being a sodomite; and after hearing of this infamy, [Moreira] saw him with a girded cloth, just as the sodomites wear in his [Manicongo's] land in Congo. Moreover, the accuser said that he knows that in Angola and Congo, lands through which he has roamed for a long time and of which he has much knowledge, it is a custom among the heathen negroes to wear a girded cloth with the corners at the front forming an opening, the negro sodomites who act as passive women in this evil sin, being called in the language of Angola and Congo *quimbanda*, which means "passive sodomites."[19]

Having seen Manicongo wearing the costume of the *quimbandas* Moreira

> immediately reprimanded him for also not having worn the men's clothes that his master had given him, [Moreira] saying to him that in not wanting to wear men's clothes he had shown himself to be a sodomite since he also wore the aforementioned cloth in such a fashion. Later, he [the accuser] again saw him two or three times in the city with the aforementioned cloth, and again told him that he should not wear it so, and nowadays he [Manicongo] dresses in men's clothes.[20]

Both the transvestite Vitória from Benin, a slave in the Metropolis, and the *quimbanda* Francisco Manicongo, a slave in Bahia, were native Africans and had already acquired their homoerotic orientation in continental Africa. Whilst Vitória offered her sexual services and attempted to find a "husband" among poor male laborers, Francisco, a *quimbanda*, "committed the said sin with other negroes." During the same Visitation to Bahia in 1591 another "Negro from Guiné" is accused of being a lover to the same sex; "Joane, a child of the heathen of Angola, inhabitant of Rio de Matoim, who, in the said sin performs the role of the women, that is, female."[21] When warned that sodomy "was punished with burning, Joane replied that Francisco Manicongo also committed the said sin with other Negroes and that he was not burned for it...And Joane, even after being arrested, tries to seduce Duarte, a 25 year old, and other Negroes with gifts."[22]

Two Italian authors unequivocally confirm the existence of a homoerotic native sub-culture[23] in Angola in the seventeenth century. The first of these authors is the Capuchin friar Giovanni Antonio Cavazzi de Montecuccolo (1621–1678), who spent a total of seventeen years in Angola and produced two volumes of the book *Istorica Descrizione dé tré Regni, Congo, Matamba et Angola*, covering the period from 1645–1670. His shocked description of the *quimbanda* at the beginning of the second half of the seventeenth century follows:

> Amongst the sorcerers, there is one who does not deserve to be remembered, should this omission not infringe the necessary information

that I, through this report, intend to provide to the missionaries. He is called nganga-ia-quimbanda, or "high priest of sacrifice." This man, completely the opposite of the priests of the true God, is morally filthy, disgusting, indecent, shameless, bestial, in such a way that, he would be the first among the inhabitants of Pentápolis.[24] To demonstrate his calling, he wears women's garments and adopts the manners and bearing of a woman, also calling him "the great mother". There is no law that condemns him, nor is there any action that is not permitted to him. Hence, he always remains unpunished, although he commits abuses with no shame for his lack of decency, so great is the affection the Devil has for him! Thus, the clearest offences that he commits against the honour of those that are married or the concubines of the most protected harems are considered favors. This deceiver also distributes belts for various superstitious uses. What is more, when there are sacrifices, he covers his shoulders with the skins of lions, tigers, wolves or other beasts, and hangs small bells called *pamba* on them. At other times, according to the various rituals, he wears a cloth of *mbondo* [baobá] leaves, covers his face with flour, paints himself with different colours and takes pride in such filthiness. Offering a sacrifice of his own, he kills a cock, a snake and a dog. Then one of those present at the sacrifice, secretly taking the head of the dog, runs to hide it in a hole. After that he asks the sorcerer to find the head, and if he is quick to discover it, he is held in high esteem, as if he were in con- tinuous communication with the spirits. Everyone then proclaims him greater than the other sorcerers, calling him *nganga-ia-quimbondi*. When this sor- cerer dies, the oldest of the sect summons everyone to celebrate his funeral. During the night, this being a propitious time to hide their depravities, only those initiated into the sect should be present, others being forbidden. They take the corpse into the middle of a wood and after many execrable ceremo- nies, which some of the recent converts revealed to me, but that I cannot describe due to their obscenity, they bury him in a very deep grave. Before this, however, the successor orders the heart and entrails to be removed and the extremities of the feet and the hands to be cut off, which they later sell in little pieces as sacred objects and for a high price. Because of the authority attributed to all these *nganga*, there is no *jaga* [warrior], whether a captain of war or a chief of the village in times of peace, who does not seek to keep one of these [*nganga*] with him; without whose approval no act of jurisdiction or resolution would dare be attempted.[25]

The second description comes from Captain Antônio de Oliveira Cadornega in his anthology *História Geral das Guerras Angolanas* (1681). Having spent forty years in Portuguese Africa, his testimony can be considered quite cred- ible. What is more, his account is less moralistic than that of his Capuchin compatriot. Cadornega asserts that:

> there is amongst the heathens of Angola much sodomy, performing with one another their filthy and sordid acts, dressed as women. They are called by a local name: *quimbandas*, who, in the district or in the lands where they reside, communicate with each other. And some of them are distinguished sorcerers, for possessing great evil and, yet, all the heathens respect them and give the no offence. And if one of this band dies, the others gather to bury him, and no one else can touch him or even come close to him, save for those belonging to

that black and dirty profession. And when they carry him from his house to bury him, they do not pass through the main entrance, but through the door at the rear of the house, for, as he served himself through rear door, in death he should also leave through this way. It is this caste of people that place the shroud over the corpse and give him a burial. And, as we said, no one who is not of the same persuasion can approach him. They are always shaved so they look like capons, and dress like women.[26]

These accounts complement one another, without contradiction, confirming several crucial factors for reconstructing the history of homoeroticism in southern Lusophone Africa. They suggest that there was "much sodomy in Angola," and that there was even a group of powerful high priests who lived openly as homosexuals. Known as the "high priests of sacrifice" they were of a higher rank than others and were universally respected. They adopted the dress, mannerisms, and bearing of women, were always "shaven so that they looked like capons" and were even given the name "great mother." The priests frequently practiced sodomy—"in Pentápolis they would be the first"—and had sex with one another, even at their crowded funerals. Referred to as a "band," "sect," or "mob," this was a highly insular group that forbade the noninitiated from attending there secret celebrations.

Whilst one could argue that these are instances of ritual homosexuality and transvestism, there is no indication that the *quimbandas* maintained heterosexual relationships outside their "sect." Furthermore, it is worth restating that the first *quimbanda* of the New World, Francisco Manicongo, did not just dress as a woman, but "was famous among the Negroes of this city as a sodomite and committed the said sin with other Negroes."

It is important to emphasize certain features of these reports. They demonstrate the respect, and even fear, that the tribal population felt toward this mob of "capons," and the skillful way in which the *quimbanda* used and abused their power. As Friar Cavazzi asserted: "There is no law that condemns him, nor is their any action that is not permitted to him. Hence, he always remains unpunished, although he commits abuses with no shame for his lack of decency, so great is the affection the Devil has for him!"

Homosexuality in Colonial Africa

Angola is a cheaper land than Brazil, and there the exiled are better treated
Antônio Lopes Saavedra, exiled sodomitic, 1652[27]

When the Europeans began to penetrate the African continent from the fifteenth century onward, they encountered native people of various regions engaging in homosexual relationships. In some cases they found an institutional form of homosexuality defined according to age—resembling the classic Greek model of *eromenos e erastes*[28] where older men have sex with younger men. In others they witnessed a form of transvestism—similar to the classic *berdaches* of the New World—in which men assumed the role of the feminine gender.[29] Additionally, we should not ignore instances of "marriage between women" documented amongst more than thirty African ethnic groups including the Bantu.[30]

With the arrival of the Europeans this undeniably "native homosexuality" received a new stimulus that led to an increase and diversification of its forms. In European kingdoms sodomy, classified as a crime equivalent to regicide or treason, was considered to be the "dirtiest, most vile and most dishonest sin," and was punished with burning at the stake. Despite this legal repression, documents confirm that during the early years of colonization many Europeans committed this "noble sin" in African lands. Some were either occasional travelers or colonizers, but the majority were exiles.

Let us begin with those who were exiled. During the almost three centuries in which the Portuguese Inquisition functioned, from a total of 124 convicted of the crime of sodomy and condemned to exile, 75 (60 percent) were banished to Africa. Brazil was the second most common destination for exiled "fanchonos" (18 percent). Until now no researcher had drawn attention to the fact that Africa was the principal destination for those found guilty of sodomy in the Lusophone world. Why such predominance? Given the strong racial prejudice of the period the Inquisitors would certainly have imagined that white sodomites would have been less tempted to copulate with black Africans than they would with the white or mixed-race people of Brazil or other places. Perhaps they really believed that such an "evil sin" did not exist in the continent of Prestes John, and, as such, were condemning the sodomites to homoerotic isolation.

The truth is that the Holy Office, founded in 1536, had already exiled the first sodomite, Antonio Coelho, in whose sentence it states that "the defendant expressed little regret for such serious offences," to the island of São Tomé in 1547. From 1595, of the Portuguese African territories, Angola received the highest number of exiled sodomites: twenty-three (32 percent). The island of Príncipe received twenty individuals, São Tomé twelve, Cape Verde two, and Guiné one, whilst fifteen were simply sent to "Africa" without a specific destination.

Although the Inquisition threatened those accused of sodomy with severe punishment upon repetition of the sin, there is evidence that many did not abandon homoerotic practices. The Inquisitors referred to these reoffenders as "incorrigible." This evaluation suggests we should discard Michel Foucault's groundless hypothesis,[31] which asserts that sodomites only occasionally practiced anal sex before the medicalization of homosexuality in the nineteenth century. The documents of the Inquisition comprehensively prove that a structured sodomitic sub-culture[32] existed in Portugal and its colonies—and not just in England and Holland[33]—from the sixteenth century onward. They even provide brief glimpses of a homoerotic identity from some of the most incorrigible sodomites.

As such, the presence of 72 notorious expatriated sodomites in several African territories during the years 1547 to 1739 should not be ignored as a factor contributing to the diffusion and diversification of homoerotic practices amongst the native populations. Apart from common people, those exiled included students, numerous pages, tradesmen, officers, clergymen and noblemen such as D. Luis de Vargas, a member of the Castilian nobility, exiled to Angola in 1632.[34]

The documentation preserved at the Torre do Tombo in Lisbon reveals that the Inquisitors were right to fear the disgraceful effect of sodomites from the kingdom of Portugal, who, like "rotten apples," were responsible for the "contamination" of African settlers and natives, many of whom were unaware of or had no contact with the "evil sin." In 1633, the Bishop of Cape Verde sent a representation to the Holy Office of Lisbon denouncing the execrable sodomitic practices of the Governor of Cape Verde, D. Cristóvão Cabral, a thirty-year-old, knight of the Order of S. João da Malta. His list of lascivious crimes included numerous acts of sodomy, *manustrupacão* (reciprocal masturbation, referred to generically in moral theology as *molice*), and even the extremely rare practice of anilingus. Some of these lewd acts involved physical violence and were not only with men, but also with prostitutes. D. Diogo Osório de Castro, one of the Inquisitors, suggested in his official judgment "that a medicine be searched for... with the assumption that he [D. Cabral] could, with his evil habits, infect the people of that land ...."[35] In fact the "evil sin" spread swiftly through the small island of Cape Verde. Two decades later the Canon of the diocese of Ribeira Grande, a twenty-eight-year-old priest named Gabriel Dias Ferreira was arrested, accused of having performed various homoerotic acts with eighty-two different partners. The majority of these were young black men between the ages of ten and twenty, many of whom were slaves. In his sentence, D. Pedro de Castilho, General Inquisitor and Viceroy of the Kingdoms of Portugal, made the following assessment of the terrible influence that this clergyman had upon the new colony: "the said libertine is harmful for having committed the crime of sodomy with many crude and young negro men and for having been one of the first convicted for this offence in that land, where it seems there was no evidence of such a crime before him."[36] His young partners included António and Vicente from Guinea; João, Martinho, Domingos, and Silvestre; Bento, aged fourteen; a twenty-year-old named Adão; and Chichi, a slave from Cacheu[37]: "he [Ferreira] would become familiar with all of them by holding the virile member... and he always gave them something, even if it was of little value, some vinténs,[38] paper and *ataca*."[39] With Garcia, a thirteen-year-old, "seated in some place, he laid down on the lap of the boy to catch [lice] and there he put his hand inside his fly, and held his virile member and the said boy did the same." On one occasion "a sixteen-year-old Negro that he [Ferreira] did not know and who pleased him [was] passing by his door; he called to him and persuaded him to commit the sin of sodomy; he penetrated his rear vessel and gave him two vinténs."[40] Over the course of one year, Ferreira had anal sex with his father's slave Duarte on numerous occasions. Ferreira recalled eighty-two partners. These were predominantly black or mulatto slaves and former slaves. Many were singers and musicians from the diocese of Cape Verde.[41]

It is clear that for more than two centuries Africa represented a less-controlled space in which Portuguese sodomites could practice their "abominable passions." In 1586, Priest Belchior de Medeiros, a twenty-eight-year-old native of the Alentejo and inhabitant of the islands São Tomé and Principe, fell into the hands of the Inquisition. He was infamous for his "scandalous relationship with a youth called Jorge Teixeira, and spent all his money supporting this young man, because he was a dandy."[42] In his confession the clergyman stated that he had been living in Africa for eight years, having been ordained by the Bishop of Congo, and held the position of coadjutor in the church of Nossa Senhora de Guadalupe and in the diocese of São Tomé. Medeiros testified that a ship was wrecked on its way to Angola, and that the governor asked the inhabitants of the island to shelter the crew. Because of this he received many young men in his house, amongst them Jorge Teixeira. It was widely known that he had a tumultuous relationship was this youth; once, in the middle of an argument, the priest slapped him lightly and the young man responded with a punch "calling him Lutero." In his confession the priest admits to having engaged in sexual conduct with three young men. As well as kissing, *punhetas* (masturbation), and *coxetas* (a practice in which the sexual act is restricted to the thighs) he had anal sex on nine occasions, as both passive and active.[43] A year after this report was made, a man of twenty-one called Gonçalo Duarte "who traded farmland in Congo," was arrested by order of the Bishop of São Tomé, accused of committing the evil sin and of having carnal relations with this same priest.[44]

In the seventeenth century we encounter various references to those that practiced the "love that dares not speak its name" in Africa. In 1653, a forty-two-year-old Knight of Christ's Habit[45] Afonso Castelhano, admitted that during the fourteen years he had lived in Angola, he had anal sex on forty occasions with the soldier João Nunes, another forty times with the soldier Simão Róis, in this case he was sometimes passive; and five times with his nineteen-year-old slave Manoel. During his stay in Bahia he had engaged in various acts of a sexual nature with his ten-year-old slave Miguel Angola, selling the boy in Salvador before his return to Portugal.[46] At around the same time (1657), Gregório Martins Ferreira, a forty-seven-year-old Portuguese priest and former dean of the diocese of Porto, articulated the most open defense and celebration of homosexuality that is to be found in the entire history of the Inquisition. The manuscripts do not tell us how long he spent in Africa or what contacts he maintained with other sodomites. Likewise they do not tell us whether he made the same arguments in Luanda. Ferreira affirmed that "the sin of sodomy was punished by laws for preventing natural procreation, but, like simple fornication, it was in itself a sin, with exacerbating circumstances, but it was more pleasurable and once one started [the practice], it was impossible to amend ones ways; these claims he instilled and preached licentiously and scandalously…"[47]

There were numerous soldiers living in Angola whose names were included in the Cadernos do Nefando da Inquisição Lisboeta, proving that homo-eroticism, as Alexander the Great demonstrated perfectly in ancient history, is not synonymous with effeminacy or cowardice. Rather it is a sexual orientation encountered in all social and professional categories including those that demand fearlessness and combativeness. In 1652, André Dias, a widowed thirty-nine-year old barber and soldier from Evora, was arrested. A public scandal was provoked when he was discovered sleeping with Antônio de Brito, another soldier, "under a blanket in a man-of-war of the Navy,"[48] inviting numerous soldiers to kiss and sleep with him and giving them wine and gifts in order to seduce them. Without shame he said that "with a bottle of wine and a bottle of spirits he could do with the young men whatever he liked, because the wine and the spirits made them take leave of their senses."[49] Even when imprisoned in the gaol in Luanda, André Dias committed the "vice" with a boy called Lourenço de Sousa, "who only consented in exchange for money and a barber's set."[50] In his confession, he at first denied but later admitted having copulated with five partners, including once "in Quicongo lands, under a blanket."[51]

There are frequent cases of Portuguese sodomites who, like this Knight of the Order of Christ, first experienced homoerotic relations in Africa and then later in Portuguese America, sometimes crossing the South Atlantic with their lovers. In 1697 Juliana, a slave "of the pagans of Guinea," made an accusation to the Commissary of the Holy Office of Bahia regarding her ex-master, the hermit Antônio de Oliveira Ramos, keeper of the beautiful little Benedictine church of Monte Serrate in the outskirts of Salvador. She said that Ramos used to commit the "vile sin" with a young male soldier, Francisco de Brito, brought from Angola five years back. Ramos "had a deep friendship [with Brito], and that the said [Brito] always slept in his bed in Angola, and here in Bahia continues the same custom, committing the vice, being the hermit the agent, and many times they locked themselves in the room and behaved indecently, and when the soldier left the house, the hermit neither ate nor rested, until he brought him [Brito] back, and gave him food, clothes and boys to serve him…"[52]

In 1700, at a time when the Court of the Holy Office was increasingly loosing its repressive power, the local chaplain of the small Island of Principe testified to the Holy Office that "it was well known in this land that Rodrigo Lopes Gago, Francisco Pinheiro and Manuel Dias had committed the vile sin, and have been very immodest going to the fields and to the house of Francisco Pinheiro, who is married, and his wife caught him in bed with Rodrigo, who gave poison to kill Maria Quaresma (the wife) for her not to report them; but God saved her and they were exiled by the Chief captain of the Island."[53] The reader observes that this and other reported episodes of sodomy became "public" knowledge, some of them generating "widespread scandal," some sodomites having had a much wider visibility than one might imagine during a period in which such acts could be punished with burning at the stake. Some of these *fanchonos* (gay men) occupied high ranks in the local colonial structure, as illustrated by the case of another governor of Portuguese Africa, accused of the same sin. In 1780, Friar Boaventura de Veneza, mayor of the Capuchin Missionaries, informed the Inquisitorial Board of Lisbon that the governor of the Island of São Tomé, João Manuel Azambuja, "is a well-known sodomite, performing this execrable evil with a subject of feminine figure, Joaquim Lopes, who came as an artillery soldier in the Frigate Nossa Senhora da Graça, of your Loyal Majesty, and [as] he had already practiced [sodomy] on board the said frigate, which is very clear at present and from which results widespread scandal."[54]

Another episode involves Rodrigo Manoel, a forty-three-year-old Brazilian-born native of Rio de Janeiro who was accused of the crime of sodomy whilst serving as a soldier in Luanda in 1750. When arrested he confessed that five to six years earlier, whilst serving in the prison of São Felipe de Benguela, "he went with another soldier Antônio Gonçalves Joaquim and some blacks [*sic*] to the estate of Catumbelha, to smoke a pipe and, once both were there, the confessant provoked, and made them commit the sin of the *molices*—his partner consented and both committed the sin of sodomy, consummated, being him, the confessor, agent only once." He stated in the second confession that he did not ejaculate inside "for his heart gave him a jolt, in such a way that it made him feel horror to consummate such guilt inside."[55] The imperfect sodomy, or "coitus interruptus," according to the Inquisitorial casuistry, was a grave sin. However, it did not constitute a crime to be punished with death.

Homophobia in Africa and in the African Diaspora: Yesterday and Today

It is better to have the corpse of my child, than for me to accept that my child is gay

African saying as quoted by Rowland Macauley,
a gay Nigerian Christian theologian

The oldest reference we can find regarding the repression of sexual "perversion" in Portuguese Africa dates from 1582. When visiting the Ndongo kingdom (present day Angola), Priest Baltasar Barreiro of the Company of Jesus, informed his superiors that

> in the *libata*[56] of the soba Songa, I found a great sorcerer who was dressed as a woman, and even being a man he was considered a woman: the ugliest and most awful thing I have seen in my life. Everybody was fearful and nobody dared to speak to him, because he was considered the god of water and of health. I commanded him to be brought to me and they brought him bound. When I saw him, I became astonished and everyone was scared to see such a hideous thing. He was dressed as a priest of the Old Law, with

a *caraminhola*[57] made of his own hair, with *michembos* [sic] so many and so long that he looked like the Devil indeed. When he arrived, I asked whether he was man or woman, but he did not want to answer. I told him to cut his hair, which had the form of a ball of wool, and to take off the cloths with which he was dressed, and for him to dress like a man. Then he confessed that he was born a man, but the demon told his mother to make him a woman, or he would die, and until now he has been a woman, but from now on, for I told him the truth, he wanted to be man. He is so old that he has a white beard, although he was shaved.[58]

Although this Jesuit chronicler does not provide the native name by which this category of sexually-perverted sorcerer was identified, unless there was more than one "band of sorcerers" that lived as women in Angola, everything suggests that he was a *quimbanda*. In forcing this *manu sacerdoti* to abandon the feminine gender role that he had experienced as a kind of berdache since his youth, the colonizers transmitted and imposed upon the natives a Judaio-Christian prejudice that sees "the man who sleeps with other man as if he were a woman" as a mortal abomination.

We have already seen that many Luso-Brazilian sodomites residing in Portuguese Africa, from governors to soldiers, as well as priests, tradesmen, and numerous pages were arrested for sodomy and condemned to different forms of punishment by the Inquisition of Lisbon. These punishments included imprisonment in the prisons of the Holy Office, confiscation of property, exile, and permanent service in the galleys.[59] With the exception of the old transvestite priest of Ndongo, who was humiliated publicly and obliged to abandon his traditional *modus vivendi*, so far we have not found any evidence of black people or Afro-descendants arrested for sodomy in southern Lusophone Africa. Research in African police and court archives will certainly reveal such cases.

On some occasions, as a way to avoid losing their capital, the masters of slaves in the Metropolis and in Portuguese America who were persecuted by the Inquisition sold the slave before his imprisonment, or were obliged by the Holy Court to trade them outside the Kingdom to prevent undesirable sodomitic contamination.[60] A greater number of African and Afro-mixed people living in Portugal or Brazil fell into the hands of the Inquisition and were accused of practicing the abominable and vile sin of sodomy. In the sixteenth century, apart from the aforementioned case of Vitória, the transvestite from Benin, there are references to a dozen other Afro-descendants living in the Metropolis who were victims of the same misfortune. For example, Jerônimo Silva, a "black slave" exiled to Spain (1647); Francisco Pires, a "manumitted black man" condemned to life imprisonment (1547); Antonio Varela, "manumitted mulatto," sentenced to perpetual service in the galleys (1560); Sebastião, "manumitted Negro who has the reputation of *fanchono* and looks more like a woman than a man, in his way of speaking as in his actions," condemned to perpetual service in the galleys (1557); João Fernandes, "manumitted Negro," sentenced to ten years in the galleys (1565).

The first case of an Afro-descendant living in Portugal who was condemned to be burnt at the stake appeared in 1575. Antônio Luiz, a "mulatto slave," was accused of having had

> many companionships and friendships with young men, who he attracted through gifts, snacks and banquets, many of whom he had touched in very embarrassing parts, involving men wherever he met them, [so that] one it was said publicly in Évora that the houses of Antônio Luiz were a brothel and a butcher's shop, [and] that men entered there to sleep with him in a carnal way like a prostitute [being] an incorrigible person, so rotten that there is no hope for him of correction and conversion, rather, it seems likely that he will be [a] person [that is] very harmful to the republic, [a] corruptor of the honesty of young men.[61]

Domingos Marques, a forty-year-old, was the second black man to be burnt at the stake by the Inquisition of Évora (1612); "black of nation," he was "found publicly in shameful acts with a donkey and also with another young man."[62]

In 1647, Timóteo da Fonseca, a twenty-three-year-old "black slave," was the third and last black man to be "transferred to the secular arm of the law": "his parents were black kaffirs from India."[63] The inquisitional judges, used to dealing with more delicate sodomites, were astonished at the stature of the "big Negro," who was described as "tall, with very large lips." They naively concluded that "being so enormous that he is notorious he should not tend towards the practice of this vice, if he were not naturally licentious and unrestrained, causing great doubt as to his correction, and he committed this sin many times after the age of twenty, and that therefore the defendant, as a convicted, self-confessed and practicing sodomite, scandalous and debauched, shall go to the autos-da-fé and be handed over to the secular justice."[64]

Conclusion

Today, according to data from the International Lesbian and Gay Association (ILGA), the practice of homosexuality is considered illegal in twenty-two African countries including Angola, and Mozambique. Information about homosexuality in Lusophone countries is practically nonexistent. With the crisis of AIDS, the first references of contamination of HIV among men who have sex with other men emerge. In May of 2004, the *Agência de Informação de Moçambique* in Maputo stated that the Conselho Nacional de Combate à AIDS had been strongly criticized by the Muslim clergyman, Sheik Aminuddin Mahomed, who had denounced the "revolução dos gays" for being responsible for the spread of AIDS. He offended many of those present when he declared that "blasphemy, heresy, homosexuality and pornography" are in opposition to ethics and morality, insisting that Sodom and Gomorra were destroyed by God because of the practice of anal coitus. He also attacked gay bars as places in which disgusting acts take place—although such open spaces do not exist in Mozambique. In reaction to this intolerant discourse, the Reverend Dinis Matsolo, from the Christian Counsel of

Mozambique, insisted on the responsibility of religious leaderships to convey accurate information about the prevention of AIDS. Despite suggesting that anti-biblical sexual behavior has been responsible for the expansion of HIV, he acknowledged that the use of condoms is important in saving lives.[65]

In the gathering of January 2005, the participants of the Fourth Forum of the Parliaments of Portuguese Speaking Countries, twenty-nine parliamentarians from Brazil, Angola, Cape Verde, Guinea Bissau, Portugal, São Tomé e Principe, and East Timor, decided to promote action to defeat AIDS. "A network of parliamentarians must be created to fight AIDS, gather information and strategies to combat the epidemic in the countries of the Comunidade dos Países da Língua Portuguesa [CPLP]."[66] The Angolans acknowledge the existence of an imbalance in the combat and prevention of AIDS in Brazil and Portugal compared to the African nations that are members of the CPLP. According to the Angolan parliamentarians, Brazilian and Portuguese efforts already demonstrate a reduction and a level of control of the epidemic, including a reduction in the number of cases. In the document delivered to the representatives of the other countries the Angolan delegation stated that "In this forum it would be useful for us to define measures of common interest [promoting] mutual, bilateral or multilateral cooperation."[67]

The publication of the text "Why does Homosexuality exist" from 2003 onward on the official site of the Ministry of Youth and Sport of Mozambique, in which freedom of sexual orientation was discussed in a politically correct and positive way, brings hope that, despite the conspiracy of silence, the intolerance of political and religious leaders, and the timidity and alienation of homosexuals themselves, Lusophone Africa moves towards respecting the citizenship of those who love members of the same sex. A vital strategy for the prevention of AIDS in the land of the *quimbanda*, is to correct the perverse effects of "heterosexism," "that has walked hand in hand with colonialism."[68]

Notes

Paper presented at the conference "The Lusophone Black Atlantic in a Comparative Perspective," March 10–11, 2005, Institute for the Study of the Americas, University of London. luizmott@ufba.br www.luizmott.cjb.net.

1. Gibbon, Edward, *History of the Decline and Fall of the Roman Empire* (1781) (London: Methuen, 1925), 506.
2. "Seria muito contra o serviço de Deus e de Sua Majestade ir para Cabo Verde um governador tão inculpado no pecado nefando e tão murmurado já de muitos tempos, para terra onde pecará sem receio, nem limite, e deixará lá introduzido este abominável pecado...Nos erros, convém atalhar nos princípios e não dar lugar que Cabo Verde se faça uma Sodoma...pois com seus maus costumes [pode] infeccionar a gente daquela terra."Arquivo Nacional da Torre do Tombo, Inquisição de Lisboa, Processo 12248, 1630.
3. "este réu devasso é prejudicial por cometer o pecado de sodomia com muitos rapazes negros e boçais, *e ser dos primeiros denunciados daquela parte donde*

parece não havia notícia do dito crime antes dele..."Arquivo Nacional da Torre do Tombo, Inquisição de Lisboa, Processo 11298, 1654.

4. "O paganismo grego conhecia esta imoralidade [pederastia], e praticou-a, mas o paganismo banto, pelo menos na nossa tribo, qualquer que seja a sua corrupção, não a conheceu. E mesmo hoje, embora se pretenda que esta forma de vício penetrou em certas partes do território por onde a tribo [Tonga] se espalha, como no Maputo, a povoação indígena tem-lhe verdadeiro horror." Pastor Henrique A. Junod, *Usos e costumes dos Bantos* (Lourenço Marques, Imprensa Nacional de Moçambique, 1944), 499.

5. Apolo Kagwa, *The Customs of the Baganda* (New York: Columbia University Press, 1918); Wilhelm Schneider, *Die Naturvolker* (Munster: Erster Theil, 1885), vol.1; Ferdinand Weine, *Expedition zur Enttdeckung der Quellen des Weissen Nil* (Berlin: G.Reimer, 1848) apud Murray, S.O. and Roscoe, W., *Boy Wives and Female Husbands: Studies of African Homosexualities* (Houndmills: Macmillan Press Ltd, 1998), XII.

6. E.E. Evans-Pritchard, *Witchcraft, Oracles and Magic among the Zande* (Oxford: Oxford University Press, 1937); A.P. Merriam, "Aspects of Sexual Behavior among the Bala," in D.Marshall and R.Suggs, eds. *Human Sexual Behaviour* (New York: Basic Books, 1971); G. Gorer, *Africa Dances* (New York: Norton, 1935), apud Murray and Roscoe, op.cit.

7. Murray, op.cit.,1998, XV.

8. Arquivo Nacional da Torre do Tombo, Inquisição Lisboa, Processo 10868.

9. "quando o chamam de homem, não gosta disso. Comumente o chamam de Vitória e só queria que lhe chamassem de Vitória, e quem lhe chamava de negro, corria às pedradas."

10. "Ratinhos": cargo porters or workers from Beira who work in other provinces of Portugal.

11. "pessoa preta, vestida e toucada como negra, que cometia os moços, mancebos e ratinhos trabalhadores que passavam e os levava detrás de umas casas derrubadas num lugar escuso, chamando-os com acenos e jeitos como mulher que provocava para pecarem. E (se) viu 7 ou 8 homens entrarem juntos enquanto os outros espreitavam e riam fora."

12. "Trazia um pano muito alvo na cabeça, com um chapéu em cima, e um açafate (cestinho de vime) em riba do chapéu, e um gibão branco atacado todo por diante, e um avental de burel cingido aberto à frente." E perguntando na rua : "Por que chama os homens se és negro? Ele disse: Sou negra e não negro! E mostrava os peitos..."

13. "se fez de negra e por tal o deitaram com as negras e só depois que se viram as cartas que notou-se o erro..."

14. "olhai, meu marido dá-me isto e ele testemunha perguntou quem é teu marido e o negro respondeu: homem branco, e disse: queres tu que seja eu teu marido? e o negro lhe respondeu; tu não tens, mostra, ora mostra, dizendo que mostrasse a sua natura, e disse mais, logo: tu ser mi marido, logo vou dar-te muita coisa..."

15. "O buraco que tem foi feito por ele ou lhe fizeram por causa de alguma inferioridade ou se nasceu com ele? Disse que nascera com os ditos buracos e que havia muitos na sua terra que tinham os mesmos buracos e nasceram com eles..."

16. "para ver se era homem, ou mulher ou *mofrodit.*" Morfrodito: contemporary Portuguese term used to characterize a hermaphrodite (note of the translator).

17. "Damos fé que o dito Antonio tem natura de homem, sem ter buraco algum nem modo algum de natura de mulher."

18. Coincidentally, while I was writing these pages, an item of news on the Internet referred to the case of a nineteen-year-old Nigerian transvestite, Abubakar Hamza from Kano, who was arrested and fined for prostitution and dressing like a women.

19. "tem fama entre os negros desta cidade que é somítigo e depois de ouvir esta fama, viu ele com um pano cingido, assim como na sua terra do Congo trazem os somítigos. Mais disse que ele denunciante sabe que em Angola e Congo, nas quais terras tem andado muito tempo e tem muita experiência delas, é costume entre os negros gentios trazerem um pano cingido com as pontas por diante, que lhe fica fazendo uma abertura diante, os negros somítigos que no pecado nefando servem de mulheres pacientes, aos quais chamam na língua de Angola e Congo *quimbanda*, que quer dizer somítigos pacientes."

20. "logo o repreendeu também porque não trazia o vestido de homem que lhe dava seu senhor, dizendo-lhe que em ele não querer trazer o vestido de homem mostrava ser somítigo, pois também trazia o dito pano do dito modo. E depois o tornou ainda duas ou três vezes a ver nesta cidade com o dito pano cingido e o tornou a responder que não usava de tal, e já agora anda vestido em vestido de homem." in Luiz Mott, "Relações raciais entre homossexuais no Brasil Colonial," *Revista de Antropologia da USP* 35, 1992: 169–190; *Primeira Visitação, Denunciações da Bahia, 1591–1593* (São Paulo: Editora Eduardo Prado, 1925), 406–407.

21. "Joane, filho do gentio de Angola, morador no Rio de Matoim, que no dito pecado usa o ofício de mulher, digo, fêmea."

22. "era caso de os queimarem, o dito Joane respondeu que também Francisco Manicongo fazia o dito pecado com outros negros e que não o queimaram por isso...E que Joane mesmo depois de ter sido preso, tenta seduzir com dádivas a Duarte, 25 anos e outros negros." *Primeira Visitação*, op.cit., 408

23. Murray, *Social Theory, Homosexual Realities* (New York: Gai Saber Monograph, 1984); A. Robert, "From Sodomy to Sub-culture: A Survey of Male Gay History," *Gay Information* 13, 1983: 7–14.

24. Pentápolis: the supposed five neighbouring cities destroyed by Jave together with Sodoma and Gomorra as a punishment for homosexual licentiousness.

25. "Entre os feiticeiros, um há que não mereceria ser lembrado, se esta omissão não prejudicasse o conhecimento necessário que eu, por meio deste escrito, pretendo dar aos missionários. *Chama-se nganga-ia.quimbanda, ou 'sacerdote chefe do sacrifício'. Este homem, tudo ao contrário dos sacerdotes do verdadeiro Deus, é moralmente sujo, nojento, impudente, descarado, bestial e de tal modo que entre os moradores da Pentápolis teria o primeiro lugar. Para sinal do papel a que está obrigado pelo seu ministério, veste fato e usa maneiras e porte de mulher, chamando-se também a 'grande mãe'.* Não há lei que o condene como não há ação que não lhe seja permitida. Portanto, fica sempre sem castigo, embora abuse sem embaraço de sua impudecência, tão grande é a estima que por ele o demônio inspira! Por isso são julgados favores os mais manifestos ultrajes que ele faz à honra dos casados ou às concubinas dos mais guardados haréns. Este embusteiro distribui, ele também, cinturas para diversos usos supersticiosos. Alem disso, quando há sacrifícios, cobre os ombros com peles de leão, tigre, lobo ou doutra fera e pendura nelas umas sinetas chamadas

pamba. Outras vezes, conforme a variedade das funções, veste um tecido de folha de *mbondo* (baobá), enfarinha todo o rosto, pinta-se com várias tintas e ostenta orgulho com semelhantes porcarias. Oferecendo o sacrifício propriamente seu, mata um galo, uma serpente e um cão. Então um dos presentes, levando às escondidas a cabeça do cão, corre a escondê-la num buraco. Depois pede ao feiticeiro que a descubra, e se este não se demora muito na descoberta, fica enormemente conceituado, como se estivesse em continua comunicação com os espíritos. Todos então o proclamam superior aos demais feiticeiros, chamando-lhe *nganga-ia-quimbondi*. Quando este feiticeiro morre, o mais ancião da seita deve convocar todo o povo para celebrar o seu funeral. Durante a noite, já que esta é propicia para ocultar suas torpezas, devem estar presentes só os inscritos na seita, sendo proibida a presença de outros. Levam então o cadáver para o interior de uma mata e depois de diversas cerimônias execráveis, que alguns dos recém convertidos me revelaram, mas que eu não posso descrever pela sua desonestidade, enterram-no numa cova muito funda. Antes disto, porem, o seu sucessor manda que lhe seja tirado o coração e as entranhas e lhe cortem as extremidades dos pés e das mãos, que eles depois vendem aos pedacinhos, como coisas sagradas e por grande preço. Pela autoridade que gozam todos esses *naganga*, não há jaga, quer capitão na guerra, quer chefe de aldeia em paz, que não procure guardar algum deles consigo, sem o conselho de aprovação do qual não se atreverá a exercer nenhum ato de jurisdição nem a tomar qualquer resolução." Cavazzi de Montecúccolo and Padre João Antonio, *Descrição Histórica dos três Reinos do Congo, Matamba e Angola* (1658), vol. I, (Lisbon: Junta de Investigações do Ultramar, 1965), 202–203.

26. Antônio de Oliveira Cadornega, *História Geral das Guerras Angolanas* (1681) (Lisbon: Agência Geral das Colônias, 1942), 259.
27. Arquivo Nacional da Torre do Tombo, Inquisição Lisboa, Processo 4005, 1652.
28. Wayne Dynes, *Encyclopedia of Homosexuality* (New York: Garland Publishing Inc., 1990), 241.
29. Murray, op.cit., 1998, 7.
30. Murray, op.cit., 1998, 255.
31. Michel Foucault, *História da sexualidade: a vontade de saber* (Rio de Janeiro: Graal, 1988), 43.
32. John Boswell, *Christianity, Social Tolerance and Homosexuality. Gay People in Western Europe from the Beginning of the Christian era to the Fourteenth Century* (Chicago: University of Chicago Press, 1980).
33. R.Trumbach, "London's Sodomites: Homosexual Behavior and Western Culture XVIIIth Century," *Journal of Social History* 2, Fall 1977: 1–33; M. Rey, "Police et sodomie a Paris au XVIIIème siècle: du peché au désordre," *Revue d'Histoirie Modern et Contemporaine* T.29, janeiro–março, 1982: 113–124.
34. Arquivo Nacional da Torre do Tombo, Inquisição de Lisboa, Processo 11530, 1632
35. "*que se buscasse algum remédio... pela presunção que pode haver, dele, com seus maus costumes, infeccionar a gente daquela terra...*"
36. "*o dito devasso é prejudicial pelo cometer o crime de sodomia com muitos rapazes negros e boçais e ser dos primeiros denunciados daquela parte donde parece não havia notícia do dito crime antes dele.*" Arquivo Nacional da Torre do Tombo, Inquisição de Lisboa, Processo 11298, 1654.
37. Cacheu: region and city in the northeast of Guinea.

38. Vinténs: old copper Portuguese coin, equivalent to 2 cents of the current currency (Note of the translator).

39. Ataca: ribbons to tie clothes.

40. "assentado em uma área, se deitou ele confitente no regaço do menino para catar (piolho) e ali lhe meteu a mão na braguilha e lhe pegou no membro viril e o mesmo fez o dito menino." Certa vez, "passando pela sua porta um negro de 16 anos, que não conhecia, e por lhe parecer bem, o chamou e persuadiu que cometessem o pecado de sodomia e penetrou-lhe o vaso traseiro, dando-lhe dois vinténs."

41. Arquivo Nacional da Torre do Tombo, Inquisição de Lisboa, Processo 12248, 1630.

42. "escandalosa conversação com um moço de nome Jorge Teixeira, e que gastara tudo o que tinha no sustento deste mancebo por ser taful."

43. Arquivo Nacional da Torre do Tombo, Inquisição de Lisboa, Processo 10990, 1587.

44. Arquivo Nacional da Torre do Tombo, Inquisição de Lisboa, Processo 12490, 1587.

45. Cavaleiros do Habito de Cristo (Translators note).

46. Arquivo Nacional da Torre do Tombo, Inquisição Lisboa, 10° Caderno do Nefando, 143-6-36, fl. 9, 1653.

47. "o pecado de sodomia era mais punido pelas leis por impedir a geração natural, mas que em si era um pecado como a simples fornicação, com circunstância agravante, e que era mais deleitoso e que uma vez o começasse, era impossível a emenda, e nesta matéria inculcava e doutrinava dissoluta e escandalosamente..."Arquivo Nacional da Torre do Tombo, Inquisição de Lisboa, Processo 11030, 1654.

48. "debaixo de um cobertor numa caravela da Armada."

49. "com uma peroleira de vinho e uma botija de aguardente fazia dos rapazes o que quisesse, porque o vinho e aguardente fazem perder o juízo."

50. "o qual só consentiu mediante dinheiro e um estojo de barbeiro."

51. Arquivo Nacional da Torre do Tombo, Inquisição de Lisboa, Processo 1467, 1652.

52. "tinha muita amizade e que dormia sempre o dito na mesma cama em Angola, e aqui na Bahia continua com o mesmo costume, vendo-os cometer o nefando, sendo o ermitão o agente, e que por várias vezes se trancavam na câmara e faziam bula, e quando o soldado se ausentou de casa, o ermitão não comia, nem sossegava até que o foi buscar, e lhe dava de comer, vestir, e moleques para o servir ...."Arquivo Nacional da Torre do Tombo, Inquisição de Lisboa, 16° Caderno do Nefando, 143-6-41, fl. 172, 1697.

53. "era público nesta terra que Rodrigo Lopes Gago, Francisco Pinheiro e Manuel Dias tinham pecado no nefando, e andavam muito decompostos indo na roça e casa de Francisco Pinheiro, que é casado, e sua mulher o apanhou na cama com Rodrigo, o qual deu peçonha para matar Maria Quaresma, a mulher do dono da casa, para que os não delatasse, mas que Deus a salvou e foram desterrados pelo Capitão Mor da Ilha."Arquivo Nacional da Torre do Tombo, Inquisição de Lisboa, 16° Caderno do Nefando, 143-6-41, fl. 164, 1700.

54. "é público sodomita, efetivando esta sua execranda maldade com um sujeito de fisionomia mulheril, Joaquim Lopes, que veio como Praça de soldado artilheiro na Fragata Nossa Senhora da Graça, de Sua Majestade

Fidelíssima, como já havia praticado a bordo da dita fragata, o que bem se manifesta presentemente e do que procede um geral escândalo." Arquivo Nacional da Torre do Tombo, Inquisição de Lisboa, Processo 11.516, 1780.

55. "foi com outro soldado Antônio Gonçalves Joaquim e uns pretos ao sítio da Catumbelha, para acender um cachimbo e estando ali ambos, o provocou ele, confitente, fez que cometessem o pecado de molicies – seu companheiro consentiu e cometeram ambos o pecado de sodomia consumado, sendo ele confitente agente, uma só vez." Ele diz na segunda confissão que não gozou dentro "por lhe dar o coração uma pancada, de sorte que lhe causou horror consumar dentro a dita culpa." Arquivo Nacional da Torre do Tombo, Inquisição de Lisboa, Processo 8900, 1750.

56. Libata: village.

57. Caraminhola: disordered hair, shag, tangled hair.

58. "na libatado soba Songa, achei aqui um grande feiticeiro que andava em trajos de mulher, e por mulher era tido sendo homem: a coisa mais feia e medonha que em minha vida vi. Todos haviam medo e ninguém lhe ousava falar, porque era tido por deus da água e da saúde. Mandei-o buscar e trouxeram-no atado. Quando vi, fiquei atônito e todos pasmaram de ver cousa tão disforme. Vinha vestido como sacerdote da Lei Velha, com uma caraminhola feita de seus próprios cabelos, com tantos e tão compridos michembos [*sic*] que parecia mesmo o diabo. Em chegando, lhe perguntei se era homem ou mulher, mas não quis responder a propósito. Mandei-lhe logo cortar os cabelos que faziam vulto de um velo de lã, e tirar os panos com que estava vestido, até o deixar em trajes de homem. *Aí ele confessou que nascera homem, mas que o demônio dissera a sua mãe que o fizesse mulher, senão havia de morrer e que até agora fora mulher,* mas que daqui por diante, pois lhe dizia a verdade, queria ser homem. É já tão velho que tem a barba toda branca o qual trazia raspada." Antonio Brasio, *Monumenta Africana*, 1ª série, Academia Portuguesa de História, vol. XV, Lisbon, 1988, 273, apud Carvalho, Virgilio. "A questão do controlo da terra e da territorialidade no antigo reino de Ndongo," in *A África e a Instalação do Sistema Colonial*, Centro de Estudos de História e Cartografia Antiga do Instituto de Investigação Tropical, Lisboa, 2000.

59. Luiz Mott,. "Justitia et misericórdia: A Inquisição Portuguesa e a repressão ao abominável pecado de sodomia," in A. Novinsky and M.L. Tucci, eds., *Inquisição: Ensaios sobre Mentalidade, Heresias e Arte* (São Paulo: EDUSP, 1992), 703–739.

60. Arquivo Nacional da Torre do Tombo, Inquisição de Lisboa, Processo 12257, 1644.

61. "muitas conversações e amizades de mancebos aos quais procurava por dádivas, merendas e banquetes, com os quais teve muitos tocamentos em partes muito vergonhosas, cometendo homens onde quer que os encontrava, [tanto] que se dizia publicamente em Évora que as casas de Antônio Luiz eram uma mancebia pública e um açougue, que ali entravam homens a dormir com ele carnalmente como uma mulher pública, [sendo] pessoa incorrigível tão estragado que nele não se tem esperança alguma de emenda e conversão, antes, parece que será pessoa mui prejudicial à república, corrompedor da honestidade dos mancebos."

62. "fora encontrado publicamente em atos torpes com uma burra e também com outro moço." Arquivo Nacional da Torre do Tombo, Inquisição de Évora, Processo 7889, 1612.
63. "seus pais eram pretos cafres da Índia." Kaffir (Cafre): name given by Muslims to the pagans and adolators, and, by extension, to the pagan Bantu populations of Mozambique, South Africa, and other countries of southeast Africa.
64. "sendo tão disforme como é notório, se não devia inclinar ao exercício deste vício, se não fora naturalmente luxurioso e incontinente, que induz grande desconfiança de emenda, e cometer por muitas vezes o dito pecado depois de ter 20 anos de idade, e que portanto o réu como sodomita convicto e confesso, exercente, escandaloso e devasso vá ao auto de fé e seja entregue a justiça secular."Arquivo Nacional da Torre do Tombo, Inquisição de Lisboa, Processo 1787, 1647.
65. *Agência de Informação de Moçambique* http://www.mask.org.za/SECTIONS/AfricaPerCountry/ABC/mozambique/mozambique_3.htm accessed on June 30, 2005.
66. "Deve ser criada uma rede de parlamentares de luta contra a aids, que congregue informação e estratégias de combate à epidemia nos países da Comunidade dos Países de Língua Portuguesa."
67. "Seria útil definirmos neste fórum medidas de cooperação mútua, bilateral ou multilateral de interesse comum," diz a delegação angolana no documento entregue aos representantes dos demais países e à imprensa. Agencia Brasil—January 28, 2005.
68. "colonialismo e heterossexualidade compulsória caminharam sempre de mãos dadas." A. Evans, *Witchcraft and the Gay Counterculture* (Boston: Fag Rag Books, 1978), 114.

Bibliography

Aldrich, Robert. 1983. "From Sodomy to Sub-culture: A Survey of Male Gay History." *Gay Information* 13: 20–35.
Boswell, John. 1980. *Christianity, Social Tolerance and Homosexuality. Gay People in Western Europe from the Beginning of the Christian era to the Fourteenth Century.* Chicago: University of Chicago Press.
Brasio, Antonio. 1988. *Monumenta Africana.* 1a série, Academia Portuguesa de História, v.XV, Lisboa, apud Carvalho, Virgilio, "A questão do controlo da terra e da territorialidade no antigo reino de Ndongo." in *A Africa e a Instalação do Sistema Colonial.* Lisbon: Centro de Estudos de História e Cartografia Antiga do Instituto de Investigação Tropical, 2000.
Cadornega, Antônio de Oliveira. [1681] 1942. *História Geral das Guerras Angolanas.* Lisbon: Agência Geral das Colónias.
Carvalho, Virgilio. 2000. "A questão do controlo da terra e da territorialidade no antigo reino de Ndongo," in *A Africa e a Instalação do Sistema Colonial.* Lisbon: Centro de Estudos de História e Cartografia Antiga do Instituto de Investigação Tropical.
Castro Junior, Augusto. 1951. "As Pinturas Rupestres dos Bosquanos." *Mensário Administrativo.* Luanda, n.43–44.
Cavazzi de Montecúccolo, Padre Joao Antonio. [1658] 1965. *Descriçao Histórica dos três Reinos do Congo, Matamba e Angola.* Lisbon: Junta de Investigações do Ultramar 1.

Dynes, Wayne. 1990. *Encyclopedia of Homosexuality*. New York: Garland.

Evans-Pritchard, E.E. 1937. *Witchcraft, Oracles and Magic among the Zande*. Oxford: Oxford University Press.

Foucault, Michel. 1988. *História da sexualidade. A voltade de saber*. Rio de Janeiro: Graal.

Garlake, Peter. 1995. *The Hunters Vision*. London: British Museum.

Gibbon, Edward. 1925. *History of the Decline and Fall of the Roman Empire* [1781]. London: Methuen.

Gorer, G. 1935. *Africa Dances*. New York: Norton.

Junod, Pastor Henrique A. 1944. *Usos e costumes dos Bantos*. Imprensa Nacional de Moçambique, Lourenço Marques.

Kagwa, Apolo. 1918. *The Customs of the Baganda*. New York: Columbia University Press.

Merriam, A.P. 1971. "Aspects of Sexual Behavior among the Bala," in D. Marshall and R. Suggs, eds. *Human Sexual Behavior*. New York: Basic Books.

Mott, Luiz. 1988. "Pagode Português: A Subculture Gay em Portugal nos tempos da Inquisiçao." *Ciencia e Cultura* 40 (February): 120–139.

———. 1992. "Justitia et misericórdia: A Inquisição Portuguesa e a repressão ao abominável pecado de sodomia," in A. Novinsky and M.L. Tucci, eds. *Inquisição: Ensaios sobre Mentalidade, Heresias e Arte*. São Paulo: Editora Universidade de São Paulo, pp.44–60.

———. 1992. "Relações raciais entre homossexuais no Brasil Colonial." *Revista de Antropologia da Universidade de Sao Paulo* 35: 169–190.

Murray, Stephen O. 1984. *Social Theory, Homosexual Realities*. New York: Gai Saber Monograph.

Murray, Stephen O., and W. Roscoe. 1998. *Boy Wives and Female Husbands: Studies of African Homosexualities*. Macmillan: Houndmills.

Rey, Michel. 1982. "Police et sodomie à Paris au XVIIIème siècle: du pechè au désordre." *Revue d'Histoire Moderne et Contemporaine* 29 (January–March): 113–124.

Schneider, Wilhelm. 1885. *Die Naturvolker*. Munster: Erster Theil, vol.1.

Trumbach, R. 1977. "London's Sodomites: Homosexual Behavior and Western Culture in the Eighteenth Century." *Journal of Social History* 11(1), Fall: 1–33.

Weine, Ferdinand. 1848. *Expedition zur Enttdeckung der Quellen des Weissen Nil* Berlin: G. Reimer. apud. Murray, S.O. and Roscoe, W. *Boy Wives and Female Husbands: Studies of African Homosexualities*. Macmillan, Houndmills, 1998.

Part II

Migrations and Colonial Cultures

Chapter 4

Atlantic Microhistories: Mobility, Personal Ties, and Slaving in the Black Atlantic World (Angola and Brazil)

Roquinaldo Ferreira

Introduction

This chapter investigates the microdynamics of the social, cultural, and commercial networks that underpinned slaving in Angola in the eighteenth and early nineteenth centuries. To that end, it uses biographical information on merchants operating out of Luanda and Benguela to explain their commercial strategies, their cultural integration into local communities, and their close commercial links with Brazil.[1] It highlights individual mobility as a central dimension to the commercial networks underpinning slaving in the southern Atlantic. Situated at the crossroad of three historiographies (African history, Atlantic history, and Brazilian history), this chapter employs a conceptual framework that relies on a close study of frequent personal movements—back and forth across the Atlantic—to study the dynamics of the trade between Angola and Brazil.[2] By focusing on the interconnections of commerce between two regions of the southern Atlantic (Angola and Brazil), it shifts away from the still dominating northern Atlantic focus in studies of Atlantic history.[3]

I begin by sketching out the specific bilateral framework that characterized the slave trade from Angola to Brazil. Like the slave trade in West Africa, the Angolan trade simultaneously gave birth to and was dependent on a highly amalgamated cultural and social milieu. In contrast to West Africa, however, where commercial links with Europe played a pivotal role in coastal slaving, the Angolan trade with Brazil was direct and largely independent from Portugal. Brazilian hegemony was particularly strong in Benguela, which witnessed the shipment of over 500,000 Africans to the Americas, primarily to Rio de Janeiro, from late seventeenth century to mid-nineteenth centuries. In order to understand the beginning of the Benguela slave trade in the early eighteenth century, I reconstruct the personal trajectory of José dos

Santos Torres, a merchant who refocused investments away from West Africa toward Angola due to the erosion of Portuguese influence on the Mina Coast. To demonstrate how commercial networks were also dependent and fueled by personal, education, and religious links between individuals in Angola and Brazil, I piece together biographical information on merchants. I then take a close look at the Benguela merchant community and Benguela links with Rio de Janeiro in the late eighteenth century and early nineteenth centuries. By devoting significant attention to Benguela, I seek to redress a well-established and imbalanced focus on Luanda within the scholarship of the slave trade between Angola and Brazil.[4]

Background

The southern Atlantic link between Angola and Brazil is important for several reasons. The Brazilians and Angolans, and some Portuguese, examined in this chapter carried approximately 45 percent of the Africans taken across the Atlantic from Angola and Kongo. Brazil was similarly the largest single American destination of slaves, receiving approximately 45 percent of the overall number of Africans affected by the slave trade, most of them from central Africa across the southern Atlantic.[5] The Angolan trade first developed in northern Angola between Loango and coastal Kongo in the early sixteenth century. Local merchants operating out of São Tomé and Kongo sidelined royal and private Portuguese groups' stakes in the business (Thornton 1998: 61–62; Klein 2003: 211–212). By the end of the sixteenth century, a southward process of decentralization of the slave trade was set in motion, eventually leading to the foundation of Luanda. As indicated by Joseph Miller, an attempt to strengthen metropolitan stakes in slaving served as the primary backdrop to the foundation of Luanda.[6]

Since the mid-seventeenth century—if not earlier—Angolan ties with Brazil were as intense as West African links with northeastern Brazil. Illustrating the intensity of the links between the two regions, Africans shipped from Angola accounted for two-thirds of those taken into Brazil. The trade between Angola and Brazil took place within a bilateral framework that undercut Portuguese influence while bolstering Angola's direct ties with Brazil. In addition to the vast trade in locally produced goods like rum, Brazilian economic dominance in Angola was also a function of a shift in the center of gravity from Lisbon to Salvador Bahia of Indian textiles, which were the main commodity used to purchase slaves in Angola. This development, which occurred in the seventeenth century, enhanced Bahia's stature in the southern Atlantic economy by turning Salvador into a focal point of the Indian textile commerce. Brazil-based merchants regularly tapped into Salvador's position in the Indian textile trade to undercut Portuguese commercial interests in Angola and carve out a hegemonic niche in Luanda and Benguela (Ferreira 2003; Miller 1986: 165–246).

While seventeenth-century Angola was primarily linked to Bahia and Pernambuco in the Brazilian northeast, the gold production in Minas Gerais turned Rio de Janeiro into the chief Angolan commercial partner. Links with Brazil were crucial to several aspects of Angolan slaving and the overall management of the Portuguese colony. These links included the deployment of soldiers from Brazil to fight wars in the Luanda hinterland, the continual flow into Angola of Brazil-based merchants, bureaucrats and political and criminal exiles, and the ownership of ships used in the Angolan trade, among others (Ferreira 2003). In 1811, for example, seven of the ten ships operating on the Luanda-Rio de Janeiro route of the Angolan trade were owned by merchants based in Rio.[7] In 1827, a consul from newly independent Brazil in Luanda estimated that the number of Brazilian-owned ships in the Luanda harbor stood at fourteen.[8]

In Benguela, Brazilian hegemony was even more pronounced than in Luanda. Here, after an early attempt to develop slaving failed in the first half of the seventeenth century, exports of slaves increased toward the end of the century and became a full-fledged independent operation in the initial decades of the eighteenth century. Benguela then became a focal point of shipments of slaves to Brazil developing lasting links with Rio de Janeiro in the wake of the discovery of gold in Minas Gerais, in the early eighteenth century, which drove the demand for labor force in Brazil upward and added significant momentum to slaving in southern Angola. In the early 1810s, for example, all ships used to transport slaves from this city to Brazil were owned by Brazil-based merchants.[9] Between 1796 and 1828, at least 80 percent of the slave ships that set sail from Benguela were bound for Rio de Janeiro (Miller 1975). Not surprisingly, Benguela accounted for approximately half of the slave ships entering the port of Rio de Janeiro between 1795 and 1811 (Klein 1978).

Cultural Milieu

Robin Law and Kristin Mann have recently coined the term "Atlantic Community" to refer to the intense commercial and cultural ties between Bahia and the Bight of Benin (1999: 307–331). Law and Mann's focus on Africa and African agency in the development of the diaspora differs from Paul Gilroy's North American-oriented analysis of white domination of the "black Atlantic" (Gilroy 1993).[10] According to Law and Mann, the slave trade between Bahia and West Africa was marked by cross-racial and cross-cultural dimensions due to the prominence of mixed-race or culturally hybrid merchants in the slave trade between these two regions. Indeed, culturally hybrid dynamics emerged elsewhere in Atlantic Africa as well. In Senegambia, for example, merchants known as *lançados*, who defined their identity by blending elements of European and African culture, controlled critical aspects of the coastal trade.[11] On the Gold Coast, the establishment of a large number of coastal fortresses by European nations directly contributed to the rise of culturally hybrid Creole communities.[12] In the Bight of Benin, a place where creolization was not a driving force in the early slave trade, the nineteenth century return of former slaves from Brazil bolstered coastal slaving and intensified links with Bahia, which led to the rise of highly creolized coastal communities.[13] Even in regions outside Portuguese and Brazilian influence, such as the Bight of Biafra, cultural hybridism provided a framework for coastal trade.[14] As demonstrated by recent work by Randy Sparks, it allowed two Efke individuals illegally enslaved to fight to regain freedom in the Caribbean, Virginia, and England (2002, 2004).

Law and Mann argue that the concept of Atlantic community cannot be applied to the Angolan case on the grounds that the Portuguese held sway in the region as a colonial power(1999: 334).[15] In reality, even in the first half of the seventeenth century, when forces fighting on behalf of the Portuguese were able to deal several military blows to African kingdoms and establish an area of influence that stretched from coastal Luanda to Mpungo Ndongo through the creation of military and administrative outposts (*presídios*), their achievements grew largely out of alliances with local Imbangala groups (Vansina 2005).[16] In the second half of the seventeenth century, Portuguese capacity to influence events in the interior of Angola dwindled dramatically as the consolidation of the Imbangala power through the creation of the kingdom of Kasanje established a political and military counterpoint that seriously undermined Luanda's capacity to conduct military operations in the Luanda hinterland (Ferreira: 2003).[17] Thus, in lieu of a strict colonial regime, the social and cultural landscape in Luanda, Benguela, and their respective hinterlands were marked by a highly amalgamated cultural and social dynamic. Africans would seize upon elements of European culture to create and reinforce social hierarchies among themselves, while key elements of the bureaucratic and legal apparatus of the colonial administration derived from African social and cultural institutions (Heywood 2000). The dynamics of the internal slave trade lay at the heart of the transformation of the social and cultural landscapes in internal Angola. This transformation seriously affected the African social fabric (Vansina 2005).

On the Atlantic side, the social and cultural landscapes in Angola also resulted from Angolan interaction with Brazil. For example, in the seventeenth and eighteenth centuries, part of the soldiers deployed in Angola were recruited in Brazil—a policy so entrenched that the Portuguese crown openly supported it at the end of the eighteenth century.[18] Furthermore, in addition to Africans and Euro-Africans, a significant number of individuals occupying positions in the administration in Luanda, Benguela, and interior of Angola had been sent to Africa as political, religious, and criminal exiles (Pantoja 2004: 117–136).[19] Details about these individuals' lives appear in records held by local Angolan archives. For example, the records state that Fernando Martins do Amaral Gurgel, a colonial administrator stationed in territories of the kingdom of Kasanje to oversee business and diplomatic relations with the kingdom, was born in Rio de Janeiro in 1749.[20] Daniel Corrêa da Silva, an officer serving in the colonial outpost in Mbaka in 1799, was recruited in Rio de Janeiro in 1785.[21] Alexandre dos Reis Pereira Barboza, a Bahian-born soldier who enlisted in the army as a volunteer in Salvador in 1761, served thirty-seven years in the military in Brazil, West Africa, and

Angola. After serving in Bahia, Barboza was assigned to West Africa in Whydah. Barboza was then appointed *capitão mor* of the Angolan military outpost (*presídio*) of Encoje and subsequently to Kakonda, located inland from Benguela.[22]

The Early Trade between Benguela and Brazil

The geopolitical circumstances that led up to the development of slaving in Benguela grew out of the erosion of Portuguese influence in West Africa due to growing slaving by Dutch, French, and British ships in the areas where the Portuguese had traditionally held an upper hand (Ferreira 2003). Law asserts that "in November 1709 there were reported to be 13 ships of several nations trading at Whydah simultaneously; in the twelve months from April 1713 to March 1714 no fewer than thirty-five ships of all nations came here, with again sometimes between twelve and fourteen at the same time; in January 1716 it was reported that eight ships (two French, five Portuguese, and one Dutch) had taken 2,800 slaves from Whydah in two months; and in September 1718 that there were ten ships (five Portuguese, three French, and two English) at Whydah" (Law 1997: 166).[23] According to Harms, "in the early 1728, for example, there were six French ships, five Portuguese ships, and three English ships waiting in the harbor beyond the forts (in Whydah), and the competition among them had driven up slave prices by a third"(Harms 2002: 212).

Due to the competition for slaving niches and the spillover of European wars to Africa, the slave trade could result in attacks pitting ships from different European nations against each other. Although authorities voiced concern about British and French attacks in 1706, the Dutch were, by any measure, the most resilient enemies of Brazilian ships along the West African coast in the early eighteenth century. They took advantage of exclusive commercial rights established by mid-seventeenth century treaties with Portugal that essentially prohibited Portuguese merchants from trading along the West African coast.[24] By the end of the seventeenth century, for example, they would not allow Brazilian ships to conduct slaving unless they paid a 10 percent fee on their cargos and refrained from carrying European goods. Between 1715 and 1756, five hundred ships paid the 10 percent fee.[25] Dutch aggressiveness might have been related to the rise of private trade in the Dutch slave trade (Emmer and Klooster 1999: 60, de Vries 2005: 9).

Although ships sought to comply with the rules established by the Dutch, many were still attacked.[26] Dutch attacks primarily affected imports of slaves to Bahia that drew heavily on West Africa. By 1718, the viceroy of Brazil openly called for a one-year ban on the slave trade with West Africa due to losses caused by the intensification of attacks.[27] In 1722, a Bahia-based merchant even requested a royal license to trade in slaves in Mozambique on the grounds that Brazilian ships could no longer sail along the West African coast.[28] However, Brazilian ships would still routinely turn to the British and purchase passports to gain free passage in case they came across Dutch ships.[29]

Despite the fact that the odds against resisting Dutch attacks were virtually insurmountable, Lisbon managed to send warships to protect ships bound for Brazil.[30] However, the weakness of military action was oddly illustrated when Portuguese warships were unable to prevent the Dutch from seizing a Brazilian ship.[31] By 1731, while the Dutch controlled fifteen of the forts on the Gold Coast, the British controlled nine forts and the Danes one fort. In the meantime, the Portuguese did not have any fort to protect Brazilian ships.[32] Between 1715 and 1756, 12,500 slaves were seized by the Dutch from Brazilian ships (Feinberg 1989: 41).

The impacts of such obstacles on the development of the Benguela trade are illustrated by the career of José dos Santos Torres. In early eighteenth century, Torres was perhaps the most prominent Bahia-based merchant operating out of West Africa. In 1721, for example, he obtained royal approval to ship 150 boxes of Brazilian sugar to the Mina Coast.[33] In addition to borrowing capital from British merchants in West Africa, Torres planned to use the sugar purchased in Brazil to trade with the Dutch back in Africa.[34] Between 1721 and 1731, Torres seized upon fears generated by Dutch attacks on Bahian ships embarking slaves in West Africa to obtain licenses to build forts on the Mina Coast (Postma 1990: 77).[35] The first of the forts was built in 1721 and was staffed by troops provided by Brazilian authorities in Bahia and guarded by two frigates maintained by Torres,[36] while between 1725 and 1727 Portuguese warships captured three Dutch slave ships.[37]

Since 1726, Dutch attacks had prompted Torres to begin dispatching ships to Benguela, but as the Portuguese were further challenged in West Africa, he completely refocused his activities toward Angola. Between 1726 and 1728, he sent four ships to Benguela that crossed the Atlantic directly without calling in Luanda to pay duties.[38] In the early 1730s, the destruction of his fort in Jakin in West Africa by the Dutch prompted Torres to move out of West Africa and relocate to Pernambuco.[39] Although Torres was still dispatching ships to West Africa in 1731, four years later, most of his business was being conducted in Angola.[40] Between 1735 and 1739, for example, his ships sailed from Rio to Benguela at least four times.[41] During the following decades and until his death in Luanda in 1774, Torres traded prominently in both Luanda and Benguela.[42] A former holder of the contract to collect duties on slaves shipped from Luanda, Vasco Lourenço, who had business in recently discovered gold mines in Mato Grosso also begin dispatching ships to Benguela, which suggests that Brazilian mining had an influence on the de facto beginning of the direct trade between Benguela and Brazil in the late 1720s.[43]

The establishment of direct trade with Brazil posed a serious threat to Luanda *moradores'* stakes in Benguela slaving, since *moradores* had traditionally benefited from the obligatory stopovers in Luanda to receive payoffs in the form of slaves for investments they had previously made in Benguela. As a result of complaints by *moradores*, the legislation obligating ships to call in Luanda to pay duties for slaves embarked in Benguela was reinstated in late 1720s.[44] By the early 1740s, however, even the holder of the contract to collect duties on slaves exported from Luanda was taking part in the direct trade between Benguela and Brazil.[45] Of a total of sixty-seven licenses issued between 1732 and 1757, Lisbon only turned down requests for ships to sail directly from Benguela to Brazil twice.[46]

Individual Mobility

Soldiers and bureaucrats notwithstanding, most of the free individuals who crossed the Atlantic from Angola to Brazil and vice versa were merchants. Mobility was a function of the complex commercial ties that linked merchants on both sides of the Atlantic. In addition to activities related to slaving, merchants would simultaneously own ships and properties in Angola and Brazil. Tereza Francisca, a resident of Bahia, and Ana Joaquina dos Santos Silva, a prominent Luanda merchant, are cases in point. In the 1820s, Silva purchased a set of houses in Luanda that belonged to Tereza Francisca.[47] The case of Brigadier António João de Menezes, who had been a prominent slave dealer in Luanda, provides further evidence of the links that merchants held across the Atlantic. While holding several positions in the Angolan bureaucracy, Menezes was active in slaving until retiring to Rio de Janeiro with his wife in the late 1820s. From Rio, Menezes remained the owner of several properties in Luanda and he bought and sold several properties there in the early 1830s.[48] Conversely, several individuals based in Luanda owned properties in Brazil, as demonstrated by Mariana de Assunção Pinheiro, who owned a house in Rio in 1808.[49]

Requests for licenses to travel to Brazil further illustrates why merchants crossed the Atlantic from Angola to Brazil and vice versa. In 1799, for example, António José da Silva, a representative of a Brazilian commercial house who had been sent to Luanda forty years earlier in 1759, decided to retire in Rio de Janeiro.[50] Other merchants would travel to Brazil to deal with financial matters with their Brazilian partners or bosses. In 1811, for example, António Francisco dos Santos, a merchant in Luanda, stated he would travel to Rio de Janeiro to settle financial accounts with his Brazilian correspondents.[51] In 1826, the *Tenente de Milícias*, Francisco Paul de Graça, received a two-year license to go to Brazil to "liquidate business with his Brazilian partners."[52] Since Luanda-based mid-level merchants lacked the connections and capital to simply ship slaves from Luanda who would then be sold by correspondents in Brazil, they would have to travel themselves in order to oversee the sale of the slaves they owned. In 1825, for example, two Luanda merchants, Francisco José Vieira and Joaquim Martins Mourão, said they needed to go to Brazil "not only because this was his custom but also because he needed to sell his slaves."[53]

In the 1820s, when the British first targeted shipments of slaves from Luanda and Benguela, merchants' mobility was affected by the rise of abolitionism in the southern Atlantic. This is suggested by the intensification of traveling in anticipation of the first prohibition of the slave trade to Brazil in 1830. This development brought to the southern Atlantic pressures against slaving that, by casting doubt about the continuation of shipments of slaves from Luanda, prompted slavers to relocate to Brazil. Slave dealers held most of their financial assets in Angola, which made the Luanda administration seek to limit their departure to protect plans to rely on their personal fortunes to make the Angolan economy move away from the slave trade and toward slavery-based legal activities (Ferreira 1996).

In order to circumvent constrictions to their traveling, merchants began using Luanda's notorious lack of proper medical facilities to push for licenses to travel to Brazil to seek medical treatment. Records from Angolan archives provide ample evidence about the practice that seemed to be a pretext for permanent departure from Angola. In 1827, for example, at least two Luanda merchants, Francisco Luis Gonçalves Ferreira and José Joaquim Ferreira Torres, were allowed to leave for Brazil for alleged health reasons.[54] In the following year, António Francisco Ribeiro and José Polilo "requested license to travel to Rio de Janeiro to undertake medical treatment."[55] Also in 1828, Francisco José Gomes "requested a one-year license to go to Rio de Janeiro to undertake medical treatment."[56] In the same year, "José Pedro de Andrade, a soldier in Dombe Grande, requested a license to travel to Rio de Janeiro to undertake medical treatment."[57] Several merchants would travel to Brazil accompanied by members of their families, which further suggests that they were seeking to relocate on a permanent basis and not merely planning to stay in Brazil for the duration of their "medical" treatment. For example, Dona Maria Ferreira da Silva, the widow of Diniz Vieira de Lima, "requested a license to leave for Rio de Janeiro with her son, Thomas, and two *agregadas*, Francisca and Rosa."[58] In 1828, Estevão da Cruz requested a license to "go to Rio de Janeiro for medical reasons, taking with him two sons and one girl."[59]

Personal, Educational, and Religious Ties

In addition to being commercially driven, the networks that merchants created across the Atlantic were also driven by family and personal connections. Since many of the merchants operating out of Luanda and Benguela had either been born or spent significant periods of time in Brazil, they would leave their families in Brazil while living and conducting business in Angola. For example, the granddaughter of José de Souza, the holder of the Benguela salt contract and the local representative of the Companhia do Grão Pará e Maranhão in the 1770s, was living in Rio when he died in 1780.[60] The will of Francisco Xavier dos Reis shows that he had fathered a child with his slave, Mariana, in Bahia before settling in Benguela.[61] In 1799, the wife and child of Joaquim António da Roza, who was a doctor in Benguela and a small-time slave dealer, were living in Rio de Janeiro.[62] In 1800, José Francisco indicated in his will that he was married in Rio and had two daughters there.[63]

The case of António José de Barros, the largest merchant in Benguela in the late 1790s, perhaps best illustrates how family ties could link Benguela merchants to Rio de Janeiro. In 1796, Barros acknowledged in this will that he had,

> spent time in Rio de Janeiro [where] [I] had sinful sexual intercourse with a mixed-race woman, Ana, who is a slave of the deceased Domingos Rebelo Pereira. After some time, [Ana] claimed she was *pejada* [pregnant], which I doubted (since she had already had several previous sexual relations) but because she insisted that I free her for the sake of the child she had in her womb and because of the promise that I made her to grant her freedom if I was the father of her child, I had to seek religious counseling with a confessor. After explaining the situation of Ana having already had sexual intercourse with other men, [the confessor] understood my uncertainty and I was exonerated of my promise to Ana. After several years, I came to know in this city [Benguela] that a boy named Feliciano was claiming to be my son [in Rio], and I decided to free him from slavery on principle and not because I was sure he was my son. The boy has been to this city [Benguela] recently and has returned to Rio.[64]

Merchants valued personal links because they provided a framework to conduct business and were seized upon when merchants faced hurdles and needed credit. In 1818, for example, the Luanda-based son of the Rio de Janeiro-based Joaquim Vieira de Souza relied on his father to avoid being drafted into the Luanda army. To help his son, Souza said he was a minor who had been sent to Angola to conduct business on behalf of his father.[65] In addition, merchants who lived on different sides of the Atlantic would seal their business partnership by marrying each others' relatives. Thus, business ties between Rio de Janeiro-based Joaquim Teixeira Macedo and his partner, Brigadier António João de Menezes, certainly became stronger when Macedo traveled to Luanda to marry the daughter of his partner. The owner of the ship *Mariana Daphne*, Macedo declared that "he was the owner of several properties [in Luanda] and that he was going on the ship to Angola to marry the daughter of Brigadier António João de Menezes."[66] Family links were also pivotal to trade in the interior of Angola, as demonstrated by the case of José António Carvalho, who traveled from Rio to Benguela and settled in Galangue in 1789. There, Carvalho strengthened connections to local African partners by fathering at least two children by African women who were subject to two African headmen named Nguingolo and Kaulokoxo.[67]

In addition to traveling across the Atlantic, merchants would also send their children to Brazil, which served to further reinforce the family dimensions of their connections. In 1828, for example, João Pedro de Andrade "requested a license to take two grandchildren, Alexandre and Martinho, whose father, Manoel Francisco de Paula, was dead, to Rio de Janeiro."[68] Andrade delayed his trip and later reapplied for a traveling license. He then "requested a license to take to Rio his grandchild Thome, minor at thirteen years old, a twelve-year-old mixed-race (*crioula*) girl named Francisca and a boy younger than eight years old named António, a son of one of his slaves."[69] In the following year, Manoel José da Costa, "recently arrived from the *sertões* [backlands of the Angolan interior], requested a license to travel on the *Patacho Leopardo* to Rio de Janeiro, taking with him his young children, José and Rosa."[70]

Many merchants' children were sent across the Atlantic—primarily to Rio de Janeiro—to be educated in Brazilian schools. In 1826, for example, Jose Pedro Cotta "requested permission to send to Rio de Janeiro on the Bergatim Flor do Mar [his] slave named Felícia and [his] child Mariana for education."[71] Sebastião Rodrigues da Silva "requested a license to send his daughter Augusta Rodrigues da Silva to Rio de Janeiro for education, together with a slave named Maria, who had already been to that city [Rio]."[72] In 1828, José Joaquim Ferreira "requested a license to send his daughter and son to Rio de Janeiro for education."[73] In 1829, Justiniano José dos Reis "requested a license to send his ten-year-old godson named Justiniano da Costa Covello to Rio de Janeiro for education."[74] In 1829, Francisco Ferreira Gomes, "tutor of Luiz, son of the late António Lopes Anjo, requested a license to send Luiz to Rio de Janeiro to be educated."[75]

The trend certainly dates back to the seventeenth century, as demonstrated by complaints by an Angolan governor in 1697 that European settlers in Luanda were forced to marry African women because young white women were sent to Brazil to be educated or to live in convents. In the eighteenth century, a governor of Benguela referred to the practice and added that many of the children sent to Brazil were the mixed-race offspring of liaisons between merchants and local African women.[76] In 1797, for example, a census of the Benguela population indicated that one of the children of the mulatto merchant, José Rodrigues de Magalhães, was studying in Rio.[77] In 1798, António José de Barros, one of the leading merchants in Benguela, sent three of the children he had fathered with slaves in Benguela to Rio de Janeiro, probably also to be educated.[78] In 1827, Justiniano José dos Reis, himself a Brazilian and one of the most powerful merchants in Benguela "sent to Rio de Janeiro for education a young, free, twelve-year old African minor named Vicente da Silva."[79] The same year, Francisco Pereira da Rocha "requested a license to send the mixed-race (*parda*) whose name is Rita to Rio de Janeiro to be educated."[80]

Finally, merchants would also retain ties with Brazil through their membership in religious brotherhoods in several Brazilian cities. To this end, they would often instruct the executors of their wills to conduct specific religious ceremonies in Rio following their deaths. António José Barros, for example, was a member of four brotherhoods located in Rio: Santíssimo Sacramento e das Almas, Nossa Senhora da Glória, Santa Luzia de Nossa Senhora do Rosário, and Jerusalém.[81] According to the governor of Benguela, the city lacked an adequate number of priests and some residents had to hold religious ceremonies in Brazil.[82] José António da Costa, for example, instructed the executor of his will that "on the occasion of my passing, masses shall be held in all convents and churches of Rio de Janeiro during two days."[83] José de Souza wrote in his will: "[I] state that the executor of my will shall make arrangements to perform 200 masses for my soul; 100 masses for my parents' souls; 100 masses on behalf of my siblings; and 100 for souls lying in purgatory. And because priests sometimes are lacking in this land [Benguela] the executor of my will is allowed to arrange for these masses to be held in Brazil, so that there is not a long delay."[84] In 1798, José António de Carvalho wrote in his will that "the executor [of my will] will make arrangements so that 20 masses on behalf of my soul are held in Rio."[85]

The Merchant Community in Benguela

While the number of *pumbeiros* (petty traders) supplying slaves to coastal Benguela was estimated at almost nine hundred individuals in 1798, only thirty-three to fifty merchants were estimated to be dealing slaves in Benguela city between 1778 and the 1790s.[86] During two judicial investigations conducted in 1780 and 1798, one-third of the thirty merchants interviewed each time had been born in Bahia, Rio de Janeiro, and Pernambuco, suggesting that many of the merchants in Benguela were in fact individuals born in Brazil.[87] One of them was a black soldier in the Benguela *henriques* (African auxiliaries, rangers) battalion, who was born in Bahia and "came to this city [Benguela] to trade in slaves."[88] These merchants were responsible for the shipment of thousands of slaves to several Brazilian ports, primarily Rio de Janeiro, as they were either owners or co-owners of half of the fleet of slave ships and dealt in slaves on behalf of Brazilian commercial houses.[89]

Most of the merchants in Benguela who had settled in the city as agents of Brazilian commercial houses were criminals and political exiles or had formerly served as crew members on ships sailing between Brazil and Benguela. Individuals born in Brazil operated as *sertanejos* in the central highlands throughout Kakonda, Kilengues, Galangue, and Huambo and in the coastal *presídio* of Novo Redondo. In 1796, for example, the first trip from Benguela to the Luvale region was undertaken by the Bahia-born José de Assunção Mello, who was regarded as the merchant most familiar with the trade and peoples of the interior of Benguela.[90] In 1800, Henrique Pedro de Almeida, a soldier born in Brazil and stationed in Benguela by the Luanda government, was allowed to trade in the central highlands with goods provided by Joaquim Vieira de Andrade from Benguela.[91] In addition, at least three of the merchants operating out of the Novo Redondo *presídio* in the late eighteenth century were born in Brazil.[92]

Many individuals from Brazil became wealthy trading in slaves in Benguela, as demonstrated by the case of Frutuoso José Cruz, a commercial agent born in Rio de Janeiro who arrived in Benguela in 1780 at the age of twenty-nine and who held several positions in the local bureaucracy during fifteen years in Benguela.[93] By the time Rodrigues returned to Rio de Janeiro in the mid-1790s, he was so well connected that several Benguela merchants continued to rely on him to oversee the offloading and sale of slaves they shipped to Rio de Janeiro. In the 1790s, Rodrigues was the contact in Rio de Janeiro of José António de Carvalho from Benguela.[94] One year later, he was the contact that Joaquim António da Roza appointed in Rio to handle slaves shipped from Benguela and pay debts in Lisbon.[95] In the same year, two children of the largest merchant participating in the Benguela trade, António José de Barros, were living in Rodrigues' house in Rio de Janeiro.[96]

Two other examples provide further evidence of merchants born in Brazil who were successful trading in slaves in coastal Benguela. The first was José Rodrigues Maia, who settled in Benguela as an impoverished criminal exile in the mid-1760s.[97] Maia became the local representative of the Portuguese company created to strengthen the slave trade to Grão Pará and Maranhão and was responsible for shipping 16,586 slaves to Brazil between 1772 and 1786.[98] By mid-1786, Maia was so influential that one of the commanders of the expedition that the Luanda government sent to Cabo Negro in 1796 remarked on Maia's role in the authorities' decision to organize the expedition. According to the commander, Maia promised to support the expedition in exchange for exclusive rights to embark slaves in Cabo Negro.[99]

Maia's career in the military suggests that he was either mixed-race or black, since before becoming the commander of the Benguela fort and an artillery captain in 1775, he was the captain of black soldiers (*guerra preta*).[100] Although he left for Rio in 1786, Maia returned to trade slaves in Benguela in the early 1790s.[101] By then, he was a close associate of two other merchants, Frutuoso José da Cruz and António José da Costa. He was so creditworthy that other Benguela merchants would rely on him for credit to purchase goods in Rio and ship to Benguela. In 1790, for example, the Benguela-based Francisco Dias de Oliveira obtained a *letra de risco* (bill of risk) from Maia that allowed him to obtain 5,073,512 réis from Rio merchants Manoel José Mesquita, José Gonçalves Marques, and António José Cunha. The money was to be used to purchase goods in Rio and was to be paid back eight months after the goods arrived in Benguela.[102]

Another successful Brazil-born merchant in Benguela was the mulatto Joaquim José de Andrade e Souza Menezes. In the 1780s, Souza Menezes was arrested on charges of trying to undermine the authority of the Benguela governor by requesting a position in the Benguela bureaucracy directly to the Luanda government. He rose to become a significant merchant in the late 1790s.[103] By then in his mid-thirties, Menezes was a captain in the Benguela militia and his business connections sprawled throughout Kakonda, Huambo, and Novo Redondo.[104] In 1799, he was reportedly providing financial support to build a new church in Benguela.[105] He was also the co-owner of a slave ship and had commercial partners in Rio de Janeiro and Lisbon.[106]

By and large, however, the Benguela merchant community was comprised of Portuguese individuals who, like the Brazilians, had come to Benguela as agents of Brazilian commercial houses. As demonstrated by José Curto, most of them had, in fact, "become" Brazilians by way of prolonged stays in Brazil before settling in Benguela.[107] In 1796, for example, the father of a merchant who had died on the way from Benguela to Bahia stated that his Portuguese son had "left for the United States [Brazil], where he lived for some time, and was coming from Benguela [where he worked as a commercial agent] to the city of Bahia."[108]

Once they settled in Benguela, merchants could still be sent to regions deep in the interior, such as Mbailundo and Galangue, to trade in slaves on behalf of financial sponsors based in Benguela. In 1789, for example, Manoel José da Cruz reported that he was a "merchant in this *praça* [Benguela] and had lived several years in Cumbira [Huambo], where I [still] conduct most of my business and where I send my agents and from where I receive most of [the] slaves [I buy]."[109] In 1826, Floriano Pires Chaves, "recently arrived from Rio de Janeiro, requested license to travel in Kakonda."[110] In 1828, "António Joaquim, a sailor who came from Rio de Janeiro, requested license to trade in Kilengues with goods of his own."[111] In the same year, "the black man José da Silva, a sailor who came from Rio de Janeiro, requested a license to trade in the *sertões* [of Benguela] with *fazendas*."[112] One year later, Domingos Rodrigues, "recently arrived from Rio de Janeiro, requested license to trade in the *sertões* [of Benguela]."[113]

As pointed out by José Curto, "that so few of the Brazilian traders residing in this central Angolan port town around 1791 were still there towards the end of 1797 points to an extremely high turnover rate within this diasporic community. One cause was certainly the disease environment in Benguela, which exacted a steep death toll amongst all foreigners. Another was far less lethal. If they survived, the trade representatives dispatched from Brazil to cattle Bay were eventually recalled home and replaced by fresh 'troops.'"[114]

The high turnover rate and the death of José Pedro Barrocas, one of the most affluent merchants in Benguela, was the reason why the governor of Benguela stated in 1796 that "the lack of former wealthy *moradores* who gave Benguela its reputation [in the trade] deeply hurts the city's economy."[115] In addition to being called back to Rio by their commercial partners, some merchants relocated back to Brazil after amassing significant fortunes trading slaves. In 1796, for example, the *sargento mor* António José da Costa, who had been dealing in slaves in Benguela since 1774 and whose business sprawled as far inland as Mbailundo, left Benguela with his wife to go back to Brazil.[116] Some merchants would also move away from Benguela to improve their business activities, as demonstrated by the case of Domingos Ferreira Leite. In 1797, Leite was listed in a census by the Benguela colonial administration as a Rio de Janeiro resident who owned a property in Benguela, but two years later, he began a successful career in Luanda.[117]

The turnover rate among merchants was so high that Lisbon unsuccessfully attempted to prohibit the colonial administration from issuing licenses for merchants to leave Benguela in the late eighteenth century.[118] The new policy was probably an effort to retain a group of merchants who arrived to the city in 1797, since they were described by the governor of Benguela as "a new group of merchants who are creditworthy and reliable."[119] Three of these merchants, Lourenço Joaquim, Francisco Alvares, and José da Silva Teixeira, came from Rio de Janeiro.[120] While Lourenço Joaquim and Francisco Alvares were ship owners, José da Silva Teixeira had reportedly amassed 25,000 *réis* during his previous career as a slave ship captain. In

Benguela, Teixeira became the partner of the merchants José Pereira Guimarães and Manoel Gomes from Rio. In addition to coming to Benguela with goods worth 200,000 *cruzados* that belonged to merchants in Rio, Teixeira was the co-owner of a ship that his partners were purchasing in Lisbon.[121] To entice Teixeira to settle in Benguela, the governor offered him a high position in the army in 1796.[122] The governor's enthusiasm was perhaps due to the fact that he wanted Teixeira to take over the commercial house previously managed by Lourenço Pereira Tavares, a prominent merchant who had passed away earlier that year. In 1797, a report by the colonial administration listed Benguela settlers and Teixeira was described as a "lieutenant of the [Benguela] militia, white, single, 37-year-old merchant."[123] As conditions in Benguela deteriorated in the late eighteenth century due to French piracy off the coast and a collapse in the illicit French supply of Indian textiles to the city, a group of merchants suggested that if the colonial administration did not take steps to improve the situation, they would leave the city.[124] Due to the fact that José da Silva Teixeira was one of three merchants living in Rio de Janeiro in 1803 who had withdrawn a *letra* written by a deceased Benguela merchant, it is possible he had relocated to Rio a few years after dealing in slaves in Benguela.[125]

Benguela Commercial Links with Brazil

In addition to Brazil, Benguela merchants also held commercial ties with individuals based in several other cities throughout the Portuguese Atlantic. In 1793, for example, António Pinto de Almeida wrote in his will that payments for credits he owned should be made in Lisbon, Rio, and Bahia.[126] In 1805, Aurélio Veríssimo Vieira, who was the owner of the ship *Nossa Senhora da Piedade* together with the Benguela-based António Francisco dos Santos, had commercial ties with Lisbon, Bahia, Pernambuco, and Luanda.[127] In 1798, António Lourenço de Carvalho, a merchant who had spent several years in Galangue, declared that he had business with the Doctor Tamagnini and Domingos Gomes Loureiro in Lisbon, as well as with Narcizo Alves Pereira and Frutuoso José da Cruz in Rio.[128]

However, the closest links that Benguela held were with Rio de Janeiro. For example, in 1794, Lourenço Pereira Tavares, a wealthy merchant born in Luanda who was also a member of the *Senado da Câmara* (Benguela municipal council) and captain of the local militia, was prevented from embarking the number of slaves he had planned to ship to Brazil on his own vessel.[129] Although Tavares instructed the captain of the vessel to embark two hundred slaves of his own and reserve the remainder of the space on the vessel for a group of Benguela merchants, his instructions were ignored by the ship's captain, who argued that he had orders from Tavares' partners in Rio to allow Tavares to embark only eighty-two slaves and reserve the remaining space on the ship for other Benguela merchants.[130]

This episode illustrates the fact that Benguela merchants were often subordinate to their primary financial sponsors in Brazil. The ship that

Tavares claimed to own was in fact owned in partnership with merchants in Rio de Janeiro, which might explain why the ship captain refused to carry the number of slaves indicated by Tavares. The subordination and dependency were so acute, argued the governor of Benguela, that the city depended on Brazil for provisions for slaves taken across the Atlantic.[131] In 1799, the governor remarked that Benguela relied on "imports of commodities and other goods traded here, including manioc flour and other supplies, both for merchants, slaves [held for shipping to Brazil] and people in general."[132]

Wills written by Benguela merchants also provide insight into the high level of dependency on Brazil—primarily Rio—for capital funding. José Souza, for example, an important merchant in the late 1790s, did business with José Ferreira da Fonseca from Lisbon, but his primary deals were conducted with Jerônimo Pereira and his brothers in Rio, with whom he co-owned the ship *Nossa Senhora da Piedade*.[133] Luiz Antonio Gomes was the co-owner of the *corveta Nossa Senhora do Rosário Santo António e Almas* together with Francisco José in Rio.[134] In 1795, José António da Costa, who was the owner of the *sumaca São Lourenço*, had commercial ties with the Rio merchants Bernardo Lourenço Vianna, António Teixeira Passos, Manoel Ferreira da Cruz, and Manoel de Souza Guimarães.[135] In 1800, José Francisco had close links with the Lisbon-based José Pereira de Souza, but also worked in partnership with Rio-based Bernardo Lourenço Vianna from Rio.[136]

António José de Barros provides an interesting example of Rio's hegemony in the trade with Benguela. Barros was appointed *sargento mor* of Benguela in 1787, after Gregório José Mendes was assigned to lead an expedition to Cabo Negro.[137] He had many debts when he arrived to Benguela in the early 1780s. He had been partners in Rio with Narcizo Luis Alves Pereira and Francisco António de Araújo Pereira, to whom he still owned 79,294 *réis* in 1796. He was paying for a debt that his father had contracted with Francisco de Araújo Pereira in Rio, in addition to still having debts from his youth. Furthermore, Barros owed money to his brother from transactions in Rio with goods shipped from Porto to Rio by his brothers. In addition, Barros owed 1,767,408 *réis* in cash to his brother-in-law, Manoel Ferreira da Silva Guimarães, who had been sent to Luanda as a political or criminal exile in 1788.[138]

In 1796, Barros appointed executors to his will in Bahia and Pernambuco and held close contacts with former Benguela merchants who had returned to Rio after decades in Benguela: "[I] declare that I have accounts with [the following Rio-based merchants] Narciso Luis Alves Pereira, Frutuoso José da Cruz, Captain José Maria Arsénio de Lacerda and António José da Costa (who left Benguela not long ago)."[139] However, his primary associate in Rio was Manoel Gonçalves Moledo, with whom he bitterly ended a commercial partnership in 1796 after receiving a letter with insults from Moledo in Benguela. Barros stated, "I had another commercial society with Captain Manoel Gonçalves Moledo, resident in the same Rio [de Janeiro]. Moledo owes me a significant amount of money, but has raised questions about the debt and has tried to damage my reputation so much that I found myself obligated to travel to Rio on my ship *Pensamento Feliz* to settle with him financial issues related to the commercial society."[140] Despite the end of the partnership with Moledo, Barros was still able to return from Rio to Benguela with a significant cargo of goods to trade in slaves.[141]

Conclusion

The microdynamic of the trade between Angola and Brazil reveals a set of multilayered and nuanced ties ingrained in family, friendship, and religion. By creating such networks, merchants compensated for the lack of institutional and legal frameworks to provide safety for business. These networks allowed them to conduct business in cultural and social environments radically different from the ones they might have known in Brazil and Portugal. Merchants born in Angola, on the other hand, benefited from the Atlantic-wide nature of such networks because they gave them sufficient cultural elements to operate outside Angola if and when they so needed. Mobility was a crucial dimension to the microdynamic of the trade. In Benguela, it is part of the early stages of slaving in the first decades of the eighteenth century. Later in that century, it frequently translated into privileged and tight-knit links with Rio de Janeiro—the origin of most of the goods and funding used to purchase slaves in that city.

Notes

1. See Carlo Ginzburg, *Clues, Myths, and the Historical Method* (Baltimore: Johns Hopkins University Press, 1989); Carlo Ginzburg and Carlo Poni, "The Name and the Game: Unequal Exchange and the Historiographic Marketplace," in Edward Muir and Guido Ruggiero, eds., *Microhistory and the Lost Peoples of Europe* (Baltimore: Johns Hopkins University Press, 1991), 1–11; Carlo Ginzburg, "Microhistory: Two or Three Things that I Know about it," *Critical Inquiry* 20, 1993: 10–36; Jacques Revel, "Microanalysis and the Construction of the Social," in Jacques Revel and Lynn Hunt, eds. *Histories: French Constructions of the Past* (New York: The New Press 1995), 493–502; Florike Egmond and Peter Mason, *The Mammoth and the Mouse: Microhistory and Morphology* (Baltimore: Johns Hopkins University Press, 1997); Matti Peltonen, "Clues, Margins, and Monads: The Micro-macro Link in Historical Research," *History and Theory* 40, 2001: 247–359.; Jill Lapore, "Historians Who Love Too Much: Reflections on Microhistory and Biography," *Journal of American History* 88, 2001: 1–40; Sigurdur Magnússon, "The Singularization of History: Social History and Microhistory within the Postmodern State of Knowledge," *Journal of Social History*, 2003 36(4) 2003: 701–735.
2. Such a framework has been utilized to examine commercial ties between West Africa and Bahia. See Pierre Verger, *Fluxo e Refluxo do Tráfico de Escravos entre o Golfo do Benin e a Bahia de Todos os Santos dos Séculos XVII a XIX* (São Paulo/ Brasilia: Corrupio, 1987); Pierre Verger, *Os Libertos, Sete Caminhos na Liberdade de Escravos da Bahia no Século XIX* (Salvador da Bahia: Corrupio, 1992); Milton Guran, *Agudás, Os Brasileiros do Benim* (Rio de Janeiro: Nova Fronteira, 1999);

Lorand Matory, "The English Professors of Brazil, On the Diasporic Roots of the Yorubá Nation," *Comparative Studies in Society and History* 41, 1999: 72–103; Robin Law, "Ouidah a Pre-colonial Urban Centre in Coastal West Africa, 1727–1892," in David Anderson and Richard Rathbone, eds. *Africa's Urban Past* (Oxford: James Currey, 2000); Robin Law, "The Port of Ouidah in the Atlantic Community, 17th to 19th Centuries," in Horst Pietschmann, ed. *Atlantic History: History of the Atlantic System, 1580–1830* (Gottingen: Vandenhoeck & Ruprecht, 2002), 349–364; Robin Law, "A Comunidade Brasileira de Uidá e os Últimos Anos do Tráfico Atlântico de Escravos, 1850–1866," *Afro-Ásia* 27, 2002: 41–77; Silke Strickrodt, "Afro-European Trade Relations on the Western Slave Coast, 16th to 19th Centuries." PhD Dissertation, University of Stirling, 2002; Mieko Nishida, *Slavery and Identity: Ethnicity, Gender, and Race in Salvador, Brazil, 1808–1888* (Bloomington: Indiana University Press, 2003); Elisée Soumonni, "Afro-Brazilian Communities of the Bight of the Bight of Benin in the Nineteenth Century," in Paul Lovejoy and David Trotman, *Trans-Atlantic Dimensions of Ethnicity in the African Diaspora* (London: Continuum, 2003); Robin Law, "Francisco Felix de Souza in West Africa, 1820–1849," in José Curto and Paul Lovejoy, *Enslaving Connections, Changing Cultures of Africa and Brazil during the Era of Slavery* (New York: Humanity Books, 2004); Silke Strickrodt, "Afro-Brazilians of the Western Slave Coast in the Nineteenth Century," in José Curto and Paul Lovejoy, *Enslaving Connections, Changing Cultures of Africa and Brazil during the Era of Slavery* (New York: Humanity Books, 2004), 213–243; Alberto da Costa e Silva, *Francisco Félix de Souza, Mercador de Escravos* (Rio de Janeiro: Editora Nova Fronteira, 2004); Robin Law, *Ouidah: the Social History a West Africa Slaving Port* (Ohio: Ohio University Press, 2004).

3. For a limited list of northern-Atlantic focused studies, see David Armitage, ed., *The British Atlantic World, 1500–1800* (New York: Palgrave Macmillan, 2002); Horst Pietschmann, ed., *Atlantic History: History of the Atlantic System, 1580–1830* (Gottingen: Vandenhoeck & Ruprecht, 2002); Peter Coclanis, ed., *The Atlantic Economy during the Seventeenth and Eighteenth centuries: Organization, Operation, Practice, and Personnel* (Columbia: University of South Carolina Press, 2005) ; Bernard Bailyn, *Atlantic History: Concept and Contours* (Cambridge: Cambridge University Press,2005). Note that Coclanis' critique of Bailyn's book glosses over the fact that the latter is skewed toward the northern Atlantic. See Peter Coclanis, "Drang Nach Osten: Bernard Bailyn, the World-Island, and the Idea of Atlantic History," *Journal of World History* 13, 2002: 169–182.

4. For studies that focus primarily on Luanda, see Joseph Miller, *Way of Death: Merchant Capitalism and the Angolan Slave Trade, 1730–1830* (Wisconsin: University of Wisconsin Press, 1988); Luiz Felipe de Alencastro, *O Trato dos Viventes: Formação do Brasil no Atlântico Sul* (São Paulo: Companhia das Letras, 2000); José Curto, *Enslaving Spirits: The Portuguese-Brazilian Alcohol Trade at Luanda and its Hinterland, c. 1550–1830* (Leiden: Brill Academic, 2004); Jaime Rodrigues, *De Costa a Costa: Escravos, Marinheiros e Intermediários do Tráfico Negreiro de Angola ao Rio de Janeiro (1780–1860)* (São Paulo: Companhia das Letras, 2005).

5. David Eltis, "The Volume and Structure of the Transatlantic Slave Trade: A Reassessment," *William and Mary Quarterly* 58, 2001: 17–42; David Eltis, "The Transatlantic Slave Trade: A Reassessment based on the Second Edition of the Transatlantic Slave Trade Dataset." Unpublished paper.

6. See Joseph Miller, "The Slave Trade in Congo and Angola," in Martin Kilson and Robert I. Rotberg, eds., *The African Diaspora: Interpretative Essays* (Cambridge: Harvard University Press, 1976); Joseph Miller, "The Paradoxes of Impoverishment in the Atlantic Zone," in David Birmingham and Phyllis Martin, eds., *History of Central Africa* (London: Longman, 1983); Joseph Miller, "Central Africa during the Era of the Slave Trade, c. 1490s–1850s," in Linda Heywood, ed., *Central Africans and Cultural Transformations in the American Diaspora* (Cambridge: Cambridge University Press, 2002). Early and equally failed similar attempts to set up sugar plantations in Africa are surveyed by David Eltis. See David Eltis, *The Rise of African Slavery in the Americas* (Cambridge: Cambridge University Press, 2000).

7. "Ofício do Desembargador Fiscal" on April 10, 1811, Instituto Histórico e Geográfico Brasileiro, hereafter IHGB, Dl 1132, 05.

8. "Ofício do Cônsul Brasileiro em Luanda" on February 24, 1827, Arquivo do Itamarati, hereafter AI, doc. 676-4-3, fls. 1–1v.

9. "Ofício do Desembargador Fiscal" on April 10, 1811, IHGB, Dl 1132, 05.

10. For alternative and critical views, see Lorand Matory, "The English Professors of Brazil, On the Diasporic Roots of the Yorubá Nation," *Comparative Studies in Society and History* 41, 1999: 72–103; Herman Bennett, "The Subject in the Plot: National Boundaries and the 'History' of the Black Atlantic," *African Studies Review* 43, 2000: 101–124; Charles Piot, "Atlantic Aporias: Africa and Gilroy's Black Atlantic," *The South Atlantic Quarterly* 100, 2001: 155–170; Patrick Manning, "Africa and the African Diaspora: New Directions of Study," *Journal of African History* 44, 2003: 487–506.

11. Walter Hawthorne, *Planting Rice and Harvesting Slaves: Transformations along the Guinea-Bissau Coast, 1400–1900* (Portsmouth: Heinemann, 2003), 59; Peter Mark, *"Portuguese" Style and Luso-African Identity: Pre-Colonial Senegambia, Sixteenth-Nineteenth Centuries* (Bloomington: University of Indiana Press, 2002); See also Philip Curtin, *Economic Change in Pre-colonial Africa: Senegambia in the Era of the Slave Trade* (Madison: University of Wisconsin Press, 1975), 95–100; José da Silva Horta, "Evidence for a Luso-African Identity in 'Portuguese' Accounts on "Guinea of Cape Verde' (six-teenth-seventeenth centuries)," *History in Africa* 27, 2000: 99–130; George Brooks, *Eurafricans in Western Africa: Commerce, Social Status, Gender, and Religious Observance from the Sixteenth Century to the Eighteenth Century* (Athens: Ohio University Press, 2003), 84.

12. See Harvey Feinberg, *Africans and Europeans in West Africa: Elminians and Dutchmen on the Gold Coast during the Eighteenth Century* (Philadelphia: University of Pennsylvania, 1989), 41; Christopher DeCorse, "Culture Contact, Continuity and Change on the Gold Coast, AD 1400–1900," *African Archaeological Review* 10, 1992: 164 ; Christopher DeCorse, "The Europeans in West Africa: Culture Contact, Continuity and Change," in Graham Connah, ed., *Transformations in Africa: Essays in Africa's Later Past* (London, Leicester University Press, 1998), 222; Rebecca Shumway, "Between the Castle and the Golden Stool: Transformations in Fante Society in the Eighteenth Century." PhD Dissertation, Emory University, 2004; Jon Sensbach, *Rebecca's Revival: Creating Black Christianity in the Atlantic World* (Cambridge, 2005); Christopher DeCorse, "The Danes on the Gold Coast: Culture Change and the European Presence," *African Archaeological Review* 11, 1993: 159; David Northrup, "West Africans and the Atlantic,

1550–1800," in Philip Morgan and Sean Hawkins, eds., *Black Experience and the Empire* (Oxford: Oxford University Press, 2004), 50; Trevor Getz, "Mechanisms of Slave Acquisition and Exchange in late Eighteenth Century Anomabu: Reconsidering a Cross-Section of the Atlantic Slave Trade," *African Economic History* 31, 2003: 79; Larry Yarak, "West African Coastal Slavery in the Nineteenth Century: The Case of the Afro-European Slaveowners of Elmina," *Ethnohistory* 36(1), 1989: 44; Richard Rathbone, "The Gold Coast, the Closing of the Atlantic Slave Trade, and Africans of the Diaspora," in Stephan Palmié, *Slave Cultures and the Cultures of Slavery* (Knoxville: University of Tennessee Press, 1995), 55–66.; Adam Jones, "Female Slave-Owners on the Gold Coast," in Stephan Palmié, ed., *Slave Cultures and the Cultures of Slavery* (Knoxville: University of Tennessee Press, 1995), 101–111.

13. For the early trade and the tight grip that Dahomey held over the slave trade, see Robin Law, *Ouidah: the Social History of a West Africa Slaving Port* (Ohio: Ohio University Press, 2004); Kenneth Kelly, "Indigenous Responses to Colonial Encounters on the West African Coast: Hueda and Dahomey from the Seventeenth through Nineteenth Century," in Claire L. Lyons and John K. Papadopoulos, *The Archaeology of Colonialism* (**Los Angeles,** Getty Trust Publications: Getty Research Institute for the History of Art and the Humanities, 2002), 96–120. For the return of former slaves from Brazil, see Pierre Verger, *Fluxo e Refluxo do Tráfico*; Robin Law, "Yoruba Liberated Slaves who returned to West Africa," in Toyin Falola and Matt Childs, eds., *The Yoruba Diaspora in the Atlantic World* (Bloomington: Bloomington and Indiana Press, 2005), 340–365; Robin Law, "The Evolution of the Brazilian Community in Ouidah," *Slavery and Abolition* 22, 2001: 23–41; Elisée Soumonni, "Afro-Brazilian Communities of the Bight of the Bight of Benin in the Nineteenth Century," in Paul Lovejoy and David Trotman, eds., *Trans-Atlantic Dimensions of Ethnicity in the African Diaspora* (London: Continnuum, 2003), 181–193.

14. See Paul Lovejoy and David Richardson, "Trust, Pawnship, and Atlantic History: The Institutional Foundations of the Old Calabar Slave Trade," *The American Historical Review* 104, 1999: 333–355. David Richardson, "Background to Annexation: Anglo-Africa Credit Relations in the Bight of Biafra, 1700–1891," in Olivier Pétré-Grenouilleau, *From Slave Trade to Empire: Europe and the Colonization of Black Africa, 1780s–1880s* (London and New York: Routledge, 2004); Paul Lovejoy, "Letters of the Old Calabar Slave Trade, 1760–1789," in Vincent Carreta and Philip Gould, eds., *Genius in Bondage: Literature of the Early Black Atlantic* (Lexington: University Press of Kentucky, 2001);Paul Lovejoy and David Richardson, "This Horrid Hole: Royal Authority, Commerce and Credit at Bonny, 1690–1840," *Journal of African History* 45, 2004: 67–89. Paul Lovejoy and David Richardson, "From Slaves to Palm Oil: Afro-European Commercial Relations in the Bight of Biafra, 1741–1841," in David Killingray, Margarette Lincoln, and Nigel Rigby, eds., *Maritime Empires: British Imperial Maritime Trade in the Nineteenth Century* (Rochester: Boydell Press, 2004). For the Slave Coast see David Northrup, "West Africans and the Atlantic, 1550–1800," in Philip Morgan and Sean Hawkins, eds., *Black Experience and the Empire* (Oxford: Oxford University Press, 2004), 51–52.

15. See also Robin Law, "The English in Western Africa to 1700," in Nicolas Canny, ed., *The Oxford History of the British Empire: The Origins of Empire*

(Oxford: Oxford University Press, 1998), vol. I, 262. For a similar view, see Eltis, *The Rise of African Slavery in the Americas*; David Eltis, "African and European Relations in the Last Century of the Transatlantic Slave Trade," in Olivier Pétré-Grenouilleau, ed., *From Slave Trade to Empire: Europe and the Colonization of Black Africa, 1780s–1880s* (London and New York: Routledge, 2004), 24. David Eltis and David Richardson, "Prices of African Slaves Newly Arrived in the Americas, 1763–1865: New Evidence on Long-Run Trends and Regional Differentials," in David Eltis, Frank Lewis, and Kenneth Sokoloff, eds., *Slavery and the Development of the Americas* (Cambridge: Cambridge University Press, 2004), 187.

16. See also Joseph Miller, "The Imbangala and the Chronology of Early Central African History," *Journal of African History* 13(4), 1972: 549–574; Joseph Miller, "Nzinga of Matamba in a New Perspectiva," *Journal of African History* 16(2): 201–216; John Thornton, "Legitimacy and Political Power: Queen Njinga, 1624–1663," *Journal of African History* 32(1): 25–40.

17. Ferreira, "Transforming Atlantic Slaving."

18. "Ofício de Rodrigo de Souza Coutinho" on September 14, 1799, Arquivo Histórico Nacional de Angola, hereafter AHNA, cód. 254, pages fls. 176v.–177v.

19. See also Ross Little Bardwell, "The Governors of Portugal's South Atlantic Empire in the Seventeenth Century: Social Background, Qualifications, Selection, and Reward." PhD Dissertation, University of California at Santa Barbara, 1974; Anne Pardo, "A Comparative Study of the Portuguese Colonies of Angola and Brazil and their Interdependence from 1648 to 1825." PhD Dissertation, Boston University, 1977.

20. "Provisão do Governador de Angola" on March 4, 1849, AHNA, cód. 299, pages fls. 350v.–351.

21. "Requerimento de Daniel Corrêa da Silva" on September 3, 1799, AHNA, cód. 254, fls. 216v.–217.

22. "Petição de Alexandre dos Reis Barboza" on October 27, 1799, AHNA, cód. 254, fls. 116–116v.

23. In 1714, for example, a slave ship bound from Lisbon to West Africa came across four Portuguese, two French, one Dutch, and one British ship in the Whydah region. See "Carta de João Diniz de Azevedo (Costa da Mina) para Francisco Pinheiro" on December 13, 1714, in Luis Lisanti, *Negócios Coloniais: Uma Correspondência Comercial do Século XVIII* (Brasília: Ministério da Fazenda; São Paulo: Visão, 1973), vol. 2, 541.

24. "CCU" on July 23, 1706, AHU, Bahia, cx. 5, doc. 433. For an overview of the Dutch-Portuguese rivalry along the West African coast dating back to the early seventeenth century, see John Vogt, *Portuguese Rule on the Gold Coast, 1469–1683* (Athens: University of Georgia, 1979); Curtin, *Economic Change in Precolonial Africa*, 100–105. For overviews of Dutch-Portuguese rivalry throughout Africa, Asia, and Africa, see Jonathan Israel, *Dutch Primacy in World Trade, 1585–1740* (Oxford: Clarendon Press, 1989); Robin Blackburn, *The Making of New World Slavery: From the Baroque to the Modern, 1492–1800* (London: Verso, 1998), 187–211. See also Stephanie Smallwood, "Salt-Water Slaves: African Enslavement, Forced Migration, and Settlement in the Anglo-Atlantic World, 1660–1700." PhD Dissertation, Duke University, 1999, 22–23, 25; Harms, *The Diligent*, 133. For the diplomatic context in which the peace treaties between the Dutch and the Portuguese were negotiated, see Evaldo

Cabral de Melo Neto, *O Negócio do Brasil: Portugal, os Países Baixos e o Nordeste (1641–1669)* (Lisbon: CNCDP, 2001), chap. 8.

25. "Carta de Antonio Marques Gomes" on December 30, 1756, AHU, São Tomé, cx. 9, doc. 83.

26. The fact that the payment of the 10 percent fee did not preclude Dutch ships from attacking ships from Brazil might account for the discrepancy in the number of detained ships recorded in Portuguese sources and scholarly analyses based on Dutch sources. Thus, while Postma indicates that only two ships were captured by the Dutch in 1715, Pernambucan authorities reported eight Bahian and Pernambucan ships captured that year. See Postma and Schwartz, "Brazil and Holland as Commercial Partners on the West African Coast," in Johannes Postma and Victor Enthoven, eds., *Riches from Atlantic Commerce: Dutch Transatlantic Trade and Shipping, 1585–1817* (Leiden: Brill, 2003); "Carta Governador de Pernambuco" on January 20, 1716, AHU, Pernambuco, cx. 27, doc. 2466. The same discrepancy is observed in the number of slaves taken from Brazilian ships. Between 1717 and 1718, for example, authorities estimated that 3,000 slaves were taken by the Dutch, differing sharply from Postma's estimation of 1,480 slaves lost during the same period. See Postma and Schwartz, "Brazil and Holland as Commercial Partners on the West African," 410–411. For the Portuguese side, see "CCU" on May 4, 1719, AHU, cód. 21, pages fls. 315v.–316v. For contemporary accounts of Dutch attacks on Brazilian ships by a Bahia-based merchant, see "Carta de Baltazar Alvarez de Araújo (Bahia) para Francisco Pinheiro" on January 15, 1719, in Lisanti, *Negócios Coloniais*, vol. 1, 93; "Carta de Baltazar Alvarez de Araujo (Bahia) para Francisco Pinheiro" on April 17, 1719, in Lisanti, *Negócios Coloniais*, vol. 1, 94; "Carta de Baltazar Alvarez de Araujo (Bahia) para Francisco Pinheiro" on October 30, 1719, in Lisanti, *Negócios Coloniais*, vol. 1, 97. For a late report of the impact of the 10 percent fee, see "Carta da Mesa de Inspeção da Bahia" on July 31, 1789, ANTT, Ministério do Reino, maço 599, cx. 702.

27. The uncertainties of attacks on the West African coast seem to have triggered a minor depression in the Bahian slave economy in 1715 by making would-be traders shy away from purchasing slave ships and entering the trade. See "Carta de Baltazar Alvarez de Araújo para (Bahia) para Francisco Pinheiro Neto (Lisboa)" on July 13, 1715, in Lisanti, *Negócios Coloniais*, vol. 1, 54; "Carta de Baltazar Alvarez de Araújo para (Bahia) para Francisco Pinheiro Neto (Lisboa)" on December 9, 1715, in Lisanti, *Negócios Coloniais*, vol. 1, 64. For the view of the viceroy of Brazil, see Verger, *Fluxo e Refluxo do Tráfico de Escravos*, 63.

28. "CCU" on August 23, 1720, AHU, Bahia, cx. 14, doc. 1185.

29. "CCU" on May 4, 1719, AHU, cód. 21, fls. 315v.–316v. In the same year, a British frigate called into Recife on the way to the Caribbean after patrolling off the West African coast on behalf of Brazilian ships. See "Carta do Governador de Pernambuco" on July 17, 1729, AHU, Pernambuco, cx. 39, doc. 3488.

30. In 1719, for example, responding to a petition sent to Lisbon by Brazilian merchants, a Portuguese frigate was dispatched to West Africa. See "CCU" on December 9, 1719, AHU, cód. 21, fls. 327–327v.

31. "CCU" on November 9, 1723, AHU, Bahia, cx. 18, doc. 1599; "Carta de Baltazar Alvarez de Araújo (Bahia) para Francisco Pinheiro" on March 25, 1722, in Lisanti, *Negócios Coloniais*, vol. 1, 106.

32. Feinberg, *Africans and Europeans in West Africa: Elminians and Dutchmen on the Gold Coast during the Eighteenth Century* (Philadelphia: University of Pennsylvania, 1989), 41.
33. "CCU" on October 17, 1721, AHU, cód. 907, fls. 160v.–161v.
34. The deal played into widely held fears that the center of gravity of the trade between Brazil and Europe was shifting to West Africa and that Portugal was gradually being excluded from it. See "CCU" on October 25, 1721, AHU, cód. 907, fls. 171–173; Carl Hanson, "Monopoly and Contraband in the Portuguese Tobacco Trade, 1624–1702," *Luso-Brazilian Review* 19, 1982: 161; Jean Dell Rae Flory, "Bahian Society in the Mid-Colonial Period: The Sugar Planters, Tobacco Growers, Merchants and Artisans of Salvador and the Reconcavo, 1680–1725." PhD Dissertation, University of Texas, 1978, 190; J.R. Russell-Wood, *The Portuguese Empire, 1415–1808: A World on the Move* (Baltimore: The Johns Hopkins University Press, 1998), 141.
35. "Parecer do Conselho Ultramarino" on February 15, 1726, AHU, Rio de Janeiro, cx. 16, doc. 1742.
36. "CCU" on May 13, 1723, AHU, cód. 908, fls. 41v.–42. For the fort built in 1731; see also Harms, *The Diligent*, 238.
37. For the fort built in 1731 see also Harms, *The Diligent*, 238. For examples of Portuguese ships seizing Dutch ships, see Postma, *The Dutch in the Atlantic Slave Trade*, 77; "Parecer do Conselho Ultramarino" on February 15, 1726, AHU, Rio de Janeiro, cx. 16, doc. 1742.
38. "Carta Régia" on December 20, 1725, AHU, cód. 546, fl. 2v.; "Carta Régia" on January 21, 1726. AHU, cód. 546, fls. 3; "Carta dos Oficiais do Senado da Câmara de Luanda" on April 17, 1728, AHU, Angola, cx. 24, doc. 36; "Carta Régia" in 1728, AHN, cód. 1, fls. 48–49. Other merchants, such as a former holder of the contract to collect duties on slaves exported from Luanda followed suit. See "Carta do Governador de Angola" on December 20, 1729, AHU, Angola, cx. 24, doc. 133; "Carta Régia" on October 23, 1730, AHU, cód. 546, fls. 49–49v.
39. For an account of Torres' departure from West Africa after his fort was destroyed by the Dutch, see Harms, *The Diligent*, 240. For a later account of the episode, see "Ofício Gaspar Caldas" on Septermber 16, 1743, AHU, Rio de Janeiro, cx. 41, doc. 44.
40. In 1735, he arrived to Luanda from Rio de Janeiro with four slave ships and began shipping slaves to Santos. See "Carta do Governador de Angola" on August 10, 1736, AHU, Angola, cx. 29.
41. "Requerimento de Manoel da Silva" on October 22, 1735, AHU, Rio de Janeiro, cx. 31, doc. 21; "Petição de Manoel da Silva" on January 26, 1736, AHU, Angola, cx. 29, doc. 12; "Requerimento de Manoel da Silva" on April 15, 1738, AHU, Rio de Janeiro, cx. 35, doc. 3; "Petição de José de Torres" on September 3, 1739, AHU, Angola, cx. 31, doc. 59.
42. "Registro de Óbitos da Paróquia de Remédios, 1748–1779," ABL, fl. 243.
43. "Carta Régia" on October 23, 1730, AHU, cód. 546, fls. 49–49v.; "Requerimento de Vasco Lourenço Veloso" on May 11, 1731, AHU, Angola, cx. 25, doc. 100.
44. "Carta Régia" in 1728, AHN, cód. 1, fls. 47–48; "Carta dos Oficiais do Senado da Câmara de Luanda" on April 17, 1728, AHU, Angola, cx. 24,

doc. 36; "Carta dos Oficiais do Senado da Câmara de Luanda" on April 17, 1728, AHU, Angola, cx. 24, doc. 36; "Carta Régia" on May 12, 1728, AHU, cód. 546, fl. 26v.; "Carta Régia" on May 19, 1729, AHU, Angola, cx. 24, doc. 133; "Carta do Governador" on December 22, 1734, AHU, Angola, cx. 27, doc. 159; "Carta do Governador de Angola" on December 20, 1729, AHU, Angola, cx. 24, doc. 133.

45. "Ordem Régia" on June 26, 1742, BNRJ, doc. I-12, 3, 31, fls. 79v.–80.
46. "Requerimento de Manoel da Silva," undated but around 1735, AHU, Rio de Janeiro, cx. 31, doc, 21; "Petição de Francisco Xavier" on February 26, 1737, AHU, Angola, cx. 30, doc. 7.
47. Biblioteca Municipal de Luanda, hereafter BML, cód. 37, fl. 17v.
48. BML, cód. 37, fls. 116v.–128v.
49. BML, cód. 37, fl. 5.
50. By then, his business was worth one hundred cruzados. See "Carta Régia" on June 18, 1799, AHNA, cód. 255, fls. 16v.–17.
51. "Carta do Governador de Angola" on November 18, 1811, AHNA, cód. 323, fl. 38.
52. "Carta para o Governador de Angola" on November 28, 1826, Arquivo Histórico Ultramarino, hereafter AHU, cód. 542.
53. "Representação de Joaquim Martins Mourão" on November 18, 1825, AHU, Angola, cx. 150, doc. 4; "Representação de Joaquim Martins Mourão" in 1825, AHU, Angola, cx. 150, doc. 7.
54. "Carta de António Manoel de Noronha" on January 23, 1827, AHU, cód. 542; "Despacho do requerimento de José Joaquim Ferreira Torres on October 6, 1827, AHNA, cód. 7182, fl. 72v.
55. "Despacho do requerimento de António Francisco Ribeiro on January 29, 1828, AHNA, cód. 7182, fl. 80v.; "Despacho do requerimento de José Polilo" on July 8, 1828, AHNA, cód. 7182, fl. 95v.
56. "Despacho do requerimento de Francisco José Gomes Guimarães" on December 12, 1828, AHNA, cód. 7182, fl. 121v.
57. "Despacho do requerimento de José Pedro de Andrade" on June 21, 1828, AHNA, cód. 7182, fl. 94.
58. "Despacho do requerimento de Dona Maria Ferreira da Silva" on September 13, 1828, AHNA, cód. 7182, fl. 105.
59. "Despacho do requerimento de Estevão da Cruz" on September 12, 1828, AHNA, cód. 7182, fl. 105.
60. Souza's will named his granddaughter as heir of two-thirds of his assets. See "Testamento de José de Souza" on April 15, 1780, ANTT, FF, JU, África, maço 21, doc. 12; ANTT, FF, JU, África, maço 2, doc. 3 B, fls. 30–35.
61. The Bahian daughter was named his heir when he wrote his will in 1789. See "Testamento de Francisco Xavier dos Reis" on December 4, 1789, ANTT, FF, JU, África, maço 24, doc. 17.
62. "Testamento de Joaquim Antonio da Roza" on September 12, 1799, Arquivo Histórico Nacional da Torre do Tombo, hereafter ANTT, FF, JU, África, maço 12, doc. 8.
63. "Testamento de José Francisco" on May 28, 1800, ANTT, FF, JU, África, maço 15, doc. 6.

64. "Testamento de António José de Barros" on September 10, 1799, ANTT, FF, JU, África, maço 2, doc. 3 A, fls. 16–17.

65. "Requerimento de Joaquim Vieira de Souza" in 1818, AHNA, cód. 361, fl. 60.

66. "Requerimento de Joaquim Teixeira Macedo" in 1818, AHNA, cód. 361, fl. 65.

67. "Carta do Capitão Mor do Presídio de Caconda" on February 20, 1789, AHU, Angola, cx. 74, doc. 49; "Depoimento de António Lourenço de Carvalho" in 1803, ANTT, FF, JU, África, maço 22, doc. 5; "Primeiro Testamento de José António de Carvalho" on January 8, 1798, ANTT, FF, JU, África, maço 22, doc. 5.

68. "Despacho do requerimento de João Pedro de Andrade" on September 9, 1828, AHNA, cód. 7182, fl. 104.

69. "Despacho do requerimento de João Pedro de Andrade" on September 15, 1828, AHNA, cód. 7182, fl. 105v.

70. "Despacho do requerimento de Manoel José da Costa" on October 5, 1829, AHNA, cód. 7182, fl. 167.

71. "Despacho do requerimento de José Pedro Cota" on October 18, 1826, AHNA, cód. 7182, fl. 23.

72. "Despacho do requerimento de Sebastião Rodrigues da Silva on October 19, 1827, AHNA, cód. 7182, fl. 69.

73. "Despacho do requerimento de José Joaquim Ferreira" on October 6, 1828, AHNA, cód. 7182, fl. 110v.

74. "Despacho do requerimento de Justiniano José dos Reis" on May 19, 1829, AHNA, cód. 7182, fl. 144v.

75. "Despacho do requerimento de Francisco Ferreira Gomes" on June 4, 1829, AHNA, cód. 7182, fl. 148v.

76. "Carta do Governador de Benguela" on February 28, 1798, AHNA, cód. 256, fls. 59v.–61.

77. "Notícias de Benguela e seus Distritos em 1797," IHGB, lata 32, pasta 2, fl. 7v.–8.

78. ANTT, FF, JU, África, maço 2, doc. 3 A, fl. 16.

79. "Despacho do requerimento de Justiniano José dos Reis" on June 6, 1827, AHNA, cód. 7182, fl. 54.

80. "Despacho do requerimento de Francisco Pereira da Rocha" on September 28, 1827, AHNA, cód. 7182, fl. 67v.

81. Furthermore, Barros left instructions to the executor of his will that he wished to be buried in Rio de Janeiro at the *Ordem Terceira de Nossa Senhora do Monte do Carmo* if he died in Rio. See "Testamento de António José de Barros" on September 10, 1799, ANTT, FF, JU, África, maço 2, doc. 3A.

82. "Ofício do Governador de Benguela" on October 24, 1799, AHNA, 441, fl. 109.

83. "Testamento de José António da Costa" on April 17, 1795, ANTT, FF, JU, África, maço 30, doc. 11.

84. "Testamento de José de Souza" on April 15, 1780, ANTT, FF, JU, África, maço 21, doc. 12.

85. "Primeiro Testamento de José António de Carvalho" on January 8, 1798, ANTT, FF, JU, África, maço 22, doc. 5.

86. "Receita do Tesoureiro do Hospital de Benguela" in 1774, AHU, Angola, cx. 61, doc. 39; "Carta do Juiz de Fora de Benguela" on July 28, 1778, AHU, Angola, cx. 61; "Ofício do Governador de Benguela" on October 12, 1788, AHU, Angola, cx. 73, doc. 44; "Relação dos Negociantes da Praça de

São Felipe de Benguela" on June 22, 1793, AHU, Angola, cx. 76; "Mapa das Pessoas Livres e Escravos de Benguela" on June 15, 1796, AHNA, cód. 441, fl. 19; "Mapa das Pessoas Livres, Escravos e Casas de Sobrado, Terras, Cobertas de Palha, e Sanzalas" in Benguela in 1796, IHGB, lata 81, pasta 2; "Mapa de Ocupações de Benguela" in 1798, AHNA, cód. 441, fl. 82; "Ofício do Governador Interino de Benguela" on August 17, 1800, AHNA, cód. 442, fls. 123v.–129. Elias Alexandre da Silva Corrêa, *História de Angola* (Lisbon: Editorial Ática, 1937), vol. 1, 38–39.

87. Autos de Residência do Juiz de Fora de Benguela" in 1780, AHU, Angola, cx. 63, doc. 2; "Devassa contra João Batista dos Santos Bonnate" in 1798, AHU, Angola, cx. 89, doc. 67.

88. "Autos de Residência do Juiz de Fora de Benguela" in 1780, AHU, Angola, cx. 63, doc. 2.

89. "Ofício do Governador de Benguela" on January 6, 1797, AHNA, cód. 442, fl. 27. In 1799, when French corsairs attacked four ships in Benguela, the city's merchants were left with only one vessel of their own. See "Ofício do Governador de Benguela" on April 18, 1799, AHNA, cód. 442, fls. 86–87. For information on French corsairs in Benguela, see "Ofício do Governador de Benguela" on March 5, 1798, AHNA, cód. 442, fls. 99v.–101; "Conta do Governador de Angola" on May 12, 1795, AHU, cód. 409; "Carta Régia" on September 22, 1796, AHU, cód. 546; "Termo de Vereação" on March 6, 1799, AHNA, cód. 258, fls. 80–84; "Ofício do Governador de Benguela" on April 28, 1799, AHNA, cód. 442, fls. 86–87; "Carta do Governador de Angola" on May 9, 1799, AHNA, cód. 247, fls. 52v.–54; "Ofício do Governador de Benguela" on July 25, 1799, AHNA, cód. 442, fls. 103–104; "Ofício do Governador de Benguela" on June 25, 1799, AHNA, cód. 442, fls. 107–108; "Ofício do Rodrigo de Souza Coutinho" on March 17, 1800, AHNA, cód. 254, fls. 159v.–161v.; "Depoimento de Thomaz Rodrigues" on June 23, 1800, AHNA, cód. 2563, fls. 17v.–19v.

90. "Relação da Viagem que fiz desta cidade Benguela para as Terras do Lovar" in 1794, AHU, Angola, cx. 80; "Notícias de Benguela e seus Distritos em 1797," IHGB, lata 32, pasta 2, fl. 6; "Ofício do Governador de Benguela" on January 2, 1798, AHNA, cód. 441, fls. 45–48; "Ofício do Governador de Benguela" on July 2, 1803, AHNA, cód. 442, fl. 238. See also Curto, "Movers of Slaves," 8.

91. "Ofício do Governador Interino de Benguela" on August 17, 1800, AHNA, cód. 442, fls. 123v.–129. For information on Joaquim Vieira de Andrade, see "Notícias de Benguela e seus Distritos em 1797," IHGB, lata 32, pasta 2, fl. 11.

92. "Notícias do Presídio de Novo Redondo" on October 25, 1797, IHGB, lata 31, pasta 9, fls. 14–15.

93. "Autos de Residência do Juiz de Fora de Benguela" in 1780, AHU, Angola, cx. 63, doc. 2; "Certidão do Escrivão da Provedoria da Fazendas dos Defuntos e Ausentes de Benguela" on April 22, 1785, ANTT, FF, JU, África, maço 8, doc. 1B; "Relação dos Negociantes da Praça de São Felipe de Benguela" on June 22, 1793, AHU, Angola, cx. 76; "Certidão de Frutuoso José da Cruz" on September 27, 1796, AHU, Angola, cx. 84, doc. 38. See also Tribunal de Contas, livro 4198, fl. 3.

94. "Primeiro Testamento de José António de Carvalho" on January 8, 1798, ANTT, FF, JU, África, maço 22, doc. 5.

95. "Testamento de Joaquim Antonio da Roza" on September 12, 1799, ANTT, FF, JU, África, maço 12, doc. 8.
96. "Testamento de António José de Barros" on September 10, 1799, ANTT, FF, JU, África, maço 2, doc. 3A.
97. "Memória sobre o Abuso Pernicioso do Comércio deste Sertão" on November 12, 1786, AHU, Angola, cx. 71, doc. 60.
98. Carta da Junta de Administração da Companhia de Comércio de Pernambuco e Paraíba" on March 14, 1781, ANTT, AHMF, livro 291; "Carta da Junta de Administração da Companhia de Comércio de Pernambuco e Paraíba" on January 23, 1782, ANTT, AHMF, livro 291; "Carta da Junta de Administração da Companhia de Comércio de Pernambuco e Paraíba" on May 17, 1782, ANTT, AHMF, livro 291.
99. "Ofício de Luiz Cândido Cordeiro Pinheiro Furtado" on September 26, 1785, AHU, Angola, cx. 70, doc. 49. Maia left for Rio shortly thereafter and never fulfilled his promise. In the end, the expedition to Cabo Negro was primarily funded by another Benguela merchant, Gregório José Mendes, who was appointed commander of the expedition after contributing five hundred slaves to work as porters. For information on Mendes' role as the commander of the expedition and his business in Benguela, see "Ofício de António José Valente" on June 29, AHU, Angola, cx. 70. "Carta Patente de Gregório José Mendes" on January 17, 1786, AHNA, cód. 311, fls. 58–58v.; "Carta do Governador de Angola" on August 3, 1786, AHU, cód. 1642; "Carta do Governador de Angola" on August 12, 1787, AHU, cód. 1642; "Carta do Governador de Angola" on February 26, 1788, AHNA, cód. 82, fl. 117v.–118; "Testamento de Domingos Rodrigues" on September 12, 1773, ANTT, FF, JU, África, maço 28, doc. 8, fls. 28v–29v. For details about Mendes' Portuguese background, see ANTT, FF, JU, África, maço 29, doc. 10.
100. "Carta Patente para José Rodrigues Maia" on July 6, 1776, AHU, Angola, cx. 77, doc. 66.
101. "Carta do Governador de Angola" on January 17, 1791, AHU, Angola, cx. 75, doc. 2.
102. "Letra de Risco" on April 26, 1790, ANTT, FF, JU, África, maço 19, doc. 13; "Testamento de Francisco Dias de Oliveira" on August 20, 1790, ANTT, FF, JU, África, maço 19, doc. 13, fls. 102–106.
103. "Petição de Joaquim José de Andrade e Souza Menezes" in 1789, AHU, Angola, cx. 74, doc. 49.
104. In 1800, for example, the governor of Benguela ordered the arrest of José Maria de Souza Ribeiro, then in Kakonda, who owed a significant amount of goods to Joaquim José de Andrade e Souza Menezes. See "Carta do Tenente Regente do Presídio de Novo Redondo" on August 7, 1797, AHNA, cód. 256, fls. 4v.–5v.; "Ofício do Governador de Benguela" on October 30, 1797, AHNA, cód. 442; "Carta do Regente de Novo Redondo" on January 12, 1799, AHNA, cód. 256, fls. 197–198.
105. "Ofício do Governador de Benguela" on October 24, 1799, AHNA, 441, fl. 109.
106. "Ofício do Governador de Benguela" on August 12, 1796, AHNA, cód. 442, fls. 13v.–14; "Depoimento de Inácio Teixeira Carneiro" on December 4, 1798, AHU, Angola, cx. 89, doc. 67;
107. Curto, "Movers of Slaves."

108. "Autos de Habilitação de António Manoel" in 1786, ANTT, FF, JU, África, maço 3, doc. 14.

109. "Petição de Manoel José da Cruz" in 1789, AHU, Angola, cx. 74, doc. 49. Cruz later clarified that he had actually lived twenty years in the interior of Benguela and that he still maintained a hub there for his agents and to keep goods used to trade for slaves. See "Depoimento de Manoel José da Cruz" on September 23, 1789, AHU, Angola, cx. 74, doc. 49.

110. "Despacho do requerimento de Floriano Pires Chaves" on September 23, 1826, AHNA, cód. 7182, fl. 19v.

111. "Despacho do requerimento de Antonio Joaquim" on March 4, 1828, AHNA, cód. 7182, fl. 84.

112. "Despacho do requerimento de Joaquim José da Silva" on April 17, 1828, AHNA, cód. 7182, fl. 89.

113. "Despacho do requerimento de Domingos Rodrigues November 28, 1829, AHNA, cód. 7182, fl. 174.

114. Curto, "Movers of Slaves," 7.

115. "Ofício do Governador de Benguela" on August 12, 1796, AHNA, cód. 442, fls. 13v.–14. For the death of Barrocas, see "Ofício do Governador de Benguela" on August 23, 1796, AHNA, cód. 442, fls. 14v.–15; "Ofício do Governador de Benguela" on December 13, 1796, AHNA, cód. 442, fls. 23–24.

116. "Depoimento de António José da Costa" on September 16, 1789, AHU, Angola, cx. 74, doc. 49; "Carta de Francisco António do Amaral" on April 21, 1789, AHU, Angola, cx. 74, doc. 15; "Carta do Governador de Angola" on December 18, 1791, AHU, cód. 1628; "Ofício do Governador de Benguela" on July 27, July 27, 1796, AHU, Angola, cx. 84; "Ofício do Governador de Benguela" on August 23, 1796, AHNA, cód. 442, fls. 14v.–15; "Ofício do Governador de Benguela" on December 13, 1796, AHNA, cód. 442, fls. 23–24. In 1797, Costa still had a property in Catumbela near Benguela. See "Notícias de Benguela e seus Distritos em 1797," IHGB, lata 32, pasta 2, fl. 50v.

117. "Notícias de Benguela e seus Distritos em 1797," IHGB, lata 32, pasta 2, fl. 7; "Carta do Governador de Angola" on March 2, 1799, AHNA, cód. 247, fls. 43–44v.

118. "Carta Geral desta Capitania (Benguela)" on March 28, 1798, AHNA, cód. 441, fls. 31v.–35.

119. "Ofício do Governador de Benguela" on March 16, 1797, AHNA, cód. 442, fls. 30–32; "Ofício do Governador de Benguela" on February 28, 1797, ANTT, Ministério do Reino, maço 604, cx. 707.

120. "Ofício do Governador de Benguela" on January 24, 1797, AHNA, cód. 442, fls. 27v.–28.

121. "Ofício do Governador de Benguela" on May 3, 1796, AHNA, cód. 518, fl. 236.

122. "Ofício do Governador de Benguela" on August 12, 1796, AHNA, cód. 442, fls. 13v.–14.

123. "Mapa das Pessoas Livres, Escravos e Casas de Sobrado, Terras, Cobertas de Palha, e Senzalas" in Benguela in 1796, IHGB, lata 81, pasta 2, fl. 8. In 1798, a Benguela merchant said, "I declare that I gave a young slave called João to captain José da Silva Teixeira to learn to be a sailor," which strongly suggests that Teixeira was living in Benguela. See "Primeiro Testamento de

José António de Carvalho" on January 8, 1798, ANTT, FF, JU, África, maço 22, doc. 5.

124. "Ofício do Governador de Benguela" on January 17, 1798, AHNA, cód. 442, fls. 58–59v.

125. "Caderno de Receita e Despesa do Inventário de António Fernandes da Silva" on June 11, 1803, ANTT, FF, JU, África, maço 4, doc. 20.

126. "Testamento de António Pinto de Almeida" on January 31, 1793, ANTT, FF, JU, África, maço 5, doc. 3 A.

127. "Testamento de Aurélio Veríssimo Vieira" on September 2, 1805, ANTT, FF, JU, África, maço 14, doc. 1, fls. 8v.–11v.

128. "Primeiro Testamento de José António de Carvalho" on January 8, 1798, ANTT, FF, JU, África, maço 22, doc. 5.

129. "Depoimento de Lourenço Pereira Tavares" on September 25, 1789, AHU, Angola, cx. 74, doc. 49.

130. "Petição de Lourenço Pereira Tavares" on August 12, 1794, AHU, Angola, cx. 80, doc. 52.

131. "Ofício do Governador de Benguela" on January 14, 1798, AHNA, cód. 442, fls. 51v.–52. In Luanda, legislation mandating ships to carry supplies for slaves from Brazil had been in place at least since 1783. See "Portaria" on January 9, 1783, AHNA, cód. 272, fls. 49v.–50; "Ofício do Governador de Angola" on September 2, 1790, AHNA, cód. 83; "Ofício do Governador de Angola" on September 2, 1790, ANRJ, cx. 502.

132. "Ofício do Governador de Benguela" on July 1, 1799, AHNA, cód. 441, fl. 107v.

133. "Testamento de José de Souza" on April 15, 1780, ANTT, FF, JU, África, maço 21, doc. 12.

134. "Testamento de Luiz António Gomes" on June 8, 1785, ANTT, FF, JU, África, maço 3, doc. 14.

135. "Testamento de José António da Costa" on April 17, 1795, ANTT, FF, JU, África, maço 30, doc. 11.

136. Francisco owed money to several Rio merchants: 900,000 *réis* to Manoel José de Mesquita, 360,000 *réis* to Antonio Pedro de Morais, and 100,000 *réis* to Antonio Francisco da Silva Guimarães. See "Testamento de José Francisco" on May 28, 1800, ANTT, FF, JU, África, maço 15, doc. 6.

137. "Carta Patente" on December 27, 1787, AHU, Angola, cx. 74, doc. 2.

138. With the exception of the first debt just noted, which were to be paid with the proceeds of ten slaves sent to Brazil, all other payments were to be in cash. See "Testamento de António José de Barros" on September 10, 1799, ANTT, FF, JU, África, maço 2, doc. 3 A.

139. "Testamento de António José de Barros" on September 10, 1799, ANTT, FF, JU, África, maço 2, doc. 3 A, fls. 13–14.

140. "Testamento de António José de Barros" on September 10, 1799, ANTT, FF, JU, África, maço 2, doc. 3 A, fl. 15. Manoel Gonçalves Moledo was one of the chief merchants in Rio in the late eighteenth century.

141. Although the ship bringing Barros back to Benguela was reputed to be one of the best sailing between Benguela and Rio de Janeiro, it was lost before it arrived back to Benguela. See "Ofício do Governador de Benguela" on March 5, 1798, AHNA, cód. 442, fls. 55v.–56 and AHNA, cód. 256; "Carta do Governador de Angola" on May 10, 1798, AHNA, cód. 247, fls. 12–14.

Bibliography

Emmer, Pieter and Wim Klooster. 1999. "The Dutch Atlantic, 1600–1800: Expansion without Empire." *Itinerario* 23(2): 48–69.

Feinberg, Harvey. 1989. *Africans and Europeans in West Africa: Elminians and Dutchmen on the Gold Coast during the Eighteenth Century.* Philadelphia: University of Pennsylvania.

Ferreira, Roquinaldo. 1996. "Dos Sertões ao Atlântico: Tráfico Ilegal de Escravos e Comércio Lícito em Angola." MA Thesis, Universidade Federal do Rio de Janeiro.

———. 2003. "Transforming Atlantic Slaving: Trade, Warfare, and Territorial Control in Angola, 1650–1800." Unpublished PhD Dissertation, UCLA.

Gilroy, Paul. 1993. *The Black Atlantic: Modernity and Double Consciousness.* Cambridge: Cambridge University Press.

Harms, Robert. 2002. *The Diligent: A Voyage through the Worlds of the Slaver Trade.* Oxford: Oxford University Press.

Heywood, Linda. 2000. "Portuguese into African: The Eighteenth-Centuy Central African Background to Atlantic Creole Cultures," in Linda Heywood, ed. *Central Africans and Cultural Transformations in the American Diaspora.* Cambridge: Cambridge University Press.

Klein, Herbert. 2003. "The Atlantic Slave Trade to 1650," in Stuart Schwartz, *Tropical Babylons: Sugar and the Making of the Atlantic World, 1450–1680.* Chapel Hill: University of North Carolina, pp.211–212.

———. 1978. *The Middle Passage: Comparative Studies in the Atlantic Slave Trade.* Princeton: Princeton University Press, pp.181–212.

Law, Robin. 1997. *The Slave Coast of West Africa.* Oxford: Oxford University Press.

Law, Robin and Kristin Mann. 1999. "West Africa in the Atlantic Community: The Case of the Slave Coast." *William and Mary Quarterly* 56(1999): 307–331.

Miller, Joseph. 1975. "Legal Portuguese Slaving from Angola. Some Preliminary Indications of Volume and Direction, 1760–1830." *Revue Française d'Histoire d'Outre-Mer* 62(1975): 145.

———. 1986. "Imports at Luanda, Angola: 1785–1823," in Gerhard Liesegang, Helma Pasch, and Adam Jones, eds., *Figuring African Trade: Proceedings of the Symposium on the Quantification and Structure of the Import and Export and Long Distance Trade of Africa in the 19th Century (c. 1800–1913).* Berlin: Dietrich Heimer Verlag, pp.165–246.

Pantoja, Selma. 2004. "Inquisição, Degredo e Mestiçagem em Angola no século XVIII." *Revista Lusófina de Ciência da Religião* 6(5): 117–136.

Postma, Johannes. 1990. *The Dutch in the Atlantic Slave Trade, 1600–1815.* Cambridge: Cambridge University Press.

Sparks, Randy J. 2002. "Two Princes of Calabar: An Atlantic Odyssey from Slavery to Freedom." *William and Mary Quarterly* 59: 555–585.

———. 2004. *The Two Princes of Calabar: An Eighteenth Century Atlantic Odyssey.* Cambridge: Cambridge University Press.

Thornton, John. 1998. *Africa and Africans in the Making of the Atlantic World, 1400–1800.* Cambridge: Cambridge University Press.

Vansina, Jan. 2004. *How Societies are Born: Governance in West Central Africa before 1600.* Charlottesville: University of Virginia.

Vansina, Jan. 2005. "Ambaca Society and the Slave Trade, ca. 1760–1845." *Journal of African History* 46: 1–27.

Vries, Jan de. 2005. "The Dutch Atlantic Economies," in Coclanis, *The Atlantic Economy during the Seventeenth and Eighteenth Centuries. Organization, Operation, Practice and Personnel.* Columbia: University of South Carolina Press.

Chapter 5

Colonial Aspirations: Connecting Three Points of the Portuguese Black Atlantic

Nancy Priscilla Naro

Introduction

Current scholarship that has revisited Portuguese colonial relationships with the Atlantic islands and mainland African countries of Guinea Bissau, Angola, and Mozambique, not to mention Brazil, is finding new ways of articulating the history of ideas with national history and microhistory, unveiling complex and multifaceted demographic, political, social, religious, and cultural strands (Pétré-Grenouilleau 2004: 16). In some instances, new findings are enriching earlier debates on unity and disunity in the long tradition of empire.[1] In others, traditional emphases on the unidirectional navigational flows of the transatlantic slave trade have been revised in the light of cultural, linguistic, and religious concerns. Revisionists highlight the multidirectional migratory patterns of returning Africans from the Americas and the Atlantic islands, and the migrations of Portuguese, Brazilians, and Africans to and from Brazil, the Atlantic islands, and Portugal during and after the Portuguese colonial experience abroad (Mann and Bay 2001; Turner 1975; Guran 2000; Carneiro da Cunha 1985; Ferreira in this volume). In some cases, the concept of the Black Atlantic has been extended to embrace Mozambique and beyond, in line with the dynamics and the interconnections of the transatlantic slave trade and other commercial trajectories in the South Atlantic (Alencastro 2000; Curto and Soulodre 2001: 243–258; Capela 2005). Although recent research engages the diaspora in terms of the cultural dynamics of the Portuguese Black Atlantic, unresolved issues include what Tiffany Patterson and Robin Kelley identify as the linkages that tie the process of the diaspora together and that also contribute to its unmaking (2000: 11–45).

The dynamics of local societies in the Atlantic framework are relevant to these linkages. In regard to the British Caribbean, Verene Shepherd raises the point that was earlier explored in reference to the southern Angolan colony of Mossamedes: unity and disunity were inherent characteristics of a system in which internal markets and local societies had an impact on each other as well as on the dynamics of the entire Atlantic system (2004: 49–65).

Local societies posited differential relationships to the broader issue of the unity of the Portuguese colonial empire. In Brazil, the transfer of the Portuguese court to Rio de Janeiro in 1808 reversed the relationship between the colony and Portugal. According to Kirsten Schultz, conflicting local agendas over constitutionalism culminated in the February 26, 1821 revolt but an eventual compromise provided the basis for the liberal constitutional monarchy that guided the state formation process following Brazil's independence on September 7 of that year (2001: ch.7). British pressure on Brazil to suspend the transatlantic slave trade was received with local resistance that delayed the implementation of the 1826 agreement and it must be recalled that Portugal responded similarly to British and French pressures.

Luiz Felipe Alencastro, author of the monumental work *O Trato dos Viventes. Formação do Brasil no Atlântico Sul Séculos XVI e XVII* (2000), explored the early dynamics of Africa in Brazil. More recently, he linked Brazil's very independence to the local dimensions of the slave trade and to commerce on both sides of the Atlantic. In highlighting the impact of British interests in the South Atlantic, he proposed the extension of the 1808 to 1822 period (that has traditionally marked the parameters of Brazil's independence) to mid-century, when local and international pressures ushered in the demise of the transatlantic slave trade (2004: 98–109).[2] Alencastro's research also broadened the boundaries of the South Atlantic to include Mozambique on the basis that ongoing British penetration into the South Atlantic affected Portuguese colonial aspirations and trade networks there.

British interests in the South Atlantic conjuncture were mainly commercial whereas the multidirectional trade connections between Brazil and Angola were bound ever tighter through personal, administrative, and kinship relations that had evolved under the colonial pact and continued well into the nineteenth century.[3] By comparison to the Portuguese African possessions, Brazil enjoyed a favorable standing in relation to Portugal, as documented in the varying terms of reference originating at the heart of empire that discriminated between the inhabitants of the different overseas colonies Whereas the colony of Brazil was elevated to a kingdom in 1815 on par with the kingdoms of the Algarve and Portugal, the African colonies were named jointly in the Portuguese liberal Constitution of 1822 and the *Carta Constitucional* of 1826 as *domínios africanos*.[4] Portuguese officialdom's terminology for the inhabitants of Portuguese Africa distinguished them from other societies within the orbit of the Portuguese colonial empire. Africans in the Portuguese colonies were termed *indígenas* unless granted the more elevated condition of assimilated citizen (*cidadão assimilado*). These unique terms distinguished African inhabitants from Portuguese subjects in Cabo Verde, Portuguese India (Goa), and Macau, who were granted the status of citizens (*cidadãos metropolitanos*) and likened in this singular respect to the colonial inhabitants of the British Empire. In Brazil, the linkage with the diaspora was evident in the identification of African slaves and freed persons of African origin as *da nação* (from Africa), or from Luanda, Benguela or their port of embarkation.

The distinctions in identifying the inhabitants of the overseas possessions reinforced the association of national identity in Portugal with the concept of a territorially bounded citizenry. This meant that to be Portuguese was to share one's land of birth or adoption as an "essentialist bond common across the people of a sovereign nation."[5] On the one hand, the breadth of Portugal's multicultural empire attested to centuries of cultural pluralism, integration, and unity under a sovereign head of state. Less apparent were the imposed boundaries of exclusion that, like the terms of reference employed to categorize differentially the inhabitants of the African *dominios*, were in evidence at the very heart of empire in Lisbon.

This chapter considers a set of events, and the reactions to them, at three points in the Lusophone Atlantic world tracing the ways in which Portugal's longstanding expansion and colonization affected political and social thinking at home and in the Lusophone South Atlantic between the 1820s and the 1850s. The institution of slavery and the transatlantic slave trade constituted the overarching connection in this period between the ports of Recife, Brazil; Mossamedes in Southern Angola; and Lisbon, Portugal. Although slavery was no longer practiced in Portugal, I have uncovered indications of a small African presence in Lisbon; in the first part of the chapter I focus on Africans and their descendants who provided a daily reminder of an institution that, despite the independence of Brazil, were still an exploitable supply of labor in various enterprises in all the Lusophone-speaking countries. I shall argue that, concealed beneath professed ideals of liberalism, there existed distinguishable limits of exclusion and inclusion during the turbulent 1830s and 1840s. The Africans in Lisbon were in general just as unequal and politically marginalized as Africans and their descendants elsewhere in the Portuguese Atlantic, in spite of their significant contributions to music, religion, and dance. The following part of the chapter deals with challenges to liberalism in the Brazilian Northeast in the late 1840s and the victimization of Portuguese residents by irate nationalistic free Brazilians. At that time, the Portuguese in Pernambuco were not perceived as agents of Portugal's long-term objectives of civilization so much as monopoly holders of jobs—clerks, artisans, retail traders—which the Brazilians desired for themselves. The third part of the chapter deals with the Portuguese government's policy for the refugees in Pernambuco to migrate to Mossamedes in southern Angola. Statesmen who were proponents of Africa as a "third empire" to replace Brazil envisaged that they would be able to establish a plantation economy there.

Africa and Africans in Lisbon

The African presence in Lisbon dated from the period of the Explorations. Africans and their descendants were longstanding residents of Lisbon, interspersed over time with a transient population of African sailors, slaves,

manual workers, tradesmen, and travelers. Freed and enslaved African laborers contributed to the intense commercial life of the port city as traders,
street vendors, entertainers, healers, artisans, and domestic servants.[6] At the
time of Marianne Baillie's visit to Lisbon in 1821, half of the Lisbon population of 300,000 "consisted of Blacks and mulattos." (1825: Letter II, Buenos
Ayres, June 30, 1821: 11). Slaves who resided in Portugal had in theory
gained their freedom in a process that was officially sanctioned under the
Marquis of Pombal in the early 1760s.[7] The transition to freedom brought
few benefits since neither long-term residence nor a subjective sense of
belonging was matched by social or political recognition. Although the
social and religious activities of the black brotherhoods in the city were integrated into the processions and festivities of the various Catholic orders, the
brotherhoods can be seen on the one hand to represent a form of assimilation to European norms, or, on the other hand, the preservation of African
rituals and customs within the metropolis.[8]

In the 1820s, Lisbon was beset by political crises that were directly related
to the independence of Brazil. In the latter years of this decade, the population responded in a nationalistic fervor to the return to power in 1828 of the
monarch, Dom Miguel, and his supporters, the *miguelistas*. An absolutist,
Dom Miguel opposed the liberal views that were espoused by Portugal's
enemy France toward the challenges to the rights of kings to rule, the
untrammeled power of the Catholic Church, and the abolition of slavery in
France's colonies. Supporters of these views rallied behind Brazil's ruler,
Dom Pedro I, and claimed him as Portugal's constitutional monarch. His
return to Portugal in 1831 after he abdicated the throne in Brazil aggravated
the political upheaval already set in train years before.

To counter political rivalries, the *miguelistas* strove to fuel patriotic sentiments. Projects like the construction of a national pantheon in Lisbon aimed
at glorifying honored heroes of the Peninsular Wars. The expected nationalistic euphoria at the inauguration of the monument was unfortunately over-
shadowed by an outbreak of cholera. Foreign visitors to the port city during
this period conveyed a sense of the turbulence and the disorder of the times
as they reported their dismay at the filthy streets, stray dogs, and hordes of
beggars who besieged passers-by in Lisbon. The writer Hans Christian
Andersen returned to Lisbon in 1866 expecting to encounter the city still in
the midst of the disarray of the 1830s. His observations express his pleasant
surprise at finding none of the earlier indications of decadence:

> I was obliged to exclaim: Where are the filthy streets that were described, the
> abandoned carcasses, the ferocious dogs and the miserable beings from the
> African possessions who grovelled about with whitened beards and sooty skin,
> with nauseating illnesses? I saw nothing of this and my mention of these things
> elicited the response that this was true thirty years before and was still recalled
> by many people.[9]

Civil order was restored under a liberal victory that legitimized Dona Maria
II's accession to the throne in 1834. The liberal governments enacted pressing

hygienic reforms that aimed to contain the spread of cholera in the capital. The implementation of the measures suggests, however, that liberal ideas were aimed at redesigning the spatial and social landscape of the city. In response to the need to bury large numbers of the epidemic's victims, burial sites were transferred from the religious sphere of the churches to the secular space of municipal areas. The cemeteries of Prazeres and the Alto de São João were created in 1833 and legitimized on September 21, 1835, making possible the spatial transfer of burials to the peripheries of the city. According to historian Fernando Catroga, the transfers effectively laicized burials and secularized the rituals surrounding death (1988: 872). Catroga also observed that despite the self-proclaimed liberal nature of the hygienic reforms, their implementation redefined the urban space along social and class lines that attested to a policy of exclusion in the socially peripheral areas of the Alfama, Mouraria, and Santo Esteves.

Exclusion was also evidenced in the widespread disregard for the regulations for secular burials. According to Rita Mega, an individual burial spot was required by law for each corpse but the practice of burial in open graves was not discontinued:

> The open trench continued to exist, in spite of the creation of new cemeteries. The bodies of the African, the slave, the impious were dumped into an open pit that was not even protected from the dogs. The Poço dos Negros was outside of the city walls enroute to Santos. This type of grave was common to both of the Lisbon cemeteries: in the cemetery of Prazeres there was an open pit and in the Alto de São Joao there was a trench (Mega: n.d.: 48). [10]

Mega's mention of slaves in this period is intriguing and is not clarified in her study. Her main point remains suggestive, as does that of Catroga: the regularization of burials under the guise of liberal hygienic reforms in the 1830s aimed to benefit the entire population but this aim was compromised in its implementation by the exclusionist treatment of the poor in general, and the African populations and their descendants in particular.

Concern about the marginalization of African residents emerged again during the following decade when Portugal was once more plagued by political turmoil. In 1842, a visiting Polish prince related the precarious conditions experienced by Africans in the city to their alienation from the political discussions of the day:

> the political furor has taken over all of the capital's inhabitants, from the noble and the royalty to the...of the common people. Only the poor Blacks from the Portuguese possessions of Africa, who wander in the thousands through Lisbon's streets, do not discuss politics; at least that is how it appears to me; they are not treated as men by the Portuguese, but as a horrible race of domestic animals. They whitewash the exterior walls of houses in the blazing sun, and when the bullfights finish, they hurl themselves at the exacerbated rage of those animals. When they become elderly, they drag themselves begging

through the streets of Lisbon, contaminated by sickening diseases, with their
hoary beards, that produce a depraved effect on their black faces (1845: 59).[11]

The prince made specific reference to one profession of Lisbon's working
class that was exclusive to Africans: the whitewasher (*caiador*) who painted
the exteriors of the private residences. The folklorist Calderon Dinis also
described the dark-skinned *caiador*, dressed in white as he roamed the streets
offering his services in the Rossio: "dressed in white they gathered in the
Rossio to negotiate white-washing work."[12] The two descriptions suggest
that, different to the *cantos* of Bahia's street-corners that united Africans
according to ethnic affiliation, the *caiador* was an occupation practiced by
individuals who plied their trade in the streets.

The gleaming whitewashed exteriors of Lisbon's buildings are suggestive
of a hygienic and sanitary urban façade that contrasts with the prince's
glimpse of a silent but visible social malaise attesting to the shortcomings of
the liberal reforms as highlighted during the cholera epidemic in the 1830s.
To an outsider, the African population not only suffered a literal invisibility
in the city streets; their precarious social condition also went unnoticed. The
city's African inhabitants were observed but were "exorcized" from political
expression. Uday Mehta has pointed out that among the legacies of liberal
politics are "liberal strategies of exclusion" or the "inclusionary pretensions
of liberal theory and the exclusionary effects of liberal practices that got written into the universalistic theoretical framework of liberalism." Mehta's findings suggest that liberal politics "reveal the truth of the ambivalence of liberal
ideas about universality."[13]

Popular Venues, Popular Classes

In the 1830s, slaves were no longer sold in the markets and ports of
Lisbon, although ships occasionally brought African laborers to Lisbon
and it was not unknown for slaves from Brazil to remain in bondage to
their returning Portuguese masters. (Tinhorão 1994: 61). Prince
Lishnowsky's diary apart, travelers to Lisbon did not generally report on
African traditions or African-derived cultures despite newspaper coverage
of the participation of the religious black brotherhoods in Catholic ceremonies and public processions through the streets of the port capital.
The portraits of Africans, depictions of African customs, daily routines,
and street life that Jean Baptiste Debret and Johann Mauritz Rugendas
documented in great detail in Brazil are largely absent from descriptions
of Lisbon. Peter Fryer claims that there was a black community in Lisbon
and that they were in close and constant touch with the rest of the city's
"lower orders": "the working people, beggars and other poor inhabitants
of Alfama, on whose quays the ships from Angola and Brazil tied up, of
Mouraria, and of the other lower-class districts of the city" (2000: 3).
Census entries for Lisbon do not include either ethnic or racial break-downs
and it is likely that the nonwhite population was merged with the varied

lower classes of Portuguese inhabitants. But conjecture is not unreasonable along the lines proposed by Patterson and Kelley, to the effect that "Europe exorcized blackness in order to create its own invented traditions, empires, and fictions of superiority and racial purity." (Patterson and Kelley 2000: 13).

Popular entertainment and pastimes, such as musical events at theaters and dancehalls, are suggestive of a robust African or Afro-derived cultural presence (Tinhorão 1994: 13). Questions remain as to whether music and dance were dynamic cultures and whether they originated in Lisbon. If so, were they the offspring of African origins, transatlantic fusions, or were they derivative of the juncture of an Afro contact with a dominant European milieu? Historian Mary Karasch attributes to Lisbon's African population of dancers and musicians the *batuque* and *lundu* that entertainers brought from Angola (1987: 244). José Ramos Tinhorão identifies elements of African music and dance during the continual process of cultural exchange that he documents among the lower social classes of Portugal (1994: 13). He states that a Portuguese form of the Spanish fandango (of possible American origin) competed with the *fofa* and the *lundu* from Brazil for the attentions of the popular groups (*povo miudo*) in the eighteenth century (1994: 16)[14] The fado was at that time a popular dance whose choreography and rhythm were the pride of the common people (and soon of the emergent middle classes). Forerunners of the sung fado of the nineteenth century, these dances shifted with changing class preferences from the venue of the tavern to the dancehalls. Tinhorão suggests that, on the basis of an 1825 stage farce in which the lundu was danced in the setting of the kitchen of a wealthy family, the dance spread at that time to socially superior groups (1994: 36).

Mário Vieira de Carvalho confirms that Africans were among the "lower social groups" who attended the Teatro de San Carlos, a popular venue that dated from 1793 (1993: 95).[15] One way to attract audiences in a city of low literacy rates was through the circulation of colorful posters with scenes from current attractions that, like billboards today, were displayed throughout the city. For Vieira de Carvalho, the Teatro de San Carlos served an important social function by establishing "norms of appropriate behavior for the audiences" in order to acculturate the popular classes to acceptable comportment in public spaces (1993: 98).[16] The Teatro Nacional de Salitre was a second popular venue where, according to Vieira de Carvalho, the common people gave thunderous acclaim to successful productions or vociferously repudiated undesirable theatre troupes.[17] The third popular venue was the Circo Olímpico (named after the Cirque Olimpique of Paris) with its main attraction of skilled horsemanship. Vieira de Carvalho cites one example of the appeal of political themes that engaged audiences: the enactment of the popular struggle against the dictatorial usurper of the throne, D. Miguel I. The grand finale of the performance was a shower of fireworks as the audience rose to acclaim the triumphant entrance of the hero, the liberal king D. Pedro I.[18]

The diversity of attractions at the three Lisbon theatres confirms a market for popular cultural entertainment that included Africans among the

common people in the city. Tinhorão's findings further suggest that
Brazilian-derived and African-related music and dance were highlights of the
common peoples' cultural life. Although Vieira de Carvalho does not delve into
the relationships between the cultural venues and the officialdom of the city,
official endorsement of public theaters suggests a tolerant liberal stance toward
popular culture and a possible source of needed revenues for the city's coffers.
By the time of the 1860s visit to the city by Hans Christian Anderson, the
widespread turmoil of previous decades was no longer generalized in the
urban milieu. The officially sanctioned urban spaces that the lower classes
occupied for entertainment and social enjoyment did not threaten the rigid
hierarchical set of social relations or encroach upon the select venues that
provided enjoyment for more elevated social groups.

A Third Empire

According to Omar Thomaz, pessimism about Brazil's independence and
the downfall of the Liberal regime in 1823 generated a profound sense of the
loss of empire.[19] In the port city of Lisbon, a theater for concerns about the
welfare, preservation, and unity of empire, divisions among official views
included the future of African slavery and the transatlantic slave trade in the
South Atlantic. According to W.G. Clarence-Smith, bourgeois strategists
claimed that the government was bereft of solutions to remedy the disintegration of overseas missionary activity and the decadence of the overseas
possessions (1979). Faced with Brazil's 1826 treaty with Great Britain to
abolish legal transatlantic slaving in 1830 (an agreement that was not officially implemented until mid-century), Portugal's priorities in the South
Atlantic needed to be revamped to enable the African colonies to eventually
take on what Joseph Miller has referred to as "a role in a reformed post-slave-
exporting nineteenth-century empire" (1988: 635).

Although liberals in general expressed little interest in the development of
Africa or the emancipation of involuntary labor there before 1870, João
Pedro Marques argues that "some of those who proposed the end of the
slave trade in the 1820s did so under the presupposition that this would
reinforce slavery in Africa in order that the African labour, under European
guidance, could nourish the dreamed-of development of *New Brazils*."[20] For
Valentim Alexandre, heightened expectations emerged at this time over the
future of the African overseas possessions, as government incentives were
made available to Portuguese merchants to establish direct links with the
African colonies. Such attempts were not fruitful given the widespread
Brazilian control over the lucrative coastal slave trade (2004: 112).

Advocates of a unified empire looked to a potential third empire in Africa
for projects that did not require substantial investments of metropolitan capital and that, in addition, would become a source of revenue and a trading
preserve to develop the metropolis.[21] According to Omar Thomaz, Portugal
redefined its imperial interests to "create a 'new Brazil' in Africa [that] meant
transforming the territories that Portugal claimed in that continent into

colonies to produce raw materials and import manufactured goods from the metropolis" (2000: 48).[22]

In the aftermath of the victory of the Liberals in 1834, official consideration again turned to the imperial plan that for the statesman and imperial minister, Bernardo de Sá Nogueira (the Marquis of Sá da Bandeira), would preserve the independence and the national dignity that Portugal had enjoyed since the fifteenth century and ensure the preservation of Portuguese hegemony in the South Atlantic (Clarence-Smith 1979: 12). Sá da Bandeira's proposals emanated outward from Lisbon to the far reaches of African local societies. Of utmost importance was the strengthening of the commercially viable fortified African coastal strongholds and the development of communication networks to link the coastal networks to the raw materials and precious metals to be extracted from the vast Angolan hinterland. The taxation of peasant commodity production and the settlement of white colonizers would contribute to the development of a local plantation sector that would replace Brazilian sugarcane, cotton, and tobacco.

The proposal naturally took into account the ready supply of local African labor. Implementation of this plan posed two fundamental challenges to Portuguese colonial authorities: 1) the maintenance of a viable military presence, and 2) the preservation of colonial boundaries and frontiers in Portuguese hands. In 1848, the year that France and Denmark officially abolished slavery in their Caribbean colonies, timely events on the Brazilian shores of the Atlantic played into the minister's strategic considerations of the coastal port of Mossamedes, sparsely inhabited by slave traders and an unregulated outlet for the ivory trade from the interior.

Recife, Pernambuco

In the northeastern port of Recife in the Brazilian province of Pernambuco, leaders of the Praia radical local faction of the established Liberal Party who had ruled in Pernambuco since 1844, took up arms when ousted from power four years later. Demanding universal suffrage and popular elections to public office to counter the interventions of Brazil's centralized government under the emperor, Dom Pedro II, the Praia directed its immediate hostility at the Conservative Party partisans who replaced them in local and national office. The rebellious Praia faction aggravated social tensions by demanding a land reform that would divide large sugar-producing estates into parcels of land to benefit small producers. Resonating with the pressing social concerns of the French working classes during the 1848 revolutionary Spring of the People, the Praia demands also brought national attention to Brazil's free working people, who were said to face unfavorable competition from Portuguese artisans and sales clerks in a labor market already heavily supplied with unpaid slave labor. The provincial social movement heightened anti-Portuguese sentiments in Rio de Janeiro and other cities where resident Portuguese creditors and moneylenders were also associated with the monopoly of the local retail commerce.

On June 26 and 27, 1848, and in the following year, Praia supporters singled out and assaulted Portuguese shopkeepers in the port city of Recife while Praia political leaders mobilized battalions of common people who targeted the sugar-producing estates of Conservative planters. The Portuguese consul in Recife, Joaquim Moreira Baptista, and the future leader of the settlers of Mossamedes, Bernardino Freire de Figueiredo Abreu e Castro, made urgent appeals to the Lisbon government to rescue the victims of local hostilities that were spreading to traders, merchants, estate overseers, and their families.[23] The central government in Lisbon authorized two Portuguese men-of-war to sail to Recife where British naval vessels had taken refugees on board. From Recife, the ships were to transport the refugees to the distant shores of Mossamedes in southern Angola where the settlers would implement the Portuguese governmental aims for a plantation society.[24]

The Colonial Exercise: Mossamedes

The colonization of Mossamedes furthered a centuries-long tradition of colonial settlement with the aim of expanding the confines of the empire and promoting Angola as a viable plantation economy. According to José C. Curto, "between the 1830s and the early 1910s, the Portuguese, taking full account of the acquired taste [for sugar brandy] established hundreds of sugar cane plantations throughout Angola with one specific objective: to produce cane brandy, which became the major industrial activity of the colony" (2004: 200). Transfers of European patrimonial institutions—the Roman Catholic Church, military fortifications, and bureaucracy—were made to overseas territories and operated under the aegis of the metropolitan government in Lisbon. A.J.R. Russell-Wood has argued that the most apparent feature of Portuguese colonization was a highly centralized administration that functioned in Portugal:

> Despite the diversity of climate, topography, religions, ethnic groups, and prevailing economic, social, and political contexts, each settlement bore the Lusitanian imprint and shared common characteristics. (2002: 129)

Events surrounding the migration of the Portuguese from Pernambuco contrasted in some ways with earlier sixteenth-century colonization undertakings. For example, Brazil's early settlements were initially financed by private merchant capital under royal provision of crown land grants in the form of donataries to the settlers. In 1849, the Portuguese overseas settlement initiative not only originated with the colonial minister of the Portuguese state in Lisbon, who authorized the dispatch of warships to Recife for the transoceanic voyage to Angola, but also made provisions for the local supervision of the project. Official instructions emanated from the corridors of power in Lisbon to the governor of the district to prohibit slave traders, criminals, and anyone who was banished to Angola from residing in Mossamedes, "to avoid contamination of the settlers."[25] Bernardino Freire de Figueiredo Abreu e

Castro, the leader of the settlers, handled the distribution of land for the cultivation of sugarcane as outlined on the map that was deposited with the Câmara Municipal of Mossamedes. Following a longstanding tradition of harnessing locally available labor to the production of agricultural products, local African labor was recruited for the undertaking.

Administration of the colony was delegated by Lisbon to the naval official, lieutenant captain of the Armada, António Sérgio de Sousa by the Secretary of State of the Ultramar who sent the following instructions:

> If it is necessary to employ African labour to aid the white settlers, without vexing the Africans who live on the outskirts of the colony, with whom all efforts to exist peacefully must be employed, you will request from the Governor General, any freed slaves in Luanda who have been reduced to slavery.[26]

On November 2, 1849, an article entitled "As Sociedades florescem, quando a Religião triunfa" was written and published in the *Boletim Oficial* a month later, anonymously signed "One of the Settlers." Acknowledging Lisbon's authorization for local government officials in Angola to provide basic tools and supplies to the settlers, the account reported on the interpersonal relationships that evolved during the early days of the colonization of Mossamedes, and went on to describe a portable altar that was erected in the fortress for a Roman Catholic Mass. In attendance were officials of the navy, local inhabitants and their families, the settlers all decently dressed with their slaves attired in European garb, and the African chief (*soba*) of Giraulo with members of his tribe. Music was played during the ceremony, a fanfare marked the raising of the Host and a display of fireworks followed. The description concluded: "Esteve luzido e edificante o concurso."[27] In his account of the Roman Catholic Mass, the settler suggested that the Africans with their *soba*, the settlers' slaves who were dressed in European clothing, and the officialdom of the Portuguese government all attested to the general acquiescence to European colonial norms.

The detailed instructions that accompanied the appointment from Lisbon of Major José Herculano Fereira da Horta as superintendent of the colonization project are illustrative of the ultimate benefits that it was expected to bring:

> I am confident that you have zealously devoted all of your efforts to promote the welfare and the prosperity of the said colony, to further its usefulness to the nation through the improvements that the government of His Majesty has attempted to implement in that place…[28]

Compromised Imperial Aspirations

The colonization of Mossamedes illustrates some of the longstanding practices that accompanied Portuguese colonization. Elisa Silva Andrade has observed with reference to Cape Verde that "European social and cultural traditions, dominant as they were because of colonial rule, were all adapted and transformed as a small number of Portuguese overlords lived in close proximity with a large number of slaves and *mestiços*'(Andrade 2002: 265). The close proximity of European administrators to Angolan traders and others in a slave-labor society can be contrasted with the Cape Verdean experience of coexistence. In southern Angola, the establishment of a plantation society was aimed at the production of sugarcane, cotton, and tobacco to ultimately contribute to the economic well-being of Portugal. The transcultural exchanges between colonizer and colonized that were envisioned by the optimistic settler in his published accounts of the colonization of Mossamedes proved to be incompatible with the projected ideals of a plantation economy as envisaged by the Marquis of Sá da Bandeira. One of the reasons for the failure of the development of Mossamedes was the disparity between the aims of the bureaucrats in Lisbon, powerful local merchants in Benguela and Luanda (examined in detail in the Ferreira chapter in this collection), and the inability of the settlers to execute the colonial policies in line with Sá da Bandeira's aims. Chronic tensions between those different interest groups are indicative of a lack of consensus between Europeans, prominent Luso-Africans, and African *sobas* to realize this objective.

For Clarence-Smith, following Ralph Delgado, "local societies were far from powerless, but in the last instance they had to bow to the dictates of Lisbon" (cited in Clarence-Smith 1979: 14). For Clarence-Smith, "the initiative throughout the period lay with outside forces, and in particular the Portuguese bourgeoisie in the colonial ministry in Lisbon." They shaped colonial policy after it "consolidated and entrenched its hold over the state apparatus as a result of the civil wars of the early nineteenth century"(1979: 12–14). Valentim Alexandre bases his alternative viewpoint on the economic and political realities of the time and argues that Lisbon had very little sovereignty during the second quarter of the nineteenth century: "Lisbon sovereignty was little more than nominal, with the government of the colonies being *de facto* in the hands of the dominant local interests" (2004: 11).

Research to date has not considered the African dimension of the local scenario or the African reaction to the Pernambucan colonists' appropriation of land, or the impact of this market-oriented project on communal and historical African claims to the lands. I would suggest that these processes exacerbated local European and African tensions in Mossamedes and eventually compromised the desired unity of Portuguese colonial endeavors both there and in the highlands of southern Angola. These, in turn, informed the panorama of the following decades when, according to Patrick Chabal, the state preceded the nation, creating wholly artificial nation-states with no "natural" roots or even antecedents (2000: 4).

Conclusion

In different ways, the events considered above in three Atlantic ports can be articulated with the broader conjuncture of the Portuguese Black Atlantic.

Specifically localized conflicts involving 1) Portuguese settlers in Pernambuco who became the colonizers in a different environment, 2) the colonial apparatus of the Portuguese metropolis, and 3) the colonized in Angola, attest to tension-ridden relationships rooted in the inequalities underlying Portuguese expansion in the Atlantic world, as determined to a great degree by the realities of slavery and the transatlantic slave trade. While political discussions in Portugal and Brazil centered on the implications of continuing or suspending the transatlantic slave trade, Portugal was seeking ways to safeguard its colonial relationships by developing the African possessions, ever mindful of intensifying British concerns over the institution of slavery and the British commercial interest in the burgeoning overseas trade in the South Atlantic. On both sides of the Atlantic divide, local free and nonfree agents experienced the realities of the "peculiar institution" and their silences have hindered historians from fully assessing the relationships of the Portuguese with the multidirectional movements across the South Atlantic.[29] The ethnic and racial details that have been cited in the reports and descriptions about Africans in Lisbon and in the African overseas possessions, contrast Africans as "others" and underscore the exclusivist, essentialist vision of the Portuguese for whom cultural unity, national dignity, language, and European ethnicity were the bases of nationality. Described as different and noticed as such, Africans and their descendants in Lisbon and abroad were discrete cultures that existed but were socially bypassed and collectively excluded by the limits of liberal measures and reforms intended to improve the welfare of the Portuguese and the success of the colonial enterprise. As historians reassess the dynamics of the Lusophone Black Atlantic, we need to draw attention to the agency of Africans and their descendants, beyond the spheres of music and dance and religious life, in the making of the Lusophone Black Atlantic in Portugal, in Brazil, and in the former Portuguese African possessions. To date, with the few exceptions that derive from careful historical research in Brazil and in Portuguese Africa, the dynamics of colonial relations have been mainly restricted to conflict—warfare and trade—that demand a broader matrix encompassing daily practices of diet, healing, dress, language, beliefs, leisure, social life, and family life, so as to further the exploration of the multidirectional flows involving the Lusophone Black Atlantic.

Notes

Paper presented to the conference "The Portuguese Atlantic: Africa, Brazil and Cape Verde," July 2005, Mindelo, Cape Verde.

1. The Portuguese relationship with the Atlantic, of longstanding interest to scholars of the transatlantic slave trade, remains largely ignored or overlooked in many English-language publications. In the 2004-launched journal *Atlantic Studies*, for example, despite one contributor's declared intentions to deal with the state-of-the-art of past and current research on the Atlantic, the Portuguese contribution to the Black Atlantic is largely unaddressed.. The article draws on the issues of division and unity of national identities on either side of the

Atlantic, prioritizing the North Atlantic and, specifically, studies concerning the United States. Donna Gabaccia, "A Long Atlantic in a Wider World," *Atlantic Studies* 1(1), 2004: 1–27. See also, Augusto Nascimento, "Crioulidade versus santomensidade: evolução política e processos identitários em S. Tomé e Príncipe," paper presented to the conference "The Portuguese Black Atlantic: Africa, Cape Verde and Brazil," Mindelo, Cape Verde, July 7, 2005; Malyn Newitt, "The Port City of Mindelo in the World of the South Atlantic." Paper read at the conference, The Portuguese Atlantic: Africa, Cape Verde, Brazil. Mindelo, Cape Verde, July 8, 2005.

2. See also a more detailed treatment of the relations between Mozambique and Brazil in Capela 2005: 243–258.

3. Headway into the understanding of Brazil's relationships with Portuguese Africa has been made in recent work by Roquinaldo Ferreira, who documents the predominant influence of Brazilians over the transatlantic slave trade and over transatlantic commerce in the late eighteenth century. "Atlantic Microhistories: Mobility, Personal Ties, and the Slave Trade from Angola to Brazil," unpublished paper, presented to the Center for Latin American Studies, Harvard University, April, 2006.

4. Although provinces and districts were later defined specifically as such, specific attributes to local jurisdictions were not mentioned. Biblioteca Nacional de Lisboa. *História de Portugal*. Dir. José Mattoso. Vol. 5, "O Liberalismo," (1807–1890), coord. Prof. Doutor Luís Reis Torgal Prof. Doutor João Lourenço Roque (Lisbon: Editorial Estampa), 294.

5. The construction of a popular sense of identity is taken from Marc Szuchman, *Journal of Latin American Studies* 36, 2004: 153–154.

6. For histories of Africans in Portugal, see José Ramos Tinhorão. *Os Negros em Portugal. Uma presença silenciosa* (Lisbon: Caminho, 1988).

7. A full text of the Pombaline *alvarás*, of September 19, 1761 and January 16, 1763 regarding slavery in Portugal is reproduced in Didier Lahon, *O Negro no Coração do Império. Uma memória a resgatar. Séculos XV-XIX* (Lisbon: Ministério da Educação. Entreculturas, 1999), 78–81. Lahon drew on Zurara who stated that African slaves were first introduced into the Algarve in 1444. Didier Lahon, "Black African Slaves and Freedmen in Portugal during the Renaissance: Creating a New Pattern of Reality," in T.F. Earle and K.J.P. Lowe, *Black Africans in Renaissance Europe* (Cambridge: Cambridge University Press, 2005), 261.

8. For a comprehensive evaluation of the black brotherhoods in Lisbon, see Didier Lahon, *Esclavage et Confréries Noires au Portugal durante l'Ancien Regime (1441–1830)*, unpublished doctorate thesis. EHESS, Paris, 2001.

9. "Fui obrigado a exclamar: Onde estão as ruas sujas que vira descritas, as carcaças abandonadas, os cães ferozes e as figuras de miseráveis das possessões africanas que, de barbas brancas e pele tisnada, com nauseantes doenças, por aqui se deviam arrastar? Nada disso ví e quando dessas coisas falei, responderam-me que correspondiam a uma época de há uns trinta anos, de que muitas pessoas se lembravam ainda perfeitamente." Hans Christian Andersen. *Uma visita em Portugal em 1866* (Lisboa: Instituto de Cultura e Lingua Portuguesa, 1884), 39.

10. "a vala comum continuou a existir, apesar do estabelecimento dos novos cemiterios. O negro, o escravo e o impio eram atirados para uma fossa, nem sequer vedada aos cães, que estava sempre aberta fora das portas das cidades,

a caminho de Santos. Era o Poço dos Negros. Ambos os cemiterios de Lisboa possuiam este tipo de enterramento: nos Prazeres existia um poço e no Alto de São Joao uma vala." Despite the legislation, open graves continued to exist for decades until the Camara Municipal extinguished them in 1878. Rita Mega. *A Escultura funerária do século XIX nos cemitérios de Lisboa e Porto* (monografia, Biblioteca Nacional, Lisboa), 48. João José Reis has examined popular reactions to the liberal reforms that included the secularization of cemeteries in Salvador, Bahia in the 1830s in *Death is a Festival. Funeral Rites and Rebellion in Nineteenth-Century Brazil*. Translated by H. Sabrina Gledhill (Chapel Hill: University of North Carolina Press, 2003). Lahon suggests that the origins of the Poço dos Negros date to the orders of King Manuel in the early sixteenth century to have deceased corpses of presumably unbaptized slaves placed in an enormous pit and sprinkled with quicklime to hasten the decomposition of the remains. Lahon, "Black Africans and Freedmen," 272. Regarding the secularization of cemeteries in Salvador, Bahia in the 1830s, see João José Reis. *Death is a Festival. Funeral Rites and Rebellion in Nineteenth-Century Brazil*. Translated by H. Sabrina Gledhill. University of North Carolina, Chapel Hill, 2003.

11. "a mania politica tem acommettido todos os habitantes da capital, desde o fidalgo e o par do reino até as f.... da plebe. Apenas os pobres pretos das possessões portuguezas da Africa, que passeiam aos milhares pelas ruas de Lisboa são os unicos que nao discutem em politica, ao menos segundo me consta; mas tambem nao são tractados como homens pelos portuguezes, porem como uma raça ruim de animaes domesticos. Caiam durante o ardor do sol as paredes exteriores das casas, e no fim das corridas de touros, lançam-se contra a furia exacerbada d' aquelles animaes. Quando chegam a envelhecer, arrastem-se mendigando pelas ruas de Lisboa, contaminados de enfermidades nauseabundos, com barbas encanecideas, que produzem um effeito hediondo nos seus rostos negros." Biblioteca Nacional do Rio de Janeiro. Secção de Obras Raras. Principe Lichnowsky. *Portugal. Recordações do Anno de 1842* (Lisboa: Imprensa Nacional, 1845), 59.

12. "vestido de branco aglomeravam-se no Rossio onde os iam contratar para os trabalhos de caiar." A popular saying illustrates the marginal status of the *caiador*: "Hey, don't bother me, go paint the roof of the Rossio!" The popular saying: "Olha, não me chateias, vai mais é pintar o tecto do Rossio!" Calderon Dinis. *Tipos e Factos da Lisboa do Meu Tempo* (Lisboa: Dom Quixote, 1986), 198.

13. Uday Mehta, "Liberal Strategies of Exclusion," in Frederick Cooper and Ann Laura Stoler, eds. *Tensions of Empire: Colonial Cultures in a Bourgeois World* (Berkeley: University of California Press, 1997), 59–86, quoted in Zine Magubane. *Bringing the Empire Home. Race, Class, and Gender in Britain and in Colonial South Africa* (Chicago: University of Chicago Press, 2004), 6, 96.

14. "O fado era destinada a dividir em Portugal no século XVIII com as danças da fofa e do lundu – estas importadas do Brasil, mas com ela aparentadas – o brio das mais populares formas rítmico-coreograficas do povo miúdo (e logo da incipiente classe média), antecipadores daquela que, sob o nome de fado, viria no século XIX realizar a sua síntese, passando da taberna às salas, para virar canção." Tinhorão dates the appearance of the Creole-Brazilian lundu in Lisbon to the end of the 1770s.

15. "Powerful connections linked the habits of Africans with the popular beliefs of the popular classes of Portugal." See also Thomaz 2000: 135.

16. "Efectivamente, a verificação de que África e Brasil estavam presentes na plateia significava dar relevo, não às reacções deste ou daquele espectador, mas sim a um processo de aculturação que emprestava certos traços ao comportamento de massa durante o espectáculo." (Vieira de Carvalho 1993: 98).

17. The German visitor, Gustav von Heeringen, who arrived in Lisbon in 1836 as part of Fernando de Saxe-Coburg's entourage, commented that in Lisbon's popular venues: "Brasil e Africa estão presentes na plateia" ("Brazil and Africa are visible in the audience"). Gustav von Heeringen, *Meine Reise nach Portugal in Frühjahr* 1836. 2 vols. (Leipzig: Brockhaus, 1838). 144; (cited in Vieira de Carvalho 1993: 98). Tinhorão also claims that the popular Teatro was dominated by blacks (1994: 35).

18. "A luta há pouco acabada contra o usurpador (Miguel I) terminando o espectáculo com a vitória do herói – o rei liberal Pedro – e uns fogos de artifício" (Carvalho 2000: 99).

19. Omar Thomaz cites Eça de Queiroz, Herculano, Júlio Diniz, and Camilo Castelo Branco among the Portuguese writers who viewed the empire as something of the past and made the Portuguese returnees from Brazil the object of their ridicule. (2000: 49).

20. "…alguns dos que, na década de 1820, propunham o fim do tráfico faziam no no pressuposto de que a esse fim corresponderia um reforço da escravidão em Africa para que a mão-de-obra negra, dirigida pela inteligência europeia, pudesse alimenta r o sonhado desenvolvimento de *novos Brasis*." "As Cortes perante o problema de escravidão (1836–1875)," *Análise Social* 36(158/159), 2001: 215.

21. W.G. Clarence-Smith argues that from 1870, the initial phase of colonial revenue collection changed to one that established protectionist tariffs to *preserve* the colonial markets under Portuguese control (1979: 12).

22. "criar um 'novo Brasil' na África [que] implicava transformar os territórios deste continente reivindicados por Portugal em colónias produtoras de matérias-primas e importadoras de manufaturas da metrópole."

23. On July 13, 1848, Figueiredo Abreu e Castro sent a communication to the Secretario de Estado dos Negocios da Marinha e Ultramar in Lisbon (cited in Padrão n.d.: 63).

24. The minister, José Joaquim Gomes de Castro through Portaria 2063 of October 26, 1848, concerned over German interest in Southern Angola, supported the endeavor. Cited in Padrão n.d: 65.

25. 10-04-1849. Rainha, D. Maria II decree to Governador do Distrito to nominate Cap. Ten. De Armada António Sergio de Sousa. Cited in Cerviño Padrão, p.67.

26. "Se para ajuda dos braços dos brancos for necessário o emprego dos braços dos pretos, V. Senhoria, fugindo quanto possível de vexar o gentio limítrofe à colónia com quem alias fará sempre todas as diligências para viver em boa harmonia, requisitará do respectivo Governador Geral, quaesquer libertos que em Loanda tenham sido subtraídos à escravatura." Visconde de Castro, Sec. Do Estado do Ultramar to António Sérgio de Sousa. Cited in Padrão n.d: 67.

27. Biblioteca Nacional de Lisboa. *Boletim Oficial do Governo Geral da Provincia de Angola* 220, December 15, 1849: 3. The *Boletim Oficial de Angola* was

first published in 1845 as an official organ but also published literary pieces and essays, and travel accounts of exploration of the interior of Angola. See Fernando Augusto Albuquerque Mourão. *A Sociedade Angolana através da Literatura* (São Paulo: Atica, 1978), 15.

28. "Confio em que V. Senhoria dedicava toda a sua actividade e zelo a promover o melhor bem para a dita colónia e a sua prosperidade, para que assim V. Senhoria se torne mais útil à nação a que pertence e às vistas de melhoramentos que o Governo de Sua Majestade tem intentado levar a efeito náquelle ponto…" Arquivos de Angola. Offício do Governo Geral de 9 –IV-1849, ao Min. De Marinha e Ultramar, cited in Cerviño Padrão, 66.

29. In Brazil, the issue of emancipation figured in the violent confrontations between slaves and masters in the Cabanagem movement in 1835–1840, in the Balaiada movement in Maranhão and Piauí from 1838–1841, and in a slave revolt in Vassouras in the coffee-producing Centre-South in 1846. Slave emancipation, despite external pressures from Great Britain and France at mid-century, would not begin to gain momentum until the 1860s.

Bibliography

Alencastro, Luiz Felipe de. 2000. *O Trato dos Viventes. Formação do Brasil no Atlântico Sul Séculos XVI e XVIII.* São Paulo: Companhia das Letras.

———. 2004. "Continental Drift: The Independence of Brazil (1822), Portugal and Africa," in Olivier Pétré-Grenouilleau, ed. *From Slave Trade to Empire. Europe and the Colonisation of Black Africa 1780s–1880s.* London: Routledge.

Alexandre, Valentim. 2004. "The Portuguese Empire, 1825–1890: Development and Economics," in Olivier Pétré-Grenouilleau, ed. *From Slave Trade to Empire. Europe and the Colonisation of Black Africa, 1780s–1880s.* London: Routledge.

Andrade, Elisa Silva. 2002. "Cabo Verde" in Patrick Chabal, David Birmingham, Joshua Forrest, and Malyn Newitt. *A History of Postcolonial Lusophone Africa.* London: Hurst and Company.

Baillie, Marianne. 1825. *Lisbon in the Years 1821, 1822, and 1823.* Lisbon: John Murray, Albemarle Street, vol. 1.

Capela, José. 2005. "Mozambique and Brazil: Cultural and Political Interferences through the Slave Trade," in José C. Curto and Renée Soulodre-La France, eds. *Africa and the Americas: Interconnections during the Slave Trade.* Trenton, NJ: Africa World Press, Inc.

Carneiro da Cunha, Manuela. 1984. *Negros Estrangeiros. Os escravos libertos e sua volta à Africa.* São Paulo: Brasiliense.

Catroga, Fernando. 1988. "A militância laica e a Descristianização da Morte em Portugal," in José Mattoso, ed. *História de Portugal (1865–1911).* Lisboa: Coimbra.

Chabal, Patrick, David Birmingham, Joshua Forrest, and Malyn Newitt. 2000. *A History of Postcolonial Lusophone Africa.* London: Hurst and Company.

Clarence-Smith, W.G. 1979. *Slaves, Peasants and Capitalists in Southern Angola 1840–1926.* Cambridge: Cambridge University Press.

———. 1985. *The Third Portuguese Empire, 1825–1975. A Study in Economic Imperialism.* Manchester: University of Manchester Press.

Curto, José C. 2004. *Enslaving Spirits. The Portuguese Brazilian Alcohol Trade at Luanda and its Hinterland, c.1550–1830.* Leiden: Brill.

Curto, José C. and Renée Soulodre-La France, ed. 2000. *Africa and the Americas: Interconnections during the Slave Trade.* Africa Trenton, NJ: World Press, Inc., 243–258.

Delgado, Ralph. 1948–1953. *História de Angola*. 4 vols. Benguela: Edição da Tipografia, do Jornal de Benguela.

Fryer, Peter. 2000. *Rhythms of Resistance. African Musical Heritage in Brazil*. London: Pluto.

Guran, Milton. 2000. *Os Agudás. Os "brasileiros" do Benim*. Rio de Janeiro: Nova Fronteira/Universidade de Gama Filho.

Karasch, Mary. 1987. *Slave Life in Rio de Janeiro 1808–1850*. Princeton: Princeton University Press.

Mann, Kirstin and Edna G. Bay, ed. 2001. *Rethinking the African Diaspora. The Making of a Black Atlantic World in the Bight of Benin and Brazil*. London: Frank Cass.

Marques, João Pedro. 2001. "As Cortes perante o problema da escravidão (1836–1875)." *Análise Social* 36(158/159): 209–247.

———. 1998. *Os Sons do Silêncio. O Portugal de Oitocentos e a Abolição do Tráfico de Escravos*. Dissertação de doutoramento em História, Universidade Nova de Lisboa.

Mega, Rita. n.d. "A escultura funerária do século XIX nos cemitérios de Lisboa e Porto" (monograph) Biblioteca Nacional Lisboa.

Miller, Joseph. 1988. *Way of Death. Merchant Capitalism and the Angolan Slave Trade 1730–1830*. Madison: University of Wisconsin Press.

Padrão, F. Cervino.n.d. *A colonização do Sul de Angola. 1485–1974*.

Patterson, Tiffany Ruby, and Robin D.G. Kelley. 2000. "Unfinished Migrations: Reflections on the African Diaspora and the Making of the Modern World." *African Studies Review* 43(1), Special Issue on the Diaspora: 11–45.

Pétré-Grenouilleau, Olivier, ed. 2004. *From Slave Trade to Empire. Europe and the Colonisation of Black Africa. 1780s –1880s*. London: Routledge.

Russell-Wood, A.J.R. 2002. *Slavery and Freedom in Colonial Brazil*. Oxford: One World.

Schultz, Kirsten. 2001. *Tropical Versailles. Empire, Monarchy, and the Portuguese Royal Court in Rio de Janeiro, 1808–1821*. London: Routledge.

Shepherd, Verene. 2004. "Unity and Disunity: Creolization and Marronage in the Atlantic World: Conceptualizing Atlantic Studies," in *Atlantic Studies* 1(1), April: 49–55.

Thomaz, Omar Ribeiro. 2000. *Ecos do Atlântico Sul*. Rio de Janeiro: Editora da Universidade Federal do Rio de Janeiro and FAPESP.

Tinhorão, José Ramos. 1994. *Fado, Dança do Brasil, Cantos de Lisboa*. Lisboa: Editorial Caminho.

Turner, Michael Jerry. 1975. "Les Brésiliens—The Impact of Former Brazilian Slaves upon Dahomey." Unpublished PhD Dissertation, Boston University.

Vieira de Carvalho, Mário. 1993. *Pensar é Morrer ou O Teatro de São Carlos na mudança do sistema sócio comunicativo desde fins do século XVIII aos nossos dias*. Lisboa: Imprensa Nacional, Casa da Moeda.

Wheeler, Douglas and René Pelissier. 1971. *Angola*. London: Pall Mall Press.

Chapter 6

Agudás from Benin: "Brazilian" Identity as a Bridge to Citizenship

Milton Guran

"Are you a Brazilian? So, you are not a foreigner in Benin: you are like a relative of Uidá!" I heard this everywhere I went in Benin. In this area of Western Africa, Portuguese was the trade language when the French colonial administration was established at the end of the nineteenth century. Even today Agudá people greet one another with a loud "*como passou?*" (How are you doing?). As in Bahia, Nossa Senhora do Bonfim is celebrated in January. In Porto Novo, one of the cities of Benin in which the presence of the "Brazilians" is most marked, the celebration begins with a true carnival procession in which everybody wears a special costume and two great Brazilian flags open the parade. People sing songs in a particular kind of Portuguese (also in Yoruba, Fon, or Gum[1]) reaffirming the Brazilian origins of this festival. The celebration of Bonfim is completed by the performance of *bourian*, a popular show that is simply an African version of the *burrinha*, an old festival that was very popular in late-nineteenth-century Bahia (in its original form it has now almost disappeared).

The old African Slave Coast, especially Benin, is probably unique as an example of Brazilian cultural implantation that developed its own independent existence[2] without a direct connection to Brazil. The Brazilian presence was so marked in this area during the eighteenth and nineteenth centuries that it could certainly be characterized as a type of informal colonization. It was mainly through the Brazilians that this area had systematic access to manufactured goods, such as firearms, and to Portuguese, a language of universal expression.

It is noteworthy that the capital of Benin (home to the national parliament) still retains the Portuguese denomination of Porto Novo, rather than its two traditional names. Known as Hogbonou or Adjacè (a name used by the many Yoruban residents) Porto Novo was once the center of the old kingdom of Adja de Ardes. The city, which offered excellent opportunities for the expansion of the Portuguese slave trade, was "discovered" in 1745 by Echaristis Campos. Campos, a Portuguese who had settled in Brazil, called it simply Porto Novo, a name that pleased the king who adopted it. Some years later, the "Brazilian" João de Oliveira, a slave trader and former slave from Brazil, settled there, permanently connecting the kingdom of Adja with Bahia (Verger 1968: 194). "Brazilians" began to settle in the city and for more than a century played a special role in the political, economic, and religious life of the kingdom. Porto Novo, also known as the "Brazilian Dream" (Tidjani-Serpos and Caffe 1993), has become the preeminent example of the cultural contribution made by returned former slaves. This important patrimony is exemplified by the Brazilian architecture in Benin.

In economic terms the "Brazilians" contributed significantly to the development of agriculture and trade in this area of the Gulf of Benin. Pierre Verger (1968: 611) cites an edition of March 1, 1882, of the *Journal Officiel des Etablissements Français du Golfe du Benin*, "7 of 25 dealers (wholesalers) established in the country (the old French colony of Daomé) were 'Brazilians' and that 78 of 154 merchants (retailers) were also 'Brazilians'; in other words, a third of the dealers and half of the merchants."

In 1845–1846 the English traveler John Duncan vividly described his impression of the level of organization attained by the "emancipated Brazilian" community in the report of his journey:[3]

> The Portuguese part of Whydah excels, in every sense of the word, both the English and the French. This I consider attributable to their superiority in the knowledge of agriculture and domestic economy and comfort of those returned slaves. Great numbers of them have small farms in a very fair state of cultivation; and they are much more cleanly in their habits and person than those who have never left their native country as slaves. They also live in comfort and plenty, and occupy good and well-furnished houses, while the latter are wallowing in dirty wretchedness, ignorance and poverty. ([1847], 1968: 138–139)

He continues:

> They are by far the most industrious people I have found. Several very fine farms, about six or seven miles from Whydah, are in a high state of cultivation. The houses are clean and comfortable, and are situated in some of the most beautiful spots that imagination can picture. It is truly gratifying to find unexpectedly a house where you are welcomed in European fashion, and asked to take refreshment. I invariably found upon inquiry that all these people had been slaves. This would seem to prove that to this country slavery is not without its good as well as bad effects. ([1847], 1968: 185–186)

Undoubtedly Mr. Duncan's own prejudices shape his consideration of what he witnessed. His conclusions seem to be permeated by a certain ethnocentrism. However, he provides us with valuable information about what he observed and gives us an idea of the social and economic characteristics of the area at the time.

The political importance of the Brazilian presence in Benin from the beginning of the nineteenth century is reflected in the history of the area's most powerful Bahian slave trader, Dom Francisco Felix de Souza. After helping Prince Gapké, future king Guêzo, to deprive his brother Adandozan of the throne in 1818, Souza became viceroy with the title of Chachá.[4]

At this time the majority of white residents in the country were either Brazilian or Portuguese traders, and were principally involved in the slave trade. However, the human landscape was profoundly altered when there was an increase in the numbers of returning former slaves from Brazil who were deported for participating in the great slave revolt of 1835 in Bahia. A significant number of former slaves found their way back to their ancestral land from Brazil for various reasons until the beginning of the last century. Once in Africa, these former slaves, who were originally of different backgrounds, organized themselves socially according to their experiences in Brazil and became assimilated into the already established Brazilian community. Today the descendants of both former slaves and free Brazilians are known as "the Brazilians," or, in the local language, as Agudás.

In some senses, to be "Brazilian" in Benin today is similar to being Yoruba, Fon, or Mina. Being "Brazilian" implies an ethnic differentiation and constitutes a social identity alongside the groups that make up the nation state of Benin. Contemporary Benin owes its composition to the designs of European colonial geopolitics and as such unites several ethnic groups. The country is defined[5] as a "youthful nation composed of twenty social groups that, from a linguistic and cultural perspective, generated homogeneous entities which have a territorial base: in the southwest: Adja, Xwatchi, Gen, Xwéda, Xwla;—in the south: Fon, Toli, Toffin;—in the southeast: Gum and Yoruba; in the center: Yoruba, Fon, Mahi;—in the north and northeast: Botombu, Dendim Fulbe; in the northwest: Betamaribe, Waaba, Yowa." According to this account "Brazilians" do not constitute a "social and cultural" group. They do not possess a language (the use of Portuguese disappeared following the imposition of French during colonization) or their own territory. However, they do possess a distinctive social status, a fact demonstrated by the greeting cited in the introductory sentence of this text. Most obviously, they are easily recognized by last names that are of Portuguese origin. Unfortunately, there is no way to know their accurate numbers but it is thought that they constitute no less than 5 percent of the total population of the country, considering that women lose their last name when they marry (as do their children).

Given that the descendants of Brazilians and former Brazilian slaves maintained no familial, political, or administrative relationships with Brazil for almost a century, it is worth considering how they preserved their distinctive ethnic identity and why they were not incorporated into the groups that constitute the rest of Benin's population.

Upon returning to Africa, a former slave from Brazil would no longer be the same person he had been before becoming a slave. He was no longer somebody's son or husband, the native of a certain village, or the subject of a particular king. Indeed, all his family and social ties were destroyed by slavery making him a sort of generic African, to employ Darcy Ribeiro's term to describe detribalized Indians in Brazil (1995: 318).

There are also numerous instances of those who were sold into slavery by members of their own family or by rival political factions. In such cases returned African slaves would avoid or be prevented from reestablishing themselves in their native village. As Kátia de Queiroz Mattoso explains (1982: 30), "it was a custom to marginalize the village troublemakers, those who broke the community's laws by theft or adultery. Equally marginalized were the children who were seen to be nothing but hungry mouths, difficult to feed in periods of crisis; those who were in debt, or even those who were due for service in battle; and children who were not potential heirs to the throne."[6]

The most famous example of this practice is that of king Guêzo's mother who was sold by Adandozan (Verger 1953, et Hazoumé 1937: 31). During my research I was able to substantiate several similar cases illustrated by the following. Mrs. Amélia Sossah (née Olympio), youngest sister of Sylvanus Olympio (Togo's first President), explains how marginalization was experienced by the populations of the old Slave Coast.[7] "People here did not realize at the time of slavery, that there was so much suffering across the ocean," she continues. "There were parents who gave their children to the traders. They said: 'if you are not obedient, I will sell you to the whites,' believing that the child would return well behaved, with a different upbringing and culture that would honor them. The fathers gave away their stubborn children, those who stole or who were recalcitrant: 'I make you a present of my son'. Unfortunately the children never returned. Although the parents hoped that their children would come back to relieve their suffering, they were, in fact, sending them away to suffer."

According to Mr. Hilário Bandeira,[8] a resident of Lomé, Togo, conflicts among families seem to have been very frequent:

> The fact is that our grandfather who came from Brazil with the name of Bandeira was not Brazilian. You heard correctly. He was not Brazilian. We came from Savalou.[9] We are Mahis. His village was Mokpa. You know that sometimes there are disputes between the families. If somebody is clever they try to marginalize him. Why? Because of inheritance. If he is clever, he can take everything or almost everything from those who are less gifted. So, they eliminate this clever person. This is what happened with our ancestor.

In fact, whether sold or given away, those individuals who had been sent into slavery—and were therefore already excluded—were subsequently alienated from the native social structure. They were different from the others, they dressed as white people, ate with silverware, and were self-proclaimed Catholics (in most cases) or Muslims. They were bricklayers, joiners, carpenters, tailors, and merchants in the capitalist sense that these terms suggest. They were frequently literate and considered themselves modern and progressive in the face of a society that they saw as primitive and savage. Nevertheless, despite their "white lifestyle" they continued to be seen as slaves.

Ethnic identity is built upon difference (Poutignat and Streiff-Fenart, 1995: 41), or to put it another way, in relation to the Other. As Manuela Carneiro da Cunha suggests (1985: 206), "what we have achieved with the study of ethnicity was precisely the notion that identity is constructed situationally and through contrast, in other words, that identity constitutes a political answer to a certain conjuncture, an answer that articulates with the other identities, with which it forms a system." The construction of identity is based upon a strategy of valorizing differences. In this respect it is clear that the returned former slaves considered the native population to be savages, whereas they continued to be seen as slaves imitating a "white lifestyle." The only things that the former slaves (Yoruba, Fon, Mina, and others) had in common were slavery in Brazil, the Portuguese language, a "white lifestyle," and their Catholicism. Thus they identified and established alliances with white people (the Brazilians who had been established for so long on the coast) and in turn were themselves regarded as "Brazilians."

On the basis of their common life experience in Brazil, the former slaves were assimilated to the Agudás (as the established Brazilians were known in the region) and shared their place in local society. Above all, this experience allowed them to occupy positions of authority higher than those of common laborers in the local economy. When the confrontation between traditional culture and expanding capitalism intensified in the region, they were able to assume a central role in driving the economy alongside merchants and Brazilian traders. The latter groups welcomed them warmly and employed them to develop their businesses. The meeting of these two groups (one composed of merchants and Brazilian or Portuguese traders and the other of the returned former slaves) created the profile of the Agudá community as we see it today. In this community, we encounter the haughtiness of high-ranking slaves (a condition that most of them only acquired once they returned to Africa) and the customs they acquired in Brazil.

One of the most important features in the study of this social group is the unique way that these former slaves incorporated themselves into a society that had excluded them. Whereas they were freed slaves in Brazil, in Africa most of the population considered them to be slaves. It was precisely in their condition as slaves, or in other words, in the experience of slavery in Brazil, that they sought out the foundations of a new collective identity. This identity granted them a social and economic purpose and gave them full citizenship in the very society that had rejected them.

Social origin, religion, and language are usually considered to be the principal foundations for the constitution of an ethnic group. In fact, to integrate into the local society, the former slaves valued their "former life" in Brazil—the only factor that was common to a group of people with different ethnic origins. Life as a slave was common to the group of people and is in the author's words a former life to the one they found in Africa. It was as if slavery was taken as the starting point for a new life, chosen as the new mythical point of common origin. The culture acquired in Brazil thus propelled the process of identity formation.

As we have seen, the integration of former slaves into the broader society as citizens took place through their identification with the members of the Brazilian colony who called themselves Agudás. Slave traders and former slaves overcame the contradiction of their original social status to constitute a single social group powerful enough to consolidate the economic and social advantages that had already been acquired by their Brazilian predecessors.

To be an Agudá nowadays in Benin is to share a common memory relating to a set of achievements and to a specific way of being "Brazilian." To gain a greater understanding of this situation, we can divide the process by which this social identity was constructed into three successive periods.

The first begins in the initial years of the nineteenth century when the presence of the Brazilian *negreiros* (slave ships) on the Slave Coast of Africa intensified. At this time the Bahians did everything to undermine the increasing restrictions placed on the transatlantic slave trade. They maintained commercial and political relations with the natives with whom they were in some respects related by way of marriage. Their numbers were small despite their economic and political importance. They prospered and lived according to their own culture. They were white in a black society, their mixed-race children were considered white like their parents, and were known as Agudás, a designation that had been used for several generations.

A second important juncture is the arrival of large numbers of former slaves in 1835. They were black but they had "white habits." They discriminated against the natives who they considered "savages." At the same time they were rejected by these natives for whom they would always be excluded as "slaves."

The subject of slavery, practically absent from schoolbooks and very frequently played down in the erudite works of the old kingdom of Dahomey, is always present in the social and personal relationships of the Agudás. In fact, as underlined by Claude Meillassoux (1986: 107), "the capture (or the purchase that presupposes the capture) marks the slaves with an unforgettable stigma." For centuries the slave trade drove the local economy where slavery had been a long-standing institution. As such it is not surprising that the label of former slave continues to be a means of discrimination in relations amongst the Agudás and between them and other groups.

All of the "Brazilians" with whom I conversed during my research said that they had been pointed at and called "slaves" in various situations. This is practically commonplace in the context of the school and the market. In contrast, in their private lives, as the Agudá historian François de Medeiros explains, "there is a tacit agreement to not speak about their slave origins."[10] It is precisely this agreement that has held the "Brazilians" together as a unit since they began to construct their new ethnic identity. However on the basis of my close association with the Agudá families, I can suggest that the stigma of slavery may be deeper than it appears.

Uniting these former Brazilian slaves was the common memory of a social experience. This memory translated itself into a way of life, a personality, and also into a professional qualification in accordance with the new European cultural and economic parameters that were increasingly being imposed on the country. They used "white peoples'" surnames and they assumed the culture of the "white man" (acquired in Brazil). This culture was a considerable advantage allowing them to associate with Bahian slave traders and to engage in modern economic activity. These activities, originally based on the slave trade, developed into a more varied international and local trade and into the production and exploitation of local resources such as palm oil (*dendê*).

In the eyes of Benin society, they would always have the lifestyle of the "white man." They were self-proclaimed Catholics and they spoke Portuguese. Together with the native slaves in their service their numbers were increasing and they were also acquiring a more significant position in the demography of the area. They formed a community of their own, in which the original white men and their mestizo descendants were a type of elite. During the second half of the nineteenth century they constituted an endogamous[11] society and constructed a social identity around that of the first Brazilians. They created schools in which the children learned to read and write in Portuguese, whilst the subjects of Abomé were forbidden from attending the classes.

The Agudás—composed of the descendants of slave traders, returned slaves, their descendants and their slaves—were behind practically all modern economic activity and were responsible for the penetration of Western culture into the area. In fact, at that time they represented the future, since their "European culture" (their so-called "white lifestyle") was eventually imposed on other groups.

If we examine the Agudá culture of this second period more closely, we can see that it is different from that of the first Brazilians. Whilst there are cultural transformations, the main change that takes place among the Agudás is the social change. The slave traders from Bahia were white, and their difference from the native people allowed them to create their own space in the autochthonous society. Their place was assured by their economic alliance with the king of Daomé and expressed symbolically by the role of Chachá and other Brazilians who occupied positions within the local power structure.

The former returned slaves were forced to create a place for themselves in a society that did not accept them. They had not only been expelled—sold as slaves—but they returned as foreigners with "white ways." The construction of a new social identity based upon their experiences of Brazil functioned as a means of integration, allowing them to occupy a space that had already been established for the whites. The notion of "foreigner"—as explained by Meillassoux (1986: 105)—"is common to all African populations. It is usually opposed to the notion of 'man', in other words to the concepts of 'citizen' or 'patrician', a person who possesses all the prerogatives of that social environment.... The foreigner must be the responsibility of a protector somebody who will testify in his favor in the society in which he wishes to reside (one initial bond that allows the formation of others). Without this protection the foreigner is isolated and condemned to servitude." In the situation being analyzed here, it is exactly this "Brazilian" identity, already endorsed by king Guêzo (through his pact with Dom Francisco) and by other potentates, that guarantees the effectiveness of the former returned slaves' strategy of social inclusion.

They become Agudás, but not exactly like their predecessors. It is true that their masters provided a model and that they had adopted a culture that was very similar to that of the original Agudás. But they had also brought to Africa a particular culture developed in Brazil by common people and slaves. As such, most visible indicators of "Brazilian" identity (except with regard to architecture and the presentation of the self) are practices that are more associated with slaves than with their masters in Brazil. Such is the case with *feijoada* (originally a slave staple of black beans that was transformed into a Brazilian national dish), the celebration of *Nosso Senhor do Bonfim* (originally an African and Creole celebration in Bahia that has become a popular celebration), and the *burrinha* (a popular form of folklore that was never truly practiced by the elites). From its original proximity to a European model, the Agudá culture was acquiring features of a truly Brazilian culture.

Although the French colonial presence imposed "white ways" upon the entire country, the cultural option of the Africans from Brazil was preserved. The ones who had departed as slaves returned as masters and owners of the culture that was being imposed in the country. It is at this time that the opposition between the notions of "civilization/modernity" and "primitivism/ savagery" acquires new outline with the incorporation of the former slaves into the local society.

Contemporary Benin is the third important stage in understanding the identity of the Agudás in Benin. Today the memory of the time spent in Brazil has given way to the memory of their accomplishments in Benin. In the same way that the original memory allowed the inclusion of these returned slaves' into local society, this second memory also has a precise social function. In fact, the opposition between "slaves, imported people/ savages" continues in the daily politics of social interaction. With reference to the memory of their accomplishments ("we made everything in this country...") the "Brazilians" defend the legitimacy of their position in contemporary Benin.

The relationship between the Agudás and the French administration produced several configurations. The "Brazilians" were primarily allies of France and used as middlemen in relations with autochthonous groups. From the installation of the protectorate of Porto Novo in 1861, they supported France against Great Britain (Costa and Silva, 1989a: 61–62). The great families of Porto Novo participated directly with France in the war against Behanzin. Ignacio Paraíso, the most important Agudá of Porto Novo and the only African to have a seat on the Colony's Council from its inception. Several other "Brazilians" were employed directly by the French administration at several levels (Sanvi 1977). In a certain sense, the "Brazilians" still play the role of middlemen today (with slight variations). In fact, they cannot affirm their Agudá identity since they have established alliances with other ethnic groups through marriage, a circumstance that integrates them into the core of large extended families and clearly illustrates their new status as middlemen.

However, beginning with the French occupation of the country the "Brazilians" were being progressively squeezed out of the more profitable economic activities; firstly from the wholesale trade, and subsequently from small trade and the retail sector, both of which were monopolized by French companies. The most well-established Agudá merchants were forced into bankruptcy.

The social and political influence of the "Brazilians" truly begins to decline from 1946 onward when the political and economic life of Benin changes radically with the implementation of a new political system that provided representation in the Territorial Assembly and in the French National Assembly. As one of Benin's historians Karl Emmanuel Augustt explains:[12] "Brazilians and the mestiços in general, seen as having assimilated to the colonial administration, were dislodged from power." This trend became more marked at the time of independence when the Agudás, already traditionally considered to be foreigners, were widely seen as allies of France. Another historian from Benin, Professor Adrien Djivo, summarizes the situation thus: "They were accused of having helped the whites, and from the outset they were on the same side as the white people."

The democratization process initiated in 1989 in Benin was linked to a movement that reevaluated the traditional leaderships, voodoo cults, and other religious manifestations. Examples of this included the international festival of the arts and of the voodoo cultures "Ouidah 92" that took place in January 1993 (Tall 1995a, 1995b), and the institution of the national voodoo cult day that was also to be commemorated in January. The crowning of Honoré de Souza as Chachá VIII in October 1995, twenty-six years after his predecessor's death was a reflection of this shift toward valorizing the traditional political leadership.

The analysis of the process by which the ethnic identity of the Agudás is constructed in Benin allows us to understand the part they played in the transition from a traditional society to the constitution of a "modern" state. It is in this sense that, in my opinion, we have to evaluate the breadth of their contribution in cultural, economic, and social terms.

It is important to emphasize that this "bricolage" of a new ethnic identity allowed the social inclusion of the returned former slaves as citizens with full civil rights. In fact, this inclusion was possible because African society as a whole was undergoing a process of evolution that enabled the Agudás to contribute with their own culture. Furthermore, we can say that the admission of this excluded group was absolutely necessary in making this process possible and more effective. Firstly, the Agudás were the "bridge" between traditional African societies and Western culture, and they soon became the representatives of the natives to the colonial power. Mixed and overlapping with traditional cultures by way of marriage, always existing between several cultures, they continue to perform their role as a bridge between the different native ethnic groups. They continue to be seen and to see themselves as the principal actors in the process of constructing a modern Benin.

Notes

I analyze the process of the construction of the social identity of the Agudás from Benin more thoroughly in the book *Agudás—os "brasileiros" do Benin,* Rio de Janeiro: Ed. Nova Fronteira/Ed. Gama Filho, 2000. See also Almeida Prado (1954), Braga (1968, 70), Castro (1965), Costa e Silva (1989a, b, c, 1994), Cunha (1985a, b), Freyre (1990), Rodrigues (1962), Rossi (1965), Turner (1975), Verger (1953a, 1968, 1992). This article was translated by Alexandre Leite Souza Farias (researcher and translator of Mokiti Okada Foundation and of the Instituto de Humanidades - UCAM). Revision by Daniel Stone, King's College London.

1. Fon or Fongbè is the language of Abomey (the most commonly spoken in the country), and Gum is the language spoken in Porto Novo.
2. Brazilians and former slaves who had returned from Brazil were found throughout the Gulf of Benin, stretching from the city of Lagos (in Nigeria) to Accra (in Ghana), home to the Tabon community (which is distinct from the other groups analyzed here). This article focuses on the region that is now the Republic of Benin.
3. Travel in Western Africa (1845–1846), 2 vol., London, 1847, Tome I p. 200, quote by Verger (1968: 604) These citations were translated into Portuguese. The editors have reproduced the original English from the republished account, John Duncan. *Travel in Western Africa in 1845 &1846, Comprising a Journey from Whydah, through the Kingdom of Dahomy, to Adofoodia, in the interior.* Vol. 1.
4. For a more complete version of the Chachá history see Costa e Silva (2004).
5. Le Bénin et la Route de L' Esclave, published by the comité national pour le Bénin from the project "A rota dos escravos" (UNESCO), Cotonou, 1992: 17–18.
6. Era hábito livrar-se dos 'cabeças quentes' das aldeias, os que infringiam as leis da comunidade, dando-se ao roubo ou cometendo adultério; eram igualmente vendidas as crianças consideradas 'bocas' inúteis, difíceis de alimentar em períodos de crise, ou os endividados e ainda os vencidos de guerra que com freqüência se livravam dos irmãos nascidos de mães diferentes, por ocasião da morte do rei seu pai.
7. Interview with Mrs. Amélia Sossah, Lomé (June 29, 1995).
8. Compiled by his nephew Priest Augusto Bandeira in Lomé (February 12, 1996) and translated from Mina by Simplice Dako.
9. Departement of the City of Zou (in the southwest of Benin) which borders on Togo.
10. Interview with François de Medeiros (June 28, 1996 in Paris).
11. Elisée Reclus in his work of 1887 observes that "in the colored families (Agudá) the flesh and blood marriages, even between brothers and sisters from different mothers were very common and the community is not opposed to it" (quoted by Verger 1953: 12). Among the twenty daughters of Dom

Francisco F. de Souza, listed by Souza (1992), eleven were married to Agudás in their first or second marriage. We can verify many cases of this kind of marriage: four children with uncles or cousins, three children with nephews, seven with brothers, and one between father and daughter.

12. Interview with K.E. Augustt (September 4, 1995 in Cotonu).

Bibliography

Almeida Prado, J.F. [1950] 1954. "Les relations de Bahia (Brésil) avec le Dahomey," in *Revue d'Histoire des Colonies*, Tomo XLI, segundo trimestre, pp. 167–226. Paris. (Translated in *Revista do Instituto Histórico e Geográfico Brasileiro*)

Braga, Júlio Santana. 1968. "Notas sobre o 'Quartier Brésil' no Daomé," in *Afro-Ásia*, 6–7: 55–72. Salvador, Bahia: Centro de Estudos Afro-Asiáticos/UFBA.

Castro, Yêda Pessoa de. 1965. "Notícia de uma pesquisa em África." *Afro-Ásia* 1. Salvador, Bahia: Centro de Estudos Afro-Asiáticos/UFBA: 41–57.

Costa e Silva, Alberto. 1989a. "As relações entre o Brasil e a África Negra, de 1922 à primeira guerra mundial," in *O vício da África e outros vícios*, op. cit., pp. 25–65.

———. 1989b. "Os habitantes brasileiros de Lagos," in *O vício da África e outros vícios*, op. cit., pp. 13–18.

———. 1989c. "Os sobrados brasileiros de Lagos." *O vício da África e outros vícios*. Lisboa: Ed. João Sá da Costa, pp. 9–12.

———. 1994. "O Brasil, a África e o Atlântico no século XIX." *Studia* 52: 195–220.

———. 2003. *Um rio chamado Atlântico*. Rio de Janeiro: Nova Fronteira.

———. 2004. *Francisco Felix de Souza, mercador de escravos*. Rio de Janeiro: Ed. UERJ/Nova Fronteira.

Cunha, Manuela Carneiro da. 1979. "Etnicidade: da cultura residual mas irredutível." *Revista de cultura e política* 1(1): 35–39.

———. 1985. *Negros, estrangeiros – os escravos libertos e sua volta à África*. São Paulo: Brasiliense.

Freyre, Gilberto. [1962] 1990. "Acontece que são baianos," in *Bahia e baianos*. Salvador, Bahia: Fundação das Artes/Emp. Gráfica da Bahia. [1st edn. in *Problemas Brasileiros de Antropologia*. Rio de Janeiro: José Olympio].

Guran, Milton. 1996. *Agoudas – les "bresiliens" du Benin – Enquête anthropologique et photographique*. Doctorate thesis. EHESS – Ecole des Hautes Etudes em Sciences Sociales.

———. 2002. "Agudás, os 'brasileiros' do Benim." Rio de Janeiro: Ed. Nova Fronteira/Ed. Gama Filho.

Guran M and J.J. Reis. 2002. "Urbain-Karim Elisio da silva, um Agudá descendente de negro malê," *Afro-Ásia* 28(2002): 77–96.

Hazoumé, Paul. 1937. *Le Pacte de Sang au Dahomey*. Paris: Institut d'Ethnologie.

Law Robin. 2002. "A comunidade brasileira de Uidá e os últimos anos do tráfico atlântico de escravos, 1850–1860." *Afro-Ásia* 27(202): 41–77.

Mattoso, Katia de Queiroz. 1982. *Ser escravo no Brasil*. Rio de Janeiro: Ed. Brasiliense.

Meillassoux, Claude. 1986. *Anthropologie de l'esclavage. Le ventre de fer et d'argent*. Paris: Presses Universitaires de France.

Poutignat, P. and J. Streiff-Fenart. 1995. *Théories de l'thnicité*. Paris: PUF.

Reis, João José. [1986] 1987. *Rebelião escrava no Brasil – A história do levante dos malés (1835)*, São Paulo: Brasiliense.

Ribeiro, Darcy. 1995. *O povo brasileiro – A formação e o sentido do Brasil*. São Paulo: Companhia das Letras.

Rodrigues, José Honório. 1962. "The Influence of Africa on Brazil and of Brazil on Africa." *Journal of African History* 3(1), 1962: 49–67.

Rossi, David A. 1965. "The Career of Domingos Martinez in the Bright of Benin 1933–64." *Journal of African History* 6(1), 1965: 79–90.

Sanvi, Anne-Marie Clementine. 1977. *Les métis et les Brésiliens dans la colonie du Dahomey 1880–1920.* Dissertation of *Maîtrise* em História, Université Nationale du Bénin.

Sinou, Alain and Bachir Oloudé. 1988. *Porto Novo – Ville d'Afrique Noire.* Marseille: Parenthèse/Orston.

Sinou, Alain. 1995. *Le comptoir de Ouidah – Une ville africaine singulière.* Paris: Karthala.

Souza, Simone de. 1992. *La famille De Souza du Bénin-Togo,* Cotonou: Les Editions du Bénin.

Tall, Emmanuelle Kadya. 1995a. "Dynamique des cultes voduns et du Christianisme Céleste au sud-Bénin." *Cahiers des Sciences Humaines* 31(4): 797–823.

———. 1995b. "De la démocracie et des cultes voduns au Bénin." *Cahiers d'Etudes Africaines* XXXV(1), n. 137.

Tavares, A.J.C. 1999. Marcos fundamentais da presença portuguesa no Daomé. Lisboa: Universitária Editora.

Tidjani-Serpos, Noureimi and Jean Caffe. 1993. *Porto Novo – Un rêve Brésilien,* Paris/Cotonou: Karthala/Assocle.

Turner, Michael Jerry. 1975. "Les Brésiliéns—The Impact of Former Brazilian Slaves upon Dahomey." PhD Dissertation, Boston University.

———. 1995. "Identidade étnica na África Ocidental: o caso especial dos afro-brasileiros no Benin, na Nigéria e em Gana nos séculos XIX e XX." *Estudos Afro-Asiáticos* 28: 85–99, Rio de Janeiro: CEAA-UCAM.

Verger, Pierre. 1953. "Le culte des vodun d'Abomey aurait-il été apporté à Saint-Louis de Maranhon par la mère du roi Ghézo?" *Les Afro-Américains—Mémoires de l'Institut Français de l'Afrique Noire* 27: 157–160, Dakar.

———. 1968. *Flux et reflux de la traite de nègres entre le Golfe du Bénin et Bahia de Todos os Santos du XVIIè. Au XIXè. Siècles.* Paris/Le Haye: Mouton & Co.

Weber, Max. [1921] 1995. *Economie et Société.* 2 vols. Paris: Pocket/Plon.

Chapter 7

Emigration and the Spatial Production of Difference from Cape Verde

Kesha D. Fikes

The migratory context in which Cape Verdean racial politics historically emerged provides a unique opportunity for observing how spatial movements create social meaning. Interestingly, this particular inquiry urges that the sending and the recipient contexts of migratory communities should not be assessed in isolation; in the case of Cape Verde, for instance, both spatial contexts mutually shaped a generalized perception of Cape Verdean racial identity under Portuguese colonialism. Subsequently, an understanding of Cape Verdean raciality, or the possibilities of raced identification within Cape Verdean communities, at least until independence in 1975, requires a dialogue on how the sending and the recipient contexts cumulatively produced a racially "flexible" Cape Verdean subject under colonialism. This chapter, thus, contributes to methods of analysis, like labor and psychology, which describe how race operates in practice. I focus on travel or spatial mobility as a medium that produces and recognizes "difference" at state and popular levels.

What follows is an overview of competing narratives of Cape Verdean history, with attention to the importance of the concept of indigeneity within it. Indigeneity is referenced as the sign for Africanity and/or "absolute" blackness. The concept is important because it was used to legally discern voluntary from forced labor status. As such, I try to show how local ideals of raced difference were conceived through one's legal relationship to free or indentured travel. I discuss how Cape Verdeans' varied use of Portuguese nationality documentation (from the late nineteenth century through 1975) became a means to entering voluntary and non-Portuguese regulated labor activities.

From the abolition of slavery (1853–1878) to independence, the idea of the migrant Cape Verdean subject was commonly problematized within discussions of racial ambiguity—whether from Portuguese colonial ethnologies or popular racial discourses within and beyond the Portuguese empire.[1]

Portuguese colonial antimiscegenation arguments on the unstable emotional and social destiny of the Cape Verdean "mulatto" (especially in the 1930s and 1940s) (see Tamagnini 1934; Corrêa 1943; Lessa and Ruffié 1960) and G. Freyre's suggestion that Cape Verde occupied the infant stages of a miscegenation process like Brazil's (Lopes 1956),[2] have contributed to scientific and popular statements that emphasize a racial-cultural crisis. Such argumentation, cumulatively, positioned the Cape Verdean subject as disconnected from its political reality. But under what logics were claims of racial ambiguity made intelligible? What aims were serviced by politics that targeted racial practices deemed unstable? In short, at the same time that this chapter observes the mutual importance of sending and recipient locations within the production and perception of Cape Verdean raciality, from the abolition of slavery to independence, the chapter also questions the political productivity of ambiguity. Specifically, if states (the Portuguese metropolis and the countries that received Cape Verdeans) created policies with effects that simultaneously but differently managed perceptions of Cape Verdean raciality, how can we rethink the circulatory value of narratives of racial ambiguity? Or, how might attention to transnationally coordinated emigrations recast narratives of ambiguity as institutional resources?

The Emigrant Logics of Cape Verdean Raciality

The Cape Verdean archipelago—annexed by the Portuguese in the late fifteenth century, and consisting of ten islands, nine of them inhabited—is located within the Sahel wind belt. It has subsequently suffered from vicious drought and periodic famine cycles that date from occupation through the mid twentieth century. This ecological circumstance was so drastic that most Cape Verdeans had to emigrate to survive. Over time, as described below, the blending of local practices of difference recognition and the development of state-managed emigration made travel a social and political tool. For instance, Portuguese subjects born in Cape Verde, and those from Cape Verdean nonslave communities (prior to emancipation), were able to travel under desirable conditions. In other Portuguese African locations (Angola, Mozambique, São Tomé e Príncipe, Guinea-Bissau) these same individuals worked as administrative officials. Beyond Portuguese space—in the Americas and in Western Europe in particular—they led lives that evaded the confines of their colonial origins. By contrast, enslaved populations were forced to emigrate; they were sent to plantations in Portuguese Africa where they labored under harsh conditions. In short, how, where, and whether one moved made and unmade one's social essence; and one's essence—by the late sixteenth century—was interpretable through raced discourse. I argue that these forms of raced recognition were activated and materialized through travel.

Between 1861 and 1863 preabolition labor codes created a link between migration and island geography. One's island affiliation within the archipelago was legally attached to one's migratory status as voluntary or indentured labor.

For example, the first series of legislation on indentured emigrations named and targeted the island of Santiago (see Meintel 1984) as an ideal source of workers. And subsequent legislation in the early twentieth century protected targeted northern islands from participation in indentured work. Accordingly, for emigrants, one's racial location—as negro and indigenous-like, or mestiço or branco—was confirmed or transformed once one was distributed (forced or voluntarily) as unit of mobile labor. Additionally, the Portuguese colonial administration partially sustained the Cape Verdean economy through forced and voluntary labor remittances. What mattered to the Portuguese state, thus, was the potential exchange value of Cape Verdean raciality within the recipient labor markets of Cape Verdean migrants; specifically, their recognition as racially viable migrants (particularly in the early-twentieth-century U.S. and in western Europe) affected Portuguese profits. Further, Azorean and continental Portuguese nationals carried the same nationality passports as Cape Verdeans; and visible "diversity" within a single national community meant that their identification as racially uncertain could facilitate their entry into places that racially profiled potential immigrants. Hence, at the same time that the metropole demanded financial returns from remittances, the Cape Verdean migrants' survival depended upon the ability to assume a "white" identity that could safeguard one's entry and residency. In short, race was a political object that state and society acted upon for profit and survival, respectively.

Perhaps the vagueness surrounding the "racial character" of Cape Verdean communities begins with the popular narrative of Cape Verdean history, a product of colonial ethnology. The most widely known ethno-historical accounts suggest that the recognition of racial difference in Cape Verde is self-evident. Specifically, they treat interracial unions across the archipelago, within the eighteenth and nineteenth centuries, as naturally occurring, self-selective practices whose "frequencies" varied by island. These stories of degrees of miscegenation are then oddly mapped onto the notion that some islands were more civilized—as evidenced by the development of advanced school systems on select islands—while others remained more "African." These self-evident distinctions prompt one to question the aims of the standard historical narrative. I begin then by presenting the popular version; next I propose an alternate one.

Competing Racial Narratives

In the popular version, the Portuguese discovered the ten-island archipelago of Cape Verde in 1460, uninhabited. Portuguese colonial administrators and Cape Verdean and Portuguese physical and social scientists created a narrative that explained processes of settlement between the sixteenth and eighteenth centuries. They produced volumes of ethnological texts that categorized and distinguished racial, cultural, and ecological differences by island, over time. (For colonial ethnologies see Pusich 1860–1861; Senna Barcellos 1899–1900, 1904; Lessa and Ruffié 1960; Mariano 1959). Settlement experiences are organized into linear progressions, the point of origin being the colonization of the island of Santiago by crown-appointed Portuguese administrators and slaves from the Senegambia region. Next, subsequent colonizations of the islands of Fogo and Brava by Santiaguense slaves and European travelers and administrators suggest the ways that racially and culturally mixed descendants from these three southern islands (or the Sotovento group) slowly populated the last southern island of Maio and the remaining five islands or the northern or Barlavento group. Over time, the development of schools (especially a seminary school in São Nicolau) in the Barlavento group, in addition to the emergence of lucrative port activities on the island of São Vicente, from the late eighteenth through the early twentieth centuries, allowed for creolized-mulatto communities to develop a self-reflexive sense of community. This worked in a nation-like sense that early-twentieth-century Cape Verdean writers, the Claristas, defined as the essence of creolidade (creolization): it made them neither African nor European, but somewhere in-between. This experience was coupled with a defining sense of saudade (longing) which these writers treat as the emotional response to physical separation from those who emigrated or were left behind; this understanding is intertwined with the experience of creolidade[3] for these important writers. Celebratory representations of hybridity— shifting vaguely between biology and culture[4]—were recognized in juxtaposition to attempts to promote civility on the island of Santiago. Santiago was the port of entry for new slaves from the continent and it was represented as a haven for "unruly" maroons and maroon-descended peoples.[5]

An alternate version of this narrative begins with the same date, 1460. However, according to unedited accounts that António Carreira found, dated in the late eighteenth century, the island of Santiago was already inhabited by people from the Senegambia region (Carreira 1977: 281–320). Thus rather than focus on "origins," which requires identity-situated truths (see D. Scott 1999), I emphasize how particular engagements with travel constituted ways of understanding social difference across the archipelago and beyond. In particular, I address how indentured and voluntary migrations— in response to the crisis of drought and famine—organized and deciphered the significance of social life in Cape Verde.

From as early as the sixteenth century, if and where one moved were treated as racially inscribing practices. Those whose "origins" tied them to the Senegambia region tended to be divided into different classes of slaves. Literate and Christianized slaves were generally sent to Europe from Cape Verde, while "underskilled" slaves were divided into those who would be shipped to the Americas and those who would remain within the archipelago for experimental agrarian projects. Others were captured and then released to work as official bureaucrats or traders. Such individuals often had access to property and slaves which would confuse the imaginaries of European maritime personnel and traders who stopped temporarily in the islands to refuel and/or to pick up slaves. By the mid- to late eighteenth century this economy had officially extended into voluntary and involuntary migrant markets (especially to the cacao plantations of São Tomé and Príncipe) in a process that coincided with Portugal's deteriorating imperial economy. By the eighteenth and nineteenth centuries, one's potential for mobility—be it forced or voluntary, labor- or government-related, temporary or permanent, or within or beyond Portuguese colonial space—cumulatively organized a field of tangible power recognition. One's racial positionality would be conceived in connection to the spaces one had occupied or could inhabit, via island and family origins and/or one's migrant labor status.

Thus, in contrast to the standard narrative which approaches migrant labor opportunities and racial positionality within an evolving island settlement schema, letters and records dating from the sixteenth through the nineteenth centuries indicate that Santiago always hosted a diverse community of free Africans, in addition to freed, self-liberated, and enslaved communities whose experiences with Portuguese planters and administrators were no less diverse—in a "contact" sense—than those on other islands. Repetitive famine crises, particularly since the metropole only marginally protected planters and administrators, meant that drought cycles affecting the lives of slaves and planters alike disrupted the social order: between the eighteenth and mid-twentieth centuries during famines, streets and plantations were commonly lined with the corpses of slaves, planters, and elites, alike (see Carreira 1983). In addition, each of the newly settled islands that were represented in the conventional narrative as hosting creolized-mulatto populations continued to absorb new slaves from the continent until the mid-nineteenth century. In fact, to conceal any "demographic" similarities between Santiago and the northern islands, Amaral (1964), drawing from Barcellos's work (1899–1890), suggests that one way of controlling the growing mulatto populations in Santiago was to send them to Brazil.

My objective here is not to represent these racial communities—African Negros and creolized-mulattos—in fixed terms, nor to assume that Negro meant slave or that mulatto signified freedom. Rather, I hope to point to ways that such representations signified categorical realities: race and the limits of freedom were made recognizable in relation to different practices of labor mobility, over time. More specifically, these practices required the idea and presence of racial ambiguity for the purpose of being able to respond to the labor demands of different Portuguese African and non-Portuguese markets, especially in the early twentieth century when migration policies were inspired by eugenics. Thus skewed representations of geography (which mapped racial progress and degeneracy through island affiliations) are reflected in the uneven history of the making and dismantling of migrant labor practices. Indeed, it would be the representation of African Negros and creolized-mulattos as absolute categories that produced the façade of racial certainty. As such, the idea of Cape Verdean racial ambiguity was produced when Cape Verdean workers changed markets and spaces (internally and externally). Arguably, it is for this very reason—the transit circumstances that yield recognition of racial ambiguity—that the interdependent political system of migration and labor requires close examination: race and island origins could mutually signify each other; they "blackened" or "hybridized" communities as necessary.

Racializing Island Origins

Colonial practices of "blackening" in Cape Verde were essential to the eighteenth-century economic development of São Tomé and Príncipe, a set of cacao-producing islands whose export earnings and contracted labor profits (from non-Portuguese companies) would be used to support the metropole. The problem, however, was that by the late eighteenth century substantial numbers of men who were avoiding contracted labor began to participate in various undocumented maritime activities, namely the Atlantic whaling industry. Subsequently, dependable pools of labor dwindled. By the mid- to late nineteenth century, as the colonial administration contemplated the consequences of the abolition of slavery, it called for the greater management of the labor, raw materials and plantation cultivation on the continent and especially within the islands of São Tomé and Príncipe. The implementation of policies of forced labor recruitment for disciplinary purposes camouflaged the continuation of slave labor. In reality, by the turn of the twentieth century, the new "freed" peasantries from each of the islands participated in forced labor emigrations, particularly to the cacau plantations. Their numbers by island varied considerably, with the majority representing Santiago (Carreira 1977; Meintel 1984). But only one island was designated in the preabolition indentured labor laws that would protect cacau production;[6] that island was Santiago (Meintel 1984).

As of 1910, Cape Verdeans were no longer Portuguese citizens (Fernandes 2002)—though travelers recognized by the Portuguese state continued to carry Portuguese nationality passports—neither were they indigenous subjects of the empire. Legally, they were provisional subjects of the Portuguese state. But the process of targeting Santiaguense workers into labor networks that legally named and targeted indigenous continental Africans (from Angola, Mozambique, and Guinea-Bissau) unofficially transformed Santiaguense workers into indigenous subjects. Accordingly, the colonial administration related to them as continental Africans, or persons whose origins by law forced them to contract themselves to plantations to avoid criminal punishment. Santiaguense would be treated as indigenous workers until forced labor laws were abolished in 1959. In practice, curiously, other islanders from Santo Antão, Fogo, and Maio, who were likewise contracted to the same plantations, were also treated as indigenous workers. This is evidenced in the language of their individual labor contracts, the outlined terms of their working conditions, and how they were identified within documented complaints by planters and administrative officials. But racialized narratives of their labor potential in Portuguese colonial labor legislation never matched descriptions pertaining to Santiago.

References to island origins should not be treated as real or absolute; Cape Verdeans migrated between the islands and hence always had family or social connections that linked communities across the archipelago. Hence, ideas about island space were produced through migrant labor practices that were intelligible through the fixating effects of race. In this sense the argument is not simply that island origins determined spatial mobility; island particularity was likewise an ideological production that relied upon the perceived certainty of racial essence.

Race and Indigeneity

The legal aims of the discourse on indigeneity, within the context of eighteenth and nineteenth century Cape Verde, focused on the benefits of turning nonassimilable vadios (vagrants) throughout the archipelago into productive workers of the Portuguese Empire (see Moutinho 2000; Silva 1953; Pereira 1984). Significantly, the term vadio was used to describe any individual who appeared "idle" (see Perreira 1984). But by the nineteenth century, as evidenced within the travelogue section of the Cape Verdean Boletins—weekly colonial administrative reviews—popular references to Santiaguense islanders emerged as interchangeable with a new category of identity—"Badiu"—derived from vadio.[7] Badiu was then used to identify primarily Santiaguense islanders who refused to participate in domestic and migratory slave labor.

The historical literature on Santiago describes absentee landlord patterns on plantations as the underlying reason for Santiaguense "ruggedness." Likewise, the mountainous areas of Santiago that often served as a refuge for run-away slaves are used to substantiate this argument. But Fogo and Santo Antão also had mountainous areas and absentee landlord practices. What is more, Santiaguense residing in the interior of the island never lived in isolation because the constant threat of famine meant that they were always connected to the urban center for food security purposes. Bravan and Barlavento island life, in contrast, are described as "close-contact" farming situations between slaves and plantation owners that "naturally" provided the ideal environment for assimilation experiences to occur on their own over time.

These juxtaposed narratives have lead many to argue or presume that Santiago remained the most "racially" and "culturally" African of all of the islands in the archipelago. While it is true that as a primary port of "African entry" Santiago experienced its own cultural particularity, future studies of Santiago will have to contend with the political implications of such representation, particularly since Santiaguense (though black-identified) do not necessarily articulate their daily Cape Verdean experience as African (though "black" and "African" can be treated as synonyms) and since the legacies of such representation are intimately tied to colonial economic interests. For example, the colonial bureaucrat and anthropologist Mendes Corrêa (1943) made the following remark (see Andrade citation 1998: 31); it contributed to the rationale linking indentured status to Santiaguese identity: "For them (referring to designated mestiços) manifestations of African origins did not survive and nor are they remembered, being that they (African manifestations) exist only [survived] in Santiago; on the other islands, what's been proven, in reality, was a simulation with a predominant Portuguese element."[8]

Representations of Santiaguense islanders fixated upon Negro identity while understanding "other" islanders to be creolized-mulattos. Future studies will need to assess the discursive history of race distribution and categorization within the archipelago, from colonial settlement through independence in 1975. Notably, the works of Daniel Pereira (1984), Gabriel Fernandes (2002), and José Carlos Gomes dos Anjos (2002), in particular, have already contributed considerably to this line of discussion. In that color is also a symbolic reference to power, a discursive legacy of colonial and plantation politics, it is also, as Frantz Fanon (1967) and Stuart Hall (1996) remind us, a sliding signifier whose meaning is politically situated. Given this sliding significance, phenotype is marginally treated in this analysis; the categories "mulatto/a," "mestiço/a," and "Negro/a" are not entertained as solid realities. As Santiago is centered within the history of Cape Verde, and its spatial signification within labor migrations, Badiu identity (in relation to Santiago) is treated as a temporal and spatial signifier that was essential to supporting Portugal and especially its cacau industries after emancipation. Notably, the treatment of Santiaguense inhabitants as Badius not only guaranteed the availability of Santiaguense workers but likewise became an infinite solution to camouflaging or "blackening" the realities of contact in Santiago.

Labor Emigration to Portugal

The signifying capacity of Santiago, from the colonial administration's perspective, continued until approximately the mid-1960s when Portugal began to reroute workers from each of the islands to Portugal. At this moment, racialized worker distinctiveness is slowly removed from the language of labor policies on migration to Portugal. Cape Verdean men were recruited to replace male Portuguese workers who emigrated to the northern parts of western Europe and/or to the Americas during the 1940s and 1950s, or who were killed or injured in battle during the colonial wars on the African continent between the late 1960s and the early 1970s. Cape Verdean men worked primarily in construction, mining, and carpentry. Simultaneously, Cape Verdean women from each of the islands and from different class locations also immigrated to Portugal; some middle-class women were employed as nurses, while poor working women received family reunification visas to help "domesticate" their working male partners or family (Fikes, n.d.).

Cape Verdean women's' migrations to Portugal were key to the transformation of the idea of indigeneity; as noted by Meintel (1984), Santiaguense women were represented as masculine and ferocious. In part, these discourses emerged in connection to their scrutinized participation in state-documented food revolts that date from the early nineteenth through the mid-twentieth centuries.[9] Subsequently, the relocation of Santiaguense women to the metropole would challenge how ideals of feminine respectability would likewise foreground the association of Santiaguense identity with indigeneity (Fikes, n.d.).

The discussion that follows attends to such voluntary Santiaguense movements as a way of illuminating not only the operative qualities of Badiu identity but also the fragility and uncertainty of Creole-mulatto status as revealed in Portugal's changing relationship to Santiago. The eventual change in Cape Verdeans' nationality status—because of the loss of Portuguese passport privileges at independence—diminished the international exchange value once attributed to internally recognized racial heterogeneity. At independence those who could not hold onto their passports legally became "sovereign" African nationals.

But in addition to Portugal's engagement in practices that would transform its labor relationship to the Cape Verdean archipelago, what else was serviced by recruitment of Cape Verdeans to the metropole? From the Portuguese colonial administration's perspective, or so it seems, the objective was to disrupt the possibility of Cape Verdean anticolonial activity while filling construction, mining, and carpentry jobs that were vacated by Portuguese workers who went abroad. As fighting never occurred in Cape Verde but rather took place in Guinea-Bissau, Cape Verde's independence partner, one could argue that the colonial administration's attempts were somewhat successful. However, I would also consider the importance of the consequences of the recruitment program. The recruitment program not only included workers from a racially and sexually stigmatized island-community within the archipelago—the Santiaguense—but it simultaneously disrupted cultural practices of race recognition by 1) allowing Santiaguense to enter into space (Portugal) that previously could only be occupied by Cape Verdean elites, clergy, and temporary maritime personnel, among the few, and 2) enforcing labor practices that did not acknowledge (in policy or practice) differences between workers, regardless of island affiliation. In essence, the recruitment program to Portugal (among other transitional events) disrupted the ways that the capital potential of Creole-mulatto particularity could "materialize" or be interpreted through transnational movements. Creolized-mulatto particularity, from the position of Portugal, became blurred, or simply *black*.

Immediately after Portugal's own revolution for democracy in 1974, which coincided with the independence movements in Portuguese Africa, the new democratic Portuguese government created its own constitution; the issue of overseas colonial citizenship was one of its key priorities (see Esteves 1991). The law that changed overseas nationality status and citizenship—Decreto-Lei #308-A/75—stated that Portuguese citizenship could be maintained or acquired by those who were either born in Portugal, or had at least one Portuguese parent who was born in Portugal. Portuguese parents included contemporary Cape Verdean nationals who were legally recognized and documented as Portuguese citizens—and not simply Portuguese nationality passport holders—prior to Decreto-Lei #308. Otherwise, Portugal recognized them as sovereign Cape Verdean nationals who pertained to sub-Saharan Africa.

The loss of Portuguese nationality passport privileges meant that the terms for acquiring Western visas changed, especially for new African national subjects. Subsequently, traveling Cape Verdeans who did not or could not hold onto their Portuguese status—regardless of their island origins— became African nationals overnight. The argument here is not to suggest that Cape Verdeans with opportunities to travel beyond the Portuguese Empire had not understood themselves as black and/or African when holding Portuguese documents. The point is that they lost the right of use of Portuguese nationality that had facilitated their entry requirement into select places and markets. Importantly, this process meant that Portugal also ceased recognition of differences in the cultural "potential" of Cape Verdeans, by island, in part because it had to dissolve any confusions (internationally) pertaining to similarities with Portuguese continentals and Azoreans. Subsequently, from the perspective of the international community, Cape Verde was now a sovereign African nation whose subjects—regardless of class or racial location—were one and the same.

This instance raises important questions pertaining to sovereignty after independence. In the end, the efforts of decolonization were never simply about independence from Portugal. Arguably, the dissolution of the West's recognition of Cape Verdeans as Portuguese nationals is likewise reflective of new practices for deciphering race from nationality and/or citizenship, globally. Today, with the exception of those migrants who were able to maintain or acquire Portuguese, American, or other Western citizenries, contemporary Cape Verdeans are not really moving in and out of different markets where race is managed differently. Instead, the politics of sovereignty are such that race—in light of increasingly centralized immigration technologies and the globally recognized citizen-status of the sub-Saharan African national—is increasingly operating, uniformly, across space. Digressing, one might even argue that the transnational networks that constitute this moment of globalization are merely about the spatial terrain upon which the management of social life and social difference has been expanded geographically.

Postcoloniality and Creolidade: Reconfiguring the Signifying Potential of Labor Migrations

Since independence the relationship between racial positionality and island origins has shifted. In postcolonial Cape Verde the representation of cultural diversity and racial miscegenation is subsumed under a universalizing national concept of creolidade. This contemporary concept differs from its colonial predecessor, however, as the term could previously operate as a synonym for *mestiçagem*, or miscegenation. Today it refers to pan-archipelago nation building and it is thought to be politically neutral; it is used to celebrate Cape Verde's unique form of Africanity in connection to its historic transatlantic experiences of contact and cultural hybridity. In theory, creolidade includes the Santiaguense. Likewise, the Santiaguense embrace this term as they situate their Cape Verdean identity both within and beyond the archipelago. But in practice something different seems to be happening and there is tremendous uncertainty around the representational role that Santiaguense identity may or may not be playing within the contemporary makeup of democratic cultural and political practices in Cape Verde (see Furtado 1993, 1997, Dos Anjos 2002, Fernandes 2002). This ambiguity, arguably, is grounded in migration-related demographic transformations in Santiago where some 60 percent of the nation's inhabitants from across the archipelago now reside. Santiago hosts the archipelago's capital city, Praia.

Today, creolidade, as a pan-archipelago experience, could be interpreted as trivializing the unequal historical circumstances that racially encoded voluntary and forced migrant labor practices. Not only is there little political space for debating island politics in conversation with race, but the state's agenda is so focused on the dilemmas of urban and rural poverty throughout the archipelago—as it should be—that poverty can only be criticized within a pan-archipelago context. In essence, after independence, class—which is treated as mutable and potentially controllable by the state and supporting donor agencies alike—is that which is recognized as being at stake; race is effectively blocked from debate. Hence, this pan-archipelago vision is not the only idea that is grounded in the transitioning status of the discourse of creolidade. In consideration of the real poverty that affects Cape Verde, and the difficulties with access to water that continue to disrupt the possibilities for normalcy, it is important to acknowledge how the transimperial and transnational circumstances that once racially empowered creolidade through emigrant practices are increasingly dissolving, from the outside.

Conclusion

Understanding the legal capacity of race in transnational perspective is essential to the study of transmigratory phenomena. Such perspective not only enables us to question the social logics of settlement in recipient settings but it also enables us to assess how local imaginaries of social distance and proximity were institutionalized in tandem with those very settlement possibilities. The absence of this attention makes it difficult to historicize how politically diverse Cape Verdean communities were collapsed into a single nation according to the entry guidelines of Western receiving nations at Cape Verdean independence. For the process of recategorizing new Cape Verdean nationals as sub-Saharan Africans versus Portuguese nationals is central to understanding how external legal frameworks are intimately and globally connected to Cape Verdean forms of social practice. Moreover, current local struggles are about the assertion of control over one's relationship to the possibilities of spatial movement, and hence one's livelihood, and the ways that such control outside of Cape Verde can mediate local experiences of national belonging in the archipelago. In brief, subjects do not simply emerge in connection to the spaces in which they "originate"; the relational or dialectic quality of subjectivity is always constituted within the relationship that binds different geopolitical locales.

These arguments should not be read as appeals to any form or practice of raciality; this is not the point. Rather, this engagement is simply about questioning how the representational value of Cape Verdean raciality has historically serviced diverse transnational interests: the mutual consequence, in the end, has been the production of a dehistoricized or "questionable" racial subject. Plainly, the production of the Cape Verdean subject as a unit of mobile Portuguese labor is obscured at the same time that politicized ideals of racial consciousness are construed independent of the emigrant logics that textured Cape Verdean subjectivity. As a consequence, little room is left for considering how whiteness—the effaced possibility through which difference and ambiguity are made recognizable (Fanon 1967), and which renders the interpretation of Cape Verdean raciality questionable in the first place—remains obfuscated in the company of conversations that emphasize "passing." Significantly, degrees of difference can only be constituted or recognized in reference to nonwhite racial subjects. How thus should we interpret the project that requires or compels recognition of Cape Verdean raciality as ambiguous? In what ways do discourses of racial appropriateness produce synchronized forms of regulation that institutionally stabilize appearances of race and racial order across space? Responses to these questions might best be framed within what David Scott (1999) has referred to as the moral-political dimension of criticism, or the politics that ideologically shape how we interpret events and practices. Narratives of Cape Verdean colonial politics and history are accompanied, compulsively, by questions aimed at fixating who Cape Verdeans are, racially; as such, one is not only required to confront the potential effects that such narratives had on the representational status of Cape Verdean identity before independence but to consider how such circulating discourses have in fact produced racially ambiguous Cape Verdeans in advance of the political histories that have positioned this community as such.

Notes

This essay is the fruit of various commentaries, invited speaking opportunities, and funded support. I would like to thank Beth Povinelli for her rigorous and challenging comments on an earlier draft, and Donald Moore for sharp comments on an oral version of this essay in 2002. The Wenner-Gren Foundation, the Ford Foundation, and Division funds from the University of Chicago funded my trips to the archives in Portugal and in Cape Verde. The information in this essay would not have been possible without their financial support. Further, I am especially grateful to Kamari Clarke, Deborah Thomas, Judith Farquhar, Danilyn Rutherford, Jessica Cattelino, and Jennifer Cole for their detailed and challenging comments on writing and translation.

1. With the exception of a few texts (cf. Halter 1993; Meintel 1984) that attend to popular ideologies pertaining to Cape Verdean racial subjectivity in the United States, there is little textual "proof" that can speak to the prevalence of popular ideas regarding Cape Verdean raciality. What is significant, however, is the circulatory or oral nature of this information. When giving talks I am often asked "What they are?" or "What do they think they are?"

2. See Lopes (1956), a transcribed radio interview in Mindelo, São Vicente (Cape Verde). Here, Lopes, a Cape Verdean intellectual, criticizes Freyre's perception of Cape Verdean identity politics, arguing the Freyre could not conceive of the

idea that Cape Verdeans were already culturally evolved and defined versus being in the early states of cultural or racial evolution.

3. Here it is essential to note that this colonial, prenationalist experience of "in-betweenness" was not conceived in terms of a logics of whitening or what it means to continue to evolve, "upward" or racially. Instead, as stressed by Baltasar Lopes, the founding intellectual of the Clarista movement, creolidade was understood to be a stable cultural experience that had already arrived or evolved. It was a cultural phenomenon in and of itself.

4. Notably, the Lessa and Ruffié reference is the collaborative product of Cape Verdean and European intellectuals and social scientists. The articles in this volume are driven by research questions that link biology, or rather blood studies, to ideas about culture.

5. See a critique of this idea in Pereira (1984).

6. See the proposed articles for legislation and letters to the governor of Cape Verde on the recruitment of Santiaguense workers, in the Boletins Officiais do Governo Geral de Cabo-Verde, 1862 through 1878.

7. This idea is also suggested in Pereira's work (1984) on Santiaguense identity politics in late eighteenth Century Santiago. See also Fernandes (2002) and Gomes dos Santos (2002).

8. Original Portuguese text: "Para eles, as manifestações de origem africana não passam de sobrevivência ou de reminiscências, existentes sobretudo em Santiago; nas outras ilhas, o que verificou, na realidade, foi uma simbiose com predominância do elemento português."

9. Popular narratives of Badiu identity were intertwined with fantastic stories of resistance and vulgarity. While archives and letters documented the presence of slave uprisings on other islands (namely Fogo and Santo Antão), stories of trickery, aggression, and violence commonly characterized "Badiu" revolts. The reality is that Santiago was always the most densely populated island. During drought crises that led to famine, infamous Santiaguense revolts occurring in 1811, 1822, and 1835 (see Tomazinho 1996), coincided with periods of mass death. Moreover, the politicized participation and leadership of women in rebellions further served the purpose of representing Santiaguense as savages, particularly at a time when "other" women began participating in migrations to the United States (see Halter 1993 on migration to the United States). Romanticized and antagonistic tales of self-liberated and fierce "Negro" women with knives and machetes, coupled with the sudden deaths of food-hoarding landowners (see Meintel 1984) consummated the idea of Badiu identity. Gendered representations of Santiaguense identity as "Negro" and aggressive were essential to discursively discerning "mestiço" from "Negro" identity. And it was the racialization or rather "blackening" of Santiaguense identity that served the purpose of the illusion of Badius as masculine and vulgar, regardless of sex. Thus, as "mestiço" identity was imaginatively constitutive of ideas of mutability, Badiu identity controlled Santiago by "blackening" it. Further, as the fetishized synthesis of black and indigenous status, and mestiço and assimilated status were solidified, these discourses systematically racialized necessary pools of mobile labor, such that travel simultaneously situated one's racial and gender positionality within local politics.

Archives

Boletim Official do Governo Geral de Cabo-Verde, 1862 through 1910.

Bibliography

Albuquerque, Luís de and Maria Emília Madeira Santos. 1991. *História de Cabo Verde*. vol. I. Lisbon: Tropical Institute.

———. 2003. *História de Cabo Verde*. Vol. III. Lisbon: Tropical Institute.

Amaral, Ilidio do. 1964. *Santiago de Cabo Verde: A Terra e os Homes*. Lisbon: Junta de Investigaçao do Ultramar.

Andrade, Elisa. 1998. "Do Mito a Historia," in *Cabo Verde: Insulariedade e Literatura*. Paris: Editions Karthala.

Carreira, António. 1977. *Migracoes nas Ilhas de Cabo Verde*. Praia-Santiago:Instituto Caboverdiano do Livro.

———. 1983. *Cabo Verde: Formação e Extinção de uma Sociedade Escravocrata (1460–1878)*. Praia-Santiago: Instituto Caboverdiano do Livro.

Corrêa, Mendes. 1943. *Raças do Império*. Lisbon: Junta de Investigações do Ultramar.

De Andrade, Lelia Lomba. 1996. "Voices from the Margins: The Construction of Racial and Ethnic Identity for Cape Verdean Americans." PhD Dissertation, Syracuse University.

Esteves, Maria do Céu. 1991. *Portugal, País de Imigração*. Lisbon: Instituto de Estudos para o Desenvolvimento.

Fanon, Frantz. 1967. *Black Skin, White Masks*. New York: Grove Press.

Fernandes, Gabriel. 2002. *A Diluição da África: Uma Interpretação da Saga Identitária Cabo-Verdiana no Panorama Político (Pós)Colonia*. Florianopolis, Brasil: Ed. Da Universidade Federal de Santa Catarina.

Fikes, Kesha. 2000. "Santiaguense Women's Transnationality in Portugal: Labor Rights, Diasporic Transformation and Citizenship." PhD Dissertation. University of California, Los Angeles.

———. n.d. *Managing African Portugal*. Manuscript on Cape Verdean Migrant Labor in Portugal.

Furtado, Cláudio Alves. 1997. *Génese e (Re) Produção da Classe Dirigente em Cabo Verde*. Praia-Santiago: Instituto Caboverdiando do Livro.

———. 1993. *A Transformação das Estruturas Agrárias numa Sociedade de Mudança–Santiago, Cabo Verde*. Praia-Santiago: Instituto Caboverdiano do Livro.

Gomes dos Anjos, José Carlos. 2002. *Intelectuais, Literatura e Poder em Cabo Verde*. Praia, Cabo Verde: INIPC.

Gottfried, Stockinger. 1990. *Crónicas de Campo II: Ilha de Santiago*. Praia: Instituto Caboverdiano do Livro e do Disco.

Hall, Stuart. 1996. "The After-life of Frantz Fanon: Why Fanon? Why Now? Why Black Skin, white Masks?" in Alan Read, ed. *The Fact of Blackness: Frantz Fanon and Visual Representation*. London: Institute of Contemporary Arts, pp. 12–37.

Lefebvre, Henri. 1991. *The Production of Space*. D. Nicholson-Smith, trans. Cambridge: Blackwell Publishers.

Lessa, Almerindo and Jacques Ruffié. 1960. *Seroantropologia das Ilhas de Cabo Verde: Mesa Redonda Sobre O Homen Cabo-Verdiano*. Lisbon: Junta de Investigações do Ultramar.

Lopes, Baltasar. 1956. *Cabo Verde Visto por Gilberto Freyre. Apontamentos lidos ao microfone do Radío Barlavento*. Praia: Imprensa Nacional.

Loude, Jean-Yves. 1999. *Cabo Verde: Notas Atlânticas*. Mem Martins-Portugal: Publicações Europa-América.

Mariano, Gabriel. 1959. "Do Funco ao Sobrado ou o Mundo que o Mulatto Criou," in Jorge Dias, ed. *Colóquios Cabo-Verdianos*. Lisbon: Junta de Investigações do Ultramar.

Meintel, Dierdre. 1984. *Race, Culture and Portuguese Colonialism in Cabo Verde*. Syracuse: Syracuse University.

Moutinho, Mario. 2000. *O Indígena no Pensamento Colonial Português: 1895–1961*. Lisbon: Edições Universitárias Lusófonas.

Pereira, Daniel. 1984. *A Situação da Ilha de Santiago no Primeiro Quartel do Século XVIII*. São Vicente-Cape Verde: Edição do Instituto Caboverdiano do Livro.

Pusich, António. 1860–1861. *Memória ou Descrição Fisico-Politico das Ilhas de Cabo Verde – 1810*. Lisbon: Anais do Conselho Ultramarino – Parte não oficial – Serie II.

Sánchez, Gina. 1999. "Diasporic [Trans]formations: Race, Culture and the Politics of Cape Verdean Identity." PhD Dissertation, University of Texas, Austin.

Scott, David. 1999. *Refashioning Futures: Criticism after Postcoloniality*. Princeton: Princeton University Press.

Senna Barcellos, Cristiano José de. 1899 e 1900. *Subsídios para a História de Cabo Verde e Guiné, I–II*. Lisbon: Tipografia da Academia Real das Ciências.

———. 1904. *Alguns Apontamentos Sobre as Fomes de Cabe, desde 1719 a 1904*. Lisbon: Tipografia da Academia Real das Ciências.

Silva, J.M. da. 1953. *O Sistema Português de Política Indígena*. Coimbra: Coimbra Editora Lda.

———. 1955. *O Trabalho Indígena*. Lisbon: Agência Geral do Ultramar, 1955, 2nd ed.

Soja, Edward. 1989. *Postmodern Geographies: The Reassertion of Space in Critical Social Theory*. New York: Verso.

Tamagnini, Eusebio. 1934. "Os Problemas da Mestiçagem," (Speech) I Congresso Nacional de Antropologia Colonial.

Veiga, Manuel. 1998. *Cabo Verde: Insularidade e Literatura*. Paris: Editions Karthala.

Chapter 8

African and Brazilian Altars in Lisbon—Some Considerations on the Reconfigurations of the Portuguese Religious Field

Clara Saraiva

Scenarios: Moving People and Spirits

A long queue of people jams the staircase at the entrance of the Portuguese Consulate in Bissau, while outside a crowd waits at the building gates for a chance to contact someone inside. This daily scenario reflects the desire of Guineans to migrate to Portugal, hopeful of socially and economically improving their living conditions.

In Lisbon, the families of these individuals seek the help of religious ritualists (*djambakóss*) to solve the problems that arise in their lives and are often connected to their condition in the diaspora. They offer gifts to the ancestors and the *irãs* (divinities) so that their relatives succeed in obtaining the much-desired visa.

In April 2006, the mayor of a city in the interior of Portugal appeared on the front page of a well-known Portuguese journal as he welcomed Brazilian migrant families. They came there under a cooperation program that envisioned the introduction of sixty young families to live and work in an aged and deserted district.

In the meantime, not far from Lisbon, a *pai de santo* (religious ritualist) gathered followers in his *terreiro* (ritual grounds) during the performance of *Umbanda* rituals and consultations. Of the almost fifty believers present that night, nearly all were Portuguese.

From Country of Emigration to Country of Privileged Destination

In the late 1970s and during the 1980s, Portugal became a destination for immigrants and inverted the emigration movements that for centuries had characterized the demography of the nation (Barreto 2005).[1] The face of the country changed as it became the locus of a multicultural and multiethnic society on an unprecedented scale. Several circumstances that were related to the social, political, and economic changes that the country underwent from the late 1960s explain this reversal (Barreto 1996) and the increases in immigration after the 1974 revolution, the defeat of Salazar's dictatorial regime, the end of the colonial war, and the subsequent independence of the overseas colonies.[2]

For the African populations, this reversal was particularly important. Until 1974, contingents of Africans who were mainly Cape Verdeans came to Portugal as workers. It was largely after that period that migrations of Africans and Asian families from the former African colonies increased. From the 1980s immigrants included Brazilians and Chinese; from the late 1990s Eastern Europeans also migrated to Portugal in search of work in low-paid jobs (Barreto 2005; Malheiros 2005).

Much of the seminal work that Khalid Koser has edited on the exuberance for the revitalization of the diaspora concept, and the conception of diasporas as a "new social form characterized by special social relationships, political orientations and economic strategies," emphasizes that this is also a phenomenon that demands an increased awareness of its multi-locality and its condition as a "novel mode of cultural production that interacts with globalization." (Koser 2003: 9) Although some research has been done in Portugal on its recent condition as a host-nation for migrants from other continents (Barreto 2005; Bastos and Bastos 1999, 2006; Bastos 2000; Garcia 2000a, 2000b, 2000c; Gusmão 2004; Machado 2002; Malheiros 2005; Padilla 2003; Pires 2003; Quintino 2000; Saint-Maurice 1997; Vala 1999), much remains to be done as the numbers and the diversity of the immigrants increase annually.

In addition to the freedom of expression, the 1974 revolution introduced religious freedom to the country, consecrated in the 1976 constitution and recently emphasized in the 2001 law on religious freedom. In a country where the Roman Catholic religion was the official religion during the fifty years of the Salazar regime, most other religious groups—with the exception of the Jewish and Islamic communities, together with the case of the evangelical churches, the Jehovah witnesses, and the Mormons (Vilaça 2001: 88)—were forbidden or given few opportunities for expansion. The new post-1974 religions accompanied the migration movements and at the outset of the twenty-first century, Portugal has become a home to Jews, Islamic groups (Sunnis and Ismaelis, for instance), several Pentecostal and Neopentecostal churches (such as the Igreja Universal do Reino de Deus[3] and Maná churches), Afro-Brazilian religions, such as several variations of *Umbanda* and Candomblé and animistic practices introduced by a variety of African migrants (Bastos and Bastos 2006; Vilaça 2001; Mafra 2002; Pordeus 2000; Saraiva 2006). These groups appear to peacefully coexist in a multicultural and multireligious context: Roman Catholics, Hindus, Shiita Muslims, and Sikhs make pilgrimages to Fatima (the most important Roman Catholic pilgrimage destination in Portugal) to pray to the supreme Mother-goddess, who is personified in the image of Our Holy Lady of Fatima (Bastos and Bastos 2006: 77; Mafra 2002).

The material presented here highlights the need for awareness of the impact on Portuguese contemporary reality of the religious movements that accompany recent migrations. Within these migrations some hidden social and economic aspects like the practical effects of religion and therapeutical practices, as well as ritual performances that fall into the realm of the symbolic, are the very bases for the religious constructs.

Based on 1) the field work that I conducted among the Pepel of Guinea-Bissau from 1997 to the present, 2) on an ongoing case study of a religious healer from Guinea-Bissau in Lisbon, and 3)my research with followers of the Afro-Brazilian cults (specifically *Umbanda* and Candomblé), this chapter highlights transnational religions and the relations—namely, the constant flow of goods and symbols (people, money, goods, practices, and ideas, as well as spirits that circulate and create bridges) between Portugal, Africa, and Brazil, the three points of the "Portuguese Atlantic."

Africa in Lisbon

In some of the former African countries where civil wars exploded in the aftermath of independence, social and economic living conditions worsened. People of Portuguese origin and Africans with Portuguese nationality were among the thousands of families who fled the social and political turbulence and civil wars in the new nation-states. The first movement of *retornados*, literally "people who returned" was followed in the late 1980s and the beginning of the 1990s (after the Portuguese integration in the European community) by citizens of the former colonies who were searching for jobs in Portugal or who benefited from the peripheral status of Portugal as they sought ways to migrate to other European Community countries. These migratory waves form part of the wider movements of sub-Saharan Africans toward the wealthier European countries in the northern hemisphere. The significant increase over the last decades justifies the discussion in the old continent about the social implications of the "new African diasporas" (Koser 2003).

The first wave of out-migration from Guinea coincided with the return to Portugal from the former colonies that occurred after the 1974–1975 period. In the aftermath of decolonization and the affirmation of independence and in the post-Luís Cabral (pro-Soviet) regime, Guinea's economy was opened to the outside world and the country adopted a more Western economic and democratic model. (Machado 2002; Quintino 2004) In spite of several development plans and international aid, the country never emerged from its severe poverty levels and local populations faced extremely difficult living conditions. The second migratory flow took place after 1984 when Guineans migrated to Senegal and France. Portugal rapidly became a preferred destination because of existing ties with families or friends who were already in the country, as well as some knowledge of the language.[4]

In 1996, the estimated population in Portugal of official and illegal immigrants from Guinea-Bissau was about 23,000 (Machado 2002: 86).

The number of people seeking refuge increased due to 1) the internal political instability caused by the 1998 crisis and armed conflict in Guinea-Bissau and 2) because of the worsening of social and economic conditions related to the departure of many national and international investors and companies. The official 2004 data[5] lists 25,148 legalization processes. If illegal immigrants are considered, the estimate rises to 50,000 individuals, as per the SEF 2003 figures (Có 2004).

In Guinea, political and economical instability continues to be the rule and the urge to obtain a visa or a way to leave remains a constant. Portugal is perceived as a symbolic paradise, providing employment that allows for remittances to be sent back to families of immigrants. Many struggle and invest considerable sums to obtain the much-desired visa, often resorting to claims for urgent medical treatment to bypass complicated bureaucratic procedures. Skilled laborers will often accept low paid and low status jobs and young people resort to student visas to gain entry into Portugal.

As a consequence, practically every family in Guinea has one or more relatives who reside in Portugal. The constant flow of peoples and goods back and forth is an important reality and one that is observable in the movement of people at the Lisbon airport on the days of flights to and from Bissau. The airport becomes a gathering place for relatives or friends, for goods *di tera* (from home), to send things home, and to bid farewell to those who depart with their modern Western products.

Guineans recreate their identity through the reelaboration of the references and codes from home. Once related to those of the host country, new networks and forms of interaction, institutions, symbols, and cultural practices are created. These allow for a re-creation of the past and a construction of the present through a permanent negotiating process that takes place within their own community and within the encompassing Portuguese society (Quintino 2004: 26).

According to Quintino (2004: 263), the *tchon* (original grounds) is an important territorial and ethnic reference that cuts across the different social and economic groups, as well as ethnic appurtenance. Its symbolic construction is based on language and a common past, rooted in the social organization of the *tabanka* (village) and the duties one has toward the lineage and members of the *moransa* (extended family living together in a compound). An "ethnicity package" is thus constructed, comprising several elements that are manipulated in the highly symbolic process of relating to their origins. These elements (territory, language, skin color, dress codes, commensality, music, dance, religion, and healing practices) are manipulated in order to construct one's identity in relation to other Guineans and in relation to the Portuguese. In the midst of all these, religious and healing practices are of paramount importance. In the sacralization of the new dwelling, the relationship with the ancestors must be acknowledged through the placement of the *testos* (altars) for the forefathers and the protective *irãs* (spirits), as well as all the magical-religious ceremonies that go along with such emplacements. The most significant is the *darma* (to pour beverages and food for the ancestors) owing to its symbolic connection with the ancestors in the other world. Only after the consecration of the ancestor's altars may a ritual healer start his/her practice inside the house.[6]

Brazil in Portugal

Across the Atlantic, Brazil presents an inverse migration pattern to that of Portugal. Historically an importer of people, including large numbers of Portuguese, Brazil became an exporter of people in the 1980s and 1990s. Internal economic, social, and political situations contributed to this reversal of the migratory trend that singled out Portugal (along with other European countries, the United States, and Japan) as a preferential destination. As occurred with the populations from Africa, a common language, the existence of cultural and political ties, special conditions based on bilateral agreements for those from the "sister-nation," and the existence, for some families, of consanguineous or affinity ties, enabled Brazilians to believe that they would have an easier integration in Portugal than they would elsewhere. In 1990 there were 20,851 legal Brazilians; in 2004 the figures had increased to 66,907 individuals, making Brazilians one of the most numerous groups, accounting for 14 percent and 9 percent of the total migrant universe.

Each wave of Brazilians included different social groups. The first group came in the late 1980s when Brazilian enterprises also invested economically in Portugal in search of a European market for their products and services (Vianna 2003). This group was mainly made up of professionals belonging to liberal professions, such as dentists, computer science technicians, and publicity agents.

The second wave toward the end of the 1990s followed the worsening of the social and economic conditions in Brazil. An image of Portugal as a place of employment and good salaries in a 1999 Brazilian television show portrayed Portugal as a paradise for Brazilian migrants. From 1999 to 2001, an average of 12,000 to 15,000 Brazilians per year entered the country (Vianna 2003). In this second large flow, there were more unskilled workers who were employed on construction and restoration projects (Padilla 2003). Like the Africans, most Brazilians relocated in the proximities of the two largest urban centers, Lisbon and Oporto or near to other regional capitals.

Although Brazilians claim they interact mainly with other Brazilians, associative initiatives of Brazilians do not abound.[7] Of the three associations listed in the ACIME, only one is considerably active and provides a social service through its monthly newsletter. Known as *Brazil House (Casa do Brasil)*, it had about 3,000 associates in 2006 but the number of active members was less than one third.

Long before the immigrants arrived there, Brazil entered Portuguese homes through television programs and Brazilian soap operas. The first one, broadcast nightly from May to November 1977 on one of Portuguese television's two channels, was *Gabriela Cravo e Canela (Gabriela, Clove and Cinammon)*, an adaptation of the famous novel by Jorge Amado and one of

TV Globo's most classic productions. Brazilian soap operas became a daily form of family entertainment and a channel for the introduction of Brazilian slang into the Portuguese language. Brazilian lifestyles and religious beliefs had a greater impact on the life of the Portuguese than Portuguese migration to Brazil had ever done. Owing to the paucity of television sets at that time, gatherings in local cafes, bars, and at the homes of neighbors engendered new forms of interaction and sociability that were intertwined with the acquisition of Brazilian usages and culture. Acting as the agents of globalization, Brazilian soap operas portrayed life in Brazil to audiences across the Atlantic. They also showed Brazilian lifestyles and demonstrated values to the rising Portuguese middle classes that were common to other modern Western societies but not to Portugal. Furthermore, this phenomenon recovered elements of Portuguese colonial history that enabled the Portuguese to view themselves through the lenses of the Brazilian other, albeit a very close "other" (Cunha n.d.: 19).

A television series based on Jorge Amado's book *Tenda dos Milagres* as well as a soap opera based on *Porto dos Milagres* portrayed the worlds of Candomblé and *Umbanda*. The image of Iemanjá became so familiar to the Portuguese that today it is sold in religious shops alongside the images of Our Lady of Fatima (at the best known and most important Roman Catholic pilgrimage site in Portugal) and among other saints of the Portuguese Roman Catholic pantheon.

Migrants saw Portugal as an ideal place where integration would be easy, due to language, culture, and a common past that was based on colonial relations and the constructed idea of the special relationship. The identification of self among Brazilians and Portuguese thus reflects ambiguities that were inscribed in the complex historical process and includes the emigration of the Portuguese to Brazil, the bilateral treaties and the rhetoric of an ideal Luso-Brazilian brotherhood (Padilla 2003; Machado 2002; Feldman-Bianco 2001).

In the eighteenth and nineteenth centuries, Brazil portrayed a paradise that attracted the Portuguese. Those who returned with considerable fortunes became the well-known *brasileiros de torna-viagem* (returning Brazilians) (Santos 2000). The situation whereby the Portuguese in Brazil suffered the stigma of being in a foreign country (especially from the beginning of the twentieth century onward) has now reversed itself and Brazilians are the victims of ostracism in Portugal. In fact, the Portuguese have constructed an image of Brazilians based on the stereotype of a carefree gay life that blends with other preconceived ideas about the sensuality of Brazilian women or the laziness and charlatanism of Brazilian men. The paradise for making a living became a tropical paradise transposed to Portuguese reality—most Brazilians, namely the younger ones, work in restaurants, bars, discos, or other occupations directly connected with leisure activities, not to mention professions with an even stronger connotation with the idea of pleasure, such as Brazilian prostitution. In fact, the Brazilian reputation for good humor and cheerfulness has become a necessity for the Portuguese labor market (Machado 2002).

African Spirits in Lisbon

Celeste is a Pepel woman,[8] who followed her second husband to Portugal in the late 1980s and like him, found employment. However, some years after her arrival she was afflicted with illness and bad luck, and was hearing voices at home that spoke to her and her husband. She was diagnosed as possessed by a spirit and returned to Biombo where she underwent the first set of initiation ceremonies in order to become a religious ritualist. Upon her subsequent return to Lisbon, she quit her job to devote herself entirely to her spirits and with time she became a respectable and known *djambakóss*.

The process of becoming a fully initiated *djambakóss* entails several periods of seclusion and initiation in the original grounds in Guinea-Bissau. Becoming a healer implies that the chosen person has no free will. A spirit who decides someone is to be possessed wants to work "through" him/her and if the person refuses such a call she risks dying or having someone in her family suffer severe retaliation.

The Pepel religion serves as a pillar for the collection of norms that rule the society. As elsewhere in Africa, there is an infinity of small spirits who are invoked in Creole, *irãs*, and who are pervasive in houses, in trees, or on land and may acquire the most varied forms. Religion is thus intrinsically connected to all aspects of local culture and may be analyzed as a phenomenon that is based on human interaction, given the relevance that actions, gestures, and performances acquire over dogmas and theologies (Blakely and Blakely 1994; Blakely, van Beek, Thomson 1994).

The daily observances of religion provide the means for the permanent and constant relationship that the living maintain with the world of the dead. The ancestors' altars, named in Creole *testos* and *firkidjas di alma*, are placed in both the interior and the exterior of the household. Together with the different types of sanctuaries (*balobas*, *kansarés*), they are the primary locus for the relationship with the supernatural and the operations of religious specialists, *baloberos* and *djambakoses*. In addition to the rituals performed for specific purposes or on special occasions, the relationship with the ancestors is present in everyday life and gestures. Before starting a meal, rice is prepared and drinks are poured for the ancestors (an operation called *darma* in Creole, a derivation of the Portuguese *derramar* (to pour)). In the same sense, no ceremony or rite can begin without a previous consultation of the ancestors. The most common form of consultation of the ancestors or of the *irãs* involves the inspection of the gonads of a sacrificed rooster: white gonads signify approval of the past actions and of future plans.

Religious beliefs and practices are intimately related to death and the other world. The Pepel believe that the world of the dead constitutes a replica of the social structure of the world of the living. When someone dies, his soul undertakes a voyage to the beyond, to join the deceased who have ascended to the condition of ancestors. Furthermore, the destiny of the soul of the deceased relates to and reproduces, directly or indirectly, the person as they were in life.

In order for an elder to become an ancestor (Kopytoff 1971), his/her funerary rituals have to be fully and correctly performed. Funerals are thus among the most important ceremonies of Pepel cultural and social life. The initial funerary ceremonies (*chur*) entail the cleaning of the corpse and wrapping it in cloths for days before inhumation; the secondary rituals (*toka chur*) are signaled by the beating of the bombolom drum and involve the sacrifice and bleeding of animals, specific divinatory processes, and wide commensality.

These rites aim to assure a harmonious relationship between the living and the dead and that is only possible if the deceased is correctly integrated into the sphere of the ancestors and ultimately turns into a good spirit who will watch over the living (Saraiva 1999, 2003, 2004a, 2004b).

There are constant and pressing relations between the two worlds and the deceased is perceived as a messenger who bears the cloth offerings from the funeral to the ancestors in the other world. According to this logic, all funeral attendees wish to offer gifts of cloths to the dead person in order to contribute to the success of the ceremony. They do this for reasons of reciprocity and because every household has ancestors in the other world who would be furious if their descendants in this world sent them nothing (Saraiva 2004a, 2004b).

When the *toka chur* takes place, the sacrifice of the animals (cows, pigs, and goats) is accompanied by dancing, feasting, eating, and drinking and is one of the most important features to celebrate the entrance of an elder into the ancestral world. To demonstrate their respect for the rules of reciprocity, each family who has previously received gifts for their own funeral feasts from the bereaved group must reciprocate with a more valuable gift, such as a cow for a pig, or a better or bigger cloth. Such gifts reinforce kinship and family ties. The individual and social gains involve both real and symbolic aspects. Firstly, the social prestige of offering something more costly than the gift that was received publicly displays the strength of the lineage and the *moransa*. The second gain is related to the relationship between the living and the dead since the gifts are offerings to the ancestors: "When one kills an animal, his ancestors receive it in the other world." Ritual sacrifice allows for the communication with the other world, necessary for survival (De Heusch 1986). Hence, these two elements—cloths and cattle—are essential to understanding the connection between funeral rites, the importance of the relations between the two worlds as a pillar of Pepel religion, and the "construction" of a transnational spirit. Of these two main sources of wealth and prestige for the Pepel, the cloth is mainly feminine, the cattle is masculine.

Ceremonies are more effective if performed in the primeval ground where they must fulfill the many restrictions on performances with high symbolic meaning. The *toka chur* should always take place in the original *tchon* and this implies the return of the families for this specific purpose. As a result, a *defunto* (spirit of a dead person) can never reach the category of a transnational spirit unless his/her *toka chur* has been performed back home and has conformed to the sequences and ritual principles described above: primeval ground may therefore be considered the foundation for the existence of a transnational religion.

Among the several spirits who possess the Pepel spiritual leader, Celeste, the most important and recurrent one is a male named Antonio. Antonio is a *defunto* who died very old, an *omi garandi*. Celeste emphasizes that he was highly educated (in the context of Guinea-Bissau, where illiteracy prevails) and held the position of teacher (*professor*) in Bolama, the ancient capital of Guinea. The fact that he was an educated person influenced his decision to become a *defunto* here in Portugal. She explains that Antonio decided to possess her in Lisbon in order to divulge and spread the Pepel religion and the knowledge of the *balobas* and *iras*: "he wants educated people, which is why he decided to come here to Portugal and not to Guinea. Antonio is a very smart and intelligent *defunto* and he knows how important these practices are and he wants them to become known and respected here in Portugal; he is also a very good person and wants to help people."

Antonio is given all the good qualities of a human being: he is respectable, educated and a "good defunto": he never does evil things (witchcraft), but desires only to help people. Also, he is extremely honest and any money given to him is returned if he is not able to help. There is clearly an identification between the spirit and the healer, observable in the overlapping of the mutual discourses. In the same way in which Celeste praises Antonio's honorable qualities when she talks about him, I found that during the times I conversed with Antonio when he possessed Celeste, he also stressed her good qualities both as a woman (hard working, honest) and as a healer (her good relation with him and all the spirits, her will to do good, to help people and to perform all the rituals in the best possible way).

People seek the aid of a *djambakóss* to solve the usual problems, connected with wealth, health, family disputes, emotional life, and often worries related to their migrant condition, such as difficulties in obtaining official documents or work permits.

The clients arrive with roosters, cloths, beverages, and cuts of sacrificed animals that are cooked at the outset or half way through the session. No one begins to eat before the beverages and some rice are spilled on the ground as an offering to the ancestors, to the spirit, and then shared communally. Everyone sits on the floor in the middle of the living room and all eat together, grabbing *bianda* (rice) and *máfé* (the meat or fish that accompany the rice) with their hands from the same pot. Commensality, so important in any ceremony at home, helps in recreating the setting and the proper atmosphere for the rituals that follow.

In the room where the consultations take place, a cassette player continuously reproduces the sounds of the ritual drums and traditional songs from Guinea. The setting is prepared with the *darmar* of beverages (all sorts of beverages are accepted, from soft drinks to schnapps, wine or beer) on the altar of the family ancestors (*testos*) and on the *irã*. Following the veneration of the ancestors, the healer, dressed in traditional *djambakóss* attire with a predominance of white and red, especially prominent on the cloths wrapped around her head, sits quietly by the *irã* altar and waits for the spirit.

In a normal consultation, the gifts of beverages, cloths, and the roosters for sacrifice follow another set of *darma*. After payment, the client who is barefoot (as in the sacred grounds in Guinea-Bissau) explains his/her problem and a dialogue is established between the client and Antonio in order to clarify the complaints and the reasons for the request for his assistance. A literate client is asked to write down his/her problems and secret wishes on a piece of paper that is sprinkled with rum and placed on the altar where it remains until the next consultation. Of the several *djambakósses* observed in practice, Celeste is the only one who places great importance on the written paper. This is most likely due to Antonio's specific status as a professor, a fact that Celeste emphasizes in every consultation. His intellect and higher social status are also the warranty of his skills, goodness, and good intentions.

Next, the rooster is sacrificed and its blood is poured over the *testos* and the *irã*. The rooster's insides are inspected and on the basis of the interpretation of all the signs, the *defunto* prescribes a treatment against witchcraft or maledictions; commonly known in Creole as *trabadjo*. The ritual congregates the forces of both good and evil and is crucial to clarify the use to be made of these forces. As therapy, *trabadjo* includes the *mezinho* and magical prophylactic charms, the sacrifice of animals, techniques of recovery, the cessation of sorcery, and the periodic communication between the ritualist and the supernatural (Quintino 2004: 281). The *trabadjo* may include one or several actions. The performance of these actions is preferably done at a crossroads and may entail variations such as wrapping a cloth around a piece of iron or rolling it in ashes and throwing it over one's head in order to recover from and undo the spell (Quintino 2004: 282).

The treatment often begins immediately and is performed with the spirit's assistance. The treatment includes specific libations (with water and salt or water with specific plants), lengthy conversations with the patient, the creation and consecration of lucky charms, and other practices. Considerable attention is given to the objects that are brought for the healer to transform into protective lucky charms. The goods used in the consultation must be, for the most part, *di tera*, from Guinea-Bissau, although adaptations are made when it is impossible to use goods from home. A Portuguese herb might be substituted for an African herb.

Given the importance of the goods and materials from the home country, certain areas of Lisbon have been appropriated by Africans and principally by Guineans as the locales for commercial exchanges. In the old central downtown area of Lisbon, the *Centro Comercial da Mouraria* shopping center is known for its range of shops that supply anything from Indian to African foods and artifacts. This is also true of the weekly street market, Feira do Relógio, and of certain areas near the train stations that serve the periphery of Lisbon (where many Guineans reside). Almost everything from Guinea-Bissau can be bought in such places, from traditional cloths, to artifacts, to food and medicinal products, including fresh fish and other products of the sea. Among the most important goods that are traded are the objects, artifacts, herbs and portions of dirt from the original *tabanka* since these are necessary for religious practices. An example is the *mezinho*, or the goat's horns that are used for the lucky charms that the *djambakóss* prescribe and manufacture for the patients. The downtown area of Lisbon—around the Rossio and Praça da Figueira—is also a meeting place where news circulates, and where the contractors and sub-contractors collect workers. The degree of interaction is so pronounced that Guineans themselves consider this area to be an extension of *tchon Pepel*. This was the center of Bissau and was historically the territory of the Pepel group, which gave it the name "Pepel grounds" (*tchon Pepel*), a usage that continues to this day.

Returning to the ceremony, if there is trouble, the source is often a spirit who is interfering and causing evil in order to remind the living of their obligations toward him. For example, an ancestor of the same lineage whose *toka chur* has not yet been performed demands its performance in *tchon* Pepel. As a result, to assure the healing of the person's affliction, many are advised to return home and perform the rituals. The preponderance of such diagnoses brings me back to the funeral rites and to their importance in mediating communication between the two worlds.

In the final part of the consultation, the cloths brought by the clients come into play. The cloths are offered to the *defunto* in a ceremony that is crucial to the success of the treatment. The cloths may be common European cloths, such as tablecloths, towels or sheets, or they may be African cloths, including both *panos di penti*, traditional cloths woven on the loom (*legosse*), or industrial cloths with multiple and colorful motifs. The spirit indicates the color and the type of cloth to be used as these can influence the treatment.

The patients kneel, holding the cloth over their heads and simulate a fight with the spirit, who tries to grab the cloth from them, while they repeat "It's mine! It's mine!" Only at the third attempt are they supposed to let go. The meaning of this performance is that the spirit attempts to remove evil from the person, but that he/she holds on to it until the third time, when the victorious spirit deposits the evil upon the *irã* and frees the person from its spell.

The cloth offerings are placed in Antonio's *mala*. When Celeste attends the ceremonies back home (whether for funerals or for initiation), she is supposed to take the cloths indicated by Antonio and they become his contribution to the performances. Once the deceased person has fulfilled his/her funerary rituals and becomes a protective spirit, he/she must contribute cloths for the rituals to increase the community of spirits in the other world. Wrapped around a dead person's body, the cloths that are offered to the *defunto* in Lisbon become offerings to the lineage members in the other world: they thus return back home and back to the world of the ancestors.

Umbanda in Lisbon

The well known Brazilian Igreja Universal do Reino de Deus—Universal Church of the Kingdom of God (IURD) was established in Portugal in 1989 and spread from there to the rest of Europe. A Neopentecostal church that incorporates diffused forms of spirit possession, the IURD immediately attracted Brazilian and African residents in Portugal (Mafra 2002).

Before the establishment of the IURD, Virginia, a Portuguese woman who had been an immigrant worker in Brazil for decades, returned in the 1970s and began to offer *Umbanda* consultations in the Lisbon area. Ismael Pordeus (2000) narrates her life story with extensive biographical chapters that relate in her own words the events of her life and the doctrine of *Umbanda*. In 1950, Virginia traveled to Brazil where she worked as a seamstress, married a Portuguese migrant and, after unsuccessful business pursuits and recurrent misfortune, she joined the *Umbanda* cult. At her first consultation she was diagnosed as a chosen daughter of *Omulu*. Over time, she found relief through this religion, attended the *gira* sessions (cult sessions), passed the initiation rites, and was possessed by her *boiadeiro* (herdsman). She became a *mãe de santo*. Eventually, she joined a *terreiro* and was fully initiated in *Umbanda*.

She tells that she inherited the gift of communication with the spirits from an aunt, her grandfather, and her father. She recalls possessing these faculties as a child and later as a young woman. Only a few hours before the death of her father she saw and spoke with her dead grandmother, who claimed she had come to take him. A few hours later the father died suddenly but peacefully in bed at home and Virginia spent the night in conversation with him, just as she had done upon the death of her mother-in-law.

Some years latter, she returned to Portugal with her children and against her husband's wishes decided not to go back to Brazil. Her association with a Kardecist group did not satisfy her spiritual needs and she then began to give *Umbanda* consultations in her home.

After the 1974 revolution, she inaugurated her own *terreiro* and started to perform *Umbanda* rituals there. In her biography she mentions the Portuguese eagerness for everything that was new in the social and political areas and in the field of religion she also stated how easy it was to find followers. Her first followers, *filhas* and *filhos de santo*, went on to found their own *terreiros* and to spread the practice of *Umbanda* and Candomblé. At present, Mother Virginia has one *terreiro* in Lisbon and one in the city suburbs.

Although the first centers were established by Portuguese women like *Mãe* Virginia, who in the process of emigration had become a follower of these cults, the first waves of Brazilian immigrants to Portugal included charlatan *pais* or *mães de santo* who used their nationality as an authoritative claim to practice such cults.

Gradually, the *Umbanda* and Candomblé cults became well known and spread throughout the entire country. Nowadays, there are more than six thousand *Umbanda* and Candomblé sites on the internet and over twenty *terreiros* are advertised on the internet or in newspapers for the Lisbon area alone. Many of them have branches in the northern, central, and southern parts of the country.

There is a stable core group in each center but the general clientele moves from center to center as personal needs or preferences dictate. The attitudes and performance of the cult leader dictate the direction of the center, not the directives from a central authority. Followers move to another center when they are dissatisfied with the *pai* or *mãe de santo*, the guidelines set for the *terreiro*, or on the basis of the economic orientation of the center. Visitors who seek help at a center may make a monetary contribution although each *terreiro* determines whether or not this is obligatory. The fee of the *trabalho* (therapeutical ritual) is also an important component in evaluating the honesty of the cult leader.

The rituals in a Lisbon *Umbanda terreiro* generally follow the descriptions concerning this religion. The interior space is clearly divided into two large areas separated by a wooden or iron railing. The cult leader and the initiated stand inside the sacred zone that is reserved for the ritual activities of the spirits. There are always several altars with statues of the various *orixás*, saints, and spirits, together with flowers, candles, and receptacles of water for absorbing evil fluids. In most *terreiros*, drums stand ready next to the altar to invoke the spirits.

Clients sit in the rear of the *terreiro*. Some bear flowers, cigars, pipe tobacco, or food for the spirit. Following an ordinary bath at home, mediums take a ritual bath with seven herbs. They appear in the sacred grounds dressed in festive white clothes and wearing strands of beads that represent the spirits of each medium. When everybody is assembled, the cult leader opens the session as the smoking with ritual herbs, the drumming, and the singing create the proper atmosphere.

The audience joins in the chants to intone the various *orixás* and lesser spirits. As he/she approaches the altar, an assistant swings a silver thurifer with incense to purify and protect the drummers, the mediums, and the audience against the presence of evil fluids from the outside world. The mediums prostrate themselves before the altar, receive the blessing of the cult leader, and respectfully kiss his/her hand. Sometimes, there is a collection and after more singing and drumming the cult leader gives a brief sermon and offers prayers to Oxalá and some other *orixás*. With renewed drumming the protective *orixás* are summoned and only then do the spirits (*entidades*) possess the initiated, *filhos*, and *filhas de santo* and receive clients for consultation.

During the consultations, the client explains her/his problems, and the entity enters in dialogue with the person. The consultations generally include *descarrego*, the cleansing of the fluids surrounding a person and affecting his/her well-being. These fluids can be either positive or negative energy. The positive fluid entails qualities such as good, pleasant, healthy, beautiful, and honest; the presence of the negative ones are indicated by the appearance of suffering, the qualities of evil, degeneration, fear, or sickness. Mediums move their hands, the *passes*, to draw the negative fluids away from the patient (*descarrego*). The prescription for healing that includes ablutions and gifts for the *orixá* usually ends the consultation.

Within the sacred area of the *terreiro*, several consultations take place simultaneously since many of the initiated become possessed by the same type of entity, who is invoked by the specific *pontos*. The entities are aided by the *cambonos*, who serve as helpers by writing down the specifics of each case, the comments and the prescriptions of the *orixás*. At the conclusion of the session, they converse with the client to make certain that the *orixá's* advice was clear. They make certain that the client has understood the treatment, the exact way to carry it out, the proper ingredients to use, and the proper venue, and so on.

The *terreiros* share some commonalities but each one has its own specificities on its organization and performances. This is also the case in their homeland, Brazil, as Stefania Capone (2004) emphasizes. What interests us is the clear tendency for some *terreiros* to accentuate the Roman Catholic side of their rites and performances. For instance, Mother Virginia's *terreiro*, Ogum Mejê, is much more related to the Portuguese Catholic practices and ideals. During Easter 2006, the ceremony of the Maunday Thursday foot-washing was incorporated in the Easter Saturday Umbanda rituals, illustrating Ismael Pordeus's assumption of the "Portuguese Umbanda" as a "bricolage of pre-existing practices" (Pordeus 2006). In other *terreiros* belonging to Portuguese *pais* or *mães de santo* there is no drumming and the singing follows a melody closer to the chanting of the Catholic Mass. In general, their *terreiros* developed around the charismatic figure of the Portuguese *pai* or *mãe de santo* who were once emigrants to Brazil and conceive of *Umbanda* as a religion that is close to the Portuguese Catholic matrix. The main altars incorporate all the *Umbanda* images of Father Oxalá, Mother Iemanjá side by side with the Catholic saints among which the image of Jesus Christ is preeminent and is identified as Oxalá.

Most of those who take part in the performances in these *terreiros* are exclusively middle-class Portuguese. Even in *terreiros* where the *pai* or *mãe de santo* are Brazilian, the initiated who incorporate the spirits are Portuguese, Very few Brazilians frequent these temples and the initiated (*filhos* and *filhas de santo*) are mostly Portuguese.

In contrast to the African populations in Portugal, Brazilians in Portugal rarely select the religious options that are available in the context of the diaspora. They join the IURD or other Neopentecostal churches. During the course of my fieldwork, I discovered that this attitude is directly related to the stereotypes and stigmatization that Brazilians feel in Portugal. They state that the Portuguese would look down upon them if they were known to frequent *Umbanda* or Candomblé cults so they prefer to avoid this possibility: "The Portuguese would think we go to do *feitiçaria* (witchcraft), they would disparage us even more..."

In the contexts of assumed "brotherhood" and affinities between the two cultures, it is striking how one stereotype reflects the other and entirely inverts the situation. The Portuguese are attracted by the exotic Afro-Brazilian cults and by the proximity to their Catholic matrix and respond to the appeal of Iemanjá by becoming followers of those religions.

The sessions at the *terreiros* are festive and colorful. *Umbanda* coexists in harmony with Catholicism; most of the practitioners were baptized in the Roman Catholic Church and are regular practitioners. The Portuguese are proud of their new religion and consider it to be quintessentially Brazilian without defying or distorting their Catholic matrix. People speak of the figure of Oxalá as being Jesus Christ and claim the principles of *Umbanda* are "peace and love in the world," as dictated by God. They conceive of it as a religion of goodness and light, where people meet in harmony. The spiritualist side of *Umbanda* is also very appealing since the spirits through the medium offer aid and counsel for life crises of the adherents.

Umbanda rituals are exotic, but not so exotic that they cannot be refused. They can be thought of as channels for the expression of emotions and paradigms that were imprisoned by the Catholic matrix (Pordeus 2000). *Umbanda* offers individuals an opportunity to communicate directly with the other world and to be an active partner in all of the rituals. The *pontos* that are sung to summon the spirits are intoned with a Brazilian accent but the melody is closer to the Catholic chants. The lyrics in the *pontos* clearly accentuate the messages of light, peace, and love and appeal to a Catholic population. Internet sites that advertise for the *terreiros* or for consultations emphasize love and brotherhood and convey these sentiments in one of the *pontos* from one of the sanctuaries on the *terreiros'* site:

> Reflecting divine light / in all its splendour / comes the kingdom of Oxalá / Where there is peace and love
>> Light that reflected itself on earth / light that reflected in the sea / Light that comes from Aruanda / to illuminate the world
>> Umbanda is peace and love / it is a world full of light / it is the force that gives us life / and the glory that leads us
>> Onwards, sons of faith / there is no other law like ours / taking to the whole wide world / the flag of Oxalá (http://homepage.oniduo.pt/teu/index1.htm accessed May 29, 2006)

Brazil always appears as the mother-land, the origin of the *Umbanda* cults. In order to assert his/her authority, a *pai* or *mãe de santo* is either a Brazilian or has lived in Brazil in order to acquire the knowledge and expertise necessary to perform his/her role. Just as Africa appears as a symbolic paradise and a source of legitimation of the cults in the New World, in a way that makes the discourses of both the initiated and the social scientists coincide (Capone 2004: 30), so too Brazil emerges in Portugal as the source of these Afro-Brazilian cults. As a potent means of empowerment, this works above all for the cult leaders, who must prove their efficiency and justify their reputation if they wish to increase the number of followers. But, it is also vital to the clients' concept of the honesty and respect for the cult leader. Since religious identity is continuously negotiated among the social actors (Capone 2004: 21), the fame of a *terreiro* is proportional to its success in the religious market: the greater the number of *filhos de santo* attracted by the force of the cult leader, the greater is his/her ability to manipulate the magical powers.

This situation extends beyond the life in the *terreiros* and encompasses what is listed in the Portuguese newspapers advertisements as the "esoteric" field: specialists who claim their training in Brazil or in Africa to publicize their expertise in tarot card games, interpretations of the tossing of sea shells, and other consultations to solve all problems related to wealth, love, or health.

Outside of the *terreiros, mães* and *pais de santo* periodically travel from Brasil to Lisbon to give consultations. They develop a regular clientele through word of mouth and do not generally advertise their services in newspapers or elsewhere. As Pordeus (2006b) stresses, such cases illustrate "the anti-communitas," since these persons operate alone, without the ritual framework of a religious community: the consultations are personal and there is no associated collective ritual.

When *Mãe* Virginia returned from Brazil, she read everything available on Afro-Brazilian religions and found that a lot was missing. She began to write her thoughts and to codify the doctrine of *Umbanda* as she conceptualized it and taught it to her *filhos de santo*. Toward the end of the 1990s, she stated that the literary production of the *terreiro* included four different collections of books, one subdivided into four sections and dozens of shorter pamphlets and brochures (Pordeus 2000) that she targeted to insiders as well as the clientele from outside.

Within the Omolocô tradition, Pordeus emphasizes how aspects of Candomblé and *Umbanda* doctrines come together, and how Mother Virginia's writings project the paradigm of a Portuguese ideal of the symbolic union Portugal-Africa-Brazil (Pordeus 2000: 249). In her discovery of new religious instances in postrevolutionary Lisbon, Mother Virginia stressed how writing could become a founding memory, an entirely new starting point (Pordeus 2000: 250). Her writings thus became a metaphor of her new life in Lisbon, her standing as a *mãe de santo*, and her founding of a *terreiro*.

Pordeus (2000: 15) analyzes the transition to the writing of the teachings of *Umbanda* as a field (beginning in the early twentieth century with Nina Rodrigues's writings) where both practitioners and scholars interact. He explores how this written material returns to its original sources (the *terreiros* and their practitioners) and thus legitimizes the imaginary and the religious practices in the *terreiros*. This is even more important in the writings of Mother Virginia that are a codified set of doctrines and practices that orient the life and ceremonies in the *terreiro*—synthesizing religious doctrine, rites, myths, defining the nature of ritual time and space, and explaining the Candomblé-*Umbanda* synthesis that is Omolocô.

Three Worlds Meet: Africa and Brazil in Portugal

As with any group that has been displaced from its original setting, the Guinean and the Brazilian communities in Lisbon may be regarded as structured on the basis of invented communities. They are thought of as an ensemble of permanently reorganized and reelaborated cultural symbols that promote and symbolize social cohesion, legitimate institutions, status, and power relations. They act as factors of socialization, providing individuals with value systems, beliefs, and behavior patterns (Anderson 1991; Hobsbawm 1983; Quintino 2004: 34). Quintino refers to the concept of "trans-identity" adopted by Berque (Quintino 2004: 35) as an identity forged in a permanent relationship between the migrants and the host society. This identity is also forged with the original community and its desire to "go back home one day," a frequently uncertain possibility that may never become a reality and often denotes a constant back and forth movement between the original and the host countries (Rocha-Trindade 1983). The ethnic group and the nation may be thought of as a symbolically constructed imagined community since its members share a sentiment of belonging, but they cannot interact as a real community (Anderson 1991).

Both Guineans and Brazilians are attracted toward the "Portuguese paradise," a land where they can improve their lives and eventually return home to enjoy an improved social and economic lifestyle. These two groups of migrants suffer discrimination and are, to some degree or other, stigmatized (Bastos 2006; Machado 2002; Quintino 2004).

But what is the role of religion in these diaspora situations? In the two cases described above we see instances of transnational religions, where religious healers travel from their spiritual grounds to Portugal and bring along the divinities of the original pantheons, as well as the spirits and entities that possess the initiated. In both cases, the connection with the "motherland" is a source of empowerment and authority for those religious ritualists who either regularly return to their homeland to strengthen their power or continue to live there and travel to Portugal for specific celebrations.

The relation of each group to religions that originated in their respective homelands is different. The two groups of religious ritualists attempt to acquire Portuguese followers but only one is successful. In the midst of the recent multicultural and multireligious environment in Portugal, *mães* and *pais de santo* attract mainly Portuguese clients whereas *djambakósses* from Guinea-Bissau basically receive Africans.

For the people from Guinea-Bissau who live in Lisbon, religion is a major ethnic reference and around it cluster other elements that help to reconstruct an identity in the diaspora. In fact, when Guineans migrate to Portugal, their religious performances, performers, and the spirits who operate to help people in their life crises come along; but the links with the original setting remain and are a means of empowerment for all those who intervene (the clients, the religious healers, and the spirits). They all become transnational characters in a complex set of relations between the living and the dead in Africa. Transposed to the diaspora universe, such relations incorporate transnational circumstances. African practices are "translated" in order to accommodate a different context and they give rise to a continuous flow of people, spirits, and goods that move back and forth between Guinea-Bissau and Portugal.

Whereas consultations with the *djambakóss* and the cultural setting that this encompasses help Guineans in Lisbon to feel that they are among their own people, closer to their home and their traditions, *Umbanda* rituals are disregarded by Brazilians who instead lead the Portuguese into a world that was previously foreign to them.

Umbanda and Candomblé have become universal religions that are codified in writing and their followers are spread over vast regions from Brazil to Europe. In contrast, the Pepel religion represents a minor religious system that is strongly connected to a world where kinship and lineage play a decisive role. The Pepel religion is not codified and is followed by a relatively small number of people. The two cases invite reflection about people's ability to manipulate the plurality of their available identities as these are placed in various levels of categorization according to the different contexts or social stages in which they interact while attempting to match social expectations (Bastos and Bastos 2006: 37; Goffman 1963).

Within the diaspora movement, several authors have stressed how the strengthening of attitudes toward territorialized origins (the "roots") are used to align identities (Clarke 2004 in Capone 2004: 11), and how the passage from the local to the global reveals a tension zone where multiple codes enter into contact, sometimes striving to differentiate themselves, and in other instances, mingling together (Capone 2004: 12). Spaces where migrants gather are places for continuous negotiation of individual and collective identities and for permanent processes of cultural interpenetrations and reconfigurations.

Capone makes the claim (2004: 16) that individuals in the diaspora who have taken routes to foreign places and are deprived of their roots will follow their original religions. This is a useful claim but we need to further examine the ways in which people and their religions adapt to the new social and cultural contexts of the nation-states that receive them. What happens with Brazilians and Guineans in Lisbon—and, more specifically, with their religious systems—illustrate these points.

Engendered in a context where the population movements have been a tradition for centuries, the Brazilian case illustrates how important the historical processes are to the understanding of the current situation. Portugal, a nation that exported people to Brazil becomes an importer of individuals, but it is a returned Portuguese emigrant who introduces the Afro-Brazilian religions that attract Portuguese adherents. In contrast, the rituals and beliefs from the West African coast that are not so distant from the Afro-Brazilian ones in their origins, essence, and doctrine, maintain a closed identitary connection with the populations of African origin. The coexistence of the religions in Lisbon makes this a field where the transnationalization of religions inspires reflection upon the interweaving of historical and symbolic processes within the Lusophone Black Atlantic.

Notes

This text would not have been possible without the collaboration of Ismael Pordeus Jr., who has worked on the *Umbanda* cults in Portugal for the past ten years, and who first took me to the terreiros in the Lisbon area. I want to express my gratitude for all his help in compiling the information that is being presented.

1. Some authors (namely Malheiros 2005) stress, however, that Portugal continues to export mainly temporary workers to some European destinations within the European community and Switzerland. In accordance with this data, Barreto (2005) correctly stresses that within less than half a century Portugal was faced with all the possible ramifications of migrant movements: an exporter and importer of people within different scenarios—transatlantic, European, definite and temporary, integration problems, black market strategies, and precarious lives.
2. At the time, all of the remaining Portuguese possessions were in Africa, except for Macau and Timor.
3. Universal Church of the Kingdom of God, hereafter abbreviated as IURD.
4. Although Portuguese is spoken by only roughly 10 percent of the population, it is nevertheless the official language and the one used in official or public interactions.
5. Sources: SEF (Serviço de Estrangeiros e Fronteiras—Service for Foreigners and Frontiers) and ACIME (High Comissariat for Immigration and Ethnic Minorities).
6. I refer here to the "animists" coming from the coastal area of Guinea-Bissau; toward the interior of the country Islamic groups prevail, and the number of Islamized Guineans in Lisbon is high, but not the subject of this text.
7. Compared with the high number of associations of migrants from Guinea-Bissau (around twenty) or African, in general (over ten).
8. One amongst the over twenty-three ethnic groups in Guinea-Bissau, the Pepel occupy the area corresponding to the former Bissau island and the Biombo peninsula, and belong to the animist groups of coastal populations, in opposition to the Islamized groups in the interior of the country.

Bibliography

Anderson, B. 1991. *Imagined Communities: Reflections on the Origin and Spread of Nationalism*. London: Verso.

Ariés, P. 1989. *Sobre a História da Morte no Ocidente desde a Idade Média*. Lisbon: Teorema.

Barreto, A., ed. 2004. *Globalização e Migrações*. Lisbon: Instituto de Ciências Sociais. 1996.

Barth, F., ed. 1969. *Ethnic Groups and Boundaries. The Social Organization of Culture Difference*. Oslo: Universitetforlaget.

Bastos, J. 2000. *Portugal Europeu. Estratégias Identitárias Inter-Nacionais dos Portugueses*. Oeiras: Celta.

Bastos, J. and S. Bastos. 1999. *Portugal Multicultural. Situação e Identificação das Minorias Étnicas*. Lisbon: Fim de Século.

Baudry, P. 1999. *La Place des Morts. Enjeux et Rites*. Paris: Armand Colin.

Blakely, P. and T. Blakely. 1994. "Ancestors, Witchcraft and Foregrounding the Poetic: Men's Oratory and Women's Song-dance in Hemba Funerary Performance," in T. Blakely, W. van Beek, and D. Thomson, eds. *Religion in Africa. Experience and Expression*. London: James Currey; Portsmouth, NH: Heinemann, pp.398–442.

Blakely, T., W. van Beek, and D. Thomson, eds. 1994. *Religion in Africa. Experience and Expression*. London: James Currey; Portsmouth NH: Heinemann, pp.398–442.

Bloch, M. and J. Parry, eds. 1982. *Death and the Regeneration of Life*. Cambridge: Cambridge University Press.

Capone, S. 2004. *A busca de África no Candomblé. Tradição e Poder no Brasil*. Rio de Janeiro: Pallas Editora.

Capone, S., ed. 2004. *Civilisations. Revue Internationale d'Anthropologie et de Sciences Humaines. Religions Transnationales*. Bruxelles: Université Libre de Bruxelles.

Có, J. 2004. "As associações das comunidades migrantes em Portugal e a sua participação no desenvolvimento do país de origem: o caso guineense." *SOCIUS Working Papers* 12, 2004.

Coppet, D. de. 1992. *Understanding Rituals*. London: Routledge.

Cunha, I. n.d. "A revolução da Gabriela : o ano de 1977 em Portugal" accessed May 29, 2006 at www.bocc.ubi.pt/pag/Cunha-isabel-ferin-revolucao-gabriela.pdf.

Déchaux, J.H. 2001. "Un nouvel âge du mourir : La mort en soi." *Recherches Sociologiques* 32(2): 79–100.

De Heusch, L. 1986. *Le Sacrifice dans les Religions Africaines*. Paris: Plon.

Einarsdottir, J. 2000. *"We are tired of crying." Child Death and Mourning among the Pepel of Guinea-Bissau*. Stockholm: Stockholm University.

Feldman-Bianco. 2001. "Brazilians in Portugal, Portuguese in Brazil: Construction of Sameness and Difference." *Identities* 8(4): 607–650.

Garcia, J. 2000a. *Portugal Migrante. Emigrantes e Imigrados. Dois estudos introdutórios*. Oeiras: Celta.

———. 2000b. *Migrações e Relações Internacionais. Uma Bibliografia*. Oeiras: Celta.

———. 2000c. *Estranhos. Juventude e Dinâmicas de Exclusão Social em Lisboa*. Oeiras: Celta.

Goodman, F. 1988. *How about Demons? Possession and Exorcism in the Modern World*. Bloomington, IN.: Indiana University Press.

Gusmão, N. 2004. *Os Filhos de África em Portugal. Multiculturalismo e Educação*. Lisbon: Instituto de Ciências Sociais.

Hertz, R. 1960. "Contribution to the Study of the Collective Representation of Death," in Hertz, R. *Death and the Right Hand*. Glencoe: The Free Press.

Hobsbawm, E. and T. Ranger. 1983. *The Reinvention of Tradition*. Cambridge: Cambridge University Press.

Horowitz, D. 1985. *Ethnic Groups in Conflict*. Berkeley: University of California Press.

Kopytoff, I. 1971. "Ancestors as Elders in Africa." *Africa* 41(2): 129–142.

Koser, K. 2003. *New African Diasporas*. London: Routledge.

Machado, F. 2002. *Contrastes e Continuidades. Migração, Etnicidade e Integração dos Guineenses em Portugal*. Oeiras: Celta.

Machado, I. 2002. "Cárcere público: os estereótipos como prisão para os brasileiros no Porto, Portugal." *Revista Temáticas Revista dos Pós Graduandos Em Ciências Sociais do IFCH, Unicamp*, Campinas 10(19/20): 120–152.

Mafra, Clara. 2002. *Na Posse da Palavra. Religião, Conversão e Liberdade Pessoal em dois Contextos Nacionais*. Lisbon: Insituto de Ciências Sociais.

Malheiros, J. 2005. "Jogos de relações internacionais: repensar a posição de Portugal no arquipélago migratório global," in A. Barreto, ed. *Globalização e Migrações*. Lisbon: Instituto de Ciencias Sociais, pp.251–272.

Metcalf, P. and R. Huntington. 1991. *Celebrations of Death. The Anthropology of Mortuary Ritual*. Cambridge: Cambridge University Press.

Motta, R. 1995. "Sacrifício, Mesa, Festa e Transe na Religião Afro-Brasileira." *Horizontes Antropológicos* 3: 31–38.

Padilla, Beatriz. 2003. "Os novos fluxos migratórios: tipos e respostas no velho e no novo mundo." Paper delivered at the 8th Metropolis Conference, Vienna 2003.

Pais, J.M., M.V. Cabral, and J. Vala, eds. 2001. *Atitudes Sociais dos Portugueses. Religião e Bioética*. Lisbon: Instituto de Ciencias Sociais.

Pina-Cabral, J. 1984. "A morte na Antropologia Social." *Análise Social* 20(2–3): 349–356.

Pires, R. 2003. *Migrações e Integração*. Oeiras: Celta.

Pordeus Jr., I. 1997. "Lisboa de caso com a Umbanda." *Revista da USP* 31: 90–113. São Paulo.

———. 2000. *Uma casa luso-afro-brasileira com certeza. Emigrações e metamorfoses da Umbanda em Portugal*. São Paulo: Terceira Margem.

———. 2004. "A Umbanda Portuguesa na Internet." *OPIS - Revista do NIESC: Universidade Federal de Goiás - Catalão - GO* 4: 7–24.

———. 2006a. "Lava-pés na Umbanda portuguesa." Paper presented at the V *Congresso de Estudos Africanos do Mundo Ibérico. África: compreender trajectos, olhar o futuro*. Covilhã, May 2006: Universidade da Beira Interior.

———. 2006b. "Mujeres ejemplares. Mães de santo em Lisboa." Paper presented at the conference *Colóquio Género, sexualidad y práticas religiosas populares*, Universidade de Cádiz, May 2006.

Portes, A. 1998. *Migrações Internacionais. Origens, tipos e modos de incorporação*. Oeiras: Celta.

Quintino, C. 2000. *Migrações e Etnicidade em Terrenos Portugueses. Guineenses : Estratégias de Invenção de uma Comunidade*. Lisbon: Universidade Técnica de Lisboa-Instituto Superior de Ciências Sociais e Politicas.

Rocha-Trindade, M. 1983. "O regresso imaginado." *Nação e Defesa* 28: 3–13.

Saint-Maurice, A. 1997 *Identidades reconstruídas. Cabo-Verdianos em Portugal*. Oeiras: Celta.

Santos, E. 2000. "Os brasileiros de Torna-Viagem no Noroeste de Portugal." *Os Brasileiros de Torna-Viagem*. Lisbon: Comissão Nacional para as Comemorações dos Descobrimentos Portugueses.

Saraiva, C. 1999. "Rios de Guiné do Cabo Verde. Rituais Funerários entre Portugal e Africa. Uma Etnografia da Morte em Cabo Verde e nos Papéis da Guiné-Bissau." Dissertação para Provas de Acesso a Investigador Auxiliar. Lisbon: Instituto de Investigação Cientifica Tropical.

———. 2003. "Rituais funerários entre os Papeis da Guiné-Bissau (Parte I)." *Soronda. Revista de Estudos Guineenses* 6: 179–209.

———. 2004a. "Rituais funerários entre os Papeis da Guiné-Bissau (Parte II)." *Soronda, Revista de Estudos Guineenses* 8: 179–210.

———. 2004b. "Embalming, Sprinkling and Wrapping Bodies: Death Ways in America, Portugal and Guinea-Bissau." *Symposia Journal for Studies in Ethnology and Anthropology 2004* publication of The International Conference Death and The Orient, May 2004, Center for Studies in Folklife and Traditional Culture of Dolj County: 97–119.

———. 2006. "Transnational Migrants and Transnational Spirits: An African Religion in Lisbon." *Journal for Ethnic and Migration Studies* (in print).

Téchio, K. 2006a. "Conhecimento de alterne: a outra diáspora das imigrantes brasileiras." *SOCIUS working papers* 2, 2006.

———. 2006b. "Imigrantes brasileiros não documentados: uma análise comparativa entre Lisboa e Madrid." *SOCIUS working papers* 1, 2006.

Thomas, L.V. 1985. *Rites de Mort. Pour la Paix des Vivants*. Paris: Fayard.

Vala, Jorge, ed. 1999. *Novos Racismos. Perspectivas Comparativas*. Oeiras: Celta.

Vale de Almeida, M. 2000. *Outros destinos. Ensaios de Antropologia e cidadania*. Lisbon: Campo das Letras.

Vianna, C. 2003. "A comunidade brasileira em Portugal" accessed May 29, 2006 at http://www.casadobrasildelisboa.rcts.pt/arq-artigos/comunidade-brasileira.doc.

Vilaça, H. 2001. "Identidades, práticas e crenças religiosas," in J. Pais, M. Cabral, and J. Vala, eds. *Atitudes Sociais dos Portugueses. Religião e Bioética.* Lisboa: Instituto de Ciencias: Sociais, pp.75–128.

Wilson, B. 1982. "Sympathetic Detachment and Disinterested Involvement." *Sociological Analysis* 44: 183–188.

Wilson, W. 1963. "Talking Drums in Guiné." *Estudos sobre a Etnologia do Ultramar Português* 102: 200–219.

Part III

Hybridity, Multiculturalism, and Racial Politics

Chapter 9

History and Memory in *Capoeira* Lyrics from Bahia, Brazil

Matthias Röhrig Assunção

Over the last years, British television has shown clips of *capoeira* almost daily. One of the "idents" used by the British Broadcasting Corporation to advertise multiethnic "Cool Britannia" features *capoeira*, and is usually broadcast at prime time just before the ten o'clock news. This is just one example of how globalized *capoeira* has become, and it also demonstrates how much young Brazilians from modest backgrounds and with no formal education can achieve through *capoeira*. Yet *capoeira*'s very success also entails the danger that the art might become just another commodity marketed by global capitalism. *Capoeira* is not just a different type of aerobics or flashy acrobatics accompanied by exotic music. It is a multilayered art form of amazing cultural density, with its own worldview and a history closely linked to that of the African Diaspora. The lyrics are central to the *capoeira* game to stimulate players or to comment on their performance and are thus worth an analysis on their own.

Slaves and freed people widely practiced combat games in late colonial and imperial Brazil. Different modalities, known under the generic name *capoeira*, developed according to both the vicissitudes of the transatlantic and internal slave trades and the local contexts in Pará, Pernambuco, Bahia, Rio de Janeiro, and other regions. *Capoeira* usually involved some form of mock combat in a circle, the *roda* (ring), accompanied by instruments, hand clapping, and singing. Whilst friendly games were part of slave and popular diversions, rougher games could end in brawls, injuries, and even death.

Throughout the Brazilian Empire (1822–1889), authorities considered that playing *capoeira* was "unacceptable behavior" requiring immediate correction in the form of whipping and forced labor in the Navy dockyards. The Republican Penal Code (1890) outlawed it together with vagrancy. Repression of the *capoeiras*,[1] although brutal, was often unsystematic and inefficient.[2]

Where and how did *capoeira* originate? This is a question twentieth-century practitioners often raised and still discuss with passion since *capoeira* is paramount to the construction of several identities. Since primary sources referring to *capoeira* or anything similar in Brazil only extend back to the early nineteenth century, adepts have advanced theories about its origins that suit their particular aspirations and world views. They therefore emphasize either the "Brazilian," or the "African" character of *capoeira*, and eventually tend to fabricate the appropriate foundational myths.[3] The narratives of its origins intersect (though not entirely overlap) with discourses of purity versus miscegenation and these are also paramount to the definition of contemporary styles.

To simplify, we can distinguish three theories. Brazilian nationalists insist that *capoeira* was invented in the Portuguese colonies in America. Authors such as Burlamaqui suggested that runaway slaves, living close to nature in the distant backlands, were inspired by the movements of animals. He therefore concluded that *capoeira* originated entirely within the Brazil environment.[4] In contrast, Afrocentric theories emphasize the importance of the slaves' original cultural backgrounds. One theory defends a single African origin of *capoeira* from the Kongo/Angola region (1928: 11–12). A third hypothesis suggests that in Brazil *capoeira* resulted from the amalgamation of different African combat traditions.

In my opinion, at the present state of knowledge on the subject, the last theory is the most convincing and consequently enjoys the most widespread support among the *capoeira* community. No early modern source documents the existence of any art in Africa that is similar to *capoeira*, even though there are specific formal similarities in some contemporary phenomena. Yet the coexistence of various combat games practiced by enslaved Africans in one location is clearly documented in Brazil. In Bahia, for instance, *capoeira* was practiced alongside *batuque* and *maculêlê*, and eventually incorporated and absorbed the latter two during the twentieth century. The existence of different styles within *capoeira* and the struggle over what movements should or should not be allowed also suggests that these might derive from different and conflicting martial traditions. Moreover, specific rhythms and associated types of games were often identified with a particular neo-African "nation" (*nação*), for example, Angola, Benguela, or with Catholic saints (São Bento, Santa Maria). The worship of saints, as practiced by lay brotherhoods, equally fulfilled the function of aggregating slaves and freed people from similar ethnic backgrounds in the Catholic colonies of the Americas. The coexistence of these different types of rhythms and games also suggests that—analogous to Candomblé—different African combat traditions came together in Brazilian *capoeira*.

In the particular case of Bahia, *capoeira* evolved further during the last decades of the nineteenth and the first decades of the twentieth century, especially among porters, stevedores, sailors, and fishermen in the port areas of Salvador and the towns of the adjacent sugar belt around the Bay of All Saints. "Vagrancy" (*vadiação*), as its adepts called it, was played in breaks during work or in popular neighborhoods on Sundays. It provided entertainment and relaxation from hard labor. Playing *capoeira* or "being idle" (*vadiar*) became an integral part of a broader Afro-Bahian popular culture. Together with *samba-de-roda* and *batuque* it had a prominent place in the multicultural cycle of celebrations to honor Catholic saints and associated African divinities (from December to Carnival). At least by the end of the nineteenth century, *capoeira* had become a complex manifestation with elaborated rituals.

During the twentieth century, *capoeira* underwent a process of modernization. Paramount to this development were the "Regional" and "Angola" styles that developed in Bahia from 1930 onward. These styles were exported to other regions of Brazil, in particular to Rio de Janeiro and São Paulo, where they underwent further changes and fused into what is known as "contemporary *capoeira*." Since the 1980s, *capoeira* has experienced an impressive process of globalization and is now played across the five continents.

This chapter examines how *capoeira* lyrics tell the history of the Afro-Brazilian experience. In my analysis of some core themes—Africa, slavery and abolition, wars and famous fighters—I intend to show how *capoeira* maintains a complex and dynamic relation with the past that still provides inspiration and models for contemporary practice. As adepts and scholars have pointed out, the *capoeira* game reenacts the past, a "sinister" past of oppression and betrayal, but also one of resistance and playfulness (Downey 1998: 121).

The Lyrics in the Game

Even though *capoeira* could become a lethal weapon in street fights, everyday practice in Bahia took the form of a game in which it was more important to show the harm one could do to the other player rather than actually cause injury to an opponent. Adepts in Bahia explicitly referred to it as *brincadeira*, or *jogo* ("playing" or "game") and even today the performance in the *capoeira roda* (circle) is called a game. *Capoeira* took place in an imaginary *roda* that was formed by the orchestra (*bateria*) and the other participants or spectators. Two players knelt in front of each other and next to the orchestra at the "foot" of the *berimbau* (percussion instrument). They listened to preliminary chants until the lead singer intoned one standard phrase such as "turn around the world" ("volta ao mundo"). That was the signal for the game to begin. Players genuflected, drew signs on the ground, and started their game. Many *capoeira* groups today still comply with that basic structure.

We do not know what African slaves sang in the nineteenth century *rodas*, but they must have chanted in their own languages. Yet, unlike Candomblé, where secrecy and initiation are paramount, and where the core of religious chants are still based on African languages, more profane celebrations such as *samba-de-roda*, *batuque*, and *capoeira* aimed to reach and appeal to wider, multiethnic audiences. We can thus assume that *capoeira* songs creolized more rapidly, even though we still do not know how that process took place. It is possible that early *capoeira* songs in Portuguese were translations of original African songs. They may have merged verses from various languages and literary traditions from several cultures. Since no nineteenth century transcripts are known, it is difficult to make any definitive statement on the matter although a systematic comparison with African and European genres might shed more light on this issue. Antônio Risério, for instance, has highlighted the influence of Yoruba *oriki* on contemporary Brazilian writing and the lyrics of MPB (Popular Brazilian Music) (1995: 165–183). Waldeloir Rego has emphasized the influence of medieval Portuguese genres on *capoeira* lyrics (1968: 235, 240, 245).

Capoeira lyrics sung in twentieth century *rodas* touch on many themes. They articulate the everyday struggle for survival or reflect on human relationships and sentiments such as love and friendship, envy and competition. They fulfill a range of functions within the game and beyond it. In formal terms, four basic types of *capoeira* songs can be distinguished. The introductory "litany" (*ladainha*) consists of a monologue by the lead singer who is usually one of the more experienced players or a respected teacher (*mestre*). Since everyone is expected to pay particular attention at this time, the singer uses the moment to pass his personal message to the audience. This is followed by the "praise" (*louvação, canto de entrada* or *chula*), where the chorus repeats the verse of the lead singer. At this time, praise is offered to deceased *mestres* and then to living *mestres* or teachers who might be present ("Iê, long live my *mestre*"). The audience is then informed that the game is about to begin, or that the players are wicked or particularly good at using head butts (*mandingueiro, cabeçeiro*). The praise can also be used to warn one player about the strengths of his opponent. When the lead singer starts a *corridor* (short verses that the audience answers with a refrain) the players begin their game.

These three types of song and their sequence are still part and parcel of many of the contemporary *capoeira rodas* that attempt to closely follow tradition. It is therefore difficult to assess to what extent earlier practices departed from this structure. Evidence does suggest that there was at least a fourth type of song, a *quadra* that was commonly executed in early-twentieth-century Bahian *rodas*. According to Greg Downey, the *quadra* is "a type of short solo that is followed by call and response and can be sung during play, unlike the solo *ladainha* which will stop play"(1998: 124). M. Bimba, among others, excelled in *quadras* and has recorded some of them.[5] Finally, the *cantiga de sotaque* represented a variation or sub-type of the *ladainha* mode. Instead of one player, it consisted of two players who improvized verses alternatively to challenge each other. The *cantigas de sotaque* usually preceded a game between *mestres* or experienced players able to improvize. (Lewis 1992: 169–172) They thus resembled the verbal challenges (*desafios*) common in the popular culture of northeast Brazil.

As Lewis wrote, "the introductory *ladainha/chula* complex clearly establishes a ritual framework for the play to follow" (1992: 217). This ritual framework was maintained during the game in a number of ways. Many *corridos* that were sung during play continued to ask for spiritual protection or referred to a wider religious context. A *roda* was usually closed by a specific *corrido* ("Adeus, adeus"), announcing that the players were about to depart with the protection of God and Our Lady the Virgin Mary. Many *corrido* lyrics take the form of proverbs, which transmit an important insight: "Whoever can't cope with *mandinga* (witchcraft) should not carry an amulet" ("Quem não pode com mandinga, não carrega patuá").[6] Since lyrics frequently use metaphors or allusions, their meaning is never straightforward, but often ambiguous and multilayered. *Mandinga*, for instance, also refers to a particular twisted manner of moving in *capoeira*, which is considered an important asset for good style.

Capoeira lyrics also only acquire their full meaning in the context of the *roda*. The particular situation of the game often explains why the orchestra intones a specific *corrido*. For example, when a small player fells a bigger one, the lead singer might sing: "Baraúna caiu, quanto mais eu" (Baraúna [a huge tree] has fallen, even more so do I). When a player dislikes the jiu-jitsu-type grabbing used in some styles but frowned upon in others, he or the lead singer might start singing: "Ô Dona Alice não me pegue não" (Oh, Dona Alice don't grab me).[7] *Capoeira* lyrics can thus tell an episode from the past but at the same time use this episode to comment on the present.

Furthermore, the song will never provide a detailed account of an historical episode. It will only allude to some key moments of a story that the *mestres* or the older players previously made known to the audience in conversations that took place after the *roda,* the training sessions, or on other occasions. Songs therefore relate to broader narratives that have been transmitted in other ways and forms. The polysemy of terms and the ambiguity of a particular episode alluded to in a song allows adepts to play with meanings.

The lyrics entertain a complex relationship with the game as it develops in the *roda*. Songs induce players to "let out their *mandinga*," to play slowly using all their resources, or to play fast and aggressively. The songs exhort the players and the audience to respect and to follow the traditions of *mestres* who have long since died. The lyrics may also ironically comment on the actual game by drawing comparisons with the past or by improvising critical remarks that are directed toward the players in the *roda*. The possibility of using tradition to interpret the present and to improvise new verses that are adequate for any situation is seen by adepts as a key aspect of *capoeira* lyrics. It allows them to channel emotions and to control aggression within the framework of the *roda*. It places the actual performance within a broader, almost timeless sequence of games that stretches back to an immemorial past. And, finally, it allows practitioners to critically comment on distance themselves from events that are taking place inside and outside the *roda*.[8]

History and Memory in *Capoeira* Lyrics

Waldeloir Rego made it clear that no clean division is possible between the "old" and the "present day" *capoeira* songs. Many lyrics that are considered new are in fact based on very old songs, whereas songs called traditional sometimes have quite recent origins. He also pointed out the difficulty of distinguishing between *capoeira* songs proper and songs of other provenance (*samba*, Candomblé, etc.) that are used in a *capoeira roda* (1968: 89). The distinction between "traditional" and "new" songs is difficult because of the tension that exists between tradition and innovation in any *roda* performance. *Corridos*, for example combine a verse by the solo singer with a refrain by the chorus. Whilst the refrain is often traditional, experienced solo singers begin with a couple of traditional verses and then add their own verses or improvise them on the spot. The same happens in the praise songs, where the solo singer can add new verses to the traditional ones that are then repeated by the chorus.

When Rego published his classic account in 1968, he had witnessed the modernization of the art since the 1930s and thought it necessary to warn his readers against a simplistic distinction between traditional and new songs. The transformations of *capoeira* since its spread throughout Brazil in the 1960s and, more recently into other countries were even more substantial than the changes that Rego observed. The following example illustrates the way songs are disseminated. Every *capoeira* group can now record its own CD and this constitutes a source of prestige and further income if other groups and the wider *capoeira* community adopt the new songs.

For historians, it is nevertheless important to try to distinguish the lyrics that were used at different moments of *capoeira* history. Since the beginning of the last century, for example, some ethnographers and folklorists have transcribed the lyrics that they collected on the spot. Manuel Querino, Edison Carneiro, Antônio Viana and some others have provided us with precious examples from the first decades of the twentieth century. In 1941, Lorenzo Dow Turner recorded *capoeira* songs from two Bahian *mestres* (Bimba and Cabeçinha).

The samples were, however, very limited and unsystematic. Rego's book, which contains over 150 *capoeira* lyrics that he registered from many different *mestres*, represents the first systematic attempt at compilation. The texts he collected reflect what was being sung in Salvador during the 1950s and 1960s. His compilation already contains some important innovations that relate to the emergence of the two modern Regional and Angola styles. I believe, however, that these songs are still relatively traditional when compared to the impressive quantity of new songs that have been composed, performed, and recorded over the last forty years. Together with the songs performed by the "old guard" of Bahian *mestres* such as Waldemar, Traíra, Canjiquinha, Caiçara, Pastinha, Bimba, João Pequeno, João Grande, Paulo dos Anjos, and others (recorded during the 1960s or later) they constitute a corpus that can be considered traditional in opposition to the many and entirely new *capoeira* songs.

It is nevertheless important to emphasize that traditional does not mean unaltered. In the case of the *ladainhas,* a set number of verses of different length are recognized as coming from the public domain. Many *mestres* combine them in their own, original way, often adding or inserting some verses of their own composition. In the case of the *louvação,* a set of well-known praises from the public domain is often followed by a number of new ones that closely follow the established model. The traditional *corridos* start with a basic refrain and some well-known solo verses from the public domain. Every performer may or may not add some new solo verses that still use the traditional refrain. Each performance can therefore consist of an original combination of traditional elements and the eventual addition of new or more recent verses. In other words, although the core of the older lyrics can be considered traditional, their performance always allows for innovation. This dynamic has led to the existence of many different versions of one *ladainha* or the recurrent use of the same verses in different *capoeira* songs.

Once we recognize the importance of creative bricolage through which traditional songs are complemented and enriched by new additions and interpretations, it is difficult to maintain a strict separation between old and new. Instead of attempting to neatly separate traditional and recent lyrics, it is better to distinguish those from the public domain from entirely new songs by a known composer.[9] The core structure of these songs from the public domain may be very ancient but this does not exclude recent additions. Unfortunately, it is only sometimes possible to document older versions and in any case, we cannot track them farther back than the first decades of the twentieth century. With regards to the new songs, some *mestres* of the Angola style, such as M. João Pequeno, João Grande, Boca Rica, Paulo dos Anjos, Moraes, or Roberval create entirely new songs that remain within the parameters of tradition, although what exactly tradition entails can still be the subject of heated debates. Composers who represent other contemporary styles take much greater liberties so that some recent *capoeira* lyrics and songs have a greater resemblance to contemporary Brazilian funk or rap.

Since *capoeira* lyrics thematize human relations in specific historical contexts, they can be considered, at least in the broadest sense, to constitute an historical source. Yet, many songs also have a universalizing message about human behavior that evades historical examination. I will therefore concentrate on four themes that seem to me particularly suited to the analysis of the relationship that practitioners have with history and memory: Africa, slavery and abolition, wars involving Brazilians, and famous *capoeira* fighters. For reasons of space I will limit my discussion to the lyrics, and exclude the narratives that *mestres* told before or after the *rodas*, during classes or during other events.

Africa in *Capoeira* Lyrics

There can be no doubt that Brazilian *capoeira* is linked in many ways to the cultures of the enslaved Africans. *Capoeira* in Rio de Janeiro and Bahia has been repeatedly associated with the Angolas and Benguelas, the slaves deported from Western Central Africa.[10] The origin of the *berimbau*, the "soul" and main symbol of the art, is the musical bow that many ethnic groups in the Angola/Kongo region use. On the other hand, the *berimbau* does not appear to have been used for any martial art in Africa and the instrument is played today with a *caxixi* that scholars have traced to the Bay of Benin. The composition of the *capoeira* orchestra is clearly a New World reinvention that combines instruments from various cultures, including the Arab *pandeiro* (tambourine).[11]

Whilst swift change characterized instruments, audiences, and texts in *capoeira*, the rhythmic patterns seemed to have remained more stable. Ethnomusicologists insist that in contrast to instruments that were used across various culture zones, rhythmic patterns marked more specific regional identities (Kazadi wa Makuna 2000: 132). G. Kubik has called time-line patterns "the metric back-bone" of African music. "They are orientation patterns, steering and holding together the motional process with participating musicians and dancers depending on them. In this quality the removal or even slight modification of a time-line pattern immediately leads to the disintegration of the music concerned" (Kubik 1979: 18) He asserts that these rhythmic key signatures enjoyed great constancy over time. Thus a twelve-pulse pattern in its seven-stroke version played on a bell can be identified as a West African Coastal tradition (Akan/Fon/Yoruba) or a sixteen-pulse pattern as coming from the Kongo/Angola region (Kubik 1979: 124–127).

It is much more difficult to establish transatlantic links regarding the movements, the rituals, and what some adepts call the spirituality of *capoeira*. In my view, any debate over these issues should take into account the lyrics.[12] The texts of *capoeira* songs are always in vernacular language and, in particular, those from Bahia are greatly influenced by the speech of African slaves and their descendants. No creole language developed on a large scale in the Portuguese colonies in America[13] but even in its mainstream version Brazilian Portuguese has retained important influences of African, mainly Bantu languages. Bahian Portuguese, in particular, is shaped by the way Africans pronounced it. Rego has shown with painstaking detail how words are systematically altered; for instance, the l substitutes the r or is dropped from the end of words.[14]

Furthermore, many African terms have entered colloquial Brazilian speech and are used in *capoeira* lyrics. For example, *muleque*—a boy in Kimbundo—has acquired the slightly altered meaning of a street kid in Brazil. Thus the song "The *muleque* is you" ("Muleque é tu") provocatively states that one's opponent—to whom the song is addressed—is a badly behaved street kid.

Despite the many formal and ritual aspects that link *capoeira* practice to Africa in general, and to the Kongo/Angola region in particular, relatively few songs from the public domain contain explicit references to things African. One frequently used term is "Aruandê" (or "Aluandê," "Aloanguê"). It is sometimes employed in association with the interjection Iê!, which is a call for attention, and also the ritual way to start or finish a *roda*, or to introduce the *louvação* (praise song). There seems to be no doubt that the term is derived from Luanda, the capital of Portuguese Angola, an important port in the transatlantic slave trade to Brazil (Rego 1968: 49, 93, 145, 184). *Capoeira* lyrics also use a number of expressions of likely African origin, such as *jacatimba, camunjerê,* or *calumbi*.[15] They might or might not be onomatopoeic but for many of these terms no meaning is known among contemporary adepts.

One reason for the relatively limited references to Africa is the repression of *capoeira* and any African cultural manifestation prior to the 1930s. This led to dissimulation and deception. In the case of Afro-Bahian religion, it is possible to identify hidden references. For example, a *corrido* which mentions *dendê* (palm oil) can also refer to spiritual energy or the messenger deity Exú.[16] Many songs worship Catholic saints such as Santo Antonio, São Benedito, and São Bento. It is well known that slaves chose devotion to particular saints to hide their worship of African Gods to the extent that Candomblé practitioners in Bahia called themselves "the people of the Saints."

I believe that references to Africa might have been more frequent in nineteenth-century lyrics but disappeared after the end of the transatlantic slave trade due to the growing distance between *capoeira* practitioners and Angolan origins. Although Bahia continued to maintain a number of important links with the Bay of Benin after 1850, it seems that this was less true of Angola. For instance, the *corrido* "Ô lembá, ê lembá. Ê lembá do Barro Vermelho" ("Oh lembá, eh lembá, eh lembá of red clay").[17] Lemba is a small place in Angola, but also, and more importantly, a feminine spirit associated with procreation, and the birth of twins. Lemba furthermore became the denomination for a specific cult that existed in the Kongo region between 1650 and 1930. Lemba has also been identified in the diaspora, for example as a *lwa* in Haitian Vodou (of the Kongo or "Petro" line) (Ribas 1994: 2, 144; MacGaffey in Heywood, ed. 2002: 214, 223).[18] However, very few contemporary *mestres* associate that *capoeira* song with a specific religious meaning. Lembá is often altered to "lembra" (= remember in Portuguese) and new verses are added that relate to the act of remembering. In other words, in this particular case the original African referent has been lost.

It is possible, on the one hand, to observe the loss of certain African references in twentieth-century *capoeira*. On the other hand, contemporary *capoeira* lyrics, and in particular those of the revivalist Angola style, have systematically reintroduced links to Angola. Traditionalists who aimed to preserve *capoeira* refused its modernization along the lines of M. Bimba's Regional style in the 1930–1940s. Angola was chosen as their rallying concept, based on the historic association of the art with the Angolan slaves. Hence adepts of the Angola style dubbed themselves *angoleiros*,[19] and invented refrains such as "Angola-Ê" or "Eu sou angoleiro/Angoleiro sim senhor/Angoleiro de valor" ("I am *angoleiro*/an *angoleiro* yes Sir/An angoleiro of value").[20]

When the Angolan artist Souza e Neves visited Pastinha in Salvador in 1965, he must have told the old *mestre* his theory regarding the single origin of *capoeira* in southern Angola. M. Pastinha thus added the verse "*Capoeira* came from África" to his *Ladainha* "Bahia, Our Bahia."[21] Yet after he went to the *Festival des Arts Nègres* (First World Festival of Black Arts) in Dakar, in 1966, he also proudly sang: "Pastinha has been to Africa, to show *capoeira* from Brazil."[22] In other words, older *mestres* did not necessarily see Afrocentric approaches and one's pride in being Brazilian as mutually exclusive.

The reestablishment of links with Africa or the re-Africanization (a term commonly used for analyzing similar trends in Afro-Brazilian religions) includes a recovery of African locations. M. João Grande, a disciple of Pastinha who moved from Salvador to New York during the 1990s, sings:

Saí do Congo	I left Congo
Passei por Angola	I passed by Angola
Cheguei aqui hoje	I arrived here today
Quero vadiar Angola	I want to play ["be idle"] Angola[23]

His disciple M. Moraes has created lyrics that provide a careful definition of Angola as opposed to mainstream *capoeira* styles:

Na Angola, na Angola	In [the] Angola [style], in Angola
Tudo é diferente, na Angola (Refr.)	Everything is different, in Angola
Jogo de Mandinga, na Angola	The game is *mandigueiro*, in Angola
A viola responde, na Angola	The *viola* answers, in Angola
A pergunta é do gunga, na Angola	The question comes from the *gunga*, in Angola
Berimbau afinado, na Angola	The *berimbau* is tuned, in Angola
O jogo é de baixo, na Angola	The game is low, in Angola[24]

This *mestre's* belief in the need to reaffirm the African character of *capoeira* has lead him to study Bantu languages and compose new songs that intermingle Bakongo and Portuguese terms in similar fashion to the uses by adepts in the old days of the *vadiação*:

Ngolo, Nguzu	Ngolo, Nguzu
Força e poder	Strength and power
Kiatálua não	[Envy?]
Vai me vencer	Will not kill me[25]

For the period for which we have evidence, these few examples illustrate the extent to which the role of Africa in *capoeira* lyrics has undergone major changes.

Slavery and Abolition

It is possible that many *capoeira* lyrics originated during slavery although only a few songs from the public domain make explicit references to the institution and to the relation between slaves and masters. The most famous one is:

Vou dizer a meu senhor	I am going to tell my master
Que a manteiga derramou	That the butter has spilled
A manteiga não é minha	The butter is not mine
A manteiga é de ioió (DP)	The butter belongs to the master (PD)

This song conveys the malice of the slave. He relates an accident but at the same time one feels that he is gloating over what happened because he stresses that the butter does not belong to him, but to the master.

The covert resistance of the slave coalesced into *malandragem*, malice that has since become a strategy of survival of the urban poor. It is not surprising that *malandro* (rogue, spiv) and *capoeira* became synonyms around the turn of the nineteenth century. The cunning of the *malandro* is alluded to in a number of *capoeira* songs.

Slavery and its abolition are still themes of recent *capoeira* songs. The thirteenth of May, the day of slave emancipation in 1888 became a day of festive celebration in the aftermath of abolition. For example, *capoeira* was prominently played in Santo Amaro in the sugar plantation belt in the market square alongside *maculêlê* (stick fighting dance) and Candomblé. In his *ladainha* performed in the 1980s, the Bahian *mestre* Canjiquinha was among many others in his praise of the princess Isabel who signed the "Golden Law":

Salve! Salve a nação	Hail! Hail the nation
Salve a nação brasileira	Hail the Brazilian nation
Salve Princesa Isabel, ô meu Deus	Hail Princesa Isabel, oh my God
Que me livrou de cativeiro	Who delivered me from captivity!

(M. Canjiquinha)[26]

The abolition of slavery underwent a major reassessment during the celebrations of the Centenary in 1988. Black consciousness groups (usually referred to as Movimento Negro) pointed out that black people in Brazil had nothing to celebrate. They opted for the date of the death of the maroon leader Zumbi to commemorate black resistance. Accordingly, the views of many capoeiristas on Abolition changed considerably and references to marronage became common:

Dona Isabel, que história é essa	Lady Isabel, what story is this
De ter feito abolição?	That you made abolition?
De ser princesa boazinha	That you are the nice princess
Que acabou com a escravidão?	That finished with slavery?
Estou cansado de conversa	I am tired of that idle chat
Estou cansado de ilusão	I am tired of that illusion
...	...
Viva Zumbi, nosso guerreiro	Long live Zumbi, our warrior
Que fez-se herói lá em Palmares	Who became a hero in Palmares
Viva a cultura desse povo	Long live the culture of this people
A liberdade verdadeira	The true freedom
Que já corria nos quilombos	Already existed in maroon settlements
Que já jogava *capoeira*	Already played *capoeira*

(M. Toni Vargas)[27]

Slavery and its abolition are not the only explicit historical references used in *capoeira* lyrics. The "classic" form of Bahian *capoeira* developed during the second half of the nineteenth and the first half of the twentieth century. *Capoeira* lyrics from this time referred to Brazil's important steps in nation building and to its participation in two international wars.

The Wars Brazilian *Capoeiras* Fought

Since the seventeenth century, Brazilian masters and colonial authorities used the martial skills of their slaves in times of need. Black troops or *Henriques* (named after Henrique Dias (?–1662) the famous commander of a black battalion in the wars against the Dutch in northeastern Brazil) offered one possible path to emancipation. During the Paraguayan War (1865–1870) when the National Guard and voluntary battalions had to reinforce the relatively reduced Brazilian army, there was a renewed offer of freedom for slave volunteers. The province of Bahia sent hundreds of Brazilian-born slaves as well as thousands of free blacks the 15,000 soldiers to Paraguay. The surviving slave veterans were subsequently freed for serving the fatherland.[28] Manuel Querino stated that the *capoeira* soldiers distinguished themselves in bayonet assaults and presented profiles of two of them (1946: 78–80).[29]

The Paraguayan War resulted in unprecedented patriotic mobilization, a growing awareness of belonging to a Brazilian nation that profoundly altered Brazilian civic culture. In the capital of Bahia the war was behind popular manifestations such as the "pilgrimage of the police" which celebrated the return of the police corps from the battlefields (Querino: 244). Streets and squares of Salvador and other cities were christened with the names of famous battles in which the Brazilian armed forces were victorious.

Given the participation of *capoeiras* in the wider context of an international war, it is no surprise that places and events associated with the Paraguayan War, such as "Humaitá," "City of Assunción" and possibly "Paranaê," are among some of the oldest identifiable references in *capoeira* songs.[30] The song "I was at home" tells the story of how one man was recruited:

Iê, tava em casa (ô meu bem)	Iê, I was at home (oh my love)
Sem pensar nem imaginar	not thinking nor imagining anything
Quando bateram na porta (meu bem)	when someone knocked on the door
Salomão mandou chamar	Solomon asked for him
Para ajudar a vencer (ô meu bem)	To help win (oh my love)
A Guerra do Paraguá (DP)	The War of Paraguay (PD)[31]

During the Second World War Brazil sent an expedition corps to Italy to fight under United States command against Nazi Germany. The *ladainha* "Brazil said yes, Japan said no" is still sung in contemporary *rodas* and invokes the participation of an anonymous *capoeira* in that conflict:

O Brasil disse que sim	Brazil said yes
O Japão disse que não	Japan said no
Uma esquadra poderosa	A powerful fleet
Pra brigar com alemão (DP)	To have a fight with the German (PD)[32]

The *ladainha* often includes a passage that clearly expresses the patriotic sentiments of the *capoeira* fighting for his country:

O Brasil já tá na guerra	Brazil is at war
Meu dever é ir lutar (DP)	My duty is to fight (PD)[33]

Since the end of the nineteenth century, nationalist intellectuals and politicians have sought to instrumentalize *capoeira* for their own purposes. During Brazil's major surge of nationalism from the 1930s to the 1950s, *capoeira* developed into a recognized art form. *Capoeira* was decriminalized during the dictatorship of Getulio Vargas (1937–1945). Vargas, who was later reelected president (1950–1954), attended an official *capoeira* exhibition and endorsed *capoeira* as the national Brazilian martial art. Complex links between *capoeira* and nationalist politics were thus established and even today many *capoeira* adepts use the national colors yellow and green on their uniforms.

Famous *Capoeira* Fighters

"Tough guys" who confront local police or armed groups that outnumber them are more admired in *capoeira* lyrics from the public domain than the Brazilian soldiers who fought abroad. The two outstanding examples are Besouro Mangangá and Pedro Mineiro.

A number of *capoeira* songs recall the death in 1914 of Pedro Mineiro inside a police station.[34] This famous troublemaker may have been a pimp in the port area and its red-light district where he had his base. He was prosecuted several times and owed his own violent death to disputes such as his violence against women and fights with other men over women. According to M. Noronha, he was the lover of the waitress Maria José who went out one day with a sailor. Pedro Mineiro followed them, killed one marine, and threw another one from a window. He was arrested and detained at the police station. The captain of the sailor's ship was dissatisfied with the arrest since it was known that the police chief, Alvaro Cova, was a known protector of *capoeiras*.[35] The captain's men therefore invaded the police station to kill Pedro Mineiro. One *ladainha* tells the story as follows: "The Warship Piauí, anchored in the port of Bahia. An insubordinate sailor jumped off to create mayhem. They ordered Pedro Mineiro to be killed inside the police station, comrade!"[36]

A number of different versions of this *ladainha* are sung in *rodas*, all emphasizing the death of Pedro Mineiro inside the police station:

Prenderam Pedro Mineiro	They arrested Pedro Mineiro
Dentro da Secretaria	Inside the police station
Para dar depoimento	To give testimony
Daquilo que não sabia(DP)	About what [something] he did not know (PD)[37]

The episode of Pedro Mineiro reveals several important facets that help to explain the links between *capoeira* and violence: the use of its techniques to subject women, the rivalry between different corporate bodies such as the navy and the police, and the involvement of *capoeiras* in clientelism. The records in the archives do not always reveal the complex web of wider social significance that lie behind the individual fights and their immediate motives.[38]

Innovation and Tradition in *Capoeira* Lyrics

Tradition is handed down in *capoeira* through song lyrics and the rituals of the game. Yet tradition is never static or rigid. With regard to lyrics, each new generation of *capoeira* practitioners recombine textual elements into something original and also something new that is still within the boundaries of tradition. Every performer thus adds to the script of tradition: by deleting some components and introducing new ones, he (since almost all are men) produces some change in the texture without fundamentally altering the structure.

The *ladainha* sung by M. Caiçara (1923–1997) might serve as an example of how *capoeira mestres* adapted and merged traditional elements into a new song:

Iê!	Iê! (Attention!)
Iê tava em casa	I was in my home
Sem pensar nem imaginar	Without thinking nor imagining
Delegado no momento	The police chief
Já mandou foi me intimar	Sent me a warning
É verdade meu colega	Is it true my friend
Com toda diplomacia	With all diplomacy
Prenderam o *capoeira*/Caiçara	They put the *capoeira*/caiçara
Dentro da secretaria	In jail
Para dar depoimento	To testify
Daquilo que não sabia	About what he did not know
Camará	Comrade[39]

This text combines the beginning of the Paraguayan War *ladainha* with the story of Pedro Mineiro, but Caiçara replaces Pedro Mineiro's name with his own and adapts the outcome to his own needs. He is no longer killed, only jailed to testify what he did not know. Caiçara therefore establishes a direct link between the veterans of that war, the famous tough guy, and himself. He somehow becomes them or at least places himself in the direct continuation of these epic heroes. Anybody who has known Caiçara will easily confirm that he could do this because he was one of Salvador's last tough guys (at least in the old sense of the term). He was arrested many times for disorderly conduct during the street festivals or in the red-light districts of the port area. He even challenged Bimba in his academy and had his jaw broken by the inventor of the Regional style.

Yet modernization of *capoeira* meant that the practice was transferred from the streets into the academies where students paid monthly fees and trained in uniforms. Their *mestres* are no longer tough guys who were famous in street brawls, but professionals with a reputation to maintain. It is possible that for this reason the genre of stories about Besouro and Pedro Mineiro can no longer be continued, despite the continued acclaim of these famous capoeiristas. Contemporary entry or praise songs (*canto de entrado* or *louvação*) often begin by enumerating the generation of long dead *mestres* and then, as mentioned earlier in this chapter, continue to praise those who are present at the *roda*. Some new *ladainhas* are composed for the teacher or esteemed *mestre*.[40] A number of *mestres* of the older generations such as Boca Rica continue to sing about their own life and experiences:

Boca Rica é um cara legal	Boca Rica is a nice guy
Joga sua Angola, toca muito berimbau	He plays his Angola and berimbau well
Boca Rica é Mestre de *Capoeira*	Boca Rica is *capoeira mestre*
Vende tomate, cebola, lá na feira	He sells tomato, onion at the market

And they do this regardless of the fact that their exploits are now of a quite different nature:

Mestre Boca Rica	Mestre Boca Rica
Capoeira (Refrain)	*Capoeira* (Refrain)
Mestre Nobre de Valor	A noble and worthy master
Foi dar curso em Los Angeles	He gave a workshop in Los Angeles
Até a gringa chorou	Even the gringa shed tears[41]

Conclusion

Even though there is a growing importance of the role of records and text-books, *capoeira* lyrics still represent a prime example of oral transmission of traditions in the twenty-first century. Songs articulate and transmit the broader aspirations and worldviews of adepts and the wisdom of an older generation of *mestres*. At the same time they fulfill important functions within the specific dynamics of each game. *Ladainhas, louvações,* and *corri-dos* performed in historic and contemporary *rodas* provide many examples of inventive bricolage, whereby sections of older songs are used to compose new ones to suit the singers' purposes. For that reason, songs from the public domain are not rigid restatements whose contents are rigidly fixed but instead they acquire new meanings with each performance. If the *capoeira* game constitutes a kind of dialogue between the movements of two *capoe-iristas*, the lyrics help musicians to build up several other dialogues: one is with the players in the *roda,* another is with the audience around the circle, and a third one is among the musicians themselves. These dialogues are made of metaphysical proverbs, historical narratives of a glorious past, or ironic comments on a game. Verses entertain the audience, preserve *capoeira* history, provide models of behavior for younger generations, or maintain the rhythm and stamina of the game. The multitude of functions and cross-references of the lyrics contribute toward the rich texture and the cultural density of a *capoeira* performance. As is true of the entire game, *capoeira* songs are a prime example of living traditions.

Adepts consider *capoeira* practice to be an emancipating practice in itself and thus the songs provide explanations and legitimacy for the game. If on the one hand the lyrics transmit historical experiences of slavery, emancipation, acts of heroism or pride in being African, Afro-Brazilian, or Brazilian, they also express an extremely dynamic relationship with the past. The past is always reinterpreted from the needs of the present and in that respect one cannot interpret *capoeira* lyrics as immutable historical documents. The evolution of lyrics on some core themes reflects developments that are taking place in Brazil's broader society (and increasingly elsewhere) including the ongoing struggle for emancipation from racial, class, or any other oppression. The reassessment of Abolition or Africa's contribution to Brazilian popular culture is articulated in these changes in *capoeira* lyrics that also provide an important vehicle through which perceptions are readjusted.

Notes

The author would like to thank Erna von der Walde and Florence Royer (Jurema) as well as the participants of the conferences "Literary Manifestations of the African Diaspora," University of Cape Coast, Cape Coast (Ghana) November 10–14, 2003, and "The Portuguese Atlantic: Africa, Brazil, and Cabo Verde," Mindelo, Cape Verde, July 7–9, 2005, for comments on earlier drafts of this paper.

1. In nineteenth-century and early-twentieth-century sources, practitioners are referred to as *capoeiras,* whereas contemporary adepts are now called *capoeiristas.*
2. The most detailed account of this period in Rio de Janeiro is provided by Carlos Eugênio Líbano Soares, *A capoeira escrava e outras tradições rebeldes no Rio de Janeiro, 1808–1850* (Campinas: UNICAMP, 2001).
3. For a more detailed discussion of myths and fakes in *capoeira* history, see Luiz Renato Vieira and Matthias Röhrig Assunção, "Mitos, controvérsias e fatos. Construindo a história da capoeira," *Estudos Afro-Asiáticos* 34, (1998): 81–120.
4. Annibal Burlamaqui, *Gymnastica Nacional (Capoeiragem) methodizada e regrada* (Rio de Janeiro: n.e., 1928), 11–12.
5. See CD *Essência. O berimbau e a voz do eterno Bimba* (Salvador: Fundação Mestre Bimba, 2001), tracks 1–2.
6. Rego, *Capoeira Angola* 67: 106.
7. For further examples, see Lewis, *Ring of Liberation,* 163–167.
8. For a further discussion of *capoeira* as "verbal play" see Lewis, 162–187 and also Downey, "Incorporating," 127–141.
9. It is worth noting that some recent songs of known authorship seem also to have entered the public domain insofar as performers do not always recognize their authorship.
10. For Bahia, see Manuel Querino, *A Bahia de outrora* (3rd ed., Salvador: Livraria Progresso Editora, 1946), 73; for Rio de Janeiro, see Carlos Eugênio Líbano Soares, *A capoeira escrava e outras tradições rebeldes no Rio de Janeiro, 1808–1850* (Campinas: Editora da Unicamp, 2001), 124–33.

11. Elements of Arab civilization came to Brazil through both the Portuguese and enslaved West African Muslims. The tambourine has been used since medieval times on the Iberian Peninsula.

12. Some U.S. scholars have attempted to interpret *capoeira* from an "Afrocentric" perspective, by reading what they consider "traditional" Central African meanings into the contemporary Brazilian game. For the most detailed attempt, see Desch-Obi, "Engolo." Interestingly enough, these interpretations cannot rely on any evidence from the "traditional" *capoeira* lyrics.

13. *Língua geral*, derived from Tupiniquim and other Tupi languages, was the main vernacular used in colonial Brazil.

14. For more details, see Rego, *Capoeira Angola,* 126–141.

15. Quoted in Querino, *A Bahia,* 76 and in Rego, *Capoeira Angola.*

16. Rego, *Capoeira Angola* 33: 94. I have not found any older mention of these lyrics, so it is possibly a relatively recent song. For an analysis of the role of *dendê*, see Raul Lody, *Tem dendê, tem axé. Etnografia do dendezeiro* (Rio de Janeiro: Pallas, 1992).

17. Rego, *Capoeira Angola* 62: 104.

18. Óscar Ribas, *Dicionário de regionalismos angolanos* (Matosinhos: Contemporânea, 1994), 2, 144; Wyatt MacGaffey, "Twins, Simbi Spirits, and Lwas in Kongo and Haiti," in Linda M. Heywood, ed. *Central Africans and Cultural Transformations in the American Diaspora* (Cambridge: CUP, 2002), 214, 223. In Angola, the gift the groom pays to the bride's family is called alembamento.

19. NB: *Angoleiro* refers to the practitioner of Angola in contrast to *angolanos*, the inhabitants of Angola.

20. See M. Boca Rica, CD *A poesia de Boca Rica* (Manaus: Cântaro Estúdio, ca. 2001), track 14. One version of "Eu sou angoleiro" has already been recorded by Rego, *Capoeira Angola* 32: 93.

21. His manuscripts contain two versions of this *ladainha*, but without that verse about the African origins. See Vicente Ferreira Pastinha, "Manuscritos e desenhos de Mestre Pastinha" (Org. by Angelo Decanio Filho, Salvador: 1996), 46A, 60B. The added verse can be heard on M. Pastinha, *Capoeira Angola* (n.p., Fontana Stereo, 1969), track 1.

22. "Pastinha já foi a África, a mostrar capoeira do Brasil." M. Pastinha, CD *Capoeira Angola* (Fontana Stereo, 1969), track 2. I would like to thank M. Cobra Mansa for discussing these *ladainhas* with me.

23. M. João Grande, CD *Capoeira Angola*, New York: 2001, track 6. If not otherwise stated, all English versions of Brazilian songs are my translation.

24. Mestre Moraes, CD *Brincando na Roda* (Salvador: GCAP - Grupo Capoeira Angola Pelourinho, 2001), track 3.

25. M. Moraes, *Brincando na Roda*, track 7.

26. As translated by Downey, "Incorporating Capoeira," 91.

27. As sung by Alex Muniz on the CD João Pequeno de Pastinha (Salvador: WR Discos, 2000).

28. Figures from J.P. de Sousa, *Escravidão ou morte. Os escravos brasileiros na Guerra do Paraguai* (Rio de Janeiro: Mauad/ADESA, 1996), 89. Querino (*A Bahia,* 188) claims as much as 18,725 Bahians fought in Paraguay. Oral tradition has it that slave *capoeiras* were already serving in a patriot battalion during the War of Independence, but no written evidence has yet been found to confirm it. See Daniel Coutinho, *O ABC da capoeira angola. Os manuscritos do Mestre Noronha* (Brasilia: DEFER/GDF, 1993), 35.

29. Querino, *A Bahia*, 78–80.
30. "Paranaê" probably refers to the Paraná river that runs from Brazil into Paraguay and forms part of the border between both countries.
31. CD—Mestre Traira: Capoeira da Bahia (São Paulo: Sonopress-Rimo, n.d.), track 1. This *ladainha* has many different versions, not all of them mentioning explicitly the Paraguay War. See also Rego, *Capoeira Angola* 60: 103, and 103: 117.
32. Rego, *Capoeira Angola* 78: 109.
33. See for instance M. Canjiquinha, *Capoeira* (São Paulo: Sonopress-Rimo Indústria e Comércio Fonográfica Ltda, 1986), track 18; M. Moraes, CD *Brincando na roda,* track 8.
34. Newspapers also registered the case. See for instance *Diário de Notícias* (Salvador), March 3, 1916.
35. Coutinho, *O ABC*, 24. For another version see Rego, *Capoeira Angola* 126: 122. Pedro Mineiro also enjoyed the protection of the ex-governor J.J. Seabra. See Jair Moura, *Mestre Bimba. A crónica da malandragem* (Salvador: author's ed., 1991), 60.
36. Coutinho, *O ABC,* 41.
37. CD *Capoeira M. Waldemar & M. Canjiquinha* (São Paulo: Sonopress-Rimo Indústria e Comércio Fonográfica Ltda, 1986), track 14.
38. For a recent assessment of Pedro Mineiro based on new archival evidence, see Antonio Liberac Cardoso Simões Pires, "Escritos sobre a cultura afro-brasileira. A formação histórica da capoeira contemporânea, 1890–1950." PhD thesis in History, UNICAMP, Campinas, 2001.
39. M. Caiçara, LP Academia de Capoeira Angola de São Jorge dos Irmãos Unidos do Mestre Caiçara (São Bernardo do Campo/SP: Discos Copacabana, 1973), track 1. For the translation, see *Capoeira Songbook for estrangeiros,* (Washington, DC: International Capoeira Angola Foundation: n.d.), 4.
40. See for example, "Grande João Grande" by M. Moraes, *Brincando na roda,* track 6; "M. Waldemar da Liberade," by M. Luiz Renato (Grupo Beribazu), CD *Músicas de Capoeira* (Manaus: Microservice Tecnologia, n.d.), track 3; "Seu Pastinha mandou falar" by M. Pé de Chumbo, CD *M. Pé de Chumbo e convidados,* (Manaus: Sonopress, ca. 2002), track 2.
41. M. Boca Rica, CD *A poesia,* tracks 2 and 3.

Bibliography

Burlamaqui, Annibal. 1928. *Gymnastica Nacional (Capoeiragem) methodizada e regrada.* Rio de Janeiro.
Capoeira Songbook for estrangeiros. n.d. Washington, DC: International Capoeira Angola Foundation.
Coutinho, Daniel. 1993. O *ABC da capoeira angola. Os manuscritos do Mestre Noronha.* Brasília: DEFER/GDF.
Desch-Obi, Thomas J. 2000. "Engolo: Combat Traditions in African and African Diaspora History." PhD Dissertation in History, University of California, Los Angeles.
Downey, Greg. 1998. "Incorporating Capoeira: Phenomemology of a Movement Discipline." PhD Dissertation in Anthropology, University of Chicago.

Kubik, Gerhard. 1979. "Angolan Traits: Black Music, Games and Dances of Brazil. A Study of African Cultural Extension Overseas." *Estudos de Antropologia* 10. Lisbon: Junta de Investigações Científicas.

Lewis, J. Lowell. 1992. *Ring of Liberation. Deceptive Discourse in Brazilian Capoeira*. Chicago: University of Chicago Press.

Lody, Raul. 1992. *Tem dendê, tem axe. Etnografia do dendezeiro*. Rio de Janeiro: Pallas.

MacGaffey, Wyatt. 2002. "Twins, Simbi Spirits, and Lwas in Kongo and Haiti," in Linda M. Heywood, ed. *Central Africans and Cultural Transformations in the American Diaspora*. Cambridge: Cambridge University Press, pp.230–260.

Makuna, Kazadi wa. 2000. *Contribuição Bantu na música popular brasileira: perspectivas etnomusicológicas*. São Paulo: Terceira Margem.

Moura, Jair. 1991. *Mestre Bimba. A crônica da malandragem*. Author's ed.: Salvador.

Pires, Antonio Liberac Cardoso Simões. 2001. "Escritos sobre a cultura afro-brasileira. A formação histórica da capoeira contemporânea, 1890–1950." PhD thesis in History. Campinas: UNICAMP.

Querino, Manuel. 1946. *A Bahia de outrora*. 3rd ed. Salvador: Livraria Progresso Editora.

Rego, Waldeloir. 1968. *Capoeira Angola. Ensaio sócio-etnográfico*. Salvador: Itapuã.

Risério, Antônio. 1995. *Oriki Orixá*. São Paulo: Perspectiva.

Soares, Carlos Eugênio Libano. 2002. *A capoeira escrava e outras tradições rebeldes no Rio de Janeiro, 1808–1850*. Campinas: Editora da Unicamp.

Chapter 10

The *"Orisha* Religion" between Syncretism and Re-Africanization

Stefania Capone

Afro-American religions are historically distinguished by their extreme fragmentation and lack of a superior authority that could impose orthodox rules and practices on its followers. Nonetheless, some religious leaders today aim for a unification of their practices that highlights the existence of a common ground in all Afro-American religious modalities. Since the early 1980s, there have been various attempts to standardize the different Afro-American religious practices on the American continent. The International Congresses of *Orisha* Tradition and Culture (also called COMTOC or Orisa World Congresses) have helped to create a wider network between the initiates of Brazilian Candomblé, Cuban Santería or *Regla de Ocha*, Haitian Vodu, North American Orisha-Voodoo, and Yoruba "traditional religion."[1] These attempts generate new ways of religious "creolization," in which the syncretic work—the historical base of these types of religions—is resignified, giving preference to African or Afro-American endogenous variables instead of European or Catholic exogenous influences. In the *Lucumí* religion of Cubans living in Miami, the ritual borrowings of practices that originated in Brazilian Candomblé are a telling example of this founding tension between unification and fragmentation within these religious phenomena.

In this chapter, I will address the issues of tradition and preservation of a collective African memory within Afro-American religions, focusing first on Brazilian Candomblé. We will see that the tension between continuity and discontinuity, between Africa and the New World, can also be found in other religions originating in Africa, such as Cuban Santería. The COMTOC congresses are essential to the diffusion of several practices, values, and views of tradition in the core of a transnational network that unites African initiates and their diaspora counterparts in the Americas, in that translocal field referred today as the "Black Atlantic" (Thompson 1983; Gilroy 1993; Matory 2005). In this confrontation of different practices and ethics, two definitions of "African" tradition seem to represent the often difficult relationships between "*Orisha* religion" practitioners: one tradition linked to the diaspora and another to Yorubaland.

Going Back to the Roots

The COMTOC have been the first attempts to organize an international network of initiates of Africa-derived religions. Since their beginning, these congresses have set out to gather Yoruba and diaspora religious leaders in order to unify the *Orisha* tradition and fight "against the fragmentation of African religion in the world."[2] The main discussion topics at these forums are tradition, standardization of religious practices, re-Africanization, and the fight against syncretism, topics that are common to different regional modalities of the *Orisha* religion.[3]

In Brazil, the debate about religious practices originating in Africa has been based mainly on two movements: desyncretization and re-Africanization. A movement called "Back to the Roots" was launched in the 1970s. It had as its main objective the purification of Afro-Brazilian religious practices in order to take them back to their original tradition, free from the contamination of Western culture. The return to the "true African tradition" has two different formats, according to their location: in the southeast of Brazil. The re-Africanization movement has been predominant through Yoruba language and Ifá divination courses while in the northeast, especially in Bahia, the syncretism debate has changed some of the practices in Candomblé *terreiros* (shrine houses).

The best example of this is the petition against syncretism, signed by five *mães-de-santo* (Candomblé female religious leaders) from Bahia's most prestigious *terreiros* during the Second COMTOC, held in 1983, in Salvador. This petition urged the end of Afro-Catholic syncretism—the association of Catholic saints to African *orixás*—and the rejection of all Catholic rituals "traditionally" performed by Candomblé followers. The latter included masses attended by *terreiros* members on Catholic saints' days corresponding to *orixás*, the *iyawó* pilgrimage by the new initiates to churches at the end of the initiation ceremony, and the washing of the steps of Salvador's Nossa Senhora do Bonfim Church. The petitioners, led by Mãe Stella of Axé Opô Afonjá, considered all these practices as a residual heritage of slavery. It was about time to show pride in one's own roots and in one's own African ancestry. Candomblé had to cease being a religion of slaves to become an ancestral religion, "going back to Africa, not to slavery" (Capone 1999: 270). The "theory of the mask" of Roger Bastide (1960) became central to this debate: Africans would pretend to accept Catholic values to free themselves from colonial repression. And, if Afro-Catholic syncretism is only a white mask covering the faces of black gods, it is then possible to go back to the original practices, rejecting everything that does not belong to "immemorial" Africa, such as Catholic influences.[4]

Desyncretization and re-Africanization have some characteristics in common that could foster the belief that their objectives and aims are the same. It is true that both movements strive for a rejection of Afro-Catholic syncretism. The desyncretization movement, led by Axé Opô Afonjá, wants to eradicate all Catholic influence in Afro-Brazilian ritual practices. The re-Africanization movement, mainly in São Paulo and Rio de Janeiro, has the same objective but a different approach. The success of Yoruba language and civilization courses is the result of a continuous search by Candomblé initiates for all elements relating to lost religious practices. These elements should help to reconstruct a supposed "purity" of this religion originating in Africa. In reality, these two movements that are apparently so close and akin display two different views on the issue of legitimacy and hegemony in the Afro-Brazilian religious field. The key question is the same: How to preserve "Africa" in Brazil? However, Africa does not necessarily mean the same to Mãe Stella and to the representatives of re-Africanized *terreiros* in the southeast of Brazil. In Candomblé, Africa as a symbol of purity and tradition is, in fact, subject to constant redefinition in order to serve different strategies of legitimacy. In this sense, desyncretization does not necessarily mean re-Africanization.

The same longing—to go back to Africa, the cradle of tradition—can take different and politically opposing forms. In 1987, Mãe Stella criticized the "trend" of searching for one's roots in Africa such as the trips by the Candomblé initiates to Lagos or Benin, in order to look for the lost basics (*fundamentos*) of the religion. According to this prestigious *mãe-de-santo*, the true roots of the African tradition are in Brazil. Those who have neither religious roots nor any prestigious Afro-Brazilian lineage have no option but to search for their roots in Africa. The "real" Africa, however, would have survived in Brazil within the Candomblé Nagô shrine houses, the so-called "traditional temples," that would have preserved African roots from times immemorial. According to the guardians of the Nagô tradition, the desyncretization movement is not a return to Africa to relearn secret rituals. It is a purification of the Africa preserved in Brazil that, like polishing a stone, is free from everything that does not belong to its true nature: the Catholic rituals, a simple inheritance of slavery.

Since the 1960s, the ties between Brazilian Candomblé and the "land of origins," Yorubaland, have become even stronger. Thanks to the collaboration between universities and research centers of the two countries, some Nigerian teachers came to Salvador, Bahia. They organized Yoruba courses for Candomblé practitioners who wanted to learn the ritual language that had lost meaning over the years. Word about the great success of these courses rapidly reached other cities that were geographically and symbolically far away from the centers of Afro-Brazilian tradition. Therefore, in São Paulo and Rio de Janeiro, young Yoruba students became language teachers and quickly metamorphosized themselves into carriers of the *fundamentos* of the religion. These courses became *inter alia* courses on the Ifá oracle and for initiates from the southeast of Brazil who were accustomed to traveling to Salvador in search of ritual knowledge; they offered an opportunity to obtain an alternative source of religious legitimacy (Capone 1999: 272–284).

Due to the more frequent contact with Yoruba practitioners today, some Candomblé initiates in Rio de Janeiro and São Paulo go directly to Africa in search of this legitimacy.[5] This search is, above all, a political response to the predominance in the religious field of some Bahian shrine houses (*terreiros*). Over the years, the anthropologists who studied them gave these houses a label of traditionalism, putting in brackets all African cultural contributions apart from the Yoruba. Therefore, going to Africa in search of tradition is the same as rejecting traditional shrine houses of Bahia as mediators.

The dilemma is then to know which "Africa" needs to be updated in Brazilian shrine houses: the mythical land of origins that is preserved in Bahian temples, cleansed of the slavery stain by the movement of desyncretization, or the modern, postcolonial Africa represented by the Yoruba *babalawos* (diviners)? To what extent does modern Africa represent a real reference for re-Africanization, and would it not be just a political tool to confirm one's own legitimacy in the field of Afro-Brazilian religions? What is really at stake in this symbolic fight is the monopoly of this mythical Africa and who is entitled to represent "African tradition."

Hegemony and Purity

In order to understand the discomfort of many Candomblé initiates, it is necessary to clarify the hegemonic position that a small number of shrine houses, identified in anthropological texts as the guardians of African traditions in Brazil, hold in the Afro-Brazilian religious field.

One of the most striking characteristics of Afro-Brazilian studies is indeed the concentration of ethnographic research in just three shrine houses of the Nagô "nation" that claim a Yoruba origin. This amazing concentration transformed these temples into the incarnation of African tradition in Brazil. These three houses are the Engenho Velho (considered to be the first *terreiro* of Candomblé ever founded in Brazil), the Gantois, and the Axé Opô Afonjá. The latter are both offspring of the Engenho Velho. Other cities in Brazil such as Recife, São Luiz do Maranhão, and Porto Alegre have been defined as the traditional centers of three other modalities of Afro-Brazilian religions. They are respectively the Xangô, the Tambor de mina, and the Batuque. In contrast, the large cities of southeast Brazil (Rio de Janeiro and São Paulo) were always considered to be the lands of Umbanda and Macumba, "degenerated" religions (if religions at all) that came from a mixture of mainly Bantu African traditions, indigenous religions, and Kardecian spiritism.

Over the years, the harmonious systematizations theorized by anthropologists allowed for the construction of an ideal model of orthodoxy that was identified with the Nagô religion. This has found its own supporters among researchers and religious practitioners. As a result, the writings of anthropologists whose studies have always been limited with very few exceptions to these three Nagô terreiros have legitimized the hegemonic discourses of the terreiro leaders of so-called traditional religions of Bahia. According to the census of September 1997 there were 1,144 terreiros in the city of Salvador alone with just as many terreiros of Candomblé Angola as of Nagô. Nevertheless, despite the diversity of religious practices in Salvador, all research has been carried out in the same shrine houses.

The Candomblé Nagô, and more specifically Engenho Velho, Gantois, and Axé Opô Afonjá became important symbols of Bahian tradition and culture. Initiation in one of these three terreiros was, and continues to be, valued as a label of traditionalism. In this way, the Nagô culture becomes a type of meta-language or "general ideology" (Risério 1988) to which any other African cultural contribution must conform.[6] It does, however, become the ultimate expression of "Bahianness" of the traditionalism of Bahian culture. Bahia, once the colonial capital of Brazil, has since the 1930s become idealized as the embodiment of the "racial democracy" model, which is the basis for the creation of the Brazilian nation. In Bahia, if blacks can live harmoniously with whites, they can therefore maintain their traditions and preserve their cultural purity. So, alongside the myth of "racial democracy," one finds the idea of "cultural democracy" that allows blacks to cultivate their African heritage. Celebration and exaltation of Africa highlights even more this cultural democracy that has become the hallmark of Salvador (Bacelar 1989).

Whether black, white, or Mestizos, intellectuals and artists from Bahia find the inspiration required for their art in "traditional" Candomblé. The most famous religious leaders are often the protagonists of the songs of Dorival Caymmi, Gilberto Gil, and Caetano Veloso, and of the books of Jorge Amado. The orixás inspire artists from Bahia such as Carybé, Mario Cravo, Emanuel Araujo, or Tati Moreno. The presence of the "white"[7] middle class in Candomblé is also the result of a fascination with a traditional culture that was meant to be authentic and unchangeable. From the 1960s, the attraction to this African and exotic religion has taken on considerable proportions. Attendance at the most famous terreiros became a must for celebrities in search of an exotic experience. In 1958, the representatives of the president of Brazil chaired the celebrations for the 50th anniversary of the initiation of the Axé Opô Afonjá's iyalorixá (or mãe-de-santo). When Menininha do Gantois, the most famous mãe-de-santo of Candomblé, died in 1986, her public funeral was comparable to that of Tancredo Neves, Brazil's democratically elected president of the Republic (after the end of the dictatorship) who died the previous year.

The fascination for the beauty and exoticism of Candomblé, which has become the main inspiration of Bahian culture, soon transforms some religious elements such as ritual music, clothes, and instruments into folkloric merchandise. Bahiatursa, the Bahian office for tourism, began financing some of the most traditional Candomblé shrine houses to make their public ceremonies more spectacular. It even created "fake" rituals adapting the liturgical calendar to conform to the tourist calendar (Silveira 1988). In the creation of the Afoxé Ilê Aiyê, which has nowadays become the largest black group related to the Bahian carnival, one finds the same merchandising of "the exotic and the different," in which black culture, dance, and music have been transformed as a symbol of Bahia (Bacelar 1989: 94). In addition, the leaders of Candomblé Nagô are becoming significant symbols, not only for Bahia but also for Brazilian society as a whole. Menininha do Gantois was in particular extremely popular and even featured in a Brazilian advertising campaign for Olivetti typewriters (Silveira 1988).

Thanks to the diffusion of a romanticized vision of Candomblé by Bahian artists and also by anthropological books, Candomblé has been transformed from a set of "pagan" and "savage" rituals into a legitimate cultural heritage. These three Bahian terreiros have been elected as the incarnation of African tradition in Brazil. This historically established hegemony could only be questioned by another authority considered more traditional and closer to the "roots." The arrival of Yoruba religious practitioners from the late 1970s onward deeply changed the Afro-Brazilian religious field, calling into question the model of tradition preserved in Brazil.

The Memory of Tradition

The arrival of a Yoruba group, whose leader was the chancellor of the University of Ilé-Ifé, Wande Abimbola, had already threatened the predominance of Bahian *terreiros* during the Second COMTOC in Salvador. Two representatives of a prestigious Yoruba *babalawo*'s family, the Epegas, made the most of this occasion by visiting several *terreiros* in São Paulo. In their own words, they were: "very impressed with the authenticity of Candomblé in Brazil." The Epegas later returned to São Paulo to initiate in the "African-style" some *pais* e *mães-de-santo* from São Paulo, like Sandra Medeiros Epega, leader of the Ilê Leuiwyato situated in Guararema. Sandra Epega became a member of the Epega lineage, having been "adopted" by Olarimiwa Epega, father of the Yoruba *babalawo* Afolabi Epega, who is presently (2007) very active in the United States (*cf.* Capone 2005: 265–267).

The campaign against Afro-Catholic syncretism could be seen as an answer to the influences of Yoruba *babalawos* amongst some groups of Brazilian initiates. However, despite the action of *mães-de-santo* from the more traditional shrine houses of Salvador, the movement against syncretism has faced a lack of consensus among the majority of Bahian *terreiros*. In an interview to one of the most important Brazilian magazines, Balbino Daniel de Paula, a Bahian *pai-de-santo* who is meant to be one of the keepers of Yoruba tradition in Brazil, declared that "Candomblé and Catholicism are like water and oil—they can be poured into the same glass, but will never mix" (*Veja* August 17, 1983). This statement is particularly interesting because it seems to be based on Bastide's theory of the "principle of separation" (*principe de coupure*). According to Bastide (1960), Afro-Brazilians feel no contradiction by living in two separate worlds: the world of Candomblé and the world outside Candomblé. Stating that Candomblé and Catholicism do not mix in the minds of their followers is like questioning the very existence of syncretism, the reality of which is implicitly denied.

In fact, according to Bastide's theory, the principle of separation exists only in the more traditional religious groups that preserved their ties with their land of origins, reproducing "true Yoruba traditions" in Brazil. These religious groups are not the *terreiros* of the "new converts" of southeastern

Brazil who mainly come from Umbanda, but the more prestigious religious communities of Bahia, especially Axé Opô Afonjá, a *terreiro* which brings together artists, intellectuals, and Brazilian and foreign anthropologists as its members. The Bastidian principle of separation establishes therefore a difference between "traditional" black people, who have been preserving Africa in Brazil, and "syncretic" black people, who have lost all contact with their lands of origin. In his theory, Bastide highlights a "good" and a "bad" type of syncretism that he associates with these two types of black people: "mosaic syncretism" is a simple juxtaposition of different elements; "fusion syncretism" involves the merger and mixture of different elements. According to Bastide, in mosaic syncretism there is no fusion, only the separation of different rituals. It is a "fake" syncretism—a syncretism that wears a "mask"—typical of traditional Nagô *terreiros* (Capone 2001).

In his analysis of syncretism, Roger Bastide (1970) also refers to a "loss of collective memory"—*les trous de la mémoire collective*—gaps that could be filled by searching for the lost elements at the source of African tradition. According to Bastide, these *trous* or gaps that symbolize the loss of collective memory represent forms that are half full and half empty. They are "empty" because the images offered by a collective memory cannot fill them. They are also "full" because they are not real absences, but in Bastide's words are "a simple feeling that something is missing," something has been lost. If the collective memory recovers everything, it is possible to reconstitute the past thanks to the restoration of the broken ties between the diaspora and the lands of origin. The recovery of the collective memory allows the return to the lost tradition and resists the loss of an immemorial knowledge caused by slavery and by the structure of secrecy on which the foundation of Candomblé hierarchy rests.

Candomblé followers have always emphasized the preservation of cultural heritage and ancestral ritual. But such a position cannot guard against the constant practice of replacing what is lost, a practice that is much older than we might imagine today. The movement to preserve ancestral knowledge and compensate ritual loss is the true basis of the group dynamic of Afro-American religions. The journeys to the centers of tradition therefore take the form of a return to what was lost, to the "true African tradition."[8] This revisit to Africa, both in Brazilian Candomblé and in North American Orisha-Voodoo (Clarke 2004; Capone 2005) represents a reactivation that is more symbolic than real of a "pure" tradition that must be reconstructed in the diaspora. The journey to Africa hence becomes central to the process of strengthening the roots. Today this involves a search for re-Africanization at any price, via courses in Yoruba language and civilization in Brazil and the United States.

The search for tradition does not only happen in Brazil and Nigeria. If Afro-Catholic syncretism is constantly criticized, another kind of syncretism, the "Afro-African" syncretism prior to slavery, is fully accepted by followers of Afro-American religions.

The basis for this kind of syncretism between "sister religions" is the idea of a common African cultural ground. Melville Herskovits (1941), the first to declare the existence of a "cultural grammar" common to different people of western Africa, defended this idea. According to Herskovits, this "cultural grammar" allowed the formation of an Afro-American culture that took its main references from the Yoruba and Fon cultures. The persistence of an African substrate, in which religion plays a fundamental role, can also be found in the "rapid early synthesis" or "creolization" model that Mintz and Price developed (1976). In this model, we can find the same kind of tension as in Roger Bastide's work between Africa and America. On the one side is the African "cognitive orientations," the "grammatical principles" (in the sense of an African cultural grammar) that would have formed Afro-American cultures. On the other side is the idea of a "rigid core of African culture" that is immune to external influences and that would have allowed the preservation of African traditions in the New World.

The concept of a basic unity of African culture has inspired several unification projects of Afro-American religious practices. One example is the National Institute of Afro-Brazilian Tradition and Culture (INTECAB— *Instituto Nacional da Tradição e da Cultura Afro-brasileira*). This institute was founded in 1987 in Salvador, Bahia and presents itself as the expression of different "traditions that propagate the heritage left by African ancestors in the New World." INTECAB founders support the unification of different kinds of Afro-Brazilian religions as per their motto "unity in diversity" (see Capone 1999: 284–296). For unity to be possible, it is however necessary to distinguish between two types of syncretism. One type must be condemned because it mixes "exogenous" or "heterogeneous" variants that originate from different cultural worlds, such as Catholic influences. The other should be encouraged because it is composed of "endogenous" or "homogenous" variants at the source of an "inter-tribal syncretism." This syncretism would therefore highlight the African culture and its continuity in the Americas. Afro-Brazilian religions such as Candomblé and Umbanda, once free of non-African influences, would become different expressions of the same "basic cultural complex." The hegemony of Bahian Nagô *terreiros* (of Yoruba origin) would therefore be confirmed by the role they play in the preservation of African traditions in Brazil.

The Sacred Journey

This same tension between the unity of African culture and the fragmentation of Afro-American religions fuels other attempts to rediscover lost traditions. During recent decades, many African Americans have rediscovered their cultural roots thanks to a new kind of tourism that could be called "religious and cultural tourism." In Bahia, this kind of tourism is also called "roots tourism." African Americans have traveled to areas of Brazil with a dense population of African descent (mainly Salvador and Cachoeira in Bahia) to establish contact with Afro-Brazilian religious followers. These trips have contributed to the constitution of transnational networks of *Orisha* religion. Many of the African Americans who travel to Bahia are interested in Afro-Brazilian culture, and specifically in its artistic practices, such as Candomblé dance, *capoeira*, or Afro-percussion courses. The impact of this cultural tourism on African American religious practices in, for example, New York and Philadelphia, represents an interesting aspect in the understanding of current transformations within the Afro-American religious field.

Some African American priestesses who are initiates in North American *ilés* (shrine houses) with religious lineages stemming from Afro-Cuban religious families are weary of the male dominance in Cuban Santería. They have been interested in Candomblé, a sister religion that can offer alternative models for the *Orisha* religion. Since the 1930s, thanks to the work of the North American anthropologist Ruth Landes (1947), traditional Candomblé Nagô has been viewed as a *locus* of power for women. The men are mainly allowed to perform specific ritual roles, like *ogan* or *alabé* (players of divine drums). In shrine houses that preserve the "true Yoruba traditions," the leadership is composed exclusively of women but this contradicts the organization of this religion in Yorubaland, given the predominant role played by *babalawos*. Nevertheless, the confirmation of the matriarchal myth in Candomblé Nagô is the leadership of women since the foundation of the three most traditional shrine houses of Salvador—Engenho Velho, Gantois, and Axé Opô Afonjá.

On August 30, 1987, representatives of the New York Egbé Omo Obatalá, a society that unites *Orisha* initiates devoted to the worship of Obatalá, traveled to Brazil to participate in Oxalá rituals (another name given to Obatalá). These were performed in the Bahian *terreiro* of Engenho Velho, also known as the Casa Branca (White House). On this occasion, the Yoruba Society of Brooklyn proposed the "religious adoption" of the Ile Funfun (Yoruba translation of Casa Branca). The text was approved and transcribed in the golden book of the Bahian *terreiro* and established an "alliance between sister houses" in order to "strengthen the tie between Afro-American and Afro-Brazilian *Orisha* worshippers." The alliance would also encompass sharing "the rich legacy of our forefathers who landed upon the shores of Bahia," as well as the exchange of ideas and experiences in order to "teach each other about the ways in which we can keep alive the traditions of the Yoruba faith" (Curry 1997: 178).

However, the ties between North American and Brazilian practitioners are not limited to African American practitioners. Other ritual specialists are also very active in the search for lost traditions. In 1988, Miguel "Willie" Ramos, *Ilarí Obá*, a Cuban-American *oriaté*[9] living in Miami, visited Salvador to learn the rituals necessary for the consecration of the altar of the serpent god, the *orixá* Oxumarê. For many years, Ramos, an adjunct professor at Florida International University, searched for information about this *orixá* who went missing in Cuba during the first half of the twentieth century. Thanks to the help of Pierre Verger, Ramos met Mãe Nilzete of Yemanjá, the leader of Ilê Oxumarê. In this *terreiro*, he performed the *assentamento* (seating) ceremony, by which the energy of the *Orisha* is fixed onto individual altars. After that, he returned to the United States with an altar for

Oxumarê and one for Logunedê, an *Orisha* whose name is still known in Cuba, but about whom there is no available ritual knowledge.

In 1999, Ramos returned to Brazil to perform a *bori* ceremony in the Brazilian Candomblé tradition. This included the consecration of *ibá ori*, the material representation of the worshipper's head. The name of this ceremony means "to feed the head (*ori*)" and it was performed in São Paulo, in Ilé Ashé Iyamí Oxún Muyiwá, the shrine house of Gilberto d'Exu, one of the organizers of the COMTOC. This ceremony "opened the way" to various consecration ceremonies in the *ori* worship that Ramos performed in Cuba and in the United States. He is believed to have performed over five hundred *bori* with the consecration of *ibá ori*, introducing into the United States a practice that had completely disappeared in Cuba. Ramos has thus been a vital figure in the propagation of ritual practices imported from Candomblé, a sister religion that, like Santería, claims a Yoruba cultural root.

In order for other followers to "receive" Candomblé *Orisha*, it is necessary to adapt the Afro-Brazilian tradition to the practices of the initiates of the *Lucumí* religion, another name given to Afro-Cuban Santería. In this religion, *Orisha* who are not "born" or fixed during initiation rituals can be "received" from the hands of a *padrino* or a *madrina* (religious leaders), whose individual altars will "give birth" to new *Orisha*. In Cuba, these *Orisha* are thus called *Orichas de adimú*. The rituals of fixing *Orisha*'s energy and the consecration of individual altars are different in Candomblé and Santería. In 2004, Willie Ramos had already consecrated four Logunedé and five Oxumarê in the United States. He added other Santería rituals to Candomblé since without these rituals *Lucumí olorishas* (initiates) would doubt the validity of these consecrations. The Afro-Cuban rituals are called *lavatorio* (washing) and *paritorio* (giving birth). In the former, the *omiero*—an infusion of herbs softened in water, along with elements specific to each *Orisha*—is prepared. The *omiero* is used to ritually wash all of the altar parts and the instruments of the *Orisha* who is being born (*que está naciendo*) thanks to the *paritorio,* the part of the ritual that marks the affiliation ties between the *Orisha* who is "born" and the one who "is giving birth." The preparation of both the *dilogun* (divination cowries that in Santería are present on each individual altar) and the *itá* divination are not performed in Candomblé and must therefore be added. As these ritual changes are reclaimed by Santería practitioners, they represent a "lucumization" of Candomblé.

Conclusions

The Afro-American universe revolves around two types of syncretism: an Afro-African syncretism that emerged prior to slavery and originated in the belief of unity formed by "African culture"; and an Afro-Western syncretism, represented by Afro-Catholic syncretism that devotees feel must be combated. These two types of syncretism foster distinct views of the past and the African collective memory. One refers to the continuity of African and

Afro-American cultures; the other emphasizes the discontinuity, the result of slavery and the loss of real and symbolic ties with the land of origin. Afro-African syncretism is therefore "good" syncretism, a "positive" syncretism among sister religions that updates the Afro-Brazilian dream of unity in diversity. A certain type of syncretism could therefore be one way to re-Africanization.

In fact, the notion of re-Africanization does not necessarily take us to a founding "primitivism" that is free from all modern influence. On the contrary, the search today in Brazil or in the United States is for a tradition that is compatible with modernity. The process of re-Africanization, "to Africanize oneself," does not mean to be or to become "black" or "African." Most importantly, the process implies a contact with specialized publications on African and Afro-American religions (mainly Afro-Brazilian and Afro-Cuban). To Africanize oneself means "to acquire knowledge," and books are the source of a lost tradition that can and must be reconstructed. Re-Africanization is thus a "bricolage," in which each element is carefully researched in scientific publications, in particular the rich anthropological literature available on Africa. The information gathered by anthropologists and travelers over a century ago in Africa, information that is absorbed today by the ritual practitioners, could fill in the lapses of "Black-African memory," that according to Bastide (1970) would have caused the dilution of African traditions in Brazil.

Attempts to rediscover "orthodoxy," reintegrating forgotten practices and ritual knowledge, generates a fundamental paradox. Ritual purity is sought in Africa despite the awareness of the losses that European colonization on the African continent produced. As a result, the writings by Africanists such as Bascom, Herskovits, and Maupoil become the only available sources of information to reconstitute a "true" form of African worship. Without a sacred book that determines the religious dogma, the work by anthropologists becomes the base on which practitioners rediscover the "foundations," the religious secrets, which can confirm the "traditionalism" of their ritual practices.

However, the attempts to preserve African tradition also create some reorientations such as change and innovation that introduce exactly what was meant to be erased. "To re-Africanize" means in fact to redefine the tradition; a process of both interpretation and rationalization in order to make its concepts work in the present context. The African tradition changes, therefore, from apparently irrational practices to a truly scientific approach. If the revision of Santería practices in the United States has as one of its objectives the creation of a "purified" religion, this creation becomes possible through "logically" reconnecting the symbols, characteristics and animals that are associated with each *Orisha* in a coherent whole. This transformation illustrates one of the characteristics of the processes of re-Africanization: the attribution of a scientific quality to religious practices.

The majority of the initiates express a willingness to adapt an "immemorial" knowledge to a contemporary reality, irrespective of their origins or their religious traditions. The result is based not only on scientific publications but also on the exchange between sister religions, such as Brazilian Candomblé and Cuban Santería. Thanks to the exchanges between shrine houses, new ritual practices like *bori* are currently being imported into the United States and new *Orisha*, such as Oxumarê and Logunedé, are submitted to a lucumization process. In Brazil, shrine houses adopt rituals that are linked to the Ifá divination system (which follows the Nigerian tradition or the Afro-Cuban *Lucumí* tradition), and adapt them to Candomblé practices. These exchanges between sister religions seem to anticipate the creation of a common belief system that is today referred to as the *Orisha* religion. In this religion, elements of different Afro-American religions are mixed but all share the same claim to a Yoruba origin and express the same desire to retrieve original African practices.

Notes

1. The term Yoruba *òrìsà* (divinity) is spelled differently in Brazil (*orixá*) and in Cuba (*oricha*). It is pronounced *orisha* in English, the term that will be used in this paper and in all references within the international context of Afro-American religions practitioners. The terms *orixá* and *oricha* will be kept when referred to regional belief systems, such as Candomblé, Santería or *lucumí* religion.

2. See Capone 2005: 279–297 for an analysis of COMTOC congresses from 1981 to 2005.

3. At international forums, Afro-American religions, like Candomblé, Santería, or Orisha-Voodoo, are considered different sides of a same whole: the "*orisha* religion." They become thus regional variations of the same belief system, based on the worship of Yoruba divinities.

4. Actually, these criticisms of Catholic influences in Candomblé seem to forget that many Africans who arrived as slaves in Brazil had already been evangelized in Africa. This is the case of the Congo Kingdom, where the influence of the Catholic Church goes back to the sixteenth century (Thornton 1992).

5. Since the end of the 1990s, Nigerian Yoruba have been competing with other Ifá divination experts: the Cuban *babalaos*. Today, several Candomblé shrine houses in Rio de Janeiro have been under the ritual protection of *ramas* (religious lineages) of Cuban *babalaos*, being Rafael Zamora Dias the most famous one. The Cuban tradition represents thus a diaspora model meant to be closer to the African tradition, allowing new Brazilian Ifá initiates to move away from Yoruba *babalawos* (diviners), often accused of mercantilism.

6. See Capone (2000) on the reasons for this valorization of a tradition model associated to the Yoruba.

7. In Brazil, this is a social category. Somebody can be very dark-skinned but socially considered as a "white" person, just because he occupies a higher social status. See Peter Fry (2007) this volume.

8. Lorand Matory (2005) has shown the importance of trips between Brazil and Africa in the building of a transnationalism *ante litteram* whose influences have been equally important in Nigeria and Brazil. See also

Capone on the trips between Brazil and Africa and its importance in building a traditional model in Candomblé (1998).

9. *Oriaté* is the initiation rituals expert in *Regla de Ocha* or Afro-Cuban Santería. He performs *itá* divination, on the third day of the initiation, and consequently is called *italero*.

Bibliography

Bacelar, Jefferson. 1989. *Etnicidade : ser negro em Salvador.* Salvador: PENBA/Ianamá.

Bastide, Roger. 1960. *Les Religions africaines au Brésil : vers une sociologie des interpénétrations de civilisations,* Paris, P.U.F. (American edition, 1978, *The African Religions of Brazil.* Baltimore: Johns Hopkins University Press).

———. 1969. "Le problème des mutations religieuses." *Cahiers internationaux de sociologie* 46: 5–16.

———. 1970. "Mémoire collective et sociologie du bricolage." *L'Année sociologique* 21(3): 65–108.

———. [1967] 1996. *Les Amériques noires.* Paris : L'Harmattan. (American edition, 1971, *African Civilizations in the New World.* [New York: Harper Row]).

Capone, Stefania. 1998. "Le voyage initiatique: déplacement spatial et accumulation de prestige." *Cahiers du Brésil contemporain* 35–36, EHESS : 137–156.

———. 1999. *La quête de l'Afrique dans le Candomblé : pouvoir et tradition au Brésil,* Paris : Karthala (Brazilian edition, *A busca da África no Candomblé: poder e tradição no Brasil.* Rio de Janeiro: Pallas/Contracapa, 2004).

———. 2000. "Entre Yoruba et Bantou: l'influence des stéréotypes raciaux dans les études afro-américaines." *Cahiers d'études africaines* 157: 55–77.

———. 2001. "Regards croisés sur le bricolage et le syncrétisme. Le syncrétisme dans tous ses états." *Archives de sciences sociales des religions* 114, April–June: 42–50.

———. 2005. *Les Yoruba du Nouveau Monde : religion, ethnicité et nationalisme noir aux Etats-Unis.* Paris: Karthala.

Clarke, Kamari M. 2004. *Mapping Yorùbá Networks: Power and Agency in the Making of Transnational Communities.* Durham, N.C., London: Duke University Press.

Curry, Mary Cuthrell. 1997. *Making the Gods in New York: The Yoruba Religion in the African American Community.* New York, London: Garland Publishing, Inc.

Gilroy, Paul. 1993. *The Black Atlantic. Modernity and Double Consciousness,* Cambridge: Harvard University Press.

Halbwachs, M. 1925. *Les cadres sociaux de la mémoire.* Paris: Felix Alcan.

Herskovits, Melville J. [1941] 1990. *The Myth of the Negro Past.* Boston: Beacon.

Landes, Ruth. 1947. *The City of Women.* New York: Macmillan (Brazilian edition, 1967, *A cidade das mulheres,* Rio de Janeiro: Civilização Brasileira).

Matory, J. Lorand. 2005. *Black Atlantic Religion: Tradition, Transnationalism and Matriarchy in the Afro-Brazilian Candomblé.* Princeton, Oxford: Princeton University Press.

Mintz, Sidney W. and Richard Price. [1976] 1992. *The Birth of African-American Culture: An Anthropological Perspective.* Boston: Beacon.

Palmié, Stephan. 2005. "*Ackee and Saltfish vs. Amalá con Quimbombó?* A Note on Sidney Mintz' Contribution to the Historical Anthropology of African American Cultures." *Journal de la société des Américanistes* 91(2): 89–122.

Risério, Antonio. 1988. "Bahia com 'H': uma leitura da cultura baiana," in J.J. Reis, ed. *Escravidão e Invenção da Liberdade.* São Paulo: Companhia das Letras, pp.143–165.

Silveira, Renato da. 1988. "Pragmatismo e milagros da fé no Extremo Occidente," in J.J. Reis, ed. *Escravidão e a Invenção da Liberdade*. São Paulo: Companhia das Letras, pp.166–197.

Thompson, Robert Farris. 1983. *Flash of the Spirit: African and Afro-American Art and Philosophy*. New York: Vintage Books.

Thornton, John. [1992] 1998. *Africa and Africans in the Making of the Atlantic World: 1400–1800*. Cambridge: Cambridge University Press.

Verger, Pierre. 1957. *Notes sur le culte des Orisa et Vodun: à Bahia, la Baie de tous les saints, au Brésil et à l'ancienne côte des Esclaves en Afrique*, Mémoires de l'Institut Français d'Afrique Noire (IFAN), n. 51.

Chapter 11

Undoing Brazil: Hybridity versus Multiculturalism

Peter Fry

Introduction

This chapter addresses the issue of the supposed specificity of the Portuguese speaking world by examining recent changes in the way parts of the Brazilian government, certain NGOs, and intellectuals, especially anthropologists, imagine Brazil. While the idea(l)s of a biologically and culturally hybrid nation consolidated during the twentieth century continue to hold sway, recent events suggest that a rival paradigm gains strength: that of Brazil as a multiethnic and multicultural society.

Over the past few years I have been trying to come to grips with the post-colonial sequels of British and Portuguese colonialism. As a British-born and trained anthropologist who has lived and worked in England, Zimbabwe, Mozambique, and Brazil, I have been more or less forced into trying to look back critically at Britain and its imperialism at the same time that I have been forced to try to come to terms with a colonial tradition that lies behind modern-day Brazil and Mozambique.

When David Lehmann invited me to give the Smuts Lectures in Cambridge in 1998, I organized my ideas around what I saw as a continued tension through-out the colonial enterprise between ideals of "assimilation" and "segregation" (Fry 2000). Classically, Portuguese colonial dogma favored the former, while British dogma tended toward the latter. To a large extent the identities of the two colonial powers were defined by this contrast. Wary of confusing interna-tional rhetorical contrasts with the internal situation of the colonies themselves, I noted that the tension between these two dogmas marked the internal experi-ence of both colonial enterprises and continues to characterize the contempo-rary postcolonial situation not just in Mozambique and Zimbabwe, but in the modern world as a whole as tensions mount between the celebration of "ethnic" difference and the universality of the human experience. This same tension is, of course, at the basis of social anthropology itself, at once concerned with the unity of humankind and the diversity of language, meaning, and identity that has in no way succumbed to the increasing pace of globalization.

As the colonial enterprise reached its zenith at the end of the nineteenth century and the first decades of the twentieth, Portuguese and British administrators-cum-intellectuals spelled out their rival theories. Jan Christiaan Smuts spelt out his own theory on the subject:

> First we looked upon the African as essentially inferior or sub-human, as having no soul, and as being only fit to be a slave. . . . Then we changed to the opposite extreme. The African now became a man and a brother. Religion and politics combined to shape this new African policy. The principles of the French Revolution which had emancipated Europe were applied to Africa; liberty, equality and fraternity could turn based Africans into good Europeans. (Smuts 1929: 76–78 quoted in Mamdani 1996: 5)

> The political system of the natives was ruthlessly destroyed in order to incorporate them as equals into the white system. The African was good as a potential European; his social and political culture was bad, barbarous, and only deserving to be stamped out root and branch. In some of the British possessions in Africa the native just emerged from barbarism was accepted as an equal citizen with full political rights along with the whites. But his native institutions were ruthlessly proscribed and destroyed. The principle of equal rights was applied in its crudest form, and while it gave the native a semblance of equality with whites, which was little good to him, it destroyed the basis of his African system which was his highest good. These are the two extreme native policies which have prevailed in the past, and the second has been only less harmful than the first. (Smuts 1929: 92)

"If Africa has to be redeemed," he continued, so as "to make her own contribution to the world," then "we shall have to proceed on different lines and evolve a policy which will not force her institutions into an alien European mould" but "will preserve her unity with her own past" and "build her future progress and civilization on specifically African foundations." "The British Empire does not stand for the assimilation of its peoples into a common type; it does not stand for standardization, but for the fullest freest development of its peoples along their own specific lines." To achieve this end, "institutional segregation" and in consequence "territorial segregation" would be necessary.

Proud of developments in South Africa, Smuts concluded that

> [T]he situation in South Africa is therefore a lesson to all the younger British communities farther north to prevent as much as possible the detachment of the native from his tribal connection, and to enforce from the very start the system of segregation with its conservation of separate native institutions.

Smuts' advice was, of course, taken. Southern Rhodesia, for example, followed this policy to the letter while in South Africa itself the ideas enunciated by Smuts finally resulted in what Coetzee has called the "madness" of apartheid. Indeed, as Mahmood Mamdani has so cogently argued, far from representing an exception to the rest of English-speaking Africa, apartheid South Africa was in reality just a particularly rabid version of indirect rule.

> [T]he discourse of apartheid—in both General Smuts, who anticipated it, and the Broederbond, which engineered it—idealized the practice of indirect rule in British colonies to the north. (Mamdani 1996: 27)

Smuts' views, dominant as they were in the British Empire, were expressed with great clarity by the architect of British colonial policy Lord Frederick Lugard, who argued for indirect rule through the mediation of local institutions.

> Here, then, is the true conception of the inter-relation of colour: complete uniformity in ideals, absolute equality in the paths of knowledge and culture, equal opportunity for those who strive, equal admiration for those who achieve; in matters social and racial a separate path, each pursuing his own inherited traditions, preserving his own race-purity and race-ride; equality in things spiritual, agreed divergence in the physical and material. (Lugard 1922: 87)

Race purity and race-pride implied, of course, condemnation and at times prohibition of marriage and sex between conquerors and conquered. To preserve such racial pride, mulatto children were set apart as almost another distinct "race." As Coetzee has argued, the prohibition of "interracial" sex in South Africa was at the center of the madness of apartheid (Coetzee, 1991).

Portuguese rhetoric was quite distinct. The Portuguese equivalent of Lugard was the soldier-administrator António Enes and his fellow generals. The "generation of 95," as they were called, were in favor of direct colonial rule and the (very) gradual assimilation of Africans to Portuguese culture. Well aware of what was occurring in South Africa, however, they doubted the advisability of implementing a policy of assimilation tout court without taking into account ethnic diversity and the sheer difficulty of "converting" in a short space of time so many "backward peoples" to the refinements of "civilization," that is, Portuguese language and culture. Influenced by the racialist tone of nineteenth-century anthropology and by their own experience, they argued that although the ultimate goal of Portuguese colonization was the assimilation of all inhabitants of Mozambique, this required patience and caution. "[T]he peoples of Africa," remarked Enes, "must necessarily pass through an extensive period of intellectual and moral development before becoming confirmed Christians, and education will shorten this period but will not substitute it" (Macagno 1996: 2). Another administrator of the same period, Eduardo Costa commented that:

> Anthropological and social factors which demonstrate the disparity of custom and of ethnic characteristics, and the manifest inferiority of the savage suggest the necessity of applying different governmental systems to such races and to maintain in civilized hands the trusteeship of the more savage and primitive, as an unfortunate or incomplete class within human society. (quoted in Macagno 1996: 25)

The result of this ratiocination was that the Portuguese maintained the long-term goal of total "spiritual assimilation," while recognizing the need to take care not to destroy concomitantly all African *usos e costumes*. In the language of colonialism, the Portuguese carried "civilization," and the Portuguese *language*. The Africans were called alternatively *gentios* or *indígenas*, in reference to their "tribal" nature and autochthonous status. They possessed *usos e costumes*—usages and customs—and spoke not in languages but in "dialects." To this day the words *civilização, usos e costumes* and dialects are used quite unselfconsciously by all but the most politically correct urban elite.

In this way the African population of the colony was divided into *assimilados* and *indígenas*. The former enjoyed the rights and obligations (including military service) of Portuguese citizens, while the latter remained subordinated to their *usos e costumes* and their *régulos*.

Although Portuguese colonial discourse was not unequivocally assimilationist, the significant difference between Mozambique and its English-speaking neighbors, was that the principle of assimilation as an ultimate goal was never called into question. In principle, at least, all subjects could become citizens, and although many Portuguese were dubious of the value of increasingly severe African competition with Europeans for jobs, prestige, and wealth, the documents reveal less of the visceral distaste that the British displayed for "pseudo Europeans" or "Europeanized Africans." Whereas the social engineers of South Africa set out on an explicit course of racial and ethnic segregation, and the celebration of cultural difference, their equivalents in Mozambique imagined a time when all Mozambicans would have abandoned their *usos e costumes* and their dialects in favor of Portuguese civilization and language. This would be achieved through the supposedly moralizing influence of work, including forced labor, education, and conversion to Christianity, which were almost monopolized by the Catholic Church, especially after the Concordat of 1940. Unlike English-speaking Africa, schooling was only conducted in the official colonial language.[1] Furthermore, interracial sex and marriage, although in practice much criticized, were recognized as possible. Traditionally mulatto children were not set apart. Rather their paternal filiation was recognized and they became assimilated into the lower (or sometimes higher) echelons of Portuguese settler society. In general, however, they formed an intermediate zone between the Portuguese and the Africans.

However, as Lorenzo Macagno has shown, total assimilation was only to be achieved in the distant future, if at all. Portuguese colonialism could only reproduce itself in this way—assimilating, but not too much, liberating, but at the same time controlling. After all, once everyone had been assimilated there would be no room left for the trusteeship of the Portuguese themselves![2]

The development of distinct Portuguese and British colonial rhetorics took place in a situation in which the former were economically and politically subordinate to the latter. British intellectuals had little time for Portuguese imperialism. Anderson's famous indictment of Portuguese cruelty and dissimulation (Anderson 1966) belongs to a long tradition of British anti-Portuguese protest, which however justified was also larded with self-righteousness and verged on what James Duffy has called a "kind of neo-racial prejudice." He quotes Lord Palmerston as having said to Lord Russell after yet another of Portugal's evasions in the curtailment of the slave trade: "The plain truth is that the Portuguese are of all European nations the lowest in the moral scale" (Duffy 1967). Livingstone had railed not only against the Portuguese as traders in slaves, but against their "moral delinquency" (Duffy 1967: 104). Cecil John Rhodes' companion de Waal, however, made "the bluntest accusations, the final racial rejection of Portugal in East Africa." Describing a small town near Beira, "The Portuguese there, like the natives dwell in huts; and there is no difference between the hut of the Portuguese and that of the Kaffirs, and not much distinction between the two races. The Portuguese wear clothes and the Kaffirs do not, the Portuguese are yellow, the Kaffirs, black; the Portuguese are physically weak, the Kaffirs, strong—those are the only striking differences. . . . They mix with each other, take each other around the waist, and talk one language when together—Kaffir. This is certain though: the natives are more cleanly in their habits than their yellow masters. The latter are as thin as dried fish, and they die like rats" (Duffy 1967: 135).

Today

I will argue that the British distaste for the Portuguese and their colonial rhetoric and practice has not waned. The ideals of "separate development," "race pride," and "racial purity" have been transmuted into the celebration of "multiculturalism," "diversity," "empowerment," "indigenous knowledge," and a plethora of similar concepts that dominate the discourse of the international development community ranging from the World Bank and the United Nations system, through the bilateral aid agencies such as Sida, Difid, and Usaid, to the philanthropical organizations that operate internationally such as the Ford and Rockefeller Foundations. Just as Enes and his colleagues squirmed to find a form of colonial domination that preserved something of the rhetoric of assimilation and which yet incorporated notions of ethnic and racial singularity, so postcolonial Lusophone societies wrestle with their old and venerated notions of a-racialism and social and biological hybridism in a world that regards them as archaic, unjust, and therefore dispensable. The zeitgeist of "ethnic" diversity is more powerful now than ever.

Of all the Portuguese colonies, Brazil and Cape Verde are those whose societies are held to approximate most closely to colonial rhetoric. Both have a high proportion of brown citizens and, until recently, a strong national a-racial ideography. Both have homegrown ideologies of the value of hybridism (Gilberto Freyre in Brazil, the intellectuals of Claridade in Cape Verde) and nonracism. As in colonial Africa, however, the process of "assimilation" (read education) is constructed in such a way as to postpone its fulfillment into the unforeseeable future. As the statistical data shows with the starkest clarity, Brazil continues to lead the inequality stakes (together with South

Africa) (data on gini coefficients) while educational, health, and economic inequalities between blacks, browns, and whites (*pretos, pardos e brancos*) remains pretty much unaltered. Most of us recognize that the educational system is largely responsible for this iniquity, providing better education in private schools, ejecting poorer students with monotonous regularity, and doing little or nothing to foster learning.

As Brazilians and non-Brazilians contemplate these figures, two interpretations (at least) emerge, one built on the premises of traditional a-racism and hybridism, the other on the premises of racism and racial/ethnic singularity. The latter interpretation has become official government policy since the publication of Fernando Henrique Cardoso's Human Rights Program in 1995. "We wish to affirm," said the president, "and truly with considerable pride, our condition as a *multi-racial society* and that we have great satisfaction in being able to enjoy the privilege of having *distinct races* [*raças distintas*] and distinct cultural traditions also. In these days, such diversity makes for the wealth of a country."

With the Lula government, these ideas have taken a more institutional form. A Special Secretariat for Policies Promoting Racial Equality was created in the president's office to oversee the activities of all ministries, many of which have special "diversity" sections, usually run by black activists. More importantly, a series of affirmative action policies has been developed. Racial quotas have been adopted in a number of universities and are part of government policy for all private and public universities. The Ministry of Health is developing policies targeting Afro-Brazilians, presenting statistics on the "racial" distribution of illnesses. The Ministry of Agricultural Development spearheads a movement for the recognition of maroon communities (*remanescentes de quilombos*), which multiply daily and have now reached the figure of 743 that have been officially recognized. The Ministry of Education has developed new curricula aimed at promoting the self-esteem of Afro-Brazilians. Behind all these policies is a premise that Brazil is no longer a biologically and culturally hybrid society, but rather a society of "distinct races." Statistical information normally refers to blacks and whites, the former term including those who define themselves as "brown" (*parda*) or "black" (*preta*) to the census takers. By so doing, the myriad *caboclos, cafuzos, morenos,* and so on disappear. José Murilo de Carvalho has referred to this process as "statistical racial genocide" (Carvalho 2004).[3]

Let me now exemplify my argument with a few examples.

Os Quilombos

A recent documentary film produced by the Brazilian Anthropological Association (ABA) and funded by the Ford Foundation has this to say about *quilombos* (maroon communities):

> Até pouco tempo o significado do termo quilombo estava ligado as definições utilizadas no período colonial e imperial para perseguir e punir escravos

fugidos. A partir de 1988 como resultado da pressão dos movimentos sociais a Constituição brasileira passa a garantir os direitos territoriais as comunidades remanescentes de quilombos. Embora tem um conteúdo histórico o termo quilombo é resemantizado, passando a assumir novo significado tanto na literatura especializada quanto para as comunidades negras rurais que buscam hoje em todo o Brasil o reconhecimento dos seus territórios. Comunidades negras rurais que sempre lutaram por sua autonomia e pela manutenção dos seus territórios contra a invasão de particulares, de empresas e do próprio Estado buscam manter e reproduzir os seus modos de vida agora sob o amparo da constituição de 1988.

As comunidades de remanescentes de quilombos constituem grupos étnicos que se auto definem a partir de situações históricas especificas que os ligam a um passado comum e cobram do Estado o reconhecimento dos seus territórios. Os quilombos contemporâneos se espalham por todo o Brasil. . . . Buscam autonomia, liberdade de praticar os seus cultos, venerar seus santos, cantar seus cânticos, e dançar seus ritmos. O Brasil, um país plural, deve reconhecê-los como grupos em sua singularidade. (Santos, M. 2004. Terras de Quilombo—uma divida histórica)

In the 1980s Carlos Vogt and I carried out research in a small rural community in the State of São Paulo that had preserved a *língua africana*, a sort of Creole with a lexicon of African words obeying the local Portuguese morpho-syntax (Vogt and Fry 1996). Descendants of a slave called Ifigênia, they were living in lands left to them by their slave master on his death but later invaded by local land grabbers. Three members of the community were on trial for the murder of one of these land grabbers. In 1988, a new Brazilian Constitution recognized right to land on the part of descendants of *quilombos*. Article 68 of the Act of Transitory Dispositions (*Ato das Disposições Transitórias*) reads thus: "Aos remanescentes das comunidades dos quilombos é reconhecida a propriedade definitiva, devendo o Estado emitir-lhes os títulos respectivos." Cafundó was redefined as a *quilombo*, and land rights were recognized.

The process of "resemantização" (semantic reassignment) of the term *quilombo* gained greater speed through the 1990s. Jean-François Véran (Véran 2003) points to November 1995, the three hundredth anniversary of the death of Zumbi de Palmares as the starting point of a political process that has led to the official recognition of 743 (up to 2002) "comunidades remanescentes de quilombos," and the legalization of 29 (Véran 2003: 86).

The transformation of rural communities into "comunidades remanescentes de quilombos" follows a ritual process. In general a land dispute brings to the fore political mediators (Sindicatos Rurais, Comissão Pastoral da Terra, etc.) who suggest that a short cut to control over the land would be to claim a *quilombola* identity. At this point government agencies enter the scenario and anthropologists are contracted to judge the veracity of the claim. The emergence and recognition of "comunidades remanescentes de quilombos" depends basically on the coordinated activities of anthropologists, activists, the local communities and, of course, the state apparatus. Jean Francois Véran in his study of one such quilombization has drawn attention to the presence of urban intellectuals, be they anthropologists, missionaries, or state employees (Véran 2003). It is they who bring the seed of quilombization and, in the last analysis, catalyze the transformation of black rural communities into *quilombolas*. The anthropologists must demonstrate long-term occupation of the land, a certain "especificidade cultural" and "autonomia econômica." The anthropologists lend their academic authority as cartographers of cultural difference "to declare these communities "remanescentes de quilombo," "resemantizando" the term "quilombo" to signify "resistência" based on racial or ethnic solidarity and a more or less autonomous system of production.[4] Claiming an ethnic or racial identity vouched for by anthropologists and later jurists, and "resemantizando," the concept of *quilombo*, groups of families who used to be part of the "geléia geral" of the peasantry acquire distinction and specific rights.

Health

The following text which is authored Grupo de Trabalho Interministerial para Valorização da População Negra (GTI) can be found on the internet:

> A temática da saúde da população negra não havia merecido, ainda, o espaço adequado na pauta de prioridades da saúde pública brasileira.
> . . . [N]não há justificativa técnica para a criação de vários programas governamentais de saúde específicos para a população negra, como pretendiam algumas correntes do setor. A única exceção é o Programa de Anemia Falciforme, por ser uma doença incidente predominantemente sobre a população afro-descendente e já contar com sinalizadores estatísticos suficientes e convincentes para justificar sua prioridade como problema de saúde pública. http://www.planalto.gov.br/publi_04/COLECAO/RACIAL2H.HTM, accessed on June 01, 2007.

The concern with sickle cell anemia also dates from the 1995 Human Rights Program, which envisaged a series of activities in favor of the "comunidade negra" (black community). The sub-group of the GTI responsible for health issues recognized two types of illness that affect the "população negra" (black population): "doenças geneticamente determinadas" (genetically determined diseases) with "berço hereditário, ancestral e étnico" (a hereditary, ancestral, and ethnic source), and illnesses "derivados de condições socioeconômicas e educacionais desfavoráveis, além da intensa pressão social"[5] (originating from unfavorable socioeconomic and educational conditions, as well as from intense social pressure). "Influências culturais" (cultural influences) are also mentioned but no example is given. The first type of illnesses includes sickle cell anemia "por ser uma doença que incide predominantemente sobre afro-descendentes" (as it is a disease predominantly affecting Afro-descendants), arterial hypertension, diabetes mellitus e, and a deficiency of the hepatic enzyme. The sub-group recognizes that these illnesses are "incidentes sobre outros grupos raciais/étnicos, porém mais graves ou de tratamento mais difícil quando acometem pretos e pardos" (likely to affect other racial/ethnic groups, but more serious or difficult to treat when affecting black and mixed race individuals).

The second type of illness includes "alcoolismo, toxicomania, desnutrição, mortalidade infantil elevada, abortos sépticos, anemia ferropriva, DST/AIDS, doenças do trabalho e transtornos mentais" (alcoholism, drug addiction, high infant mortality, septic miscarriages, iron-deficiency anemia, STDs/AIDS, work-related illnesses, and mental breakdowns), and also "o conjunto de condições fisiológicas que sofrem interferência das condições negativas anteriormente mencionadas, contribuindo para sua evolução para doenças: crescimento, gravidez, parto e envelhecimento"(the entire set of physiological conditions that are prone to interference from the previously mentioned negative conditions, contributing to their progression into illnesses: growth, pregnancy, birth, and ageing). Of all these illnesses, sickle cell anemia was given highest priority.

Since its discovery in 1910 in a student of Caribbean origin, sickle cell anemia has been associated with the "black race." Later in the 1940s, it was found that the illness was transmitted by a recessive gene, and affected sufferers in different ways. Heterozygotes showed no clinical symptoms, although they could be immune to certain forms of malaria. Homozygotes, who inherit the gene from both parents, develop a variant of the anemia, which is incurable but whose effects may be assuaged by medicines. The mendelian logic of transmission means that the gene spread with the velocity of productive sex. Given the high incidence of "miscigenação" in Brazil, it follows that skin color is a very weak indicator of the genetic composition of individuals (Parra, Amado, et al. 2003).

Even so, the Programa Nacional de Combate à Anemia Falciforme was elaborated in 1996 with the active participation of black activists and medical specialists (one of the principal participants is both). Black activists have adopted the fight against sickle cell anemia as a major part of their political campaigning. Studies of educational materials and the press show a strong and almost exclusive relationship between sickling and the black body.

In the United States during the 1970s, in the context of the battle for civil liberties, the campaign against sickle cell anemia involved explicitly the "black community." The anthropologist Melbourne Tapper argues convincingly that an important consequence of this policy was the *formation* of a responsible "black community."

> The dilemma facing the proponents of the sickling program was . . . that no well-defined, unified black community existed at the time of the hearings and the enactment of the National Sickle Cell Anemia Prevention Act; rather it had to be produced. The proponents of the sickling initiative sought to assemble a positive image of that which was to be governed—the black community—as well as to stress government's good intentions, organizing their presentation around such key terms as neglect (to be corrected), personal responsibility (presented as a universally available category to be appealed to), urgency (the insistence on immediacy being articulated as proof of the genuineness of government's concern for a group of marginalized citizens), and self-governance

(as the crystallization of the benevolent nature of liberal democracy [and, I might add, as the legitimate inheritor of indirect rule]. (Tapper 1999: 123)

I argue that the Brazilian program has another and more basic consequence: that of naturalizing the notion of "raça negra" as such. In the United States such a concept is taken for granted on the premises of the "one drop rule" which produces wide consensus on who is black and who is not. I feel somehow that the total support of black activists for the aims of the PAF means that sickling represents much more than an illness to be detected and treated. By understating the mendelian logic of transmission, sickling becomes a potent natural symbol for the specificity of the black body, and by logical opposition, the white one also.

Racial Quotas

The following text was issued by the University of Brasília to announce the adoption of a system of quotas for black candidates in 2004:

- No segundo vestibular de 2004, os candidatos poderão concorrer pelo sistema universal ou pelo sistema de cotas, que oferecem 80% e 20% das vagas respectivamente de cada curso;
- Para concorrer às vagas reservadas por meio do sistema de cotas para negros, o candidato deverá ser de cor preta ou parda, declarar-se negro e optar pelo sistema de cotas;
- No momento da inscrição, o candidato deverá assinar uma declaração específica relativa aos requisitos exigidos para concorrer pelo sistema de cotas;
- O pedido de inscrição e uma foto, que será tirada no momento da inscrição, serão analisados por uma comissão que decidirá pela homologação ou não pelo sistema de cotas. Essa comissão terá representantes de movimentos sociais ligados à questão, especialistas no tema e membros do grupo que operacionalizou a implantação do sistema; . . .
- As inscrições pelo sistema de cotas para negros serão aceitas somente pessoalmente em cinco postos no Distrito Federal e outros sete espalhados por cidades de Goiás e Minas Gerais. Não poderão ser realizadas pela Internet, por terceiros com procuração, via fax ou via postal.

  Universidade de Brasília Agência, http://www.unb.br/acs/acsweb/ accessed March 18, 2004.

The UNB was the fourth university to adopt racial quotas, which are claimed as a temporary measure to correct the imbalance of blacks and whites (note the dichotomy) especially in highly competitive courses.

Since the introduction of quotas in the Rio de Janeiro state universities in 2002, university administrators have had to wrestle with the question of who is black and who is not in a society marked by ambiguity and situational definition. Unable to find "objective criteria" they opted for self-definition, even though the law was something of an oxymoron, stating that candidates would do so "sob pena da lei" (as required by law). Candidates for the 2002 entrance exam to the State University of Rio de Janeiro (Uerj) were obliged to fill in a form accepting the terms and conditions of the exam. Question 24 read: "De acordo com o decreto n 30.766, de 04/03/2002, declaro, sob penas da lei, identificar-me como negro ou pardo: ( )S-Sim/( ) N-Não." The instructions warn that those who do not tick either "yes" or "no" will be considered not black or brown. Those who for one reason or another did not tick either box became honorary whites.

There were many problems. More than three hundred candidates filed suits claiming that they had lost their places to blacks or public school candidates with lower scores. One candidate who refused to fill in question 24 because he was against the quota system failed to enter the faculty of law although he claimed that he would have done so if he had declared himself black. White- looking candidates were interviewed on TV claiming black ancestry. The coordinator of the NGO, Educafro, which prepares young blacks for the entrance exam, Frei David, accused the Uerj of permitting "frauds."

It was probably to avoid this kind of problem that the UNB opted for photographs and commissions. In June 2004, under rules introduced that year, candidates for the University of Brasília's entrance examination formed two queues: one for those competing for the 20 percent of places reserved for blacks and one for the rest. Those claiming to be black had their photographs taken: on the basis of these pictures a commission composed of a student, a sociologist, an anthropologist, and three representatives of Brazil's Black Movement decided whether they were really black or not. The commission rejected 212 out of 4,385. Thirty-four of these complained, and were interviewed by a second commission, composed of university teachers and members of NGOs, which asked among other things whether they had strong links to "black values and culture." One young man said afterward that they asked him whether he had belonged to the black movement and if he had ever had a *mulatta* girl friend. In the end, only thirteen of the thirty-four were denied a black identity.

Many Brazilian intellectuals expressed some astonishment that one of the leading universities in the country could have adopted racial classification techniques redolent of the eugenics movement of the 1930s. Others wrung their hands at what they saw as an affront to Brazil's identity as a mestizo republic where racial identity was formally immaterial. Defenders of the newly introduced quotas maintained that Brazil must break with its French republican tradition of color blindness. Unequal treatment was necessary, they argued, for those who were, in fact, unequal. To treat all equally was the only way of avoiding dealing with racial inequality (Fry 2004; Santos 2004).

In spite of opposition the quota policy continues to enthuse. The federal government has introduced scholarships in private universities for blacks and Indians from public schools in the proportions revealed by the census bureau. Legislation is planned to extend quotas to all federal universities.

Quotas for blacks mean that from the point of view of the legislators and black activists, Brazil should no longer be imagined as a country of biological mixture and of multiple terms used to define the citizenry. The mulattos have disappeared.

The Meaning of Change

The three examples I have given suggest a significant inflexion in official discourse on the racial and ethnic configuration of Brazil.

I would like to put forward two questions: 1) what factors led to the salience of racial and ethnic definition in official discourse? and (2) what is the future of hybridist and confusion?

A widely disseminated opinion in Brazil is that all of this is yet one more example of the submission of Brazil to the designs of the UD. A few years back, Pierre Bourdieu and Loïc Wacquant argued that "various topics which result directly from intellectual confrontations related to the social specificity of American society and American universities are being imposed in ways that seem de-historicized, to the totality of the planet." Under this argument, "multiculturalism" and "neoliberalism"—concepts developed in the United States—are transformed into natural and universal truths and premises (Bourdieu and Wacquant 1998: 109). Noting that the debate on "race" and "identity" has been subject to "similar ethnocentric intrusions" they turn to Brazil to illustrate their argument:

> An historical representation, born from the fact that American tradition arbi-
> trarily imposed a dichotomy of blacks and whites on an infinitely more com-
> plex reality, may even be imposed on countries where the principles of vision
> and division, codified or practical, of ethnic differences are completely differ-
> ent and that, as in Brazil, were until recently held as a counter example to the
> "American model." (Bourdieu and Wacquant 1998: 112)

This "symbolic violence" derives, they argue, from the utilization of American racial categories to describe Brazil coupled to the power of the United States to obtain "the collaboration, conscious or not, of all the pur-veyors and importers of cultural products with or without griffe," such as editors, directors of cultural institutions, theatres, museums, galleries, mag-azines, and similar cultural artifacts. They also emphasize the role of the great American philanthropical organizations in the "diffusion of the North American racial doxa in the heart of Brazilian universities both in terms of representation and practice" (Bourdieu and Wacquant 1998: 113).

It is true that at least one American foundation has been most generous in its support for NGOs led by the most articulate black activists and the Brazilian Anthropological Association for its work in mapping *quilombo* and Indian identities and territories. But Bourdieu and Wacquant might also have pointed to the increasing influence of the multilateral organizations, above all the World Bank and the United Nations system. The Convention

169 of the ILO on Indigenous and Tribal Peoples in Independent Countries of June 7, 1989, is a case in point, guaranteeing that they have rights to land and the conservation of "their own social, economic, cultural and political institutions, or part thereof." Three years after the publication of Bourdieu and Wacquant's article, the United Nations promoted the Third World Conference to Combat Racism, Racial Discrimination, Xenophobia and Correlate Intolerance in Durban in 2001. One hundred seventy states and 1000 NGOs participated. It had a catalyzing effect on government policy in Brazil leading immediately to the adoption of racial quotas in Rio de Janeiro's universities. The most recent UNDP report on human development has as sub-title: "Cultural freedom in a diversified world." The principle message of the report, even though it recognizes the dangers of "essentialization" is that without cultural diversity there can be no development. There can be no doubt, therefore, that Brazil finds itself immersed in a network of discourses, meanings, and relationships that are positioned against the old Brazilian ideology that formally ignored "race" in the distribution of justice and the benesses of the state. And there is no doubt that there has been a significant investment of human and material resources in support of the demands of the black activists.

Bourdieu and Wacquant's diffusionist theory so close to the common sense of many Brazilians who see racial quotas as an affront to hallowed tradition only partly does justice to the facts as I see them. The trick of personifying nations and attributing to them some kind of cultural homogeneity and objectively defined hegemonic projects may hide those themes that are really at play and that are endogenous to all contemporary societies and that derive from a tension between the post-Boazian position, that race is a malignant social artifact and the persistent survival and the increasingly powerful presence of "race" as the basis for the formation of social categories and identities. Diffusionist theories also ignore, of course, the way in which "receiving" societies "read" the messages they receive, often translating them into their own native categories.

On this point it is important to remember that racial divide always existed in Brazil, gaining strength from 1951 with the promulgation of the Afonso Arinos Law onward. Costa Pinto argued that this law inaugurated in republican Brazil the "figura judicial do negro" irrefutable argument thus establishing a binary "racial" taxonomy within Brazil's *corpus júris*. Costa Pinto affirms that the Afonso Arinos law is:

> . . . o começo de um processo que, dentro das tensões raciais existentes e em agravamento neste País, não será surpreendente se conduzir à situação que caracteriza as relações de raças nas cidades setentrionais dos Estados Unidos e que se pode resumir na fórmula *separate but equal*. De fato, até então, no Brasil, na legislação republicana, o negro vinha comparecendo como o liberto de 1888, como cidadão, em abstrato, juridicamente igual a todos os cidadãos; estava na lei por exclusão—*todos* são iguais perante a lei, independentemente de

cor, sexo, religião, etc. Agora, pela primeira vez, salvo engano, regulamenta-se em lei o comportamento de brancos em relação a negros, e atribui-se a estes, como negros, o direito específico de não terem praticamente negados alguns direitos mais gerais que a lei já atribuía a todos os cidadãos, independente-mente da condição étnica. ... a declarar que são puníveis os que violarem determinados princípios já solenemente presentes em leis anteriores e mais gerais. . . . Ora, uma tal atitude da lei . . . pode vir a ser . . . o prelúdio de uma outra legislação substitutiva desta e até inspirada no desejo de remediar sua inoperância pratica, visando assegurar a negros e brancos o direito de terem educação, recreação, distritos residenciais, obras de assistência e outro setores institucionalizados da vida social *iguais mas separados*. Para isto, tecnicamente, uma das pré-condições já existe: a entidade jurídica *negro*, presente no espírito e no texto da legislação ordinária. (Pinto 1953: 292–293)

Since then, as Fabiano Dias Monteiro has argued, the "racial divide" grew stronger with the attacks on "racial democracy," seen not even as an ideal but a cruel trick masking discrimination and Brazilian racial polarity (Monteiro 2003). In other words, one might interpret the introduction of racial quotas as the legal crowning of a long process of change in the racial taxonomy of Brazil.

The term "afrodescendente," which was introduced at the same time as the introduction of quotas represents Brazil as a racially divided country and suggests the North American one-drop rule as the basis of classification. But to affirm that this is a simple importation is no answer. Surely the increasing involvement of Brazilian intellectuals and activists in the global networks of meaning that underpin the values of "diversity" and "multiculturalism" strengthen their hand. Those who prefer to imagine alternative nonracializ-ing policies to confront inequality and discrimination are deprived of such pecuniary or moral support! In a sense, then, the argument of Bourdieu and Wacquant is partially acceptable. Those who believe in the naturalness of a racial divide between blacks and whites and who see Brazilian ideals of mix-ture and hybridism as archaic and unjust, have the right and might of the wider world on their side. And this wider world, I would like to argue, car-ries the logical meanings of difference that hark back to the indirect rule of the British Empire: racial pride and racial purity.

The Future of Hybridity

On the issue of hybridism and miscegenation the debate rages in Brazil. There is not time to resume it here, even though it is worth noting that many of the most vociferous supporters of what I have called the "undoing of Brazil" continue to exalt mixture. They argue that quotas are a temporary measure that will be abandoned when no longer needed. This utilitarian argument fails to take into account the immense symbolic charge that these measures carry and that will not evaporate. Rather they will increase.

My own feeling is that the victory of racialization and "ethnicization" in Brazil marks a major defeat for that which was considered so long a specific feature of the postcolonial Lusophone world (in particular Brazil). Powerful rhetoric in the hands of powerful institutions is powerful.

At present, there is a strong ground swell of skepticism in relation to all these policies as evidenced in informal conversation and letters to the newspapers. My own first year undergraduate students still think that multiculturalism is mixture. It does not define ethnic groups or "races" but rather each individual in his own internal cultural and biological diversity.

But one cannot minimize the consequences of the power of the state when it enters the ring of racial classification. I tend to agree with Yvonne Maggie when she suggests that the changes I have described could be the event that transforms the fragile notions of a-raciality just as the return and death of Captain Cook changed Hawaii (Sahlins 1995).

> One should not accuse Mário de Andrade of being a racist! It was his generation under his leadership which gave birth to the most radically anti-racist movement after a century of pseudo scientific racism. But maybe those who wish the end of modernist ideas are themselves as much believers in *Macunaíma* and the *Manifesto Antropófago* as she who writes these lines. Maybe they believe that we will eat multiculturalism today as Bishop Sardinha was eaten so long ago without evaluating the risks for structure when events like these occur. The structural changes produced by these events [quotas, above all] the creation of a racialized social engineering, will affect above all the mixed-up population of the immense suburbs on the peripheries of our cities. (Maggie 2005)

One might also add on the caboclos, Indians, peasants, "remanescentes de quilombos," inhabitants of Brazil's vast hinterland.

The self image of a Brazil that exalts miscegenation, hybridism, and the ambiguity of taxonomies and classifications emerged in the context of imperial conquest and domination, becoming consolidated as national doxa in the 1920s and 1930s. But it did not emerge in the context of the conquest and domination by the British! As cultural fact, it cannot be interpreted in terms of practical reason, as a conscious sleight of hand of domination. It was a specific form of colonial social organization and control. In the twentieth century it became an icon of Brazilian specificity in contrast to the pessimism and segregation in the United States and the British Empire. That this should now be condemned to the rubbish bin of history by activists and well-meaning urban intellectuals has about it a touch of irony when one notices how societies that have been historically segregated yearn for the hybridism that Brazil now appears to reject, the Rainbow Nation that South Africa would like to be. This irony becomes more pungent when one realizes that at bottom the premises of British imperialism as set out by Lord Frederick Lugard (Lugard 1922) whose apotheosis was the apartheid regime, (Mamdani 1996) underlie the contemporary eulogy of "diversity" and the celebration of "racial" and "ethnic" identities forged by those urban intellectuals who must surely know that race is a social construct and that they have a part to play in its construction or deconstruction.

Notes

An initial version of this essay was presented to the Seminário de Pós Graduação do Instituto de Ciências Sociais, Universidade de Lisboa, on September 21, 2004. I am grateful for the criticisms and the comments received from this seminar.

1. Exceptions were some protestant mission schools such Henri Junod's Swiss Mission in Mozambique where early instruction was carried out in Shangaan, the language spoken in the mission's hinterland.
2. The critics of the assimilation policy all point to the undeniable fact that rhetoric was more powerful than actual fact. Very few people did acquire *assimilado* status and even then they suffered from severe discrimination (Penvenne 1989). But statistical failure is not, in my view, the same as ideological failure.
3. Similar processes may be observed in relation to indigenous societies. But for reasons of time I have unfortunately had to leave them out of this communication.
4. Interestingly enough recent historiography has been at pains to demonstrate the relative *integration* of historical quilombos (Gomes 1993).
5. All references to this working group were taken from Negra 2004.

Bibliography

Anderson, P. 1966. *Portugal e o Fim do Ultracolonialismo.* Rio de Janeiro: Civilização Brasileira.

Bourdieu, P. and L. Wacquant. 1998. "Les Ruses de la Raison Impérialiste." *Actes de la Recherche en Sciences Sociale* 121–122, March 1998: 109–118.

Carvalho, J. M. D. 2004. "Genocídio racial estatístico." *O Globo.* December 27, 2004: 7.

Coetzee, J. M. 1991. "*The Mind of Apartheid:* Geoffrey Cronjé (1907)." *Social Dynamics* 17(1): 1–35.

Duffy, J. 1967 *A Question of Slavery.* Oxford: Clarendon Press.

Fry, P. 2000. "Cultures of Difference: The Aftermath of Portuguese and British Colonial Policies in Southern Africa." *Social Anthropology* 8(2): 117–144.

———. 2004. "A lógica das cotas raciais." *O Globo.* April 14, 2004: 7.

Gomes, F.D.S. 1995. *Histórias de Quilombolas: Mocambos e Comunidades de Senzalas no Rio de Janeiro-Século XIX.* Arquivo Nacional. 1993 (Prêmio Arquivo Nacional de Pesquisa).

Lugard, F.D. 1922. *The Dual Mandate in British Tropical Africa.* Edinburgh and London: William Blackwood and Sons.

Macagno, L. 1996. *Os paradoxos do assimilacionismo: "usos e costumes" do colonialismo português em Moçambique.* (Mestrado). Programa de Pós Graduação em Sociologia, UFRJ, Rio Janeiro.

Maggie, Y. 2005. O eu e os outros: o ideário modernista em questão. http://www.observa.ifcs.ufrj.br/trabalhosemandamento/ accessed on June 01, 2007.

Mamdani, M. 1996. *Citizen and Subject Contemporary Africa and the Legacy of Late Colonialism.* London: James Curry.

Monteiro, F.D. 2003. *Retratos em branco e preto, retratos sem nenhuma cor: a experiência do disque-racismo da Secretaria de segurança pública do Estado do Rio de Janeiro.* (Mestrado). PPGSA, UFRJ, Rio de Janeiro.

Negra—Grupo de Trabalho Interministerial Para a Valorizaçao da População Negra, 2004. *Construindo a democracia racial.* http://www.planalto.gov.br/publi04/

COLECAO/RACIAL2H.HTM: Ministério de Saúde accessed on August 3, 2004.

Parra, F.C., R.C. Amado, J.R. Lambertucci, J. Rocha, C.M. Antunes, and S.D.J. Pena. 2003. "Color and Genomic Ancestry in Brazilians." *Proceedings of the National Academy of Sciences of the United States of America* 100: 177–182.

Penvenne, J. 1989. "'We are all Portuguese!' Challenging the Political Economy of Assimilation: Lourenço Marques, 1870–1933," in L.Vail, ed. *The Creation of Tribalism in Southern Africa*. London: James Curry, pp.255–288.

Pinto, L.C. 1953. *O negro no Rio de Janeiro: relações de raça numa sociedade em mudança*. São Paulo: Companhia Editora Nacional.

Sahlins, M. 1995. *How "Natives" Think: About Captain Cook, For Example*. Chicago and London: The University of Chicago Press.

Santos, R.V. 2004. "Uma grande fraude." *O Globo*. Rio de Janeiro: 7.

Smuts, J.C. 1929. *Africa and Some World Problems, Including the Rhodes Memorial Lectures*. Delivered in Michaelman Term, 1929. Oxford: Clarendon Press.

Tapper, M. 1999. *In the Blood: Sickle Cell Anemia and the Politics of Race*. Philadelphia: University of Pennsylvania Press.

Véran, J.F. 2003. *L'esclavage en héritage (Brésil). Le droit à la terre des descendants de marrons*. Paris: Karthala.

Vogt, C. and P. Fry. 1996. *Cafundó - África No Brasil*. São Paulo: Editora da UNICAMP/Companhia da Letras.

Index